VERBS AND DIACHRONIC SYNTAX

Studies in Natural Language and Linguistic Theory

VOLUME 28

VERBS AND DIACHRONIC SYNTAX
A Comparative History of English and French

IAN ROBERTS

University of Wales

Kluwer Academic Publishers

Dordrecht / Boston / London

Library of Congress Cataloging-in-Publication Data

Roberts, Ian G.
    Verbs and diachronic syntax : a comparative history of English and
French / by Ian G. Roberts.
        p.   cm. -- (Studies in natural language and linguistic theory
; v. 28)
    Includes bibliographical references and index.
    ISBN 0-7923-1705-X (alk. paper)
    1. English language--Verb. 2. English language--Grammar,
Comparative--French. 3. French language--Grammar, Comparative-
-English. 4. English language--History. 5. English language-
-Syntax. 6. French language--History. 7. French language--Syntax.
8. French language--Verb.   I. Title.   II. Series.
PE1271.R63 1992
425--dc20   92-9768

Published by Kluwer Academic Publishers,
P.O. Box 17, 3300 AA Dordrecht, The Netherlands.

Kluwer Academic Publishers incorporates the publishing programmes of
D. Reidel, Martinus Nijhoff, Dr W. Junk and MTP Press.

Sold and distributed in the U.S.A. and Canada
by Kluwer Academic Publishers,
101 Philip Drive, Norwell, MA 02061, U.S.A.

In all other countries, sold and distributed
by Kluwer Academic Publishers Group,
P.O. Box 322, 3300 AH Dordrecht, The Netherlands.

Printed in the Netherlands.

Langagis, whos reulis ben not writen, as ben Englisch, Frensch and many otheres, ben channgid withynne yeeris and countrees that oon man of the oon cuntre, and of the oon tyme, myghte not, or schulde not kunne undirstonde a man of the othere kuntre, and of the othere tyme; and al for this, that the seid langagis ben not stabili and fondamentali writen.

Pecock (1454) *Book of Feith*

TABLE OF CONTENTS

PREFACE

This book combines several strands of my work, both individually and in collaboration with various people, over the last couple of years. To a very large extent, I have been inspired by the many talks, classes, appointments and other interactions that took place in the exciting intellectual environment that grew up among the linguists working in Geneva in the period 1989–90.

It is impossible to mention by name everyone who influenced the development of this material, but I'd particularly like to thank the students in my class 'linguistique diachronique' during that period, who had to suffer through preliminary versions of much of this book, and often seemed to understand what I was getting at better than I did.

Luigi Rizzi did more than anyone else to create the unique atmosphere here in the last couple of years, and so he deserves our gratitude for that; he was also my collaborator on the synchronic work on French inversion that inspired much of this book; he also read the whole manuscript in draft form and gave detailed comments; he is also, as anyone working in current comparative syntax knows, a wellspring of knowledge, ideas and inspiration. Maria-Teresa Guasti also read the entire manuscript and gave me invaluable comments. Sten Vikner was a great help, for much more than just Danish data. Special thanks also to Adriana Belletti, Anna Cardinaletti, Liliane Haegeman and Cecilia Poletto. For many interesting discussions, and for sharing valuable data with me, I'd like to thank the following 'non-Genevans': Paola Benincà, Paul Hirschbuhler, Ans van Kemenade, Anthony Kroch, David Lightfoot, Lorenzo Renzi and Laura Vanelli. A special thanks also to two anonymous reviewers, who made a number of valuable suggestions.

The material here was given in talks at the 1989 GLOW Colloquium, Utrecht; Going Romance 1990, Utrecht; University of Arizona, Tucson; Rutgers University, New Jersey; Universidad Autonoma de Madrid; University of Vitoria, Euskadi; Universidade Federal do Rio de Janeiro; Universidade Federal da Bahia, Salvador; Universidade Federal das Minas Gerais, Belo Horizonte; Università degli Studi di Venezia; Universität Stuttgart. I also taught earlier versions at Unicamp, Brazil, and at the University of Vienna. I'd like to thank all the audiences for their patience and comments. A particular thanks to the organizers of my 'foreign' classes: Mary Kato at Unicamp and Martin Prinzhorn in Vienna.

One person influenced this book, and all my linguistic endeavours up to now, who will never see the finished result. In November 1989, Osvaldo

Jaeggli visited Geneva. While he was here he gave me comments on a draft of Chapter One. He died on August 20th, 1990. This book is dedicated to his memory, with affection and deep sadness. I hope it is worthy of him.

Geneva, December 22nd, 1990

CHAPTER 1

THE ANALYSIS OF INVERSION

1.0. INTRODUCTION

The discussion and analysis in this initial chapter will be purely synchronic in nature. Our goal here is to develop and motivate an analytic framework in terms of which we can discuss the synchronic and diachronic phenomena of verb-placement throughout the rest of the book. This analytic framework consists of an interlocking set of assumptions about how different grammatical systems determine verb-placement. Most of these assumptions are taken from the recent theoretical literature, although we also propose certain modifications of our own. Since our purpose is just to set up a framework for discussion and analysis, the proposals we will make in this chapter are of course subject to subsequent modification.

Before going any further, however, we should present the basic facts that we are interested in. We are concerned primarily with the Romance and Germanic languages, and, among these, our focus will be mostly on English and French. Nevertheless, we will also pay a good deal of attention to other Germanic languages and dialects, as well as to Italian and various dialects of Northern Italy; Spanish and Portuguese, on the other hand, will play a lesser role.

What kinds of word orders do we find in these languages? If we consider the Romance, Germanic and Celtic languages together, we find that the three word orders which are prevalent in the world's languages are all attested: SVO, SOV and VSO (cf. Greenberg's (1963: 77) Universal I).[1] English, Yiddish, all the Scandinavian and all the Romance languages are SVO; German, Dutch and all Continental West Germanic dialects are SOV; and the Celtic languages are VSO. These different word orders are illustrated in (1):

(1) a. L' enfant vit un cheval   (French, SVO)
        the child saw a   horse

    b. . . . daß das Kind ein Pferd sah   (German, SOV)
        . . . that the child a   horse saw

    c. Gwelodd y plentyn geffyl   (Welsh, VSO)
        saw   the child horse

In (1b) we have illustrated German word order with an embedded sentence. This is because the base word-order is disguised matrix clauses by

1

the obligatory movement of the verb to second position — for a presentation of the 'verb-second' phenomenon, see below; for an analysis of it, see 1.4. These examples show that any theory of syntax which has a comparative dimension will have to say something about cross-linguistic variation in the position of the verb relative to other major sentence constituents.

However, the issue is more complex than this first look at things implies; the position of the verb in a given language in fact varies along several dimensions. These concern the morphological marking of the verb, the status of the clause containing the verb, and the intrinsic properties of the verb itself. We will now illustrate each of these factors one by one, and show how they interact to produce the fairly complex array of crosslinguistic similarities and differences that we find in the languages we are concerned with.

The most important factor, which seems to be operative in all the languages we are interested in, in one guise or another, concerns the morphological marking of the verb. Finite verbs, i.e. verbs which bear an inflectional ending marking person, number and tense, tend to occupy different syntactic positions from non-finite verbs, i.e. infinitival and participial forms. The basically morphological distinction between finite and nonfinite verb-forms has an impact on many aspects of syntax.

French provides a good example of how the finiteness of a verb affects its syntactic position. In French, a finite verb precedes the negative marker *pas*, floated quantifiers and various kinds of VP-adverbs:

(2) a.   Jean **n'aime pas**   Marie
          J.   neg loves not M.
          'John doesn't love Mary'

   b.   Les enfants **sortent tous** en même   temps
          the children leave   all   at the same time
          'All the children leave at the same time'

   c.   Pierre **comprend**   **à peine** l'italien
          P.   understands hardly Italian
          'Peter hardly understands Italian'

The reverse order of the finite verb and these elements is impossible:

(3) a.   *Jean ne **pas aime** Marie

   b.   *Les enfants **tous sortent** ce livre

   c.   *Pierre **à peine comprend** l'italien

However, with infinitivals (and participles), the order in (3), impossible with finite verbs, is the usual one:

(4) a.   Ne **pas aimer** ses   parents est une mauvaise chose
         neg not to-love one's parents is a   bad   thing
         'Not to love one's parents is a bad thing'

   b.   J'ai vu   les enfants **tous sortir** en même   temps
         I've seen the children all   leave at the same time
         'I saw the children all leave at the same time'

   c.   **A peine comprendre**   l'italien, ce n'est pas un crime
         Hardly to-understand Italian, it neg is not a   crime
         'To hardly understand Italian is not a crime'

Making the reasonable assumption that the position of *pas*, the floated quantifier and the adverbs in question remains constant, we can see that finiteness determines the position of the verb in French: finite verbs precede, and infinitives follow, these elements. These phenomena are analyzed in detail in Pollock (1989), an analysis which we will take up at several points (cf. 1.1., 1.3., and Chapter 3, especially 3.1.1.).

A more dramatic example of the way in which finiteness can determine verb-placement comes from Welsh. Sproat (1985) argues that VSO is in fact a derived order in Welsh, and is moreover related to the finiteness of the verb.[2] The basic fact is that, alongside the VSO order illustrated in (1c), Welsh allows the order Aux SVO. The auxiliaries in question may be forms of *gwneud*, 'to do', or of *bod*, 'to be', the latter combining with prepositional elements and a non-finite form of the verb to form progressives and perfects. Some examples are given in (5):

(5) a.   Gwnaeth y plentyn **weld** ceffyl
         did   the child see   horse
         'The child saw a horse'

   b.   Y   mae'r plentyn yn **gweld** ceffyl
         Prt is-the child in see   horse
         'The child is seeing a horse'

   c.   Y   mae'r plentyn wedi **gweld** ceffyl
         Prt is-the child   after see   horse
         'The child has seen a horse'

The non-finite form of the verb here is traditionally known as the 'verbal noun'. Sproat shows, on the basis of contrasts in extraction, topicalization and thematic properties, that these elements are distinct from standard derived nominals like *distrywiad* 'destruction'. He thus concludes that they are non-finite forms of verbs (cf. also Rouveret 1982, 1987, and McCloskey 1986 for the same conclusion concerning the analogous construction in Irish). The same form appears in standard infinitival contexts, cf.:

(6) a.   Dymunai Wyn i   Ifor **ddarllen** y   llyfr

        wanted   W.   for I.   read   the book

        'Wyn wanted Ifor to read the book'

        (Sproat's (75), p. 206)

    b.   Cyn   i Siôn **laddu** draig   y   mae

        before to S.   kill   dragon prt is

        rhaid iddo   **brynu** llaeth

        must to-him buy   milk

        'Before for John to kill the dragon, he must buy milk'

        (Sproat's (72), p. 205)

While more remains to be said (particularly concerning the Case-assigning properties of these non-finite verbs), the conclusion seems to be fairly clear: non-finite verbs appear in between the subject and the object, while finite verbs precede both. We will briefly sketch an analysis of this situation in 1.2.

Consider next the second factor determining the placement of verbs: the position of the clause which contains the verb. Quite prevalently in the Germanic languages and also in some Romance languages (in French, for example), we find that the finite verb occupies a different position in root clauses of various types to that which it occupies in embedded clauses. The placement of the finite verb is, then, sensitive to the root/embedded distinction. Note also that this factor interacts with the first in that only finite verbs are affected.

The most striking example of the sensitivity of verb-placement to the root/embedded distinction is the well-known 'Verb-second' constraint, found in all the Germanic languages other than (Modern) English (cf. Haider and Prinzhorn 1986, and Vikner 1990 Ch. 2 for an overview). This constraint imposes the requirement that in root declarative sentences the inflected verb or auxiliary must occupy a position immediately following exactly one phrasal constituent, while no requirement is imposed on the nature of this first constituent. This constraint, which we refer to henceforth as V2, is common to languages whose base order is SVO (North Germanic) and those whose base order is SOV (West Germanic).

In the German examples in (7) we give a simple tense and a compound tense, to illustrate that the finite verb appears in second position while the participle appears in final position:

(7) a.   Ich **las**   schon   letztes Jahr diesen Roman
          I   read already last   year this   book

    b.   Ich **habe** schon   letztes Jahr diesen Roman **gelesen**
          I   have already last   year this   book   read
          'I read this book last year already'

In (7), the subject precedes the finite verb. This is not necessary, however; other constituents can precede the finite verb as long as the subject then follows it:

(8) a.   Diesen Roman **las**   ich schon   letztes Jahr
          This   book   read I   already last   year

    b.   Diesen Roman **habe** ich schon   letztes Jahr **gelesen**
          This   book   have I   already last   year read

(9) a.   Schon   letztes Jahr **las**   ich diesen Roman
          Already last   year read I   this   book

    b.   Schon   letztes Jahr **habe** ich diesen Roman **gelesen**
          Already last   year have I   this   book   read

(10) a. *Schon letztes Jahr ich **las** diesen Roman

     b. *Schon letztes Jahr ich **habe** diesen Roman **gelesen**

In subordinate clauses, on the other hand, all the verbs appear at the end, with the finite verb coming last:

(11)   Du weisst wohl,
        you know well

    a. daß ich schon   letztes Jahr diesen Roman **las**
        that I already last   year this   book   read

    b. daß ich schon   letztes Jahr diesen Roman **gelesen habe**
        that I already last   year this   book   read   have

(12) and (13) show the operation of this constraint in an SVO language, Danish (cf. Vikner op. cit.). In (12), we see that, just as in German, exactly one constituent, the subject in (12a), the object in (12b), and an adverb in (12c), may precede the finite verb. (12d) shows that the finite verb must precede the negative element *ikke* in main clauses:

(12) a. Peter **drikker** ikke kaffe om morgenen
         P.   drinks   not coffee in morning-the

    b. Kaffe **drikker** Peter ikke om morgenen
        Coffee drinks   P.   not in morning-the

    c. Om morgenen   **drikker** Peter ikke kaffe
        In morning-the drinks   P.   not coffee
        'Peter doesn't drink coffee in the morning'

    d. *Peter ikke **drikker** kaffe om morgenen

In subordinate clauses, however, the finite verb follows *ikke*:

(13)   . . . at   Peter **ikke drikker** kaffe om morgenen
          . . . that P.   not drinks   coffee in morning-the

Similarly, the finite verb always follows VP-adverbs and floated quantifiers
in MSc subordinate clauses (cf. Holmberg 1986: 165–6). Some subordinate
clauses allow V2 (cf. 1.4. for details), but indirect questions (as in (14a))
and complements to non-bridge verbs (as in (14b); for a list of the relevant
verbs, cf. Vikner 1990: 74–5) do not, as the following examples show both
for German and Danish:

(14) a. *Jeg ved ikke hvorfor P. **drikker ikke** kaffe om morgenen
         *Ich weiss nicht warum P. **trinkt** morgens keinen Kaffee

         'I don't know why P. does not drink coffee in the morning'

    b. *Jeg beklager at P. **drikker ikke** kaffe om morgenen
        *Ich bereue daß P. **trinkt** morgens keinen Kaffee

        'I regret that P. does not drink coffee in the morning'

So, in these languages, the position of the finite verb varies depending on
whether it is in a root clause or not; in a root clause, the finite verb
occupies second position, while in a subordinate clause it either appears
between the subject and the object, or appears in final position, depending
on the 'basic' word order of the language. Another important point is that
the second position is a position which precedes the subject.

   Although the best-known cases of the V2 constraint are found in the
Germanic languages, this constraint is not limited to those languages.
Romansch (Arquint 1964: 11, Thöni 1969: 143; cf. also Haiman 1971,
1974, 1988) and various dialects in the extreme North of Italy in an area
near the Swiss–Italian border (Benincà 1986) have it. Moreover, a number
of Romance languages show some form of V2 constraint at earlier stages
in their history: French, Occitan, medieval Northern Italian dialects, Flor-
entine, Portuguese (Mattos e Silva 1989, Ribeiro 1990), see 2.1.2., 2.3.1.,
2.3.2., on French and 2.4.3. on the Italian varieties; further references

are also given there. Returning to Germanic, it is also well-known that English was formerly a V2 language (see 3.4.).

Modern French, while lacking the V2 constraint, shows the same root-embedded asymmetry in verb-placement in a more restricted form. Preposing of the finite verb is not triggered in all main clauses, but only in questions (both *wh*-questions and yes/no questions) and by a very restricted class of adverbs like *peut-être* ('perhaps'), *à peine* ('hardly'), etc. It seems hard to maintain that the verb moves to second position in these cases, since on the one hand the verb may appear initially (in yes/no questions), and on the other hand, in so-called complex inversion, both the subject NP and a *wh*-constituent may precede it (nevertheless, we will see in 1.5. that the position occupied by the verb here is the same as that occupied by the verb in V2 sentences in the Germanic languages). The basic examples are given in (15):[3]

(15) a. (Jean) **voit**-il le cheval?

      (*J.*)   *sees he the horse*

      'Does John/he see the horse?'

  b. Quel   cheval (Jean) **voit**-il?

      Which horse (J.)   sees he

      'Which horse does he/John see?'

  c. *Je ne sais pas quel cheval (Jean) **voit**-il

So, in French, finite verbs are preposed in interrogative main clauses.

In English, verb-preposing is still more restricted than in French. Here we are faced with the third factor determining verb-placement, the one which relates to the intrinsic properties of the verb. The process moving verbs in English is subject-auxiliary inversion (SAI). Like verb-preposing in French, this process takes place in root interrogatives (and also in contexts determined by a class of negative-polarity adverbs, a different and seemingly more productive class than that which triggers verb-preposing in French). However, SAI is more restricted than French verb-preposing in that it only affects modal and aspectual auxiliaries and *do*; it cannot apply to other verbs. SAI is illustrated in (16):

(16) a. **Has** John left?

  b. Which students **did** the police arrest?

  c. Only in America **can** you get away with that

  d. ***Will** be John arrested?

  e. *I wonder who **has** John seen

  f. ***Left** John?

In English, then, all three factors interact to restrict verb-preposing: the verb must be finite ((16d)), the process takes place only in main clauses ((16e)), and only auxiliary verbs are affected ((16f)).

The facts just reviewed form the core phenomena which we are concerned with in this book. The history of the French constructions of subject-clitic inversion and complex inversion are discussed in Chapter 2, along with the former V2 constraint; the origins of the English auxiliary system, hence of SAI, are the main focus in Chapter 3.

In this Chapter we lay the groundwork for the subsequent analyses by giving synchronic analyses of the constructions we have reviewed above. We begin in Section 1.1. by showing how recent extensions of the X-bar system to non-lexical categories provide a natural structural correlate of the factors relating to finiteness and to the root/embedded distinction. In Section 1.2., we show how verb-preposing interacts with the position and properties of the subject NP, by adopting and elaborating recent proposals for Nominative Case assignment made by Koopmann and Sportiche (1990). Section 1.3. deals with the technical aspects of verb-preposing by showing how this is an instance of the general rule of head-to-head movement (cf. Travis 1984, Baker 1988). Moreover, in this section we propose certain refinements of Baker's theory. In Section 1.4. we provide an analysis of the V2 constraint. We also describe and account for various differences among V2 languages along the lines of Cardinaletti and Roberts (forthcoming), and we present Rizzi's (1990b) analysis of 'residual V2' in languages like (contemporary) English and French. In Section 5 we treat the cross-linguistically more unusual case of French complex inversion. The synchronic analyses put forward in this Chapter, then, will serve as a basis for the diachronic work in the remainder of the book.

1.1. INVERSION AND X-BAR THEORY

In this section we will show how the categorial component of the grammar — X-bar theory — determines the structural positions in which verbs appear. Our exposition of X-bar theory relies on Rizzi (1988).

The categorial component of the grammar does two things: it provides an inventory of grammatical categories, and it specifies the hierarchical and linear structures of each category.

Concerning the inventory of categories, there are generally assumed to be two types: lexical categories and non-lexical categories. Lexical categories are fairly familiar from traditional grammars, and are those to which the words of a language are assigned in the lexicon: Noun (N), Verb (V), Adjective (A) and Preposition (P). These four categories exhaust the logical combinations of the two categorial features $[\pm N, \pm V]$, in the following way:

(17) a. [+N, +V] = Adjective

    b. [+N, −V] = Noun

    c. [−N, +V] = Verb

    d. [−N, −V] = Preposition

This feature system makes some predictions about natural classes of categories, which seem to be relevant for syntactic processes; for example, it has been claimed that only [−N] categories, i.e. verbs and prepositions, can assign Case (cf. Rouveret and Vergnaud 1980; Chomsky 1986a puts forward a different view).

    The non-lexical categories (also known as functional categories, cf. Fukui and Speas 1986) are the projections of morphological and closed-class elements, such as auxiliaries, complementizers and parts of the inflectional system. As we shall see in detail throughout this work, they play an important role in characterizing how morphological properties, particularly inflectional properties, interact with syntax, and are particularly prominent in the domain of verb-placement. Until fairly recently, it was assumed that there are two non-lexical categories: Inflection (I) and Comp (C) (cf. Chomsky 1986b). Other such categories have more recently been proposed, notably Determiner (D) (cf. Fukui and Speas 1986, Abney 1987), Tense (T), Agreement (Agr) and Negation (Neg) (Chomsky 1989, Pollock 1989). We will discuss the last three below, but have little to say about the 'DP hypothesis' here, as the syntax of nouns is not our concern (but cf. 2.2.1., 2.2.2., 2.3.3.). It is unclear what the nature of the feature system for non-lexical categories should be, largely since the precise inventory of these categories remains hard to determine. One proposal is that of Rizzi (1990b), which is based on the two features [±C, ±I]. These features give the following possibilities (Rizzi's definitions):

    (18) a. [+C, −I]: a category which designates a proposition, the familiar CP of non-V2 languages.

        b. [−C, +I]: a category designating a predication, the familiar IP.

        c. [−C, −I]: a category which is neither propositional nor predicational, the determiner and its projection, the DP.

        d. [+C, +I]: a category which is propositional *and* predicational.

This proposal is important for the analysis of V2 languages, since the complementizer system (which includes the landing-site for finite verbs in matrix clauses (cf. (24)) of these languages is said to be a projection of category (18d), while the complentizer system of non-V2 languages is a projection of category (18a) (cf. also Platzack 1987 for the idea that V2 languages feature a complementizer system which has a different categor-

ial status from that of non-V2 languages). We will return to this proposal
in 1.4. Note that this framework requires some further elaboration in
order to integrate Pollock's (1989) 'split Infl' proposal with it in such a
way as to distinguish the T and Agr (see below).

X-bar theory determines the linear and hierarchical structure of the
syntactic categories we have just enumerated in a category-neutral fashion.
The claim of this theory, then, is that the essential structure of all syntactic
categories is uniform. Moreover, hierarchical structure is assumed to be
uniform across languages, while linear order is subject to parametric variation.

The hierarchical structure determined by X-bar theory can be summarized by the following statements (here we borrow the presentation from
Rizzi 1988):

(19) a. $XP = \{\alpha, X'\}$

   b. $X' = \{\beta, X°\}$

Since we are abstracting away from linear order, we use set notation here
to indicate that the order in which the elements are presented is irrelevant.
Here, XP is the maximal projection of category X; X' is the intermediate
projection; and X° the head. α is known as the Specifier of X' (SpecX')
and β is the complement of X°. Where X is a lexical category, then, the
nature of β will be determined by the lexical properties of the lexical item
in X°. Where X is non-lexical, the nature of β is fixed (or so it seems;
this is an aspect of the syntax of nonlexical categories which has been
investigated very little up to now, and we will say nothing about it here).

The statements in (19) are taken to be principles of Universal Grammar
(UG), invariant in all actual and possible human languages since they are
part of the innate human linguistic apparatus. On the other hand, the
principles governing linear order are subject to variation within certain
parameters fixed by UG, i.e. parametric variation. UG makes two options
available in this domain:

(20) a.   X' precedes/follows α

   b.   X° precedes/follows β

The choice between 'precedes' and 'follows' here is made by each language. Languages are frequently coherent across categories, in that the
choice is made once for all categories. With respect to the choice in (20b),
it is thus possible to speak of 'head-final' and 'head-initial' languages. In
English, and in the Romance languages, X' follows α, and X° precedes
β, so these are head-initial languages within X'. This is true for all categories, so we have the following structural schema:

(21)

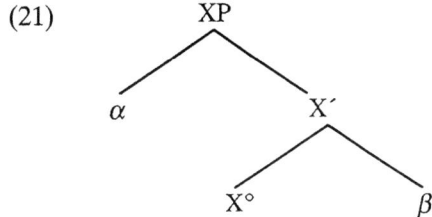

For XP = IP we get the following representation:

(22)

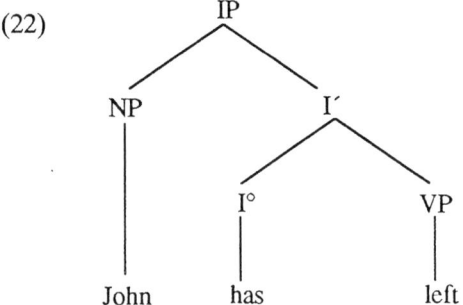

So, following Chomsky (1986b), we take it that the normal surface position of the subject is SpecI', and VP is the complement of I°. Auxiliaries like perfect *have* may occupy I° (see 1.3. and 3.0.).

German and Dutch choose the opposite order inside I' and V', with the complement preceding the head. This gives structures like the following (we illustrate with an embedded clause, to abstract away from the effects of V2):

(23)

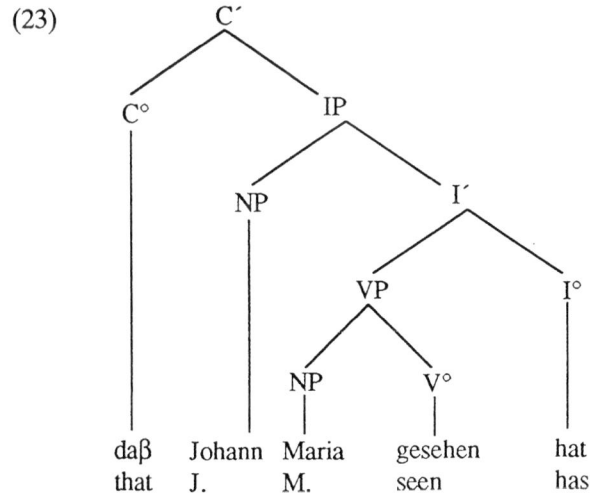

'that J. has seen M.'

We can see from (23) that complementizers like German *daß* occupy C°. Inflected verbs may also appear in C°. This can be seen from the following structure for the interrogative corresponding to (22):

(24)

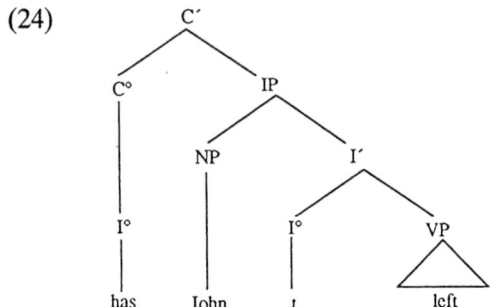

Subject-aux inversion in English can thus be treated as a rule which places I° in C°, an instance of a general schema for movement of one head to another (head-to-head movement, or incorporation, cf. Baker 1988 and 1.3.).

It is immediately apparent how the idea that a verb (or auxiliary) may move to C° could account for the root/embedded asymmetries in verb-placement that we observed in the previous section: in embedded contexts a complementizer typically occupies C°, thereby blocking movement from I° (we will give a full, technical characterization of the root/embedded distinction in 1.3. and 1.4.). For this reason, it is normal to treat V2 as involving successive raising of the verb to Infl and then to Comp, combined with some operation which fronts an XP to the SpecC' position. This gives the following general schema for V2 (on the first step of movement, V to I, see below):

(25)

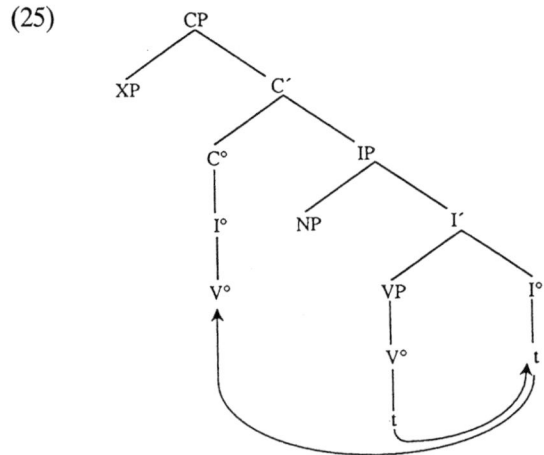

While such an analysis leaves open the question of why these operations are obligatory in all declarative main clauses (see 1.4. for a proposal), such an analysis accounts naturally for the observed derived word orders, as well as for the ungrammaticality of examples like (10) (as long as we prevent XP-adjunction to CP; see 2.3.1.). Thus, as argued in detail in den Besten (1983), it is possible to analyse SAI as exactly the same formal operation as V2 applying to a more restricted class of verbs and in a more restricted class of contexts (cf. also Williams 1974, Koster 1975). In 1.4. we will suggest an account (taken from Rizzi 1990b) of the difference between interrogative and declarative clauses which underlies the selective nature of verb-movement to C in English and French.

In (25), the verb moves first to $I°$, and then $I°$ moves to $C°$. V to I movement is another instance of head-to-head movement. Infl is the element which contains features, or affixes, realizing tense and agreement. So, for a verb to carry such affixes, it must be related to $I°$, presumably by movement, at some stage of the derivation. In general, this is the way in which differences in verb-placement due to the finiteness of the verb are captured: all other things being equal, if a verb is finite, it appears in I (at some point in the derivation). (We state this as a one-way implication because it is also true that non-finite verb forms may move, see Belletti (1990) and below: moreover, in Modern English all other things are not equal, since finite main verbs do not appear in I, cf. below, and, for account of this restriction, 1.3.). In these terms, VSO order is derived from underlying SVO order in a language like Welsh by Verb-raising to I. Welsh differs from French in that I precedes the surface position of the subject, a difference attributable to Case properties (see 1.2.).

There is well-known evidence that all finite verbs move to Infl in French, while this is impossible for non-auxiliaries in English (see Emonds 1978, Pollock 1989). Consider again the contrasts in (2) and (3), which we repeat here for convenience:

(2) a.   Jean **n'aime pas**   Marie

       J.   neg loves not M.

       'John doesn't love Mary'

   b.   Les enfants **sortent tous** en même   temps

       the children leave   all   at the same time

       'All the children leave at the same time'

   c.   Pierre **comprend**   **à peine** l'italien

       P.   understands hardly Italian

       'Peter hardly understands Italian'

(3) a.   *Jean ne **pas aime** Marie

b.   *Les enfants **tous sortent** ce livre

c.   *Pierre **à peine comprend** l'italien

We said earlier that floated quantifiers, *pas* and the adverbs in question occupy a fixed position. Assuming as a first approximation that this position is SpecV' (we will make a more refined proposal below), we get the correct results regarding verb-placement, providing that V to I movement takes place obligatorily with tensed verbs. The situation is illustrated in (26):

(26)

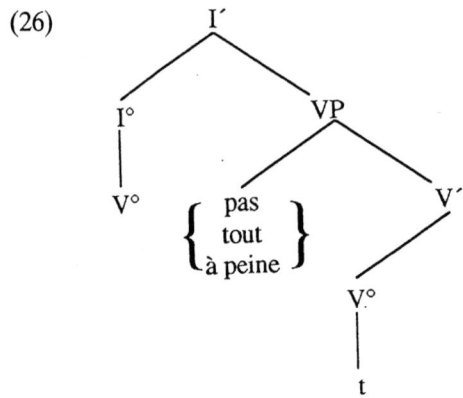

Infinitives, on the other hand, do not raise in this way, giving the data in (4).

If we now consider English, we find that similar arguments lead to the conclusion that a (non-auxiliary) verb cannot move to I. Main verbs cannot precede *not*, floated quantifiers and adverbs of the relevant type:

(27) a.   *John likes not Mary

b.   *The kids like all this book

c.   *Pete understands hardly Italian

Instead they follow these elements:

(28) a.   John doesn't like Mary

b.   The kids all like this book

c.   Pete hardly understands Italian

We thus conclude that main verbs in English do not move to I, unlike their French counterparts. This raises the question of how the main verb is marked with tense/agreement morphology, and the related question of the conditions governing the appearance of *do*. These questions form the subject matter of Chapter 3, cf. 3.0. and 3.2.1. for an account of the Modern English situation; for other accounts, cf. Chomsky 1989, Pollock 1989, Rizzi 1990a, Appendix 1, Chapter 1.

On the other hand, following the same logic we are led to conclude that the auxiliaries *have* and *be* raise to I given data like the following:

(29) a. John has not seen Mary

b. The kids have all left

c. Pete has hardly said a word

This restriction is a manifestation of the third factor governing verb-placement that we mentioned in the previous section: the intrinsic properties of the verb itself. This factor is at work in English, in that only auxiliaries can move to I; main verbs cannot. Roberts (1983, 1985a) and Pollock (1989) treat the distinction between auxiliaries and main verbs in terms of Θ-theory, claiming that the fundamental difference between auxiliaries and main verbs is that the former do not contract thematic (Θ-) relations like Agent, Patient, Beneficiary, etc., with arguments, while the latter do (cf. Gruber 1965, Jackendoff 1972, Chomsky 1981 Ch 2, on Θ-theory). We will return to this question in 1.3. and in 3.3.2.

A further manifestation of this distinction is found in French infinitives (this was first pointed out by Pollock 1989). We mentioned earlier that infinitives must follow *pas* in French:

(30)   *N'aimer   pas ses   parents est une honte

neg to-love not one's parents is   a   shame

'Not to love one's parents is shameful'

However, infinitival forms of auxiliaries can precede *pas*:

(31) a. N'être   pas heureux est une condition d'écrire

Neg to-be not happy   is   a   condition for to-write

'To not be happy is a condition for writing'

b. Ne pas être heureux est une condition d'écrire

Compare the behaviour of *être* in this respect with that of *sembler* ('seem'), which, despite its semantic similarity to *être*, cannot raise in infinitivals:

(32) a. *Ne sembler pas heureux . . .

b. Ne pas sembler heureux . . .

This difference can be attributed to the auxiliary vs. main verb distinction, and so, following the proposals of Roberts and Pollock, to Θ-theory.

The hypothesis that root interrogatives involve Infl-to-Comp movement provides an explanation of the fact that inversion is restricted to auxiliaries in English. Since in English Verb-to-Infl movement applies only to auxiliaries, this operation fails to feed I-to-C movement in English, while it plays exactly this role in French interrogatives and in all root clauses in German (the situation in the Mainland Scandinavian languages ('MSc' henceforth) is apparently more complex, cf. Holmberg and Platzack 1988, and 1.3.2.). So the ungrammaticality of an example like (16f) is due to restrictions on Verb-to-Infl movement. The rule of inversion in English is the same as in all other Germanic languages and French: I moves to C.

Implicit in the above remarks is the idea that V cannot move directly to C, 'skipping' I. This restriction is normally taken to hold of head-to-head movement in general, and is formulated as the Head Movement Constraint (HMC) of Travis (1984), which we will discuss in detail in 1.3.2. Two other general restrictions are assumed to hold of head-to-head movement: first, it is cyclic, meaning that it is possible to reiterate the movement such that it passes through several heads; this in fact happens in V2, as indicated in (24). Second, it is structure-preserving, in that heads can only move to other heads; movement which attaches a head to XP or to X′ is ruled out. It follows that when we see a verb occupying the C position, we must conclude that it has passed through I.

We mentioned above that various further non-lexical categories, in addition to I and C, have been proposed recently. In particular, Pollock (1989) has proposed that I should be replaced by two heads, Agreement (Agr) and Tense (T), each with its own full projection determined by X-bar theory. The evidence for this idea comes from the distribution of infinitives in French. Although infinitival forms of main verbs must follow *pas*, as (29) and (31a) show, they can either precede or follow adverbs like *à peine*:

(33) a.   A peine comprendre l'italien . . .

     b.   Comprendre à peine l'italien . . .

This fact led Pollock to postulate the presence of a further head position which is available as a landing site for 'short' movement of this type, a head which intervenes between the base position of the verb and the position occupied by finite verbs (for an alternative account of these data which makes them consistent with a traditional 'whole' Infl, cf. Iatridou 1990). So the 'traditional' Infl is split into two separate heads, manifesting the two kinds of features formerly assumed to be carried by I, Tense and Agr.

Pollock assumes the structure where T° is structurally higher, taking Agr as its complement. However, we adopt Belletti's (1990) proposal that Agr is the higher head. So we now postulate the following clause structure:

(34)   AgrP

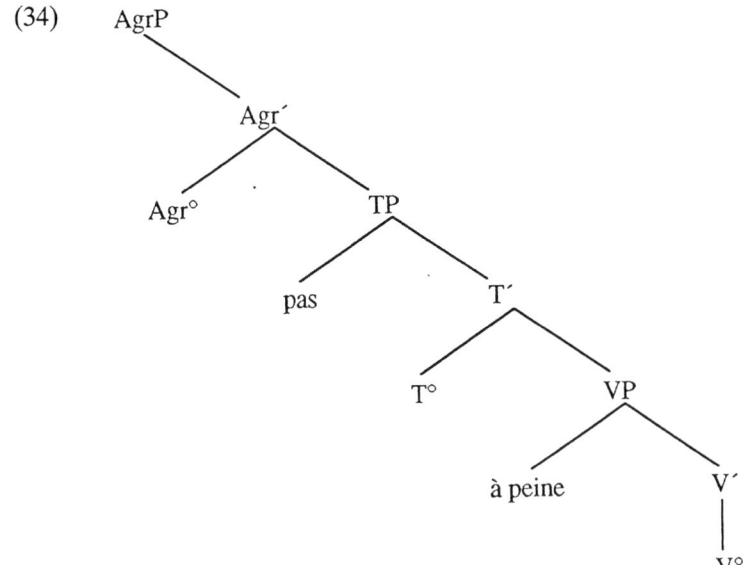

In French, finite verbs move to Agr°, while in English they remain in V°. French main-verb infinitives optionally raise to T°, and auxiliary infinitives to T° or Agr°. The normal surface position of the subject is SpecAgr'. Splitting Infl in this way appears to pose a problem for Rizzi's feature system for nonlexical categories (see (18)). However, it seems correct to assume that Agr and T are both [+I, −C], and that some further property distinguishes them; cf. 1.3.2. for a proposal regarding a fundamental difference between Agr and T.

We will assume the clause structure in (34) in what follows. However, for reasons of expository and typographical simplicity, we will occasionally refer to Agr and T together as I, and indicate them as such in tree diagrams where it is not necessary to distinguish them. In Chapter 3, we adopt Pollock's hypothesis that there is a NegP; until then, we can simplify our representations by leaving this category out of consideration. In 1.4., we see some motivation for the idea that there are two occurrences of AgrP in normal clauses in some languages, notably Icelandic (cf. Cardinaletti and Roberts, forthcoming).

1.2. INVERSION AND CASE THEORY

In this Section we will outline how Case theory interacts with inversion in different languages. The result will be an approach to Case-assignment, in particular Nominative-assignment, which provides a natural way of accounting for the various interactions between inversion and the position and realization of the subject NP that are attested in the languages we are concerned with.

The Case module of the grammar is concerned with the distribution of phonologically overt NPs. All such NPs are required to bear a Case feature. These Case features are assigned to NPs by various heads: Agr assigns Nominative Case; V assigns Accusative Case; P assigns Oblique Case; N and A either assign Genitive (Chomsky 1986a) or no Case at all (Rouveret and Vergnaud 1980). These Case features may be realized morphologically in various ways: in English, MSc and Romance, only pronouns show any actual Case morphology; in German and Icelandic, on the other hand, most NPs manifest Case overtly (although in German the actual mark often shows up only on the determiner).

A distinction is often made between structural and inherent Case. Structural Case is assigned 'blindly' by a head at S-structure under the specified structural conditions (which we will describe directly), while inherent Case is a property of particular lexical items, and is assigned at D-structure. Moreover, inherent Case is generally closely tied to Θ-role assignment (cf. the Uniformity Condition of Chomsky 1986a). Since the requirement that NPs bear a Case feature is an S-structure requirement, the difference in the level at which the different types of Case are assigned can have important consequences. However, we will have little to say about inherent Case here, as our chief concern is Nominative Case.

Sportiche (1988b) and Koopmann and Sportiche (1990) propose that structural Case can be assigned in either of two types of configuration: government or agreement. The two configurations are illustrated in (35) (order is irrelevant):

(35) a.   Case-assignment under government:

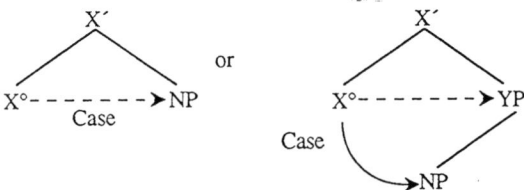

   b.   Case-assignment under agreement:

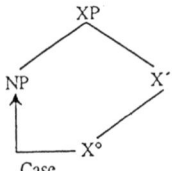

The two configurations of Case-assignment correspond to the two basic

configurations defined by X-bar theory: government is the relation between a head and its complement (or the specifier of its complement),
and agreement is the relation between a head and its specifier. We assume
with Sportiche that government is defined in terms of strict c-command,
rather than m-command, as follows:

(36) α governs β iff:
  (i) α is a head;
  (ii) α c-commands β;
  (iii) there is no head Γ which c-commands β but does not c-
        command α;
  (iv) there is no barrier Γ such that Γ includes β but not α.

We assume, following Sportiche (1988b), that α c-commands β iff α does
not dominate β and the first X'-projection dominating α dominates β.
Given this definition of c-command (which Sportiche refers to as "i-
command"), it follows from (36) that a head will not govern its own
specifier, thanks to the presence of X' which dominates the head but not
the specifier. However, a head will govern the specifier of its complement;
the lower head cannot govern this position because of the strict c-command
clause (36ii), and so the minimality clause (36iii) will not block government
by the upper head.[4] On the other hand, a head cannot govern into a non-
complement at all. This is the effect of clause (36iv); a barrier is a category
which is not L-marked in the sense of Chomsky (1986b: 14), i.e. a category
which is not a direct complement of a head. This notion distinguishes
complements (L-marked) from subjects and adjuncts (not L-marked).[5]

We consider agreement to be a purely structural relation, independent
in principle of the morphological relation of correspondence in or assignment of Φ-features. Neither is it the exclusive property of the category
Agr. The configuration of agreement is illustrated in (35b). This is the
relation of 'Spec-head agreement' in Chomsky (1986b). So we take it that
agreement is just the structural relation that holds between a head and its
specifier. The relation of morphological agreement, although standardly
attested in this configuration, is independent in principle of this structural
relation.

Our concern in this book is the application of this system to the assignment of Nominative Case in Romance and Germanic languages, in particular in the history of French. We will thus leave Accusative Case out of
consideration (but cf. Koopmann and Sportiche 1990 for the suggestion
that Accusative is assigned under agreement in Dutch). We are assuming
that the choice of configuration for Nominative-assignment in (35) is a
parametric one, in fact a non-exclusive parametric choice in the sense that
both options can be chosen together by a given language.[6] Leaving aside
the possibility that a given language may lack Nominative Case altogether

(which is probably not to be excluded a priori, cf. Note 6), this gives the following three possibilities:

(37) a.   Nominative-assignment under both government and agreement

b.   Nominative-assignment under government only

c.   Nominative-assignment under agreement only

We will now look at examples of each of these possibilities in turn.

A clear case of a language which allows Nominative-assignment in either configuration in (35) is English. Thus, in clauses without inversion, I° assigns Nominative to the subject in SpecI' in a configuration of agreement:

(38)

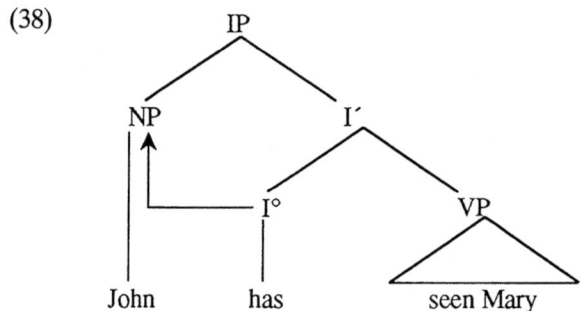

This is clearly a standard assumption common to all versions of Case theory. On the other hand, in inverted clauses, I° is raised to C, as we saw in 1.1. Here Nominative is assigned to SpecI' in a configuration of government:

(39)

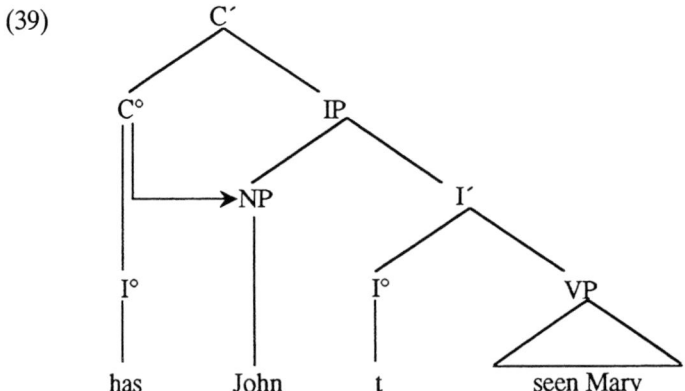

Since C° c-commands the NP in SpecI' and I does not intervene, C° governs this NP. So the raised I° governs this NP. So I° is able to assign

Nominative Case to this NP. (38) and (39) show that English allows Case-assignment in both of the configurations made available by UG, then.

A potential problem arises at this point. It is now fairly widely assumed that subjects are base-generated internally to VP.[7] Subjects are, at least in languages like English, raised to SpecI′ in the derivation (among others, this analysis is argued for by Koopmann and Sportiche 1990 and Sportiche 1988a; see additionally Zagona 1982, Fukui and Speas 1986, Kitagawa 1986, Manzini 1986). This kind of derivation is illustrated in (40) (assuming that the base position of the subject is on the left of the rest of VP in English — see below on Romance; VP* is exactly equivalent to Koopmann and Sportiche's VP^{max}):

(40) a.   DS: $[_{IP} [_{I'} I° [_{VP*} $ a man $[_{VP}$ loves Mary$]]]]$

    b.   SS: $[_{IP}$ a man $[_{I'} I° [_{VP*} $ t $[_{VP}$ loves Mary$]]]]$

The claim is, then, that I° acts like a raising trigger in a language like English. However, given that I° can assign Nominative Case under government, it is unclear at first sight why this should be so: why can I° not Case-mark an NP in the base subject position? It is clear that I° does not Case-mark this position, or else we might expect a DS like (40a) to give rise to an SS of the type in (41) (the variants in (41) depend on other factors: *do*-insertion vs. Agr-lowering (cf. 3.2.1.), and the type of expletive that occupies SpecI′):

(41) a.   *It/there does a man love Mary

    b.   *It/there a man loves Mary

Assuming that nothing prevents well-formed expletive-replacement in LF, placing *a man* in SpecAgr′ (cf. Chomsky 1989), the question is: why does I° not govern the base position of the subject? Clearly, some barrier must intervene between I° and this position. We could stipulate that VP is a barrier; however, this creates problems for raising of the subject. We adopt instead the definition of L-marking proposed by Cinque (1991):

(42)   XP is L-marked iff XP is directly selected by an X° $\neq$ [−V]

(42) has the consequence that complements to Nouns and Prepositions, as well as subjects and adjuncts, are not L-marked, and are therefore barriers. Since non-lexical categories are unspecified for [±V], their complements are L-marked and hence not barriers. Therefore VP and IP are not barriers in Cinque's system (on this we differ from Chomsky 1986b, Jaeggli and Hyams 1989, Kayne 1989a, and Pollock 1989, among others). Instead of a solution based on L-marking, we can turn the problem raised by (41) into an argument in favour of the extended clause structure given in (34). In these terms, Agr° is the assigner of Nominative Case. If we retain the assumption that the subject is base-generated in VP, we can

now see why it cannot receive Case *in situ*; the entire projection of T°
intervenes between Agr and the base position of the subject. In terms of
the definition of government we gave in (36), T° (=Γ) prevents Agr°
(=α) from governing the base position of the subject (=β). We can rule
out the possibility of the subject being assigned Nominative Case in SpecT'
(which would also presumably give rise to S-Structures like (41)) by assuming that this position is an A'-specifier position, like the Spec of C',
and so non-operators are unable to appear there (cf. Rizzi 1990a). With
these assumptions, then, we can consistently maintain that Agr° is able to
assign Case under government but cannot assign Case to the base position
of the subject. Therefore the subject must move to SpecAgr' in order to
get Case.

Given this account of English, two comparative questions arise: first,
we saw in 1.0. that declarative sentences exactly like (41) are possible in
Welsh (cf. (5a), repeated below); second, we must provide an account of
Case-assignment in the 'free-inversion' construction characteristic of Italian and other null-subject languages. We will now deal with each of these
questions in turn.

S-structures which appear to be the exact counterparts of (41) are
possible in Welsh. We repeat the relevant example here:

(5) a.   Gwnaeth y   plentyn **weld** ceffyl
          did   the child   see   horse
          'The child saw a horse'

We have just excluded (41) in terms of the definition of government and
a characterization of the nature of SpecT'. How, then, are such sentences
possible in any language? We tentatively propose that such sentences, and
in fact VSO orders generally, are the consequence of a negative choice
for the option of Case assignment under agreement (the same proposal is
made in Koopman and Sportiche 1990). So, at least in Welsh, Nominative
Case can only be assigned under government (the same proposal is made
for Irish in McCloskey and Hale 1984; cf. also McCloskey 1986, 1990).

Given the way in which we just excluded (41), it might at first be thought
that a government-only system of Nominative assignment would be impossible. We pointed out above that Agr° cannot Case-mark the base position
of the subject in this structure because it does not govern this position.
Furthermore, SpecT' is unavailable as a landing site for the subject, since
we have assumed that it is an A'-position. Finally, SpecAgr' is not available (in non-inverted clauses) since this position is not governed by Agr°
(cf. (36ii)). The conclusion might seem to be that a government-only
system cannot exist. (Note that a system with 'generalized inversion' in
all finite clauses would nevertheless be possible, as inversion would create
the context for Nominative-assignment under government. It is unclear

whether such a system exists. Certainly, for reasons we will spell out in 1.3. and 1.4., generalized movement to C is impossible in many kinds of embedded clauses. However, the option of Agr-recursion (cf. 1.4.) may make possible a system in which Agr assigns Nom only under government — see below).

A related parametric option becomes relevant at this point. Suppose that Nominative can be assigned by either component of the former Infl, i.e. by either Tense or by Agr, as a matter of parametric choice. In a system where T is the Nominative assigner, Nominative can be assigned under government to the base position of the subject. This is what we propose to be the situation in Welsh (and presumably also in Irish, see McCloskey (1990) and the references given there).

This idea receives support from a salient feature of Welsh syntax; non-pronominal NPs show no morphological agreement with the verb (these examples are from Hendrick 1988: 43; a similar proposal is made by Rouveret 1988, who assumes that Welsh lacks Agr entirely):

(43) a. Can**odd** y **plentyn** bob dydd
   sing-pst-sg the child   every day
   'The child sang every day'

   b. Can**odd** y **plant** bob dydd
   sing-pst-sg the children every day
   'The children sang every day'

   c. *Can**on** y **plant** bob dydd
   sing-pst-pl the children every day

   d. Can**on** (**nhw**) bob dydd
   sing-pst-pl (they) every day
   'They sang every day'

((43d) indicates that Welsh is null-subject language, as long as the verb shows agreement). It is natural to suppose that the morphological reflex of bearing a Nominative feature assigned by Agr is agreement for relevant Φ-features with Agr. However, if Nominative is assigned by Tense we may expect the two morphological properties of bearing Nominative Case and sharing Agr's Φ-features will be dissociated. This is exactly what we find in Welsh (and in other Celtic languages), as illustrated in (43). We conclude that Welsh, and probably the other Celtic VSO languages, exemplify the parametric option where Nominative Case is assigned only under government, and since, in a structure like (35), Agr cannot then be the Nominative-assigner, T takes on this role, giving rise to the unusual agreement system found in these languages. It is possible that a system of this sort underlies VSO more generally, since Semitic VSO languages typically have agreement systems similar to those found in Celtic (cf. Mohammad 1989, Koopman and Sportiche 1990 on Arabic. Koopman and Sportiche also point out that in Welsh the subject precedes the negative adverb, which may suggest that it raises at least to SpecNeg'; we leave this matter open pending a more detailed analysis of negation in Welsh). On the other hand, Chung (to appear) argues that VSO orders in Chamorro are derived by subject-lowering rather than by verb-raising.

A similar problem to that posed by Welsh is raised by the phenomenon of 'free inversion' found in the Romance null-subject languages. The following Italian example illustrates free inversion:

(44)   Ha telefonato Maria

        Has telephoned Mary

        'Mary has telephoned'

This inversion option exists in much more limited form in French, where it forms one subcase of the operation known as stylistic inversion (or StylInv; cf. Kayne and Pollock 1978, Kayne 1986, Pollock 1986, and 2.4.4.1.):

(45)   A quelle heure a   téléphoné Marie?

        When   has telephoned Mary?

        'When did Mary telephone?'

We assume that the subject occupies its base position in these examples. So the Romance languages differ from English and Welsh in that the base position of the subject is on the right of the rest of VP rather than on the left of it (cf. Giorgi and Longobardi 1991 for more on this idea, where the consequences of a similar proposal for nominals are explored at length).

The question that concerns us most directly here is: how does the subject get Nominative Case in its inverted position in (44) and (45)? For the reasons outlined in the discussion of English above, Agr° cannot Case-mark this position since it does not govern it. Moreover, we will see below that neither (Modern) French nor Italian allow Agr to assign Nominative under government. We therefore propose that here, too, T° assigns Nominative. This is possible since T° governs the subject position in (44) and (45), which have the following partial structures (cf. Note 7):

(46)

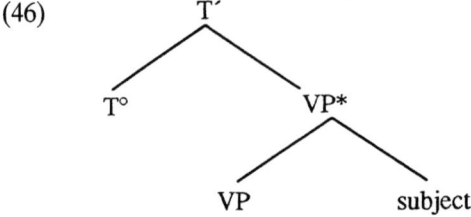

So in French and Italian (and probably other Romance languages, e.g. Spanish) T° assigns Nominative under government. What is the difference between Romance and Celtic, such that Romance languages, although they allow T° to Case-mark the subject under government, do not show the Celtic pattern of agreement? In fact, the essence of the account of Welsh just given can be retained; however, we must state that the lack of correlation between Nominative-assignment and morphological agreement in Welsh is due to the fact that Agr° **never** plays any role in Nominative-assignment in this language. In Romance, on the other hand, Agr° can assign Nominative to its Specifier, and so it is not entirely divorced from the assignment of Nominative. To capture the fact that postverbal subjects in Italian always agree, we provisionally stipulate a cosuperscripting relation between Agr° and T° (this relation may not hold in Italian dialects, where postverbal subjects typically do not agree (cf. Brandi and Cordin 1989); we will return to this question in 1.5). Nevertheless, it is T° that assigns Nominative to the subject in this construction. Further evidence that T° assigns Nominative comes from the Aux-to-Comp construction discussed in Rizzi (1982, Ch. 3), where the subject is clearly Nominative even though there is no (overt) Agr in the clause (Rizzi's (17b), p. 83):

(47)   Avendo Mario accettato di aiutarci, . . .

        Having M.   agreed   to help-us, . . .

        'Mario having agreed to help us, . . .'

We will say more about these issues directly and in 1.5. For brief remarks on Aux-to-Comp in the history of French, cf. 2.4.1.

Modern French is a language where Agr° only assigns Nominative in configurations of agreement. This has the result that sentences corresponding to English (38) are possible, but those corresponding to (39) are impossible, since Nominative cannot be assigned to SpecAgr' in the government configuration of (39). The ungrammaticality of examples like (48a) and (48b) illustrates this:

(48) a. *A   Jean pris   le   livre?

        Has J.   taken the book?

     b. *Quel film a   Jean vu?

        which film has John seen?

     c. A-t-il pris   le   livre?

        Has he taken the book?

     d. Quel   film a-t-il   vu?

        Which film has he seen?

In a language where Agr° assigns Nominative Case only under agreement, then, Agr to C movement (i.e. inversion) destroys the context in which Agr° can assign Nominative to SpecAgr'. So *Jean* cannot get a Case in (48a–b), and the sentence is ruled out by the Case Filter. We clearly need to say more about French, however, as we have to account for the grammaticality of examples comparable to (48a–b) which have clitic subjects, like (48c–d). We defer this question until 1.5. What we wish to show here is that French is an example of a language where Agr° only assigns Nominative under agreement.

Italian is like French in banning the equivalent of (48a–b):

(49)a. *Ha Gianni preso il   libro?

     Has John   this   the book?

   b. *Che   film ha Gianni visto?

     Which film has John   seen?

(The question of the Italian equivalents of (48c–d) arises in a rather different form, since Italian has no subject clitics — cf. 1.5. There we will also discuss the evidence that Agr moves to C in Italian interrogatives). However, we have just seen that Case can be assigned from C° to SpecAgr' in Aux-to-Comp constructions in Italian, and, more generally that T° assigns Nominative under government in both French and Italian. What, then, prevents T° from assigning Nominative to the subject under government in examples like (48a–b) and (49a–b)?

To answer this question, we need to sharpen our technical assumptions about how complex heads assign Case (Section 1.3. is devoted to a general introduction to the theory of head-to-head movement and complex heads). In principle, both T° and Agr° can have the feature [+Nom] in French and Italian. When T° [+Nom] incorporates with Agr° [+Nom], the result is a complex head Agr° which is able to assign Nominative Case just once. We take it that, since Agr° is the head of the complex head formed by incorporation of T° (see 1.3.), then the Nominative assigned by the complex head is Agr°'s (this is in accordance with the feature-percolation conventions for derived words proposed by Lieber 1980, 1983 and Marantz 1984). This Nominative feature cannot be assigned under government in these languages, since Agr° cannot assign Nominative under government in these languages. Thus, in (48a–b) and (49a–b), *Jean/Gianni* fails to get Case since T°'s Nominative feature is blocked by Agr°'s, and Agr°'s cannot be assigned in this configuration. This account leads to the following prediction: if T° is able to incorporate with C° when there is no other Nominative feature available, either because Agr° is absent or lacking this feature, or because T° skips Agr°, then T° should be able to Case-mark SpecAgr' (or the Specifier position that it governs, if Agr is absent) in a configuration like (49a). This is clearly true for Italian, as this gives us the Aux-to-Comp construction of (47) (and related cases involving the subjunctive (*Speravo* **fossi** *tu disposto ad aiutarci* 'I hoped that you were disposed to help us' Rizzi 1982: 85) which we then have to treat as having at the very least a different kind of Agr° from the indicative, possibly an Agr base-generated directly in C° — cf. 1.4.). Modern French lacks Aux-to-Comp, but this may be due to the independent absence of the relevant head-movement rule in these contexts. See 2.4.1. for further comments on Aux-to-Comp and related constructions in French.

A final point on free/stylistic inversion: in examples like (44) and (45) T° clearly incorporates with Agr°. However, here Agr°'s Nominative feature does not prevent T° from assigning its own Nominative feature to the position it governs in the base. This is possible because where head-to-head movement takes place, the incorporated head retains all its former government properties. Baker's (1988) Government Transparency Corollary is behind this property of derived heads. The Government Transparency Corollary (GTC) can be formulated as follows:

(50)   An X° which has an item Y° incorporated into it governs everything which Y° governed in its original structural position.

We will discuss this principle in more detail when we introduce the theory of head-to-head movement in the next section. Its effect in the free/stylistic inversion construction of Italian and French is to allow T° to assign Nominative Case to the base position of the subject even after (V-to-)T-to-Agr raising has taken place in examples like (44) and (45).

In this section we have seen how Koopmann and Sportiche's proposals for different modes of Case-assignment can work for Nominative Case. In the light of the account of Case-assignment in free-inversion constructions just given, we must reformulate the parametric choice among the three possibilities given in (37) along the following lines:

(51) a.   Agr° assigns Nominative under government? Yes/no

    b.   Agr° assigns Nominative under agreement? Yes/no

In these terms, the languages we have discussed make the following choices:

(52) a.   Government and agreement: English

    b.   Agreement but not government: French, Italian

    c.   Neither government nor agreement: Welsh

There is one logical possibility that we have not seen: the case where Agr° assigns Nominative only under government. In terms of our assumptions about clause structure so far, this is in fact impossible, since SpecT' is the only position governed by Agr and this is an A'-position. Assuming that the A' nature of SpecT' is not subject to cross-linguistic variation, the only way to allow the 'government-only' option for Agr° is to have an Agr-recursion (cf. Cardinaletti and Roberts, forthcoming). We will discuss this possibility in more detail in 1.4., and discuss its application to OF in 2.1.2. and 2.2.4. Note further that the assumption that SpecT' is an A'-position means that the parametric options available for T° are simply assignment under government (Welsh, French, Italian) or not (English).

So, counting Agr-recursion as allowing Agr° to choose the 'government-only' option, we have eight possible language-types, as follows:

(53) a. (52a) & T [−Nom]:   English

b. (52a) & T [+Nom]:   Middle French (see 2.3.)

c. (52b) & T [−Nom]:   Brazilian Portuguese

d. (52b) & T [+Nom]:   French, Italian

e. (52c) & T [−Nom]:   *(no way to assign Nom)

f. (52c) & T [+Nom]:   Welsh (etc)

g. Agr-recursion & T [−Nom]:   Icelandic (1.4.)

h. Agr-recursion & T [+Nom]:   (Early) Old French (2.1.2.)

We have discussed English, French, Italian and Welsh above. The earlier stages of French will be discussed in detail in Chapter 2. For Icelandic, cf. the brief remarks in 1.4. and the references given there, especially Cardinaletti and Roberts (forthcoming). It is unclear whether Brazilian Portuguese genuinely instantiates the system in (53c). (53c) is a system like French or Italian in ruling out (48a–b) and (49a–b), and which bans free inversion. It has been claimed that Brazilian Portuguese does not allow free inversion (Zubizarreta 1982), but the facts remain somewhat uncertain (cf. Kato and Tarallo 1986, Tarallo and Kato 1989 for relevant discussion).

This system has a number of implications and consequences. The most important consequence for our purposes here is that languages which allow Agr° to assign Nominative under government allow inversion around a non-pronominal subject, while languages in which Agr° assigns Nominative only under agreement do not. We have seen that this is a major difference between French and English. In Chapter 2, we consider the consequences of the fact, indicated in (53), that Old French and Modern French appear to differ in exactly the same way as French and English; so one of the central cases of parametric change we will be concerned with in this book involves the differing selection among the options given by (52) that we find at different periods of the history of French. We will see that an account of the differing choices in (52) that French has made in its recorded history also sheds some light on what the conditions are that lead acquirers to choose among the options that are in principle available to them (cf. in particular 2.4.).

1.3. INVERSION AND INCORPORATION

We said in 1.1. that the rule which moves the verb from its base position to I or C is the rule of head-to-head movement, or incorporation, in the sense of Baker (1988). In this section we will present our assumptions concerning the nature and functioning of this rule. In 1.3.1., we describe Baker's system in detail. In 1.3.2. we consider some consequences of the interaction of incorporation and the ECP for the analysis of verb-movement in a variety of languages. Here we also extend the distinction between A and A′ positions to the X°-level. In 1.3.3. we propose two refinements of Baker's theory: the first concerns the precise nature of the operation of head-to-head movement as adjunction or substitution (cf. Rizzi and Roberts 1989); the second concerns the possibility of successive-cyclic head-movement, or 'excorporation' (cf. Roberts 1991).

1.3.1. *The Theory of Incorporation*

In Baker's (1988) theory of syntactic incorporation, the operation which derives morphologically complex words from more basic elements (roots, stems or affixes) is taken to be head-to-head movement, i.e. the variant of move-α which applies to heads. Incorporation can thus be schematized as in (54):

(54)

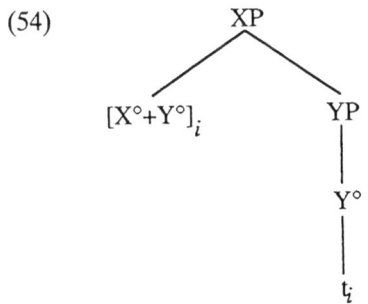

Baker analyzes noun-incorporation, applicative constructions, causatives and passives in these terms. Following proposals in Chomsky (1986b) and Pollock (1989), we treat verb-movement as a further instance of the schema in (54).

As we mentioned in the previous section, the complex head retains certain properties of the incorporated head in a derived structure like

(54). This is the effect of the Government Transparency Corollary (GTC), which we repeat here from the previous section:

(50)   An X° which has an item Y° incorporated into it governs everything which Y° governed in its original structural position.

For example, then, if Y° has a Case feature to assign to its complement under government inside Y′ in (54), this feature can still be assigned by [Y + X] after incorporation, as [Y + X] still governs the complement of Y. For this reason, V's Accusative Case can be assigned to the direct object from [V + I] after V-raising to Agr or C (the same is true of T's Nominative Case in Romance free-inversion examples like (44) and (45)). On the other hand, since (50) refers explicitly to **government**, incorporation of a head which assigns Case in an agreement configuration will destroy the relevant configuration. This is what happens when Agr is raised to C in French and Italian, as we saw in the previous section (cf. (48), (49)).[8]

Similarly, an incorporated head still head-governs its complements for purposes of satisfying the ECP. Thus (50) guarantees that V-to-I incorporation does not affect the status of the object with respect to extraction; classical subject-object asymmetries follow in the standard way from the ECP and are not affected by the operation of this rule (on the other hand, the head-government relation between the incorporation host X and its complement may be affected — cf. 1.5.). Moreover, as indicated in (54), we assume that any index possessed by Y° is associated with the complex head resulting from incorporation. This has the consequence that antecedent-government of the incorporation trace is possible. We also take it that this mechanism makes possible the formation of the chain (Y°, t) in (54) (see Note 9).

It is conceivable that the GTC is relevant for Θ-role assignment. However, we prefer to take Θ-assignment to be a property of chains. That is, we assume that the structural condition for Θ-role assignment is sisterhood, rather than government (following Chomsky 1986b), and that *both* Θ-assigners *and* Θ-assignees are abstractly represented by chains. (Similarly, we will see below and in more detail in Chapter 3 that both types of chain must be PF-identified in the sense of Baker op. cit.).

Baker (op. cit.: 66f) shows how the GTC can be derived from the definitions of government and barrierhood that he assumes. The same is true for the system we have adopted here, but we will not go through a detailed demonstration.

A major advantage of this theory of incorporation is that it allows an account of certain constraints on morphological operations in terms of well-known and independently motivated syntactic conditions, notably the Empty Category Principle (ECP). The ECP requires that all traces be both head-governed and antecedent-governed.[9]

Four major results ensue when the ECP is applied to the traces of head-to-head movement of the type in (54): (i) we can explain why incorporation is impossible from subjects and from adjuncts; (ii) the Head Movement Constraint (see 1.1.) can be derived; (iii) downgrading of heads is banned; (iv) 'excorporation' is banned.

Let us consider these points one by one. Cases where head-to-head movement takes place from a non-complement category are ruled out by the head-government portion of the ECP. The definition of government that we gave in (36) states that government is only possible into L-marked categories, while the ECP requires that all traces, including therefore traces of heads, be head-governed. Therefore only the heads of L-marked categories can satisfy the head-government requirement, as these are the only categories which allow a head to govern in from outside. Thus the heads of subjects and adjuncts cannot be moved to other heads without the ensuing trace giving rise to a violation of the ECP, as it cannot be head-governed.

Abstractly, then, the following cases are ruled out by the ECP in a system like Baker's, i.e. in each case the trace of head-to-head movement fails to be head-governed:

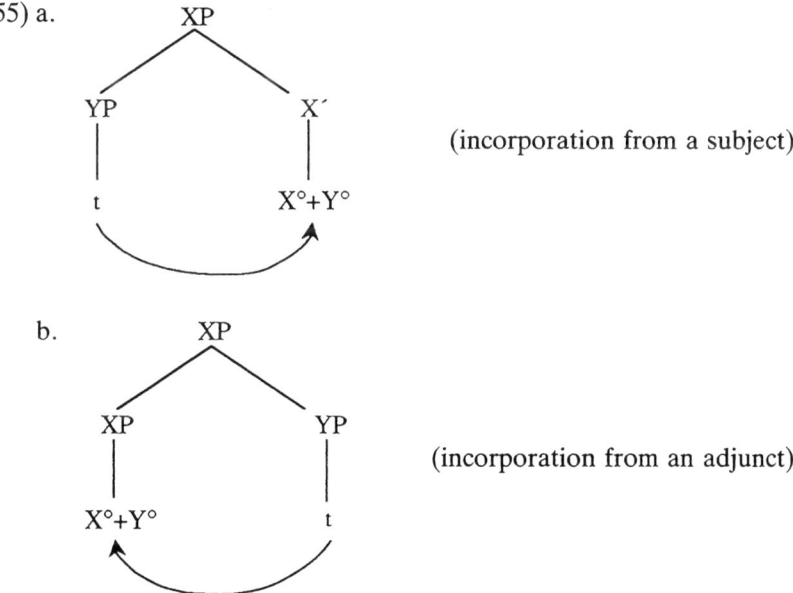

(55) a.   (incorporation from a subject)

b.   (incorporation from an adjunct)

Baker shows at length that there are indeed no instances of noun-incorporation, causative formation or applicative formation which move the head of a subject or an adjunct to another head position. Incorporation of the heads of complements of subjects or adjuncts, i.e. a Z° head of a ZP complement to Y° in (55), is ruled out by the combination of the reason given above and the Head Movement Constraint.

The derivation of the Head Movement Constraint comes out most clearly if we adopt the approach to antecedent-government based on the Relativized Minimality Condition of Rizzi (1990a). Rizzi's leading idea is to modify the Minimality Condition of *Barriers* (Chomsky 1986b: 10). The Minimality Condition, essentially clause (36iii) of the definition of government given earlier, operates in configurations of the kind shown in (56):

(56) $. . X . . [_Y . . W . . Z . .]$

Here, if W governs Z then the Minimality Condition prevents X from governing Z even if X satisfies all the other criteria for governing Z. The Minimality Condition is particularly important for the computation of antecedent-government relations; thus an intervening governor may block government of a trace by its antecedent, leading potentially to a violation of the ECP.

Rizzi proposes that the Minimality Condition be relativized such that the nature of both W and Z is taken into account. In terms of Relativized Minimality (RM), antecedent-government is defined as follows:

(57)   In the configuration (56), X antecedent-governs Z only if there is no W such that:
         (i)   W is an typical potential antecedent-governor for Z;
         (ii) W intervenes between X and Z.

Rizzi defines the class of typical potential antecedent-governors as follows.[10]

(58)   W is a typical potential antecedent-governor for Z =
         (i)   . . . in an A'-chain, W is an A'-specifier c-commanding Z;
         (ii) . . . in an A-chain, W is an A-specifier c-commanding Z;
         (iii) . . . in an X°-chain, W is a head c-commanding Z.

(58iii) is the condition that is relevant here. The Head Movement Constraint is violated in cases like the following:

(59)

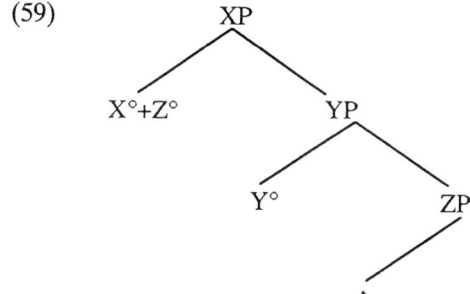

In terms of the definitions just given, $Y°$ in (59) counts as a typical potential antecedent governor for the trace of $Z°$, and so prevents $Z°$ from antecedent-governing its trace. Such configurations are thus ungrammatical. We saw in 1.1. that such a constraint is needed in order to account for the facts of verb-movement to C, in that it allows us to account for the restriction of English SAI to auxiliaries in terms of the general restriction on V-to-I to auxiliaries, and thus consider SAI to be a normal case of I-to-C (see also Travis 1984, where the HMC was originally proposed).[11]

Third, downgrading of a head to a non-c-commanding head is ruled out. This is prevented because c-command is necessary for government (cf. (36ii)), so the trace of a downgrading operation cannot be governed at all, and hence will fail to satisfy the ECP. Downgrading is illustrated in (60):

(60)

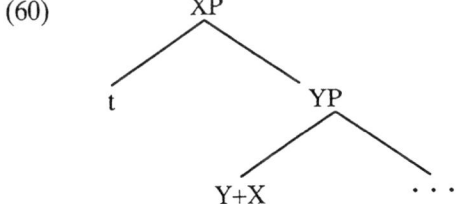

We will discuss the empirical import of this result in 1.3.2.

Fourth, excorporation is ruled out. Excorporation is successive cyclic head-to-head movement where one head simply 'passes through' another, first incorporating and then moving on. We illustrate this situation in (61):

(61)

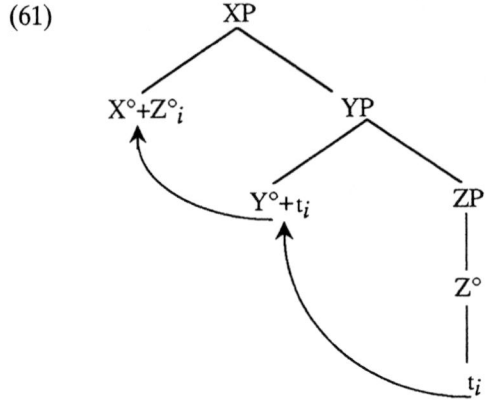

Excorporation seems to be impossible in a large class of cases of head-to-head movement. For example, assuming that *do* is inserted in English at PF in order to carry 'stranded' verbal affixes (cf. Chomsky 1957), and that *have* and *be* raise from base V-positions to I (Emonds 1976, 1978; we will have more to say about the English auxiliary system in 3.0. and 3.2.1.), we never find cases of subject-aux inversion of the following type:

(62) a. *Have John does t gone? (SS: Have John [t −s] t gone)

  b. *Be John did t arrested? (SS: Be John [t −ed] t arrested)

Instead, once the auxiliary combines with agreement, the two elements must move together to C° (giving *Has John gone* and *Was John arrested* for (62)).

Baker (1988: 73) rules excorporation out by the claim that words cannot contain traces (as Baker (ibid.) comments, "this part of the old lexicalist hypothesis still seems true"). For Baker, words can be formed by syntactic operations like incorporation, but they cannot be broken up by such operations once formed. However, the ECP can also provide this result (Baker mentions this possibility in Note 19, p. 73). Baker supposes that incorporation gives rise to derived complex heads with the following structure:

(63)

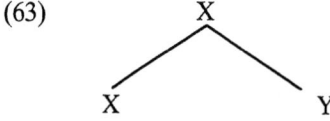

So head-to-head movement always adjoins a head to another head in Baker's system (see Baker 1988: 59; we will refine this point of view in 1.3.3.). If the incorporee Y now moves on, a trace will be left in the adjoined position. We can assume that X suffices to block antecedent-government of this trace by minimality (another point to be refined in

1.3.3.). So the ban on excorporation reduces to a variant of the Head Movement Constraint, in that both can be derived from the ECP in the same way.

The above are the standard assumptions about the nature and functioning of the incorporation rule that we will adopt here. They are either taken directly from Baker's work or modelled very closely on Baker's proposals. In what follows we will develop this initial conception of incorporation further.

1.3.2. *Constraints on Incorporation*

The above conditions on incorporation follow straightforwardly from the ECP and the theory of government. However, there are cases of verb-movement in the languages we are concerned with which appear to pose problems for the last three of these conditions. Since we want to maintain that the ECP constrains head-to-head movement in the strongest possible way (and, of course, we want to maintain that verb-movement is head-to-head movement), we should pay careful attention to these cases. We will now present the problematic data and suggest preliminary solutions, i.e. analyses of the facts in question which allow us to maintain the ECP and the theory of government as formulated. In fact, we will show that one class of problem posed for the HMC (by MSc) is probably not a genuine one. However, HMC violations in Balkan and conservative Romance languages are more problematic, as we shall see. The main case of downgrading that has been discussed in the recent literature concerns English, which we will deal with extensively. The third issue, excorporation, we defer until 1.3.3.

Let us consider first, then, putative violations of the HMC. In MSc, as discussed in Holmberg and Platzack (1988) (H & P), the inflected verb never appears in Agr. Since these are V2 languages, the inflected verb appears in C in matrix clauses. This is shown by the Danish examples we gave earlier, repeated here:

(12) a. Peter **drikker** ikke kaffe om morgenen
         P.   drinks   not coffee in   morning-the

  b. Kaffe **drikker** Peter ikke om morgenen
       Coffee drinks P.   not in   morning-the

  c. Om morgenen   **drikker** Peter ikke kaffe
       In morning-the drinks P.   not coffee
       'Peter doesn't drink coffee in the morning'

  d. *Peter ikke **drikker** kaffe om morgenen

As we saw earlier (example (13)), the finite verb follows the negation in subordinate clauses. In this respect, MSc differs from Icelandic, as the following pair (H & P's (7c–d)) shows:

(64) a. Om J´n **inte köpte** boken   (Swedish)
         if   J. not bought the-book

     b. hvort Jón **keypti ekki** bókina   (Icelandic)
         if   J. bought not   the-book

The obvious analysis of this contrast seems to be, as H & P propose, that V moves to Agr in Icelandic, but not in MSc.

In our discussion of English SAI in the Introduction, we said that SAI is an instance of Agr-to-C movement limited to auxiliaries since only auxiliaries can move to Agr and thereby 'feed' the subsequent movement. However, in MSc, it appears that all verbs can move to C, and yet we find the analogous evidence from negative-placement to that found in English that they do not move to Agr. H & P conclude from this that V moves directly to C in these languages, without passing through Agr. So, if H & P are right, MSc presents a systematic violation of the Head Movement Constraint.

However, H & P's data do not force us to this conclusion; we could simply take the view that the theory dictates that V passes through Agr on the way to C, even though one step of this movement is never visible (cf. successive cyclic *wh*-movement through Comp, whose intermediate steps are often invisible, but successive-cyclic movement is nevertheless generally assumed to take place in order to satisfy bounding theory). The question then becomes: why is V to Agr never visible in MSc, while it is in Icelandic (and French, etc.)? One possibility is that this is related to the complete absence of verbal agreement inflections in MSc (cf. 3.1.3.). This fact could be interpreted as meaning that MSc lacks an Agr-projection entirely; however, this idea leaves no position for the canonical, VP-external subject (still assuming SpecT' is an A'-position). In Chapter 3, Note 15, we will see comparative evidence in favour of an MSc Agr projection. We return to this question in 1.4. (cf. Notes 15, 19) and 3.3.2.; for now it suffices to note that there is no clear evidence of a violation of the Head Movement Constraint when V raises to C in MSc.

Another class of HMC violations has recently been discussed by Rivero (1988, 1990) and Lema and Rivero (L & R) (1989, 1990a, b). These are cases of Long Head Movement (LHM) in various Balkan and conservative Romance varieties: Bulgarian (B), Czech (C), Rumanian (R), 19th-century European Portuguese (EP) and Old Spanish (OS) (L & R also (1989: 17) mention Old Provençal, Old Catalan and Early Italian; Rivero 1990 discusses Slovak and Serbo-Croatian).

LHM constructions have the following general form:

(65)   Prt/infin$_i$ Aux + Agr t$_i$

(65) shows that some non-finite verb-form is moved over a finite auxiliary (this form may itself be an auxiliary, see below). To the extent that the finite auxiliary is a head which c-commands the base-position of the verb (and this is certainly the natural assumption to make, as well as having some evidence in its favour, see below), these are clear violations of the HMC. Some cases of (65) are given in (66) (L & R's 1990a, (4), p. 2):

(66) a. **Pročel**   sum knigata   (B)
         Read (I) have book-the
         'I have read the book'

     b. **Představil**   jsem se   mu   (C)
         Introduced (I) have him myself
         'I have introduced myself to him'

     c. **Seguir**-te-ei   por toda a   parte   (EP)
         Follow-you-will-(I) by all   the part
         'I will follow you everywhere'

     d. **Dar**te   he un exemplo   (OS)
         Give-you (I) will an example
         'I will give you an example'

     e. **Spune** mi va?   (R)
         Tell   me will (he/she)
         'Will he/she tell me?'

L & R show that LHM has the following properties in all these languages:

(67) a.   It is restricted to root contexts

     b.   It is blocked by negation

     c.   It is local (in a sense to be made clear below)

     d.   It is licensed only by temporal auxiliaries

     e.   It is triggered by a ban on first-position clitics

The restriction to root contexts is illustrated for Bulgarian and Portuguese in (68):

(68) a. *Znam   ce **pročel**   sum knigata. (cf. (66a))
         (I) know that read (I) have book-the
         (L & R (1990a), (7b), p. 4)

b. Uma historia . . onde me **referirei**   de espaço a elle. (EP)

    A   story   where me (I) refer-will at length to her

    'A history where I will refer to it at length'

    (ibid., (9a), p. 4)

In the Slav languages, the verb remains *in situ* in non-root contexts, while in the Romance languages it incorporates with the auxiliary, as (68b) shows. We follow L & R in taking the root nature of LHM as an indication that it involves movement to $C°$. L & R further point out that the fact that the verb incorporates with the auxiliary in the Romance languages indicates that the auxiliary must be in a position which c-commands the verb, and so where the verb moves over this auxiliary in matrix clauses we have genuine HMC violations.

Negation blocks this movement to C, as (69) illustrates:

(69) a. ****Pročel** ne sum knigata   (B, cf. (66a))

       '*I have not read the book*'

       (ibid., (11b), p. 5)

    b. Aqui non vos   **far**an   si non todo plazer

       Here not to-you make-will if not all   pleasure

       'Here they will not give you anything but pleasure'

       (ibid., (13b), p. 5)

Here, too, there is a difference between the Romance and the Slav languages: in the Romance languages, negation can be pre-verbal, while in the Slav languages, this is impossible (cf. L & R's ibid. (11c)).

LHM is local in the sense that it cannot take place across a second, non-finite auxiliary. This can be illustrated with the Bulgarian 'emphatic renarrated present', which involves two occurrences of auxiliary *have*, followed by a participle (ibid., (19), (21a), pp. 7, 8):

(70) a. Az sum **bil** cetjal knigata   (No movement)

       I   have had read book-the

    b. **Bil**   sum cetjal knigata   (LHM of *bil*)

       Had (I) have read book-the

       '(According to someone) I am reading the book'

    c. *Cetjal sum **bil** t knigata   (LHM of *cetjal*)

L & R show very clearly that LHM is not VP-Fronting (VPF), since some of the languages in question have a VPF process which is subject to quite different locality conditions, and which is licensed by a particular class of auxiliaries which does not license LHM. In fact, the auxiliaries which license LHM do not license VPF, and vice versa. For example, the Rumanian future auxiliary *va* allows LHM, as (66e) shows. However, this auxiliary does not allow VPF, while the modal 'can' does:

(71) a. *[Citi cartea] Maria va

      Read book-the M.   will

      (ibid., (25b), p. 9)

   b. [Citi cartea] nu   am putut

      Read book-the not (I) have could

      'I have not been able to read the book'

      (ibid., (24d), p. 9)

The auxiliaries which allow LHM and disallow VPF are purely temporal auxiliaries, while those which allow VPF have semantic content different to or additional to purely temporal content.

    LHM is triggered by a ban on clitic elements in first position. Thus LHM is connected to Wackernagel's Law (cf. Wackernagel 1892) and, in Romance, to the Tobler-Mussafia Law (cf. Mussafia 1983). The Tobler-Mussafia Law, operative in Medieval Romance languages (and, at least prescriptively, in contemporary Portuguese), bans clitic-first orders; when a clitic would otherwise come first the inflected verb is 'topicalized' and enclisis ensues (cf. de Kok 1985, Benincà 1989, 1990, Alberton 1990, and 2.1.2.). LHM is the case where a noninflected verb 'topicalizes' over the inflected verb. This 'topicalization' of the verb, although perhaps phonologically motivated, is best treated as syntactic movement, in large part for the reasons we have just seen. In fact, taking our cue from Benincà (1989), we take it to be syntactic movement to C°, presumably followed by obligatory enclisis of the clitic element which at SS occupies a functional-head position immediately below C° (arguably Agrl°, cf. Cardinaletti and Roberts (forthcoming) and 3.4.). The categorial nature of the clitic varies: in Romance, it is usually pronominal, while in Slavic it can also be verb- or auxiliary-like.

    We can treat these facts by extending further another aspect of the syntax of maximal projections to the head-level. We propose that there are two types of heads: A-heads and A'-heads. A-heads have properties that are relevant for the determination of argument structure; while A'-heads are relevant for the A'-system. More precisely, A-heads license A-chains (by assigning a Case or a Θ-role), while A'-heads license A'-chains (e.g. by licensing an operator). In these terms, we can state as a first approximation that T and C should be considered A'-heads while Agr and V are A-heads (although it should be borne in mind that at the X°-level, as at the XP-level, there is no inherent connection between category and function; just as NPs can be either arguments or operators, we may expect that a given head can be either an argument-licenser (A-head) or an operator licenser (A'-head), depending on factors other than its category (for example, its internal structure). We will develop this point further below).

Let us further apply the RM system to heads in a way that is sensitive to the A/A' distinction, just as it is in the XP-level. So we reformulate the definition of 'typical potential antecedent-governor' given in (58), as follows:

(58') W is a typical potential antecedent-governor for Z =

(i) . . . in an A'-chain: for Z = XP, W is an A'-specifier c-commanding Z.
for Z = a head W is an A'-head c-commanding Z.

(ii) . . . in an A-chain: for Z = XP, W is an A-specifier c-commanding Z.
for Z = a head, W is an A-head c-commanding Z.

In this way, RM applies to heads in a fashion analogous to the way in which it applies to maximal projections (note that Rizzi's definition is asymmetrical in that the intervener for head-movement is defined in purely structural terms, while the interveners for XP-movement are defined functionally; the reformulation just given defines the intervener for head-movement in functional terms too, eliminating this asymmetry).

Now, we have seen that LHM is movement to C°. Therefore we take it to be a case of head movement to an A'-position. As such, Agr° does not count as an intervener since it is an A-head, and so the non-finite verb is free to move over it. The elements which **do** count as interveners are negation and temporal auxiliaries.

For negation, this suggests strongly that we should adopt Pollock's NegP hypothesis, and then make the natural move of treating Neg° (naturally construable as an operator position) as an A'-head; we propose this as the account of (69a) (for (69b), it may be, as Zanuttini (1989) has proposed, that NegP is higher than AgrP in some Romance languages; alternatively, *non* here could be a clitic negation, attached to another head).

For the second case, we can say that the auxiliaries in question are members of T°, another A'-head. This accounts for cases like (70c), where *bil* in T° blocks A'-movement of *cetjal* to C°. However, we must explain two things: (i) why the auxiliaries in standard LHM, which bear tense-morphology, are not interveners; (ii) why the VPF-licensing auxiliaries are interveners (and why these auxiliaries license a VP-trace while LHM-licensing auxiliaries do not).

On the first point, we take it that these auxiliaries are either generated in T° or pass through T° in order to pick up tense morphology. However, this occurrence of T° is morphologically selected (in a sense to be discussed in detail in 1.3.3.) by Agr°. This gives rise to T-to-Agr movement, an instance of A-movement. If we suppose that A'-to-A movement is out in general (an idea which simply requires extending the standard conditions on variables to the X°-level), then we must assume that a morphologically selected T° is an A-head. Hence the T° which contributes the tense-marking to the auxiliary in the standard LHM cases is an A-head, and therefore not an intervener for LHM. On the other hand, the T° occupied by the auxiliary in examples like (70c) is not morphologically selected, and as such is an A'-head. All participles agree with the finite auxiliary (cf. L & R 1990a: 7f.); we cannot treat this kind of agreement as inducing movement to an A-head-position, however, or (70c) would be allowed as *bil* would be in an A-position, and thus would not block A'-movement of *cetjal*. So we are forced to assume that, at least for B, only **personal** agreement is associated with an (A-position) Agr°. Presumably, this is borne out to the extent that only personal Agr° licenses an A-chain by assigning Nominative or identifying a null subject.

On the second point, we can say that VPF-licensing auxiliaries are interveners for the reason just given regarding second auxiliaries in general. We assume that, since they have 'extra' semantic content, they are able to head-govern VP-traces, while purely temporal auxiliaries are not; this is what permits VP-Fronting following this class of auxiliaries.

So, to sum up, L & R's data can be used as motivation for applying the A/A' distinction at the X°-level and reformulating Relativized Minimality along the lines of (58'). We agree with L & R that the majority of cases where the HMC holds in full (for example with V-to-I-to-C movement in V2 languages, English and French, etc.) are due to the fact that I, or more precisely Agr, imposes a morphological constraint on V. We will see what this morphological constraint is in the next subsection. For the moment the important thing to note is that this constraint is independent of (58').

This system appears to predict some classes of interactions that are not attested. For example, holding constant the idea that Agr is an A-head, T is an A'-head and C is an A'-head, while lexical heads are A-heads, we might expect that Agr can move to a higher V, skipping C, or conversely that C can move to a higher T, skipping the higher V (thanks to Luigi Rizzi for pointing out these problems). However, another factor which we have not yet considered may rule out these possibilities: the fact that traces of head-movement must be head-governed. The independent nature of this requirement is obscured in a system in which the HMC holds in full since the same head — the one which is the minimal governor of the trace of incorporation — will always be both the antecedent-governor and the head-governor of the lower trace (although Rizzi's (1990a) system takes the conceptual difference into account). In a system like the one we are proposing here, however, this difference is of real empirical importance. We suggest, following the general lines of the theory of head-government in Rizzi (1990a, Ch. 2), that C is inert for head-government. For this reason, LHM will never go beyond C. This prevents movement from Agr direct to a higher V, skipping the intermediate C.

The other cases are harder to rule out. We cannot give a full discussion of them all here, but we will return to this issue when we have distinguished the different types of incorporation in the next subsection.

The issue of downgrading arises most clearly in the analysis of English. If non-auxiliary verbs do not move to Agr, and we saw ample evidence that they do not in 1.1., then how does the tense/agreement specification of T and Agr attach to V? English main verbs do not differ from (non-modal) auxiliaries in showing tense/agreement marking (although the aspectual auxiliaries of course have more suppletive forms than any main verb: cf. Chapter 3, Note 5, for a possible interpretation of this), and yet while we can maintain that auxiliaries raise, there is no obvious mechanism for attaching the inflection to a main verb. Given the incorporation-based approach to inflectional morphology that has been adopted in recent work, we do not want to adopt a lexicalist approach to inflection of the type in Lieber (1980); moreover, a solution based on feature-assignment from Agr/T to V of the type proposed in Roberts (1985) should probably only be adopted if no other approach can be made to work. So syntactic movement seems to be the mechanism which attaches Agr and T to V, in line with the initial proposal in Chomsky (1957). That is to say, Agr and T move down to V in these cases. At this point, a problem arises for the general ECP-derived ban on downward movement.

Solutions to this problem have recently been proposed by Chomsky (1989), Jaeggli and Hyams (1989), Pollock (1989) and Rizzi (1990a: Ch. 1, Appendix 1) (and cf. also Ouhalla 1990 for a different approach, which does not rely on downward movement (in syntax)). The essential idea that is common to each of these proposals is that the illicit traces which result from downgrading can be 'saved' by LF raising of the verb. Since the ECP applies to LF representations, no violation results, despite the fact that the relevant SS representations contain traces which are not properly governed.

We will return to this analysis of *do*-support and downgrading in 3.2.1., when we consider the history *do*-insertion. In terms of the theory of incorporation presented in 1.3.1., the conclusion is clearly that the general ban on downgrading of heads applies only at LF, and that downgrading in the mapping from D- to S-structure is possible as long as the representation can somehow be 'saved' at LF. In 3.2.1., we will propose a version of this idea which appeals to the distinction between A-heads and A'-heads.

1.3.3. *Types of Incorporation*

Now, however, we wish to address another aspect of the theory of incorporation, one which will lead to an account of the impossibility of V-to-Agr movement in English and MSc.

In order to see why this operation is impossible in these languages, we must first introduce the modifications Rizzi and Roberts (1989) make to the theory of head-to-head movement. As we mentioned above in connection with (63), Baker assumes that incorporation adjoins a head to another head. Rizzi and Roberts elaborate Baker's theory by assuming that head-to-head movement may be either substitution of a head into another head position, or adjunction of a head to another head position. In cases where incorporation results in a visible amalgam of the two heads, e.g. standard cases of Noun-incorporation or of V-to-Agr movement, they assume that the incorporation host morphologically selects the incorporee, hence a structural slot is created for the incorporee at D-structure as a function of the lexical properties of the incorporation host (this proposal is also made in Roberts 1985). So Agr° in a language like French has the subcategorization frame $[+T°\_\_\_\_]$ and T° has the frame $[+V°\_\_\_\_]$; an incorporating V° in Mohawk has the feature $[+N°\_\_\_\_]$, etc. In general, where an incorporation trigger X° has the feature $[+Y°\_\_\_\_]$, this means that the slot for Y° is base-generated within X°, triggering substitution of Y° during the derivation, leading to the creation of a complex head. More precisely, the complex head X° which triggers incorporation is made up of a slot for the incorporee and an X-element which selects the incorporee. We adopt the notation of Selkirk (1982), also used in Roberts (1991), and refer to the triggering element within X° as X^{-1}. This is a way of marking the internal structure of complex words which brings out the relations to aspects of phrasal syntax. With this kind of incorporation, the head of the complex formed by incorporation remains X°, the incorporation trigger, and the complex correspondingly remains of category X. Another feature of this type of incorporation was alluded in the discussion of the HMC in the previous section: a morphologically selected head position is an A-position, hence this kind of incorporation is A-movement of a head, and so the moved head must also originate in an A-position, in order to avoid the X° analogue of 'improper movement'. As we mentioned at the end of 1.3.2., it is morphological selection which is responsible for many cases where the HMC is obeyed, in a fashion in principle independent of (but, in fact, redundant with) (58').

On the other hand, if the potential host does not provide a structural slot via morphological selection, head-to-head movement may take place either as an instance of adjunction, or, if the host head is radically empty, as substitution into the empty head position. In the case of adjunction, following the proposals concerning adjunction in May (1985), the host head is realized in two segments, neither of which is a head on its own. The following three types of head-to-head movement are thus postulated:[12]

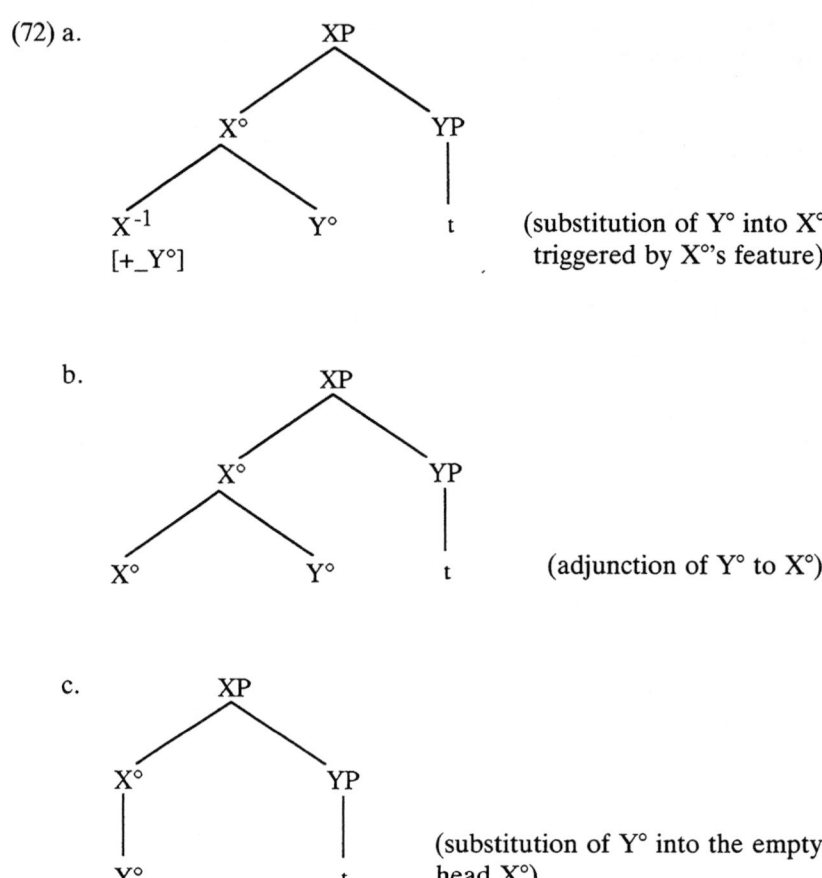

(72) a. (substitution of Y° into X° triggered by X°'s feature)

b. (adjunction of Y° to X°)

c. (substitution of Y° into the empty head X°)

What interests us in particular here is the difference between (72a) and (72c). Rizzi and Roberts propose that, while substitution into a morphologically given slot does not alter the 'external' properties of the host head (apart from the effects of Baker's Government Transparency Corollary — see (50)) substitution not triggered by morphological selection creates structures containing categories of a hybrid nature. That is, in a structure like (72c), Y° 'is-a' X°, hence X° and Y° together head 'XP' (cf. McCawley 1968). We will notate hybrid categories formed by free substitution of one head into another head in the following way:

(73)   XP/YP

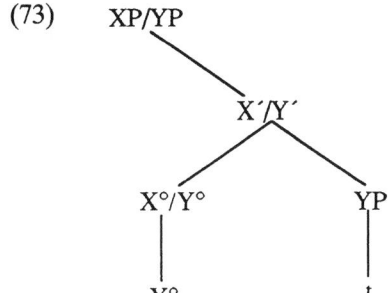

In (73), since the head is simultaneously Y° and X°, all projections are correspondingly doubly specified (cf. Haider 1989 for a similar idea).

This idea has two important consequences. First, assuming that, at least in non-V2 languages, Agr-to-C is 'free' incorporation, i.e. that Agr is not selected by C, it allows a principled account of the restriction of Agr-to-C movement to root clauses in non-V2 languages. In fact, as Rizzi and Roberts show, drawing on Kayne (1982), the correct generalization is that Agr-to-C movement is banned in selected contexts. Rizzi and Roberts claim that this generalization derives from the Projection Principle, given their proposals concerning head-to-head movement. The Projection Principle (cf. Chomsky 1981: 29) requires that selectional properties be satisfied at all levels of syntactic representation. This requirement extends to categorial selectional properties, imposing thereby a strong structure-preservation constraint on all selected contexts. The instances of Agr-to-C movement of the type illustrated in (73) are not structure-preserving in the sense required by the Projection Principle, and so are banned in all selected contexts. Although the generalized Agr-to-C movement that gives V2 is also basically a root phenomenon, we will suggest in 1.4. that this constraint holds for other reasons.

The second consequence concerns the specifier system of such complex heads. Rizzi and Roberts propose that a double head is able to license two kinds of specifier: for example, the hybrid head resulting from the free incorporation of Agr into C in a non-V2 language like French licenses a typical specifier for C° (an operator position), and a typical specifier for Agr° (a subject position). This is very important for the analysis of French complex inversion, as we shall see in 1.5.

We can extend the first consequence so as to explain the absence of V-to-Agr movement in English and MSc. As we mentioned in 1.1., the basic generalization for English seems to be that only non-Θ-assigning verbs can raise to Agr: raising of a Θ-assigning verb is ruled out.[13] Pollock (1989: 385) proposes that this is due to the fact that English Agr is opaque, precisely in the sense that it does not "permit transmission of the verb's Θ-role(s)" (ibid.), and that this is related to the morphological poverty of

English Agr. In French, on the other hand, Agr is sufficiently rich to be transparent in the relevant sense, i.e. to permit Θ-role assignment on the part of an incorporated verb. So, according to Pollock, raising a Θ-assigning verb to Agr in English leads to a Θ-criterion violation, while in French it does not.

We propose to adapt the proposals of Rizzi and Roberts concerning incorporation in such a way as to keep the basic insight behind Pollock's idea. The basic idea is this: all verbs which have Θ-roles to assign are required by the Projection Principle to be in determinate structural relations with structural positions filled by arguments bearing those Θ-roles (in the case of complements, this entails the creation of the positions as well). The Projection Principle checks the arguments in the positions in the verb's syntactic environment against the specifications of the verb's Θ-grid. If we assume that there is a thematic hierarchy in the sense originally proposed in Jackendoff (1972) and elaborated in Belletti and Rizzi (1988), a crucial aspect of this checking procedure will be the verification of whether the arguments in the various positions in the syntactic environment (probably the m-command domain) of $V°$ match the specifications in the verb's lexical entry (we saw above that one facet of this is checking the category of the verb's arguments).

Now, if the verb undergoes 'free' (non-selected) substitution into another head position, there will be two $V°$'s in the clause, both with identical thematic properties to be checked by the Projection Principle. There is then no way that both the Projection Principle and the biuniqueness relation between arguments and Θ-roles imposed by Θ-criterion can be satisfied. For example, consider the case of an unergative intransitive like *sneeze*. This verb will project a DS position for its argument, the VP-internal subject position on a theory like the one adopted here (cf. 1.2.), in order to satisfy the Projection Principle. At SS, after free incorporation with Agr, the Projection Principle will look for such a position associated both with the base position and with the derived position of *sneeze*. Such a position could exist, but the Projection Principle further requires it to be filled by an argument; if it is so filled, the argument will either receive no Θ-role or share its Θ-role with the DS subject of *sneeze*, and in either case the Θ-criterion will be violated. Hence there is no way that a well-formed structure can result from the non-selected substitution of a Θ-assigning verb into a higher head. Essential to this account is the idea that the Projection Principle only checks the syntactic environment of a 'free' $V°$, i.e. $V°$ immediately dominated by V'; so where $V°$ undergoes selected incorporation, the Projection Principle only checks the argument positions in the Θ-domain of the base $V°$.

On the other hand, verbs which have no thematic properties at all, i.e. auxiliaries, will not cause any violations if they undergo 'free' incorporation. This is why verbs which do not assign Θ-roles i.e. auxiliaries, raise

more freely than Θ-assigning verbs, hence the differences observed by
Roberts and by Pollock. This account can, still following Pollock, be tied
to the relative richness of verbal inflection; we assume that 'richer' verbal
inflection is more likely to morphologically select V. In that case, V raises
to Agr to form a complex Agr, not a V/Agr hybrid, and so the problems
with the Θ-criterion and the Projection Principle do not arise; clearly this
is the case in French (and, as we shall see in 3.1., earlier stages of both
English and MSc; the diachronic data also give us a clearer notion of what
constitutes 'richness', cf. 3.1.3.).

This approach to the restrictions on V-to-Agr in English leads us to
expect, other things being equal, that the head V/Agr that results from
have/be raising has a double specifier. This seems to be a correct prediction, as English has an 'extra' position for adverbs and floated quantifiers
which precedes the inflected verb, whether the inflected verb is an auxiliary
or not (although the reason in the two cases is different). No such position
is available in French, as the following examples show:

(74) a. The fact that John probably has made several mistakes is well-
       known

 b. *Le fait que Jean probablement ait fait plusieurs erreurs est bien
       connu

       (Kayne 1989, (22, 23), p. 8)

(75) a. I wonder   if John ever   was a   rational man

 b. *Je me demande si Jean jamais fut   un homme rationnel

       (Pollock 1989: 370, Note 8)

(76) a. The children all   will   leave

 b. *Les enfants tous vont partir

       (Sportiche 1988a: 443)

In our terms, this is related to the fact V-to-Agr movement is free incorporation in the sense just described. One aspect of these English sentences
that we cannot readily account for, however, is the order. It is not clear,
given these proposals, why the subject position should rigourously precede
the adverbial position (and, as we shall see in 1.5., why the *wh*-operator
must precede the subject in French complex inversion, which is another
case of incorporation by free substitution). We may speculate that adverbs
(of the relevant class) must be sisters of I', perhaps for reasons connected
to the fact that they are modifiers (cf. Roberts 1987, Sportiche 1988),
while *wh*-operators must take the entire clause — including the subject —
in their scope. Leaving that question aside, however, we can relate this
'extra' property of English to the nature of the V-to-Agr rule. A clear
diachronic prediction emerges from this: orders of this type were not

available as long as English allowed main verbs to move to Agr (as long as Agr was rich in the relevant sense). We will return to this point in Chapter 3.

This account also extends to the differences between auxiliaries and main verbs with respect to the possibilities of raising infinitives that we discussed in 1.1. The relevant facts were given in (30–32), which we repeat here:

(30)   *N'aimer   pas ses   parents est une honte

   neg to-love not one's parents is   a   shame

   'Not to love one's parents is shameful'

(31)a.   N'être   pas heureux est une condition d'écrire

   Neg to-be not happy   is   a   condition for to-write

   'To not be happy is a condition for writing'

   b.   Ne pas être heureux est une condition d'écrire

(32) a.   *Ne sembler pas heureux . . .

   b.   Ne pas sembler heureux . . .

These examples show that French main-verb infinitives have the properties of all English main verbs, so we conclude that they are not morphologically selected, hence they are unable to raise without violating the Projection Principle and/or the Θ-criterion. Only the Agr of tensed clauses in French has the property of morphologically selecting V^{14} (the situation is apparently different in Italian, cf. Belletti 1990; and cf. Kayne 1990 for a survey of the different positions occupied by infinitives in a range of Romance languages, and for a very interesting and suggestive analysis of this variation which goes somewhat beyond our concerns here), so in infinitival clauses V cannot raise. Pollock shows, however, that V does raise to T in such clauses; this is illustrated in (33), which we repeat from 1.1.:

(33) a.   A peine comprendre l'italien . . .

   b.   Comprendre à peine l'italien . . .

One way to account for this would be to say that infinitival morphology in French appears in T° and morphologically selects V. This seems to be an option in French; the other being either base-generation of infinitival morphology on V°, or, if we take seriously the idea that this morphology is a reflex of a [−finite] specification on T°, downgrading of T° followed by LF raising of [T + V] back to T°.

The idea that −er in T° selects V° does not give a clear idea of why continued raising to Agr should be blocked (whether or not we assume that Agr morphologically selects [−finite] T). Since T is a functional head, lacking thematic properties, the restrictions imposed on 'free' incorporation by the Projection Principle and the Θ-criterion outlined above do not apply to it, and V° will not give rise to Projection Principle/Θ-criterion violations since the category resulting from selected V-to-T movement is T (i.e. V° is not 'free' in the sense mentioned above when it is selected by T). On the other hand, if we propose instead that V-to-T is free incorporation in French infinitives, this has the result that the Projection Principle and the Θ-criterion will rule out the resulting structure (in the same way that raising of all English main verbs is ruled out). Moreover, the existence of infinitival morphology strongly suggests the presence of T^{-1}, and hence of morphological selection for V (cf. 3.1.2., 3.3.2. on the diachronic loss of the English infinitival affix, and its consequences when seen as the loss of T^{-1}). So it seems that neither free nor selected incorporation gives the right result for short movement of French main-verb infinitives.

An important clue to the way out of this dilemma comes from the diachronic data. There is clear evidence that infinitives raised to Agr in earlier stages of French. The following examples (from de Kok 1985: 335, cited in Alberton 1990) illustrate:

(77) a. car elle (. . .) commenca à ne les   **chercher pas**
         for she   began   to neg them look-for not
         'for she began not looking for them'
         (M. de Navarre, *L'Heptaméron*, M. François (ed.), Paris, Garnier, 1950: 65)

b. Le   pauvre gentilz homme (. . .) les   pria
    The poor   gentleman   them begged
    de ne les   **abandonner point**
    to neg them abandon   not
    'The poor man begged them not to abandon them'
    (M. de Navarre, *L'Heptaméron*, M. François (ed.), Paris, Garnier, 1950: 3)

Also, infinitives appear to raise in Italian (Belletti 1990). The following should be contrasted with Pollock's examples in (30) and (32a):

(78) a. Non **amare più** i propri genitori è una vergogna
         '*To love no longer one's parents is shameful*'

b. Non **sembrare mai**   contenti . . .
    '*To seem   never happy . . .*'

What we have said up to now accounts straightforwardly for infinitive-movement of the type in (77) and (78): the infinitival affix in T^{-1} selects $V°$, and the resulting complex $[_{T°} \, V \, T^{-1}]$ can then move to Agr without violating the Projection Principle (and, in Italian at least, it must move on; cf. Belletti 1990). The question is, then: what is different about Modern French?

We cannot give a full answer here, but in work in progress, I propose that this is connected with the loss of clitic-climbing and the loss of Aux-to-C (cf. 2.4.2.), which in turn, following Kayne (1989a), can be connected to the fact Agr lost the capacity to license null subjects. As a result of losing the capacity to license null subjects (cf. 2.3.4.), French Agr lost ability to head-govern a certain class of head-traces. So this is what blocks the infinitive-movement in Modern French: the trace of such movement cannot be head-governed.

The question which now arises is: why are *avoir* and *être* able to move to Agr? The answer is that, as non-Θ-assigners, they are not forced to leave traces in their base positions. So, as in English, the distributional differences between auxiliaries and main verbs can be traced to the fact that the Projection Principle treats auxiliaries differently, as they are not Θ-assigners.

As a final remark concerning the theory of head-to-head movement, consider what was said above concerning the general ban on excorporation in terms of the elaborated theory of head-to-head movement we have developed in this section. We will take each type of incorporation in turn, and consider the possibilities of excorporation for each of the different types of incorporation we have seen.

With respect to free incorporation, no issue arises as excorporation is indistinguishable from a subsequent movement of the whole head. In these cases, as there is no host for incorporation, nothing can be stranded by excorporation. Selected incorporation, i.e. substitution into the position created by the morphological subcategorization property of the host, prevents excorporation following essentially the reasoning outlined above. In terms of relativized minimality, the host head counts as a typical potential head-governor for the trace and so the excorporated head cannot antecedent-govern its trace. In terms of the approach to antecedent-government of traces summed up in (58'), we have to say, in order to get this result, that all morphologically **selecting** and morphologically **selected** heads are A-positions (a statement we have already made on independent grounds). This requirement does not necessarily extend to syntactic selection (i.e. standard categorial selection for XPs); cf. 1.4.

Consider next the situation which arises when incorporation involves the adjunction of one head to another. Following the conception of adjunction outlined in May (1985) and adopted in Chomsky (1986b), the two occurrences of the host head $X°$ in (72b) are the segments of the single head $X°$. We can thus propose that the $X°$ sister to $Y°$, since it is not itself a head, cannot count as a typical potential antecedent-governor for the trace of Y°. Therefore, Y° is able, other things being equal, to move on, stranding the host head, and its trace will be properly governed (this account replaces the one sketched in connection with (63) above). Possible cases of this kind are discussed in Roberts (1991).

The relevance of excorporation to our concerns involves the possibility of LF-excorporation of T/Agr after these elements have been downgraded to V in the mapping to SS. Given what we have said so far, excorporation should be possible from a complex head formed by downgrading. Downgrading must be incorporation by adjunction. It cannot be free substitution (at least in the case of T/Agr-to-V movement, as here V° is patently filled), and it cannot be selected since we assume, following Chomsky (1981), Stowell (1981), that selection creates base configurations: if V morphologically selected T°, TP would be base-generated as the complement of V°. Thus, by elimination, we conclude that this kind of incorporation is adjunction. The structure of a tensed verb in English is thus as follows:

(79)

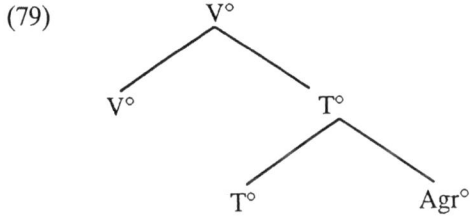

In this structure, what prevents T° from excorporating? It must be that T° must leave a variable in an A-position. If T° fails to 'pied-pipe' V°, the position of the variable left behind will be the adjoined T° position, clearly an A'-position. On the other hand, if V° is pied-piped, the variable occupies V°, an A-position. We need to say more, however, in order to rule out successive-cyclic V (or T) movement through *not* in Neg°; this is crucial in deriving the necessity for *do*-insertion in negatives (cf. 3.2.1.). For this reason, we assume that excorporation is in general banned, at least at LF. It may be that the cases of excorporation discussed in Roberts (1991) are triggered by purely morphosyntactic conditions, and so are independent of LF.

The above remarks are intended as an elaboration of Baker's theory. We see that, when certain points left open by Baker are developed, a picture of a range of different kinds of head-to-head movements emerges. We have elaborated Baker's theory in two ways in this section: by positing that incorporation may result either in adjunction or substitution structures, and that the latter may be triggered in one of two different ways (as proposed in Rizzi and Roberts 1989); and by suggesting that the distinction between A and A'-positions can be extended to heads. Both of these elaborations are held to interact with other conditions, notably the Projection Principle, in such a way as to rule out many improper examples of incorporation.

Although the theory of head-to-head movement proposed here is quite complex, it is firmly rooted in general principles of the overall theory of syntax. The modifications and refinements we have proposed here continue the program of extending the principles of syntax that are operative above the X° level to apply to those processes that are sensitive to what goes on below (or inside) this level.

1.4. *Verb Second*

In this section we will apply the system of head-to-head movement outlined in the previous section to the well-known case of movements to C. We will concentrate on the best-known and most pervasive instance of this phenomenon, that of V2. As far as we know, the phenomena are as described in the Introduction in all Continental West Germanic languages and dialects, with the notable exception of Yiddish (cf. Diesing 1988, Santorini 1988 and below). Similarly, all the North Germanic languages share this basic pattern, except for Icelandic (cf. Rögnvaldsson and Thráinsson 1990). We will also summarize Rizzi's (1990b) recent analysis of 'residual V2': movement to C in English and French interrogatives (and a few other contexts). Many analyses of V2 have been proposed in the recent literature; cf. Vikner (1990, Ch. 2) for a survey and relevant references. We will adopt a variant of the proposal in Tomaselli (1989).

The basic facts of the V2 constraint were given in the discussion of examples (7–11) in the Introduction, which we repeat here:

(7) a. Ich **las** schon letztes Jahr diesen Roman
    I read already last year this book

  b. Ich **habe** schon letztes Jahr diesen Roman **gelesen**
    I have already last year this book read
    'I read this book last year already'

(8) a. Diesen Roman **las** ich schon letztes Jahr
    This book read I already last year

  b. Diesen Roman **habe** ich schon letztes Jahr **gelesen**
    This book have I already last year read

(9) a. Schon letztes Jahr **las** ich diesen Roman
    Already last year read I this book

b. Schon   letztes Jahr **habe** ich diesen Roman **gelesen**

Already last   year have I   this   book   read

(10) a. *Schon letztes Jahr ich **las** diesen Roman

b. *Schon letztes Jahr ich **habe** diesen Roman **gelesen**

(11) Du weisst wohl,

you know well

a. daß ich schon   letztes Jahr diesen Roman **las**

that I   already last   year this   book   read

b. daß ich schon   letztes Jahr diesen Roman **gelesen habe**

that I   already last   year this   book   read   have

These sentences show that the inflected verb must appear in second position in a root clause, preceded by some phrasal constituent. Following Chomsky (1986b) and the analysis presented in 1.1., we take it that the second position is $C°$, and the position occupied by the obligatory first constituent is SpecC' (here we differ from Travis 1984; for arguments based on German against this position and in favour of Chomsky's, see Schwartz and Vikner 1989, see also 2.3.1., 2.3.2. for indirect confirmation of Schwartz and Vikner's point of view on the basis of evidence from Middle French). Essentially, then, there are three questions that any analysis of V2 must answer:

I What forces V-movement to C?

II What forces movement of some XP to SpecC'?

III What prevents the processes at work in I and II from operating in (most) embedded contexts?

We will now deal with each of these questions in turn.

Concerning I, we now have a mechanism for forcing head-to-head movement: morphological selection, as described in the previous section. Following Tomaselli (1989: 355f), we claim that C is 'pronominal' in V2 languages, in the sense that it attracts V (this idea goes back, in varying forms, to Platzack 1987 and den Besten 1983). More precisely, we take it that C contains C^{-1} with the morphological selection feature [+Agr° ____] in such languages (or rather, C has this structure wherever some other principle does not prevent it from doing so, see below). So Agr incorporates with C. Since Agr selects T and T selects V, the result is that the inflected verb ends up in C, after successive movement through T and Agr. This really amounts to a classic treatment of V-movement to C in Germanic, cf. den Besten (1983), Platzack (1987, 1988), and the references given there.[15] This view is very close to the one presented in Rizzi (1990b), which is based on the feature system for functional heads of (17), and says that V2 languages have [+C, +I] as the highest functional head of

the full clause, while non-V2 languages have [+C, −I]. In these terms, C°
[+Agr°] is equivalent to Rizzi's [+C, +I].

Tomaselli points out three major pieces of evidence in favour of the
idea that C is associated with Agr in Germanic. First, C is able to license
a null subject (although in standard German this must be an expletive,
see 2.2.3.). This is illustrated in (80):

> (80) a. Mir   wurde *pro* geholfen
>   *To-me was   helped*
>   'I was helped'
>
> b. Hier wurde *pro* getanzt
>   *Here was   danced*
>   'There was dancing here'

The null subject here is the empty pronominal *pro*. This element must be
licensed by some designated head (on the licensing conditions for *pro*, see
2.0.). If C is the licenser of *pro* here, then C certainly shares a major
property with Agr in classic null-subject languages like Italian. Since Rizzi
(1982, Ch. 4), it has been assumed that the category which licenses *pro* is
'pronominal' in some sense; hence if C is the licenser of *pro*, C must be
pronominal. The proposal that C has the feature [+Agr____] accounts
for these facts straightforwardly, since C will therefore contain Agr at S-
Structure, the level at which *pro* is licensed. Again, the possession of
some type of 'rich' agreement has classically been related to the possibility
of null subjects (Taraldsen 1979, Chomsky 1982, Rizzi 1986a).[16,17]

Striking evidence for the pronominal, or agreeing, nature of C in Continental West Germanic comes from certain dialects where complementizers
appear to agree with the verb. The clearest case of this type is West
Flemish (WF; the data and many facets of analysis are drawn from Haegeman (1990, Ch. 2) — see also Bayer 1984, Reis 1985 for similar data from
different varieties of German). In WF, we find that the complementizer
dat, which introduces a tensed [−wh] complement clause, varies in form
exactly like a verb according to the person and number of the subject of the
clause it introduces (in the pronominal forms, (81a,b), a clitic obligatorily
attaches to C, with the option of 'doubling' with a full pronoun in subject
position, cf. Haegeman (op. cit.) for details and analysis):

> (81)   Kpeinzen . . .
>   *I think   . . .*
>
> a. . . . da Valère morgen   goat
>   *. . . that V.   tomorrow goes*

b. . . . dan Valère en Pol morgen goan
   . . . *that V. and P. tomorrow go*

Here there seems to be no escaping the conclusion that C is able to agree. Moreover, Haegeman shows that this agreement is not an adjacency effect; when the subject is for some reason nonadjacent to the complementizer, the agreement still shows up (ibid., (10–12)).[18] The natural claim, then, is that C contains Agr. Our proposal, again following Tomaselli, is that C contains Agr also in varieties like Standard German and Standard Dutch where the Agr is not overt.

Third, it appears that C is the host for clitics in many V2 languages. This is the case in WF (cf. Haegeman ibid.). In Standard German, for example, subject pronouns must be adjacent to a lexical complementizer (examples from Tomaselli (1989: 367, (52–3)):

(82) a. daß **er ihm/*ihm er** ein Buch geschenkt hat
         *that he him/*him he a book given had*

   b. daß **er es/*es er** dem Jungen geschenkt hat
       that he it/it he the boy given had

Similar facts are found in Dutch. Den Besten (1983: 56f.) shows that weak subject pronouns in Dutch must occur to the immediate right of C:

(83) a. dat **je gisteren/*gisteren je** ziek was
         that you yesterday/yesterday you sick were

   b. Was **ze gisteren/*gisteren ze** ziek?
       was she yesterday/yesterday she sick?

The weak pronouns *je, ze*, etc. should be contrasted with the strong pronouns *jij, zij*, etc. These can be separated from C:

(84) a. dat **gisteren jij** ziek was

   b. Was **gisteren zij** ziek?

Again, there is a well-known correlation between the possibility for a given head to host clitics and its ability to license *pro* (cf. Rizzi 1986a). Both properties can arguably be viewed as the reflex of the presence of Agr. If so, then the data in (82–84) further indicate that C contains Agr in German, Dutch and other V2 languages (although cf. Cardinaletti and Roberts (forthcoming) and 3.4. for a slightly different interpretation of these facts).

We conclude, then, that the answer to question I is that C has a morphosyntactic feature which attracts Agr (or T in MSc, cf. Note 15), and hence the inflected verb. In V2 languages C has this feature in (at least) all matrix clauses; in non-V2 languages it does not. The presence of Agr in C at SS which results from the presence of this feature determines, directly or indirectly, the properties of C in Continental West Germanic languages in (80–84).

The incorporation of Agr in C is therefore an instance of selected incorporation. This means that the head which results is C, rather than C/Agr, and that there is only one specifier position available: the one typically licensed by C (it also means that C[+Agr] is an A-head, given what we said in the previous section; see below).

We turn now to question II: What underlies the obligatory presence of some constituent in SpecC' when the inflected verb is in C°? Our proposal is that a constituent is obligatory in SpecC' because of the following condition:

(85)   A head containing Agr must have a filled specifier

(85) is related to the Extended Projection Principle of Chomsky (1982), although we take it to hold at SS only. This condition guarantees that SpecAgr' is filled in non-V2 languages; and, as stated in (85), in conjunction with our version of Tomaselli's proposals for verb-movement to C, it similarly guarantees that SpecC' is filled in V2 languages (including MSc, as no reference is made to the content of Agr). We can assume that (85) is trivially satisfied in VSO languages like Welsh and Irish since the head containing the verb does not contain Agr; the agreement paradigm of these languages (which we saw in (43)) can be treated as resulting from the cliticization of a subject pronoun into V° (cf. McCloskey and Hale 1984 on Irish, and Rouveret 1988 on Welsh; Welsh presents the further complication of allowing a pronominal subject to co-occur with an agreement affix (cf. (43d)), but we can adopt the approach in Bennis (1984) and treat this element as an expletive pronoun, similar to the clitic pronouns in French complex inversion to be discussed in 1.5.). This view of Welsh is entirely consistent with what we said in 1.2 regarding the position of the verb and Nominative Case assignment in these languages.

As formulated, (85) interacts with our proposal that Agr incorporates with C in V2 languages in such a way as to force the movement of some XP into SpecC'. It thus provides an adequate initial answer to question II. However, there are certain cases of apparent V1 sentences in V2 languages which require further discussion. These fall into essentially four classes: yes/no questions, conditionals, 'lively narrative style' and German 'Pronoun Zap' (Ross 1982, Huang 1984, Cardinaletti 1990b). We illustrate the first three phenomena using Dutch examples from den Besten (1983), and fourth with German examples from Haider (1986):

(86) a. **Komt** je   broer   nog?
     Comes your brother yet?
     (den Besten's (22a), p. 54)

   b. **Mocht** je   nog geld   nodig hebben, . . .
     Might you still money need, . . .
     (den Besten's (ii), Note 3, p. 121)

   c. **Ging** ik laatst   naar de Swart
     Went I   recently to   de Swart's
     (den Besten's (63), p. 62)

   d. **Habe** es schon   gelesen
     Have it already read
     (Haider's (2–18a), p. 56)

We would like to maintain that these are really V2 structures; in each case, some phonologically null category occupies SpecC'. In (86a), this is the empty interrogative morpheme (which we indicate 'Q'). This morpheme will play an important role in the account of the history of French interrogatives to be presented in Chapter 2. In (86b), we postulate a null modal operator for the first position. For (86c), we tentatively suggest that a discourse or illocutionary operator of some kind occupies this position. Such a solution certainly seems to be appropriate for (86d), as argued in Huang (1984). If we can maintain these assumptions, then (85) gives a full account of the obligatory appearance of some XP in SpecC' which characterizes V2 structures.

This brings us to III: The question of the root nature of V2. Here some refinement of the question is in order, as there are well-known cases of embedded V2. The best-known kind of example is the German phenomenon of 'conjunctive discourse' (Bach and Horn 1976, den Besten 1983). Here a verb of saying takes a sentential complement without *daß*, with the verb preferentially (or at least prescriptively) marked subjunctive, and V2:

(87) a. Er sagte, **er komme**   morgen
     He said   he come (subj.) tomorrow
     (den Besten's (1), p. 108)

   b. Er sagte, **gestern wäre**   er schon   arriviert
     He said   yesterday have (subj.) he already arrived
     (den Besten's (ii), Note 11, p. 123)

The class of verbs in question is roughly the class of bridge verbs (cf.

Haider 1986: 53) which may be semantically characterizable as non-factives. This phenomenon is closely related to a phenomenon found in other Germanic languages: V2 order following the equivalent of *that*, i.e. the complementizer which introduces tensed [−wh] complements (see Platzack 1987):

(88) a. vi vet   [at [kaffe drikker Peter aldrig]]
         we know that coffee drinks Peter never
         (Danish, (Vikner 1990))

   b. Jón segir [að [Helgi hafi keypt bókina]]
       John says   that Helgi has bought the book
       (Icelandic, (Thráinsson 1986: 171))

   c. Pyt sei [dat [**hy hie** my sjoen]]
       Pete said   that he   had me seen
       (Frisian *et al.*, de Haan & Weerman (1986: 84))

As the examples show, it seems that roughly the same class of verbs is at work in (88) as in (87).

What we do not find, however, are V2 [+wh] complements. This is completely impossible in German (cf. Reis 1985, Haider 1986, 1989) and Swedish (Platzack 1987):

(89) a. Wenn man dich fragt, wo   du gewesen **seist**, . . .
         If   one you asks where you been   have, . . .

   b. *Wenn man dich fragt, wo   **seist du** gewesen, . . .
      If   one you asks where have you been, . . .
      (Haider 1989, (10c–d), p. 104)

   c. *Jag undrar om **kommer han** inte snart
      I wonder if comes   he   not soon
      (Platzack 1987, (28a), p. 39)

Two V2 Germanic languages appear to allow this: Yiddish and Icelandic. The following Yiddish example from Santorini (1988: 6) contrasts minimally with (89):

(90)   Hot im di vayb gefregt, vos **iz** di mayse?
        Has him the wife asked   what is the story?

Santorini shows, following the proposal of Diesing (1988), that V2 in Yiddish is in fact a rather different phenomenon from the more general Germanic case. Rather than obligatory V-movement to C, and topicaliz-

ation of XP to SpecC', the Yiddish phenomenon involves obligatory V-
to-Agr (or at least to some functional head below C°) and 'topicalization'
into the SpecAgr (or the Specifier of the highest functional head in the
clause ≠ C°). As such, it is completely insensitive to the root/embedded
distinction. This approach seems quite justified for Yiddish, but is clearly
not viable for German (and the other languages) given the observed
contrasts. For a detailed discussion of Yiddish in terms of this analysis,
cf. Diesing (1990).

In Icelandic, V2 orders are possible in all types of embedded clauses:

(91) a. Ég held   að þegar   hafi María lesið

     I   believe that already has Mary read

     þessa bók   (bridge)

     this   book

   b. Ég harma að þegar   hafi María lesið

     I   regret that already has Mary read

     þessa bók   (factive)

     this   book

   c. Ég spurði **hvort**   þegar   **hefði María** lesið

     I   asked whether already had   Mary read

     þessa bók   (*wh*)

     this   book

   d. sú staðreynd **að** **þegar**   **hefur María** lesið

     the fact   that already had   Mary read

     þessa bók.   (NP)

     this   book.

   e. bókin   **sem þegar**   **hefur María** lesið.   (relative)

     book-the that already had   Mary read.

   (Rögnvaldsson and Thráinsson 1990; Thráinsson, pers. comm.)

To treat this situation, holding constant our other assumptions (in particular the idea that SpecT' is an A'-position), Agr-recursion is necessary.
Cardinaletti and Roberts (forthcoming) point out (*pace* Vikner 1990) that
generalized CP-recursion is an undesirable option for Icelandic, since
there is no way in such a system to avoid unlimited recursion. Instead,
Cardinaletti and Roberts assume that Icelandic has the 'double-Agr' structure. The recursion problem does not arise on this approach since Agr1
and Agr2 are distinct categories. In this system, SpecAgr1' is a topic
position, occupied by the fronted XP, the verb occupies Agr1°, while

the subject occupies SpecAgr2' (and receives Nominative Case under government, cf. (53)). This situation is illustrated in (92) (for (91c)):

(92)

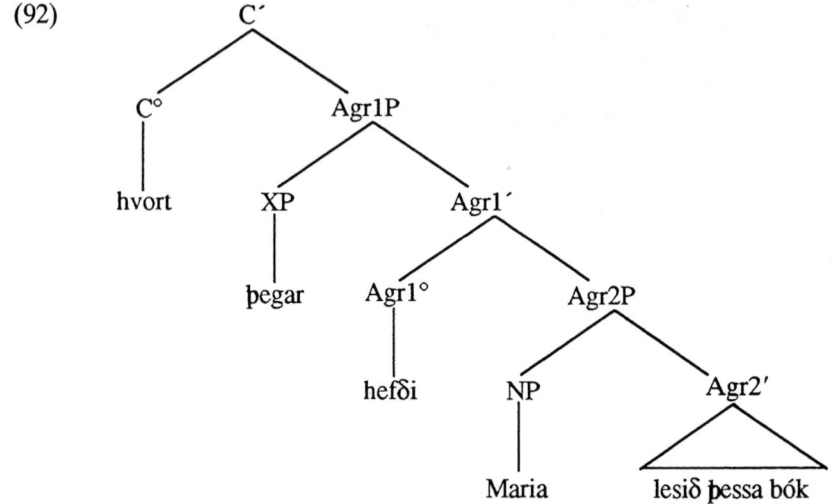

For more details, particularly regarding the similarities and differences between Icelandic and German, see Cardinaletti and Roberts (forthcoming). We will return to Cardinaletti and Roberts' proposal for clause structure in 2.1.2. and 2.2.4. when we discuss evidence that Old French may have passed through a stage similar to that represented by Modern Icelandic.

Our task now is to explain the restriction of V2 to root clauses, but our explanation should allow for certain cases in [−wh] complements, and strongly rule out Agr-to-C in [+wh] complements. At first sight, the answer we proposed to question I seems quite ill-suited to providing any account of the root nature of V2. We suggested above that the inflected verb appears in C as a result of that head's possession of the morphological selection feature. So incorporation of the inflected verb in C is an instance of selected incorporation. As such, after incorporation into C, the inflected verb is 'invisible' to syntactic processes that take place outside the C° that dominates it, except in so far as the Government Transparency Corollary is concerned (cf. 1.3.1.). In particular, any category selecting CP (or, more precisely, C°, since we assume standardly that selection is always for heads) will not 'see' the inflected verb. So there is apparently no way to distinguish a V2 CP from a non-V2 one with respect to elements outside the CP, and hence no obvious way to account for the root nature of the phenomenon, which necessarily involves considering the relation of the entire CP to things outside it (but cf. Tomaselli (op. cit.: 389f.) for a suggestion).

We can solve this problem in terms of the proposal made in 1.3.2. that the A/A' distinction should be extended to heads. There we said that all selecting heads are A-positions. So it follows, as we have already mentioned, that C° is an A-position in a V2 language when it triggers movement of the inflected verb: henceforth a 'V2 C' for short. The selection requirements of non-bridge verbs and of verbs with [+wh] complements must, in these terms, be such that the C° that heads their complement cannot trigger V-movement.[19]

This allows us to account for the fact the [+wh] complements are completely incompatible with V2. Let us refine our initial characterization of the classes of A-heads and A'-heads a little, and say that C[+wh] is an A'-head, while V2 C is an A-head. Suppose moreover that the A/A' status of heads is a matter that c-selection is sensitive to (but not morphological selection, as this always implies an A-head, as we saw in the previous section). It follows that verbs (and other predicates) that take [+wh] complements require that their complements have an A'-head. This idea is supported by the observation in Stowell (1981: 422) that verbs with [+wh] complements do not select for [±Tense], even where they disallow [−wh] infinitival complements (thus we have contrasts like the following: *Louise explained to read Proust vs. Louise explained what to read). In our terms, selection for an A'-complement (i.e. [+wh]) precludes selection among the 'A' options [±Tense] (which may perhaps be better regarded as [±Agr]). This means that verbs which take a [+wh] complement require that the head of that complement is an A'-head; as such, it cannot be an A-head, and so cannot be a V2 C. On the other hand, bridge verbs, at least, allow this C to be realized as a V2 C, since in any case it will unambiguously be an A-head.[20] So we arrive at the following typology of possible C°s, given the features [+Agr°] (i.e. C is an A-position) and [+wh] (i.e. C is an A'-position):

(93)   *Agr*   *wh*
        +   +   matrix questions (see below)
        −   +   embedded questions
        +   −   declaratives; bridge complements
        −   −   non-bridge complements.

We take it that the seemingly contradictory feature specification [+Agr°, +wh] is possible just in case the C° bearing it is not selected by anything (including another X°). This is essentially only the case with matrix interrogatives (cf. 1.5. where we claim that French matrix C° can also be simultaneously A and A', although in a rather different way).

Another construction that should be mentioned here is Stylistic-Fronting (Styl-F), found in both Icelandic and Faroese (cf. Maling 1980, Platzack 1987, Rögnvalsson and Thráinsson 1990; our discussion is largely based on Platzack). Styl-F fronts non-subjects in embedded clauses with a subject gap (either a trace or a null expletive). The fronted element is typically an adverbial (including the negator) or a participle. The following sentences (from Platzack 1987, (27), p. 394–5) illustrate Styl-F in Icelandic and Faroese, and its ungrammaticality in Swedish:

(94) a. þarna er konan sem **kosin var/var kosin** forsetí   (Ic)

b. Har er kvinnan ið **kosin varð/varð kosin** til forseta   (Fa)

c. Där är kvinnan som ***vald blev/blev vald** till president   (Sw)

'There is the woman that elected was/was elected president'

Here we see how in Icelandic and Faroese the participle may be fronted inside the relative, but not in Swedish.[21]

Styl-F appears to have existed in various medieval languages: Old Swedish (Platzack 1987, 1988), Old Danish (Vikner 1990, 2.5.), Middle English (Platzack 1990, 3.2.4.), Old French (Dupuis 1989, Platzack 1990, 2.1.2., 2.2.4.). It is possible that participle-fronting in Old Spanish and other conservative Romance varieties is something similar, which raises the possibility of connecting it with LHM in some way. However, Styl-F differs from LHM in not (a) not being triggered by any ban on clitic-first orders, (b) not being a root phenomenon (cf. Lema and Rivero 1990b: 12 on participle-fronting).

Finally, we should comment on the triggering of Agr-to-C movement in interrogatives, in English and French. We cannot claim for these languages that C[+wh] bears the feature [+Agr____], triggering selected incorporation into C by Agr because this would be incompatible with the account of French complex inversion that we will propose in 1.5. However, it is clear that the inflected verb (or auxiliary) appears in a matrix $C°$ when such a $C°$ is [+wh]. The movement does not take place in non-interrogative clauses (or only those that are introduced by a modal adverb (French) or an 'affective' element (English)); and does not take place in complements of any kind:[22]

(95) a. *Yesterday did he leave

b. *Hier est-il parti

(96) a. Who has she seen?

b. Qui a-t-elle vu?

(97) a. *I wonder who has she seen

b. *Je me demande qui a-t-elle vu

We can account for (95) by saying that in (Modern) English and (Modern) French, $C°$ does not contain C^{-1} and so does not trigger verb-movement (both languages were formerly V2 languages, cf. 2.3.1., 2.3.2. and 2.4.2. on French and 3.4. on English). (97) can be ruled out by essentially the same assumption: if C° lacks a selection feature, Agr-to-C movement will change the category of the head and so violate the Projection Principle (see 1.5.).

This leaves (96). We adopt Rizzi's (1990b) account of the facts of inversion in interrogatives in English and French. This is based on the following adaptation of May's (1985) *Wh*-Criterion:

(98) a. Each *Wh*-Operator must be in a Spec-head configuration with [+wh] X°

b. Each [+wh] X° must be in a Spec-head configuration with a *Wh*-Operator

Rizzi further assumes that I° (in our terms, T°) is the element base-generated as [+wh]. These assumptions explain the following ungrammatical versions of (96a) (we are excluding echo questions):

(99) a. *She has seen who?

b. *Has she seen who?

c. *Who she has seen?

In other words, (98) requires that *wh*-movement to SpecC' be accompanied by T-to-Agr-to-C movement. In embedded questions, T-to-Agr-to-C movement is impossible, as we have seen. However, (98) nevertheless forces *wh*-movement to the embedded SpecC', where the *wh*-operator satisfies (98) since C° bears the [+wh] feature thanks to selection.

The situation in French is more complex, since, alongside (96b), we have the following:

(100) a. Elle a vu qui?   (=(99a))

b. *A-t-elle vu qui?   (=(99b))

c. Qui elle a vu?   (=(99c))

Rizzi proposes that *wh*-movement of a *wh*-operator to SpecC' can induce a [+wh] feature on C° under Spec-head agreement. This possibility allows (100c). In (100a), C° fails to bear the [+wh] feature; similarly in (100b), hence the impossibility of Agr-to-C here.

A number of further issues arise in connection with Rizzi's proposals, notably in connection with *wh-in-situ* and the characterization of operators (Rizzi proposes a functional definition). However, for our purposes the above brief summary of the main points suffices. We will apply this system to the analysis of both Standard Italian and Northern Italian dialects in the next section.

To summarize, in this section we have proposed a preliminary analysis of the V2 phenomenon in its classic instantiation in the non-English Germanic languages. We have proposed the following answers to questions I–III that we posed at the beginning of the section:

(101) a. The inflected verb appears in C because C contains C^{-1}

b. Some XP moves to SpecC′ because of (85) (to be refined in 2.2.4).

c. The highly restricted occurrence of V2 in embedded clauses is due to the fact that clauses headed by C^{-1} can only be selected by specific classes of verbs, and never by [+wh]-taking and non-bridge verbs.

This is very far from being our last word on V2 (cf. 2.1.2., 2.3.1., 2.3.2., 2.4.2., 3.4.) but the analysis in this section will serve as an adequate framework for the discussion in Chapters 2 and 3.

1.5. COMPLEX INVERSION

In this section we will summarize the main points of the analysis of French complex inversion proposed by Rizzi and Roberts (1989). The purpose of this is to lay the groundwork for the analysis of the origins of this construction to be presented in Chapter 2.

The major cases of complex inversion are found in root interrogative sentences, as illustrated in (14), which we repeat here:

(14) a. **Jean voit-il** le cheval?

J.   sees-he the horse?

'Does John see the horse?'

b. Quel cheval **Jean voit-il**?

Which horse J.   sees-he?

'Which horse does J. see?'

A striking property of complex inversion is that there are apparently two subjects: a full NP, which occurs to the left of the inflected verb (after a *wh*-word or initially in *yes/no* questions), and a pronoun to the right of the inflected verb. The first possibility that springs to mind is that the nonpronominal subject NP is in a dislocated position. However, it can be shown that this is not so; in general, non-referential quantifiers cannot be dislocated, as (102) shows both for English and for French:

(102) a. *No-one, he came

b. *Personne, il n'est venu

(Cf. Rizzi 1986b and below on the implications of this observation for the treatment of subject clitics in Northern Italian dialects). The well-formedness of (103) then shows that this NP in (14) is not in a dislocated position:

(103)   (Pourquoi) personne n'est-il venu?

Further, the fact that the NP in question follows the *wh*-word in this construction indicates that it occupies a position internal to CP, and hence a position which is not dislocated. So we conclude that this NP is not in a dislocated position; we will argue in Chapter 2, however, that the corresponding NP in the precursor construction to complex inversion was in a dislocated position (see 2.1.3.).

An alternative approach which comes to mind is to treat the preverbal NP in (14) as occupying the normal subject position for French, SpecAgr', and consider the verb-clitic combination to occupy Agr. This approach runs into a number of serious problems, however. First, since the CP-level is not involved, it offers no natural way to deal with the root nature of complex inversion (on which see below). Second, it is clear that complex inversion, like subject-clitic inversion, is in complementary distribution with a filled complementizer:

(104) a. Peut-être **(Jean) est-il** parti
        Perhaps (John) has he left

      b. Peut-être **que Jean/ il est** parti
         Perhaps that John/he has left

      c. *Peut-être **que (Jean) est-il** parti
         Perhaps that (John) has he left

(105) a. Quoi **que Jean/il** veut?
         What that John/he wants?

      b. *Quoi **que (Jean) veut-il**?
          What that (John) wants he?

((105a) is only found in substandard varieties of French, cf. Safir 1982 and 2.4.4.4). Third, this analysis cannot account for the inextractability of the preverbal NP in complex inversion (pointed out by Kayne 1983), given the general possibility of extracting subjects in French (via the *que* → *qui* rule):

(106) a. ***Qui** t a-t-il téléphoné?
          Who did he telephone?

   b. (Je me demande) **qui t** a   téléphoné
      (*I wonder*)   *who has telephoned*

Fourth, this analysis cannot account for the incompatibility of complex inversion and stylistic inversion (cf. Rizzi and Roberts 1989: 16):

(107) a. Où   **Jean est-il**   allé?   (Complex Inversion)
         Where J.   has he gone?

      b. Où   **est allé Jean?**   (Stylistic Inversion)
         Where has gone John?

      c.*Où   **est-il allé   Jean**?   (Complex + Stylistic Inversion)
         Where has he gone John?

For these reasons, an account which supposes that the preverbal subject is in SpecAgr′ cannot work. The obvious alternative is to assume that the verb is in C (as the evidence in (104) and (105) clearly indicates) and the preverbal subject somewhere in the C-projection (but not in the usual SpecC′, as the possibility of a *wh*-constituent preceding this NP shows).

   In accordance with these conclusions, Rizzi and Roberts assume the structure in (108) for subject-clitic inversion, the independently existing construction which is identical to complex inversion except that the preverbal subject is absent:

(108)

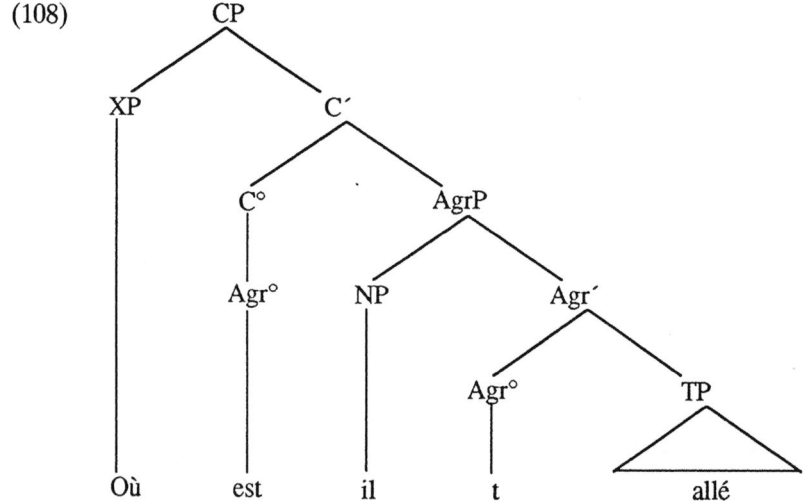

Following the initial insight of den Besten (1983) and Kayne (1983), subject-clitic inversion is thus assimilated to the kinds of Germanic verb-movement we have considered in the previous sections, as it features V-raising to C. We saw in the previous section how this is optionally triggered in interrogatives in French.

There is nevertheless a striking difference between the French case and the Germanic case (illustrated below by subject-aux inversion in English), namely that the process is restricted to pronominal subjects in French, unlike in Germanic:

(109) a. Has John spoken?

   b. *A Jean parlé?

(110) a. Has he spoken?

   b. A-t-il parlé?

We saw in 1.2. that we can rule out (109b) by assuming that French chooses a different parametric option for Nominative-assignment, one which gives the result that Nominative cannot be assigned to SpecAgr' in inversion contexts (see (48a) and the discussion following). However, as we noted in 1.2., this proposal is too strong, as it rules out the well-formed example (110b). In order to account for (110b), Rizzi and Roberts assume that the requirement that NPs be Case-marked is actually an instance of a more general requirement that nominals be associated with a Case feature. This association takes place in one of two ways: either by means of assignment of the feature from a head to the nominal, or by means of incorporation of the nominal into the head bearing the Case feature (cf. Baker's (1988) notion of PF-identification). They then assume that the pronoun in subject position in (110b) can cliticize to C°, so the clitic escapes the effects of the restricted nature of Nominative-assignment in French (as compared to English) as it is associated with a Case feature by incorporation with C°.

Against the background of this analysis of subject-clitic inversion, we can return to the analysis of complex inversion. As we said above, the striking thing about this construction is the apparent presence of two subjects. This leads to three questions:

(111) a. How are the two subjects assigned Case?

   b. Where are the two subjects base-generated?

   c. What is the structural position of the pre-C NP subject at S-structure?

Assuming that the pre-C subject occupies some specifier position, or at least some position which is in a structural agreement relation with C° (see Note 7), Rizzi and Roberts answer the first question by saying that (a) the pre-C NP receives Nominative Case from Agr under agreement, the standard configuration for Nominative-assignment in French (cf. 1.2.);

(b) the clitic is morphologically identified by incorporating with C (see above). This account allows us to see why complex inversion is impossible in English:

(112)   *Which books John has he read?

Since English subject pronouns never incorporate with C (i.e. they are not clitics), *he* and *John* cannot both be PF-identified, since both require Nominative Case (we are assuming that a Nominative-assigning head assigns Nominative to exactly one category — see below). This analysis retains the idea of Kayne (1972) that the possibility of complex inversion in French is a consequence of the existence of subject clitics in this language; a language without subject clitics cannot have complex inversion. This conclusion is important for the analysis both of Northern Italian dialects (cf. Rizzi 1986b, Brandi and Cordin 1989, Roberts 1990 and below) and of the history of French (see Chapter 2).

Concerning (111b), it is assumed that the full NP subject is the thematic subject of complex-inversion clauses, and so is base-generated internally to VP (cf. 1.2. and the references given there), and that the clitic is an expletive element base-generated in SpecAgr´ (we clearly must treat the clitic as an expletive; the availability of such expletive clitics is another important precondition for a language to have complex inversion — cf. Poletto 1990a). These assumptions give the following DS representation of an example like (14a):

(113) $[_{AgrP}$ il$_i$ $[_{Agr'}$ Agr° $[_{TP}$ $[_{VP*}$ $[_{VP}$ voir le cheval] Jean$_i$]]]].

(NB we put the base-position of the subject in VP* to the right of the 'core' VP consisting of the V and its internal arguments. This is important for the analysis of stylistic inversion in French and free inversion in Italian, as we shall see directly). The S-Structure of (14a), in which Jean occupies some specifier-like position to the left of C, is derived by several operations that we have already seen in action in this chapter: V raises to T and on to Agr, each time thanks to morphological selection by the governing head. The last step is free incorporation, as we saw in 1.4. The derivation also features NP-movement of the subject to the pre-C position; and, in cases where a *wh*-constituent is present, *wh*-movement of this element to SpecC'. The movement of the subject 'skips' the A-specifier position SpecAgr'. This does not lead to a violation of Relativized Minimality, however (cf. (58i)), since the expletive *il* is coindexed with the subject; in fact, *il* is a member of the chain headed by *Jean*.

Concerning the question of the S-Structure position of *Jean*, the assumptions made about the different types of head-to-head movement that we outlined in 1.3.3. come into play. In particular, since Agr-to-C movement is free incorporation, it results in a complex head Agr/C, and so two specifier positions can be licensed: the typical specifier of C°, the landing site for *wh* movement, and the typical specifier of Agr°, a subject position. Both positions are used in complex inversion:

(114)

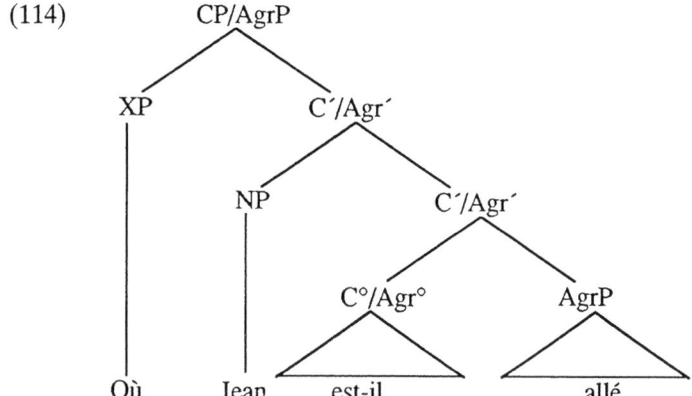

So when the new head is created by Agr-to-C movement, the extra specifier position is automatically provided and made available for the lower subject to move into. On the relative order of the two specifiers, cf. 1.3.3. and below.

Comparative questions immediately arise at this point: (i) why is the double-specifier option not taken in English? (ii) Why is the same option not taken in V2 languages? (iii) Why is complex inversion impossible in Standard Italian and in Northern Italian dialects? First note that the double-specifier option will not give rise to a complex-inversion-like structure in a language lacking subject clitics for Case-theoretic reasons, as we mentioned above. This suffices to rule out examples like (112) in English: Agr has only one Case to assign, and so cannot Case-mark both its newly created specifier and the original specifier. The other option, where the subject moves through the original specifier of AgrP and into the new one, giving (115), is more problematic:

(115)   *Which books John has t t read?

However, we can appeal to the head-government requirement of the ECP to rule out this representation. The trace in SpecAgr′ is not head-governed in the required way. So we assimilate the ungrammaticality of (115) to that of (116) (cf. Rizzi 1990a: 2.3.4.):

(116)   *Who did t see Mary?   (*do* non-emphatic)

The hybrid head C/Agr is not able to head-govern the trace in subject position here, so the ECP is violated.[23]

Turning to the second question, why is the second specifier position not available in V2 languages? This is because Agr-to-C movement in these languages, as we argued above, is selected incorporation. Hence there is no possibility of projecting a second specifier position. In general, then, complex-inversion-like constructions are incompatible with V2; this conclusion, which follows directly from the assumptions that we have adopted, is very important for the history of French, as we will see in the next chapter.

This analysis is consistent with the fact that the structure analogous to (116) is grammatical in V2 languages (cf. Rizzi op. cit.: 2.3.5.), as the possibility of examples where the subject raises to SpecC′ shows (here the demonstration by Schwartz and Vikner (1989) that subject-initial V2 clauses must be CPs with the subject in SpecC′ is very important, and cf. 2.3. on V2 and complex inversion in Middle French):

(117)   Johann hat t Maria gesehen.

The trace in SpecAgr′ here is clearly well-formed, since the sentence is grammatical. This is because C has the feature [+Agr] in V2 languages, a feature which endows this otherwise inert head with capacity of properly governing (cf. Rizzi ibid.).[24]

This analysis of complex inversion allows an account of the impossibility of extracting the preverbal subject, illustrated in (106a). The account is in fact identical to that just proposed for (116); the hybrid head C/Agr is unable to head-govern the trace in its newly-created A-specifier position. The trace of the incorporated clitic is properly governed by the clitic itself.

The fact that the two specifiers of C′/Agr′ in (114) are strictly ordered is related to the fact that a Case relation is involved only with one specifier: *Jean* must be adjacent (in the appropriate sense) to the head that assigns Case to it, hence *où* cannot intervene.

Moreover, we can give an account of the incompatibility of complex inversion with stylistic inversion, illustrated in (107c). To do this, we extend the approach to Case-assignment outlined in 1.2. to the licensing of *pro* along the same lines (cf. Rizzi 1986a, and 2.0). So, *pro* can be licensed under agreement with its licensing head or under government by this head, as a matter of parametric choice. It appears that the non-argument *pro* responsible for stylistic inversion in French is licensed under strict government from C° (probably determined by the presence of [+wh] in C°, see Kayne and Pollock 1978, Pollock 1986). But in that case *pro* cannot be licensed in a structure like (114) where it would be in an agreement configuration with the appropriate head, and would not be governed by it. We will return to the analysis of stylistic inversion in 2.3.5. and 2.4.4.1.

The third comparative question concerns the impossibility of complex inversion in Standard Italian and in the Northern Italian dialects. Let us take the dialects first. As Brandi and Cordin (1989) show, Trentino and Fiorentino, although they have subject-clitic inversion, lack complex inver-

sion (cf. Brandi and Cordin 1989, (80), p. 134). The same is true for
Veneto dialects, illustrated in (118c), from Poletto (1990b):

(118) a.*Icché la Carla ha-ella comprato?   (Fiorentino)

   b.*Cosa la Carla ha-la   comprá   (Trentino)
      What C.   has-she bought
      'What has C. bought?'

   c.*Quando Gianni vienlo?   (Veneto)
      when   G.   comes-he
      'When is G. coming?'

Rizzi (1986b) has shown that the subject clitics in these dialects have a
different status to French subject clitics in that they are located in Agr°,
rather than in SpecAgr' (the situation is slightly more complex than this
in Veneto, cf. Poletto 1990a, b). Thus, these are null-subject languages,
where the licenser of *pro* is the subject clitic (for a general discussion of
licensing null subjects, see 2.0.). In an example like (118), then, Agr°
must both license *pro* and assign Case to the subject. Given the general
similarities between licensing of *pro* and Case-assignment (cf. Rizzi
1986a), we can rule out (118) by extending the biuniqueness condition on
Case-assignment to cover both licensing of *pro* and Case-assignment, in
the following way:

(119)   *Uniqueness Condition on Licensing (UCL)*

        $X°$ cannot license two categories in a single structure.

We take 'licensing' here to cover both licensing of *pro* and Case-assignment (in terms of the distinction between formal licensing and identification, cf. 2.0., (119) is intended only to cover formal licensing). It is this
condition that is violated in (118), since Agr° must both Case-mark the
subject and formally license *pro*. For this reason, (118) is ungrammatical.

   Adopting (119) leads to the prediction that complex inversion is possible
only where a language has a subject clitic available to fill SpecAgr'.
Moreover, as we mentioned earlier, this clitic must be an expletive clitic.
Since the preconditions for complex inversion are so stringent, it is unsurprising that it is so rare cross-linguistically.[25]

   Consider next Standard Italian. Since Italian lacks subject clitics, complex inversion would give the string (120a), with the representation in
(120b):

(120) a.*Chi Gianni ha *pro* visto?
      Who G.   has (he) seen?
      'Who has G. seen?'

b. [$_{CP/AgrP}$ chi [$_{C'/Agr'}$ G. [$_{C'/Agr'}$ ha [$_{AgrP}$ *pro* [$_{Agr'}$ Agr° TP]]]]]

We assume that *pro* is always and only a maximal projection, and so the Structure Preservation Condition (cf. Chomsky 1986b) prevents it from cliticizing to C° in the manner of a French subject pronoun. However, we can rule out this representation in exactly the manner in which we ruled out (118), by appeal to the UCL of (119): Agr° cannot simultaneously Case-mark the subject and identify *pro*.

However, we want to rule out (120b) absolutely, and so we need to block the representation of (120a) where Agr-to-C movement does not take place, and the subject is in SpecAgr'. The obvious way to do this is to force Agr-to-C raising. In the previous section, we introduced a way of doing this in interrogatives in non-V2 languages. So suppose, as a first approximation, that the *wh*-criterion applies in Italian as it does in English, and so forces T-to-Agr-to-C movement in (*wh*) interrogatives.[26] This move immediately eliminates the unwanted representation of (120a).

If we say that the inflected verb is always in C° in *wh*-questions in Italian, we have to account for the null subject in SpecAgr' in examples like the following:

(121) a. Che   film ha visto Gianni?

   Which film has seen G.?

   'Which film has G. seen?'

  b. Che   film   ha visto?

   Which film (he) has seen?

   'Which film has he seen?'

(119) does not prevent us from saying that Agr is able to license *pro* under government here. However, there are two problems with this idea. First, it is generally the case that a null subject can be licensed only in positions where Case can be assigned (cf. Rizzi 1986a and 2.0.), but we saw in (49) that Agr cannot assign Nominative Case under government:

(49) a. *Ha Gianni preso il   libro?

   Has G.   taken the book?

  b. *Che   film ha Gianni visto?

   Which film has G.   seen?

Second, there is evidence that in (121b) the referential null subject occupies the postverbal position, the position of *Gianni* in (121a). This evidence comes from the fact discussed in Rizzi (1987) (and which we take up again in a different connection in 2.2.3.) that postverbal subjects cannot license floated quantifiers in Italian. Given this fact, the ungrammaticality of (122) indicates that the referential null subject is postverbal:

(122)   *Che   film   sono tutti andati a vedere?

       Which film (they) are   all   gone   to see?

       'Which film have they all gone to see?'

We can explain the impossibility of (122) if we prevent referential *pro* from appearing in SpecAgr'. We propose, then, that $C°$ is able to license a null subject in SpecAgr', and that, like other cases where $C°$ is the licenser (cf. the German examples in (80) and Styl-Inv in French, as well as the general discussion in 2.3.5. and 2.4.3.), only an expletive *pro* is possible. $Agr°$ neither licenses a null subject nor assigns Nominative Case under government in Italian. The postverbal referential null subject in (121b) is formally licensed by $T°$ and identified by Agr/T thanks to the Government Transparency Corollary (which means that we do not want identification of null subjects to be too closely tied to Case theory, as $Agr°$ clearly identifies this null subject under government − see Chapter 2). We can rule out postverbal null subjects in declaratives (cf. 2.3.2.) in terms of (119), since here Agr/T would license the preverbal expletive *pro* and the postverbal argumental *pro*. In (121b), on the other hand, $C°$ licenses the preverbal expletive.

    A further application of (119) arises in connection with Styl-Inv (cf. 1.2.). This construction, unlike subject-clitic inversion and complex inversion, is not sensitive to the root/embedded distinction, as the following examples show:

(123) a. Quand est parti ton   ami?

        When   is   left   your friend?

        'When did your friend leave?'

     b. Je me demande quand est parti ton   ami

        I wonder   when is left   your friend

        'I wonder when your friend left?'

As Kayne and Pollock (1978) observe, Styl-Inv is impossible in yes/no questions:

(124)   *Est parti ton   ami?

       Is   left   your friend?

We can account for this restriction in terms of (119), if we maintain the assumption that yes/no questions contain an interrogative element 'Q', whlch has to be licensed by $C°$. In that case, (124) violates (119) because $C°$ has to license both Q and *pro* in SpecAgr' (cf. Note 26 on Italian yes/no questions). A similar account carries over to the embedded case, (125a), as the partial representation in (125b) indicates:

(125) a.*Je me demande si est parti ton   ami

       I   wonder   if is   left   your friend

     b. .. [$_{CP}$ Q [$_{C'}$ [$_{C°}$ si] [$_{AgrP}$ *pro* ..

(Cf. Kayne (1990, Note 55), where it is suggested on independent grounds that *si* is associated with a null operator).

However, we are now led to the prediction that a head which licenses Q in yes/no questions cannot Case-mark. This is clearly false, as English (or any Germanic) *yes/no* questions show:

(126)   Has John left?

Why does the position occupied by *has* here not violate (119), since it must simultaneously identify Q and Case-mark the subject? The natural answer is to say that different components of the complex head Agr/C are licensing different things here: Agr° assigns Case to the subject, and C° licenses Q.

This solution works well for English (and the results with Styl-Inv are retained). However, we are now able to let in complex inversion in Standard Italian. In (120b), *pro* could be licensed by C°, while Agr° assigns Case to the subject. What this suggests is the following reformulation of the UCL, where X° is taken to include complex heads as a unit:

(119′)   X° cannot license:
       (i) two empty categories in a single structure;
      (ii) two A-positions in a single structure.

(119′ii) rules out (120b). Here a single X° = Agr°/C° must license the subject (Agr° assigns it Nominative) and the *pro* in SpecAgr′ (C° formally licenses it). Both of these elements are in A-positions, and so the structure is ill-formed. Thus our proposed condition (in an unsatisfactorily disjunctive form) tells us why complex inversion is impossible in Italian.

As a final remark on complex inversion, we must also rule out the possibility of a non-subject occupying the second specifier position in (114). Since this is an A-position, any element occupying this position at LF can only be licensed by being in a well-formed Θ-chain. The formation of a well-formed chain from this position is impossible for non-subject NPs, because the subject in SpecAgr′ will block chain-formation with any position it c-commands, since it will block antecedent-government of any such position, following Relativized Minimality (see (58)).[27] Thus the only way of licensing an NP in this position is by linking it to a trace in subject position. Although this is the trace of the incorporated clitic, it bears the same index as the subject and is a member of the Θ-chain to which the subject's Θ-role is assigned (see above). Therefore the only NP that can appear in this position is the subject NP itself.

In conclusion, then, we can see how Rizzi and Roberts' analysis of complex inversion fits into the overall framework that we have been developing throughout this chapter. In particular, the analysis of this structure provides important motivation for the postulation of two different kinds of substitution incorporation, as in 1.3.3. We will see in the next chapter that the developments in the history of French from a V2 system allowing Nominative-assignment under government to one with complex inversion and Nominative-assignment only under agreement provide further justification for the analyses of V2 and complex inversion and for the theory of incorporation proposed here.

NOTES

[1] Greenberg's Universal 1 says: "In declarative sentences with a nominal subject and object, the dominant order is almost always one in which the subject precedes the object." This does not imply that there are no languages where subject-object order is reversed. Such orders are attested, although they are certainly rare in comparison with languages where the subject precedes the object: Malagasy is VOS (cf. Keenan 1978, where other languages which show this order are discussed), while various Amazonian languages exemplify the OSV and OVS possibilities (cf. Derbyshire and Pullum 1986). Moreover, Greenberg (ibid., Note 5) cites the Penutian languages Siuslaw and the Salishan language Coeur d'Alene as exceptions (without, however, stating what the dominant word order is in these languages).

[2] In this respect, Sproat confirms the general position on VSO languages advocated by Emonds (1981). For similar analyses of other Celtic languages, cf. McCloskey (1986) on Irish and Stephens (1982) on Breton.

[3] Stylistic inversion (cf. Kayne 1972, Kayne and Pollock 1978, Kayne 1986, Pollock 1986) is a different kind of construction, involving, not verb-preposing, but apparent subject-postposing. The basic differences between stylistic inversion and the inversions in (14) are (a) it is not restricted root contexts, and (b) it is not possible in yes/no questions. These properties are illustrated in (i) and (ii) respectively:

(i)   Je me demande quand partira   ton ami
        I me ask   *when will-leave your friend*
        'I wonder when your friend will leave'

(ii)   *Partira ton ami?

For detailed discussion of these and other properties which clearly show that stylistic inversion is a distinct construction from subject-clitic inversion and complex inversion, see Kayne (1972). Subject-clitic inversion, on the other hand, seems to be a component of complex inversion, cf. Kayne (1983), Rizzi and Roberts (1989) and 1.5. For more on stylistic inversion, cf. 1.5., 2.3.4., 2.4.4.1.

[4] We adopt Sportiche's notion of i-command in place of standard notions of c-command defined in terms of 'first branching node' as in Reinhart (1976), in order to avoid the complication that 'transitive' heads do not protect their heads from government from outside the projection, while 'intransitive' heads do. Rizzi (1990a) proposes that lexical heads govern under m-command and functional heads under c-command. This entails that functional heads

do not in general protect their specifiers from outside government (since they usually, perhaps always, have complements), while lexical heads always do. Cf. Rizzi (1990a: 112).

[5] We have not made reference to the notion of Blocking Category (BC) of Chomsky (1986b). In Chomsky's system, barriers are defined in terms of BCs, which are in turn defined in terms of L-marking. This further complication is necessary in order to link government and bounding; since this is not our concern here, however, we leave aside the notion of BC in the interests of expository simplicity.

[6] This possibility is consistent with the idea that all parameters are binary. In that case the options in (37) represent two parameters, cf. (50) and the discussion there. It may be possible to extend this view to other structural Cases, although we will not pursue that matter here (cf. Koopmann and Sportiche 1990).

[7] Proposals differ as to where exactly 'in VP' the base position of subjects is. We follow Koopman and Sportiche (1990), Sportiche (1988b) and Manzini (1986) in assuming that VP and the subject together form a kind of small clause, with the subject adjoined to VP. We refer to this small-clause VP as 'VP*'. Note that, following the definition of government based on c-command defined as in Note 4, V does not govern the base position of the subject. It may also be necessary for the subject to be able in principle to receive Case from V in an agreement configuration. If so, then agreement should be defined more widely than in the text, perhaps as follows:

(ii) $\alpha = X°$ agrees with $\beta = YP$ iff α m-commands β, β m-commands α and α does not govern β.

If VP* is the m-command domain of V, this gives the desired result with respect to the DS position of the subject, and builds in the notion of exclusivity with respect to government.

[8] This creates the a priori possibility of assigning Accusative Case to *Jean* in an example like (48a). However, we can rule this out in one of two ways: either Agr's Nominative feature is able to block V's Accusative feature (as it blocks T's Nominative feature, cf. 1.2.), or the only verbs which have an Accusative feature are those whose objects require it. It seems to us that the second of these alternatives is the more plausible, if only because we want the solution to generalize across tensed and untensed clauses. So, we can allow *Jean* to be assigned Accusative by V in (48a), because the sentence will remain a Case Filter violation, since *le livre* now has no Case. To the extent that the direct objects of transitive verbs have no other means of being Case-marked (i.e. there is no possibility of insertion of a dummy Case-marker, no inherent Accusative, etc.), this account will work. A further possibility was pointed out by M. Kato (pers. comm.); what prevents [V + I] from assigning Accusative to the subject and Nominative to the object? Since this question could only arise in tensed clauses with transitive verbs, such a configuration of Case-assignment would give rise to a morphologically ergative system. Tentatively, then, we leave this possibility open at the level of UG: some parameter, whose precise nature is unclear, determines the distribution of Cases here and gives rise to the salient differences between 'accusative' and 'ergative' Case-marking systems. (Note that this kind of account of the 'ergative parameter' leads to the prediction that all ergative languages have V-to-Agr movement).

[9] The relevant definitions are as follows:

(i) α **head-governs** β iff $\alpha = X°$ governs β in X' (the immediate projection of X°) (cf. Rizzi 1990a);

(ii) α **antecedent-governs** β iff: α c-commands β, α is coindexed with β, no barrier intervenes between α and β, and relativized minimality is respected.

Rizzi (1990a, Ch. Three) concludes that the antedecent-government portion of the ECP is really a condition on chain-formation and that coindexation is not a requirement; in place of the coindexation requirement Rizzi imposes a non-distinctness requirement between α and β. We will continue to speak of antecedent-government in more 'traditional' terms, as part of the ECP and as involving coindexation, although Rizzi's conclusion should be borne in mind (cf. also Aoun *et al.* 1987 for a similar approach to the ECP).

[10] Rizzi (1990a, Appendix 2, Ch. 1) gives a more conceptually unified statement of (58) in terms of the notion of government-theory compatibility (cf. Chomsky 1986a on binding-theory compatibility). In the next section, we will restate (58) so that the status of head-movement with respect to antecedent-government is changed.

[11] NP-movement raising the subject from its VP-internal A-position to SpecAgr' does not violate RM, since SpecT' is an A'-position and so an element in this position does not count as a typical potential antecedent-governor for the NP-trace in VP.

[12] It is important to stress that in a representation like (72a) X^{-1} is still functionally the head of $X°$ (and so of XP). This element counts as a head for all relevant principles, most importantly RM (this is why the formulation in (58') makes reference to 'heads' rather than to 'X°s').

[13] This generalization is not entirely unproblematic. Existential *be*, the possessive *have* of conservative dialects of British English and some root modals (at least *can* and *will*) could, on semantic grounds, be considered Θ-assigners. Following Roberts (1985a: 50f.) and Zubizarreta (1982), we take root modals to assign a secondary, or adjunct, Θ-role; the account for the absence of V-to-Agr in terms of Θ-theory to be given in the text would not carry over to adjunct Θ-assigners, as such categories by definition do not create structural positions in virtue of their thematic properties. A similar analysis can probably carry over to the intentional *be* of *John was **being** obnoxious* (cf. Williams 1984, Roberts 1987, Ch. 2).

Possessive *have* is a more recalcitrant case, especially given its semantic closeness to such undoubted Θ-assigners as *own*, *possess*, etc. However, it is possible, in the spirit of Kayne (1984), Guéron (1986), Pollock (1989), that *have* takes a small-clause complement to which it assigns no Θ-role, and moreover it assigns no Θ-role to its subject, and so it effectively lacks thematic properties (of the kind relevant to the text discussion). This is the kind of analysis of *have* that must be proposed if the generalization relating V-to-Agr movement and Θ-theory is to hold up.

A similar small-clause analysis may be feasible for existential *be*. Pollock (op. cit.: 387f.) suggests that existential *be* takes a small-clause complement headed by an abstract locative marker. For concreteness, we concur with Pollock's general proposal. However, it is worth pointing out that in English, at least, existential *be* is very odd in inversion and negation contexts:

(i)   ??Is God?

(ii)   ??God isn't

This is another grey area for Θ-theory, as *exist* clearly has normal main-verb syntax, but almost identical semantics.

Finally, Jaeggli and Hyams (1989) point out that the aspectual *come* and *go* of American English are auxiliary-like in never showing inflection, although main-verb-like in not raising to Agr:

(iii)   *John goes talk to his advisor every day

(iv)   *Go you see a movie every day?

They suggest (p. 40f) that this is due to the fact that these verbs assign secondary Θ-roles. If we adopt their basic proposal, we could say that the difference between *come* and *go* and root modals is that the former also assign a secondary Θ-role to their complement VP, while the latter only Θ-mark the subject. In that case, raising of these verbs (whether at LF or S-structure) will give rise to a structure in which the configuration required for secondary Θ-role assignment is not satisfied. This suggests that the trace of these verbs cannot assign the secondary Θ-role, not unreasonable conclusion if chain-formation is only relevant for primary

Θ-roles (cf. 1.3.1.). Cf. also Pollock (in progress) for an alternative analysis of *come* and *go* based on the idea that *come* and *go* obligatorily trigger incorporation of their complement verb. On *come* and *go* in other West Germanic languages, cf. Haegeman (1990), Penner (1990) and Schönenberger (1990).

[14] More precisely, T selects V and Agr selects T in tensed clauses.

[15] MSc seems to pose problems for this approach. As we have seen, V does not raise to Agr in these languages. Assuming that Agr is nevertheless present, although always empty, if C selects Agr this will have no effect on the position of the inflected V. Moreover, the kinds of evidence that C contains Agr adduced by Tomaselli (see following text) are not found in MSc languages. We propose that the structure of $C°$ in MSc is such that it contains a C^{-1} which as usual needs to attach to some lexical element, but there is no requirement as to the category of that element. Agr being completely empty, $[_T V T]$ moves there (on movement to T in MSc, see 3.3.2.).

We could generalize this idea to the West Germanic languages as a whole if, following Cardinaletti and Roberts (forthcoming), we assume that the 'pronominal' properties attributed to C by Tomaselli are in fact properties of a functional head lower than C but higher than the Agr containing verbal agreement, a position to be identified with the Wackernagel position (cf. 1.3.2., 2.1.2. and 3.4.). This is Cardinaletti and Roberts' Agr1. In that case, we can ascribe exactly the same lexicalization requirement to C^{-1} in West Germanic as we just did for MSc, and we have a unified treatment of V2 which allows for the observed differences between MSc and West Germanic.

[16] A full consideration of the distribution of expletive null subjects in German should take into account two further facts: (a) the expletive impersonal pronoun *es* is impossible wherever *pro* is allowed; contrast (i) with (80):

(i) a.   *Mir wurde es geholfen

    b.   *Hier wurde es getanzt

(b) Null subjects are apparently impossible in initial position:

(ii)   *Pro* wurde getanzt

On (i), cf. Cardinaletti (1990a); on (ii), cf. 2.2.3.

[17] Unsurprisingly, since MSc lacks Agr, these languages do not have null subjects in these contexts. Instead we find that an expletive is always required (Roberts 1987: 292):

(i)   I går   blev *(der)   danset   (Danish)
            Yesterday was   (there) danced

The analysis of MSc V2 proposed in Note 15 accounts for this difference with West Germanic.

[18] A [+wh] C also agrees:

(i) a.   kweten nie   o: Valère dienen boek gelezen eet
            I-don't-know if Valère   your   book read   has

    b.   kweten nie   o:n Valère en Pol dienen gelezen eet.
            (Haegeman's (13c–d), Chapter 2)

These facts are quite problematic for the proposals in the text. See Notes 15 and 19.

[19] A problem now arises with respect to the kind of data we saw in (81). This kind of data can only be obtained in embedded clauses, but our proposal implies that any embedded clause allowing agreement or cliticization should tolerate V2. This prediction is false; see the previous footnote for at least one indication of this. Moreover, our interpretation of Tomaselli seems to require that Agr be in C here, and yet V clearly is not in C, although it agrees. A solution is to suppose that there are two Agrs available in these cases, and presumably therefore two Agrs are available in general in Continental West Germanic

languages. So, as suggested in Note 15, the 'agreement' properties of C are not intrinsically associated with C. See above, 2.1.2., 2.2.4., and Cardinaletti and Roberts (forthcoming).

Similarly, in order to integrate MSc, we should not make our account of the root nature of V2 depend on agreement. This further corroborates the proposal made in Note 15.

[20] This is consistent with Rizzi's (1990a) proposal that the phonologically null alternant of *that* in English is Agr, accounting thereby for the fact that the phonologically null C properly governs a following subject trace, while *that* does not; similarly, *qui* in French is taken to be the [+Agr] variant of *que*. English bridge verbs (epistemic verbs and verbs of saying) allow *that*-deletion, while factives for example do not; in French a similar pattern emerges for the *que/qui* rule. These facts suggest that allowing a C = A-head complement is a well-defined lexical property.

[21] It is unclear what the landing site of Styl-F is. Given the requirement for a subject gap, it is tempting to say that the fronted element lands in the subject position. However, this creates various technical problems concerning the subject trace in cases of movement, and also with the Strict Cycle Condition. Cardinaletti and Roberts' (forthcoming) proposal for an 'extra' topic position in languages like Icelandic suggests at least a landing site, although Rögnvaldsson and Thráinsson (1990) show that other elements can be topicalized simultaneously with Styl-F in Icelandic. For these reasons, we will not propose an analysis here; for concreteness, we assume that the fronted element adjoins to AgrP. Cf. 3.2.4.

[22] We are assuming that the Q-morpheme of *yes/no* questions is [+wh]. This seems reasonable as it corresponds to *whether, if* or *si* in embedded contexts. It is quite possible, however, that a characterization in terms of [±wh] is on the wrong track here. The modal and 'affective' clauses are not obviously [+wh], in that they cannot satisfy the selection requirements of verbs requiring [+wh] complements:

(i)   *I wonder never John has done that

       (i.e. 'I wonder if John has ever done that')

Moreover, a class of apparently [+wh] clauses disallows movement to C, namely the exclamatives:

(ii) a.   What a fast car he drives!

    b.   *What a fast car does he drive!

Exclamatives are also [+wh] in the sense that they satisfy the selection requirement of [+wh]-taking predicates:

(iii)   It's amazing what a fool he is

These predicates are of a different semantic class to those which take embedded interrogatives (cf. Grimshaw 1979).

So it seems that there are two things at work. On the one hand there is a formal [+wh] feature shared by interrogatives and exclamatives. This feature does not necessarily trigger inversion, as the exclamatives show. On the other hand, there is an "affective" feature, shared by [+wh] and negative elements, which does trigger inversion. That this feature is not [+wh] is shown by the selection facts. Interrogatives have both features.

[23] To be precise, this is because head-government is formulated in terms of government within the immediate projection of a head (cf. Note 9). We can suppose, slightly adapting a suggestion made by Rizzi (ibid.), that the hybrid head C/Agr cannot be a head-governor because (a) C is intrinsically inert for government, (b) Agr can only head-govern in its **own** immediate projection, and (c) the projections of C/Agr are not Agr's own projections.

[24] Since MSc patterns with Continental West Germanic and against English with respect to (116) and (117), the proposal in Note 15 must be adopted.

[25] Valdôtain (a Franco-Provençal dialect spoken in North-Western Italy) has both complex inversion and French-style subject clitics (in addition to Northern-Italian-style subject clitics).

This result is consistent with Kayne's (1972) original claim regarding complex inversion, and with our (119). Cf. Roberts (1990) for more on Valdôtain.

Another dialect which may have all the prerequisites for complex inversion is Friulian; it has French-style subject clitics (in inversion contexts), and expletive clitics. Moreover, it is not V2, and so Agr-to-C should create the double-specifier structure. However, complex inversion is absent (Poletto 1990b). We have nothing to say about this here. Cf. 2.4.3. on subject clitics and complex inversion in the history of Northern Italian dialects.

[26] The grammaticality of (i) suggests that Agr-to-C does not obligatorily take place in yes/no questions in Italian:

(i)   Gianni ha fatto questo?

           G.   had done this?

If this example involved Agr-to-C, it would be a further case of the 'complex inversion' structure in (120b), and so would be ruled out by (119). Therefore we take it that here *ha* is in Agr and *Gianni* is in SpecAgr'. This may not be problematic for the *wh*-criterion since it is not clear that Q is an operator in the relevant sense (in fact it is not, on Rizzi's (1990b) definition), and it is in any case clear that *yes/no* questions trigger inversion less rigidly than *wh*-questions, cf. the following contrast in English:

(ii)   *Who John saw?

(iii)   ?John saw Mary?

In both (i) and (iii) a special intonation is required, and the question has presuppositions of disbelief, etc.

There is also a version of (i) with left-dislocation of *Gianni*, which is fully grammatical without special intonation or presuppositions. That this is left-dislocation is seen from (iv):

(iv)   Nessuno ha fatto questo?

           Noone   has done that?

This example is only possible with marked intonation and presuppositions, as expected, given the general impossibility of left-dislocating non-referential quantifiers like *nessuno*.

It should also be noted that things are not quite as simple in *wh*-questions as the text implies. At least one *wh*-word does not trigger inversion, *perché* ('why'):

(v)   Perché Gianni ha fatto questo?

           Why   G.   has done this?

           'Why has John done this?'

Compare this with (120a). More generally, it seems that D-linking in the sense of Pesetsky (1987) may be a determining factor:

(vi)   ?*Quando Gianni ha fatto questo?

           When   G.   has done this?   (not-D-linked)

(vii)   A che ora Gianni ha fatto questo?

           At what time G.   has done this?   (D-linked)

D-linked *wh*-elements like *a che ora* do not seem to trigger Agr-to-C movement, while non-D-linked ones do. This clearly has consequences for the definition of operator that is relevant for the *wh*-criterion. See Rizzi (1990b).

[27] We follow Chomsky (1986b) in considering antecedent-government to be the basic condition on chain-formation. That is, the chain $C = (\alpha_1, \ldots, \alpha_n)$ is well-formed iff every α_i antecedent-governs α_{i+1}, for $n \geq i \geq 1$. Antecedent-government is defined in terms of relativized minimality, as in (58). This also works for our reformulation in (58').

CHAPTER 2

THE HISTORY OF FRENCH INTERROGATIVES

2.0. INTRODUCTION

The central topic of this chapter is the development of interrogative and inversion constructions in the history of French. The basic fact that we are concerned with was alluded to in 1.2.: in Modern French (henceforth ModFr), i.e. French texts from the 16th century on (see 2.4. for more precise dates), inversion around a non-pronominal subject is impossible. This was illustrated by (48) of Chapter One, which we repeat here:

(1)   *A   Jean pris   le   livre?
       Has John taken the book?

We interpreted this constraint as indicating that Nominative Case is assigned only in configurations of agreement in ModFr. In this respect, ModFr differs from all the Germanic languages, which allow structures like that in (1). Old French (OF), however, patterns like a typical Germanic language in that the analogue of is (1) possible:[1]

(2) a.   Comment fu   ceste lettre faitte?
          How   was this   letter made?
          (*MirND* XXXVI; Schulze 1888: 198).

   b.   Vialt   donc Yvains ocirre monseigneur Gauvain?
          Wants then Y.   to kill my lord   G.?
          (Chrétien de Troyes; Price 1971: 226).

In terms of what was said in 1.2. concerning the parameters of Case-assignment, the obvious conclusion is that OF allowed Nominative Case to be assigned under government. Consider again the parametric possibilities for Nominative assignment by Agr° that we gave in (51) of Chapter One:

(3) a.   Agr° assigns Nominative under government? Yes/no

   b.   Agr° assigns Nominative under agreement? Yes/no

In these terms, the contrast between (1) and (2) indicates that French has changed during its recorded history from a system which selected the 'yes' option in (3a) (we cannot yet say which choice was selected in (3b) — see below) to one which, as we argued in 1.2. and 1.5., chooses the negative option. This is then a clear case of parametric change. Our central goal in this chapter is to describe and explain this change. On the descriptive level, this means showing when it took place, what its causes were and what its effects were. On the explanatory level, this means accounting for how acquirers of a system choosing a positive setting in (3a) came to converge, on the basis of the output of such a system, on the negative setting. Our account of how this took place will lead us to develop a number of notions relevant for a general theory of change; cf. 2.3.2.

If we are dealing with a genuine case of parametric change here, we expect other phenomena to be implicated; the loss of the 'simple inversion' construction in (2) should be correlated with other syntactic changes. In fact, this appears to be the case; two other major syntactic phenomena which distinguish OF from ModFr are lost with simple inversion: null subjects and the V2 constraint. Our account of the change in the parametric selection in (3) explains these correlations, as we shall see. We will also argue that two further developments play a causal role in the parametric change in question: the development of two sets of subject pronouns and the development of complex inversion. Our account of the parametric change in the modes of Nominative-assignment thus brings together a number of important developments in the history of French syntax.

The null-subject parameter distinguishes languages which allow a phonologically-null referential pronoun to appear as the subject of tensed sentences from those that do not (see Jaeggli and Safir 1989, especially the Introduction, for a detailed discussion of this parameter). The classic null-subject languages are Italian and Spanish, while good examples of non-null subject languages are English and ModFr. The following contrasts illustrate the core difference:

(4) a.   Mangia la mela   (Italian)

    b.   Come la manzana   (Spanish)

(5) a.   *Eats the apple

    b.   *Mange la pomme

The null subject is taken to be the empty category *pro*, a phonologically empty pronoun. The cross-linguistic differences illustrated in (4) and (5) thus reside in the fact that *pro* is allowed (or 'licensed') as the subject of a tensed clause in Spanish and Italian, but not in English or ModFr.

(6) gives a slight adaptation of the licensing conditions for *pro* given by Rizzi (1986a: 519f.):

(6) a.   If X° is the licensing head of *pro*, X° can assign Case to the
          position occupied by *pro*

   b.   *Pro* has the grammatical features of its licensing head $X°$

(6a) is the formal licensing condition for *pro*, and (6b) is the content-licensing (or identification) condition for *pro*. (6) can be parametrized in one of two ways. First, each language contains an inventory of the heads which are formal licensers for *pro*, and it is possible that a given language may lack such heads entirely — this is generally held to be the situation in Modern English. Second, the licensing head may either have or lack the grammatical features which permit the recovery of *pro*'s content. If these features are lacking, *pro* will fail to be identified and the structure in question will be ungrammatical.

   The cross-linguistic differences in (4) and (5) can now be accounted for. In Spanish and Italian, the licensing head for null subjects, which occupy SpecAgr', is Agr, the head which assigns Nominative to this position. Agr contains person/number features which are sufficiently rich to permit full recovery of the content of a null subject, hence *pro* is allowed as the subject in (4). In English and ModFr, however, one or both of the conditions in (6) fails to be satisfied and so the sentences in (5) are ruled out as they contain an illicit *pro*.[2] This account has the advantage of capturing the frequently observed connection between null subjects and 'rich' specification of person/number features in the verbal morphology (cf. Taraldsen 1978, Chomsky 1982, Rizzi 1982), although the question of how this richness is determined is a complex one; cf. Rizzi (1986a), Jaeggli and Safir (1989), and 2.2.3. for some proposals.

   The importance of the null-subject parameter is that the simple statement that Spanish and Italian allow *pro* as the subject of tensed clauses opens the way to an account of two other properties which systematically distinguish these languages from languages like English and ModFr: 'free' subject inversion (cf. 1.2.) and apparent *that*-trace violations (i.e. long-distance extraction of the subject of a tensed clause across an unmodified complementizer — the correlation between this phenomenon and null subjects was originally characterized by 'Perlmutter's generalization' — cf. Perlmutter 1971). These phenomena are illustrated from Italian in (7):

(7) a.   Ha telefonato Maria
         has telephoned Maria

   b.   Chi hai   detto che — ha telefonato?
         Who have-you said   that   has telephoned?

The standard analysis of these correlations (see Rizzi 1982, Ch. 4) is that Italian makes available a postverbal subject position, and fills the 'usual', preverbal subject position with an expletive *pro*. The unavailability of the structure in (7a) in English and ModFr is then reduced to the general unavailability of *pro* in this position in these languages (although questions

remain concerning the postverbal subject position, we assume for concreteness that this is the DS subject position, which in languages like
Italian and Spanish appears on the right of the rest of VP, cf. 1.2.). (7b)
is taken to be a further instance of free inversion: the subject is extracted
from the properly governed postverbal position, while the preverbal subject position is occupied by *pro*. In this way the ECP is satisfied here.

It should be clear from the above discussion that ModFr is not a null-
subject language. However, it is well-known that OF allowed null subjects
(although under more restricted conditions than Italian and Spanish, as
we shall see directly). The following examples illustrate this:

(8) a.   Einsi **partirent** del port de Venise come vos avez oi

       Thus they-left the port of Venice as   you have heard

       (G. de Villehardouin *La Conquête de Constantinople*, in A.
       Pauphilet (ed.) *Historiens et Chroniqueurs du Moyen Age*, Gal-
       limard, 1952, XVI, p. 101; Adams 1987b: 1)

   b.   Ainsi **s'acorderent** que il   prendront par nuit

       Thus they-agreed that they will-take by night

       (*Le Roman du Graal*, B. Cerquiglini (ed.) Union Générale
       d'Editions, Paris, 1981, 26; Adams 1987b: 41)

   c.   Si **firent**   grant joie la   nuit

       So they-made great joy that night

       (R. de Clari *La Conquête de Constantinople*, (in A. Pauphilet
       (ed.) *Historiens et Chroniqueurs du Moyen Age*, Gallimard,
       1952, xii); Adams 1987b: 45)

It seems then that we have here a further case of parametric change
between OF and ModFr. We must account for the fact that *pro* had a
much freer distribution in OF than in ModFr.

Nevertheless, *pro* does not show the same distribution in OF as in
Italian and Spanish. The fundamental difference is that *pro* is sensitive to
the root/embedded distinction in OF, but it is not in either Spanish or
Italian. *Pro* is much more widely attested in root clauses than in embedded
clauses (Price 1971, Einhorn 1974, Foulet 1982, Vanelli, Renzi and Benincà 1983, Adams 1987a, b), a fact which has led to the claim in the
latter two works that null subjects are a root phenomenon in OF, a claim
that we will consider more closely in 2.2.4. Foulet was the first to tie this
restriction on null subjects in OF to the V2 nature of that language (the
first edition of Foulet (1982) was Foulet 1919), an insight which Adams
(1987a, b) builds on in order to develop a modified theory of null subjects.
Adams (1987a: 13) adds to the licensing conditions for *pro* given in (6)
the further condition that the directional relation between *pro* and its

licensing head must be canonical for the language in question, where 'canonical' means the same as the relation between a verb and its direct object (cf. Kayne 1984). Since OF is a VO language, this means that Agr must be to the left of *pro* in order to license it, entailing that Agr has to be in C in order to license a null subject in OF. Hence null subjects are only possible where the verb moves to C, i.e. in V2 clauses. In these terms, *pro* appears to the right of the inflected verb in the examples in (8), and the verb is thus in second position. Adams' analysis is very interesting and insightful, and represents the first serious attempt to integrate Foulet's insight into a rigourous syntactic framework. We will discuss her proposals more critically, particularly in 2.2.3.

Following the analysis of V2 that we gave in Chapter 1, *pro* is in SpecAgr' and V is in C° in (8). Thus the V governs *pro* here. We can now make the connection with the change in the Case-assignment parameter which underlies the loss of simple inversion: if *pro* can only be licensed in contexts of Case-assignment, the possibility of licensing a null subject under government depends on the possibility of assigning Nominative under government. So we can account for the loss of null subjects of the type in (8) as a reflex of the same change in the grammatical system as that which made (2) impossible. In this way, we connect the loss of simple inversion to the loss of null subjects.

The V2 nature of OF is illustrated clearly by the examples in (9) (non-nominative clitics — e.g. *en* in (9b) — are effectively part of C°, and so do not 'count' in the computation of the second position):

(9) a.   Einsint **aama** la   demoisele Lancelot

       Thus   loved the lady   Lancelot

       'Thus the lady loved L'

       (*La Mort le Roi Artu*, J. Frappier (ed.), Droz, Genève, 1964, 38; Adams 1987b: 50)

    b.   Desuz un pin   en **est** li   reis alez

       Under a pine-tree is   the king gone

       'The king went underneath a pine-tree'

       (*La Chanson de Roland*, 165; Schulze 1888: 200)

    c.   Quatre *saietes*   **ot** li bers *au* costé

       Four   boats of war had the baron at his side

       'The baron had four boats of war at his side'

       (*Charroi de Nîmes*, 1. 20)

Again, ModFr is certainly not a V2 language, so this is a further important syntactic change between OF and ModFr. It should be clear how we can

integrate the loss of V2 with our account of the other changes: cases of
V2 where the subject is not raised to SpecC' like those illustrated in
(9) require that the subject receive Nominative Case from Agr under
government, since Agr is raised to C here. This is the situation in OF
examples such as (9). Once Nominative is no longer able to be assigned
under government, however, sentences like (9) become ungrammatical.
This entails that the subject must always raise to SpecC' to receive Case,
which in an SVO language creates a strong pressure for treating such
sentences as not involving the C-level, but rather as having the subject in
SpecAgr' and the verb in Agr° (we will elaborate on the implicit assumption of a 'least-effort' principle creating pressure for this reanalysis below
(cf. 2.3.2., 2.4.2.)). So the loss of V2 is a further consequence of the
change in the selection of the options in (3).

The three syntactic features of OF that we have just reviewed: simple
inversion (see (2)), null subjects in root clauses ((8)), and V2 ((9)) all
share one property in common: the inflected verb appears in C and licenses
or Case-marks the subject from that position. Formerly this was possible
in French; it no longer is. We can account for this in terms of a change
in the value of the Nominative-assignment parameter in (3).

In Section 1 we review in detail the situation of inversion in OF. We
first look at simple inversion structures in interrogatives in representative
texts from roughly 1050 to 1300. Similarly, we will take a detailed look
at the status of the V2 constraint; here we will see some evidence that
early OF had an Icelandic-style V2 system, in that V2 clauses are found
even as *wh*-complements. Third, we consider the status of complex inversion in OF, showing, following Foulet (1921), that this construction did
not exist in OF. Apparent cases of complex inversion should be analysed
as left dislocation structures.

In Section 2, we consider in detail the status of pronominal subjects in
OF, both null and overt. It is clear that nominative pronouns could be
tonic in OF. We will suggest, following Hirschbuhler and Junker (1988)
and Vance (1989), that preverbal nominative pronouns were fully independent, but that postverbal nominative pronouns were clitics, and in fact,
following Haiman (1971, 1989), syntactic clitics. We then consider in detail
the status of null subjects in OF, and consider the recent claims (Adams
1988a, b, c, Dupuis 1988, 1989, Hirschbuhler and Junker 1988, Hirschbuhler 1990, Vance 1989) that null subjects were not a uniquely root
phenomenon in OF. Although, then, neither null subjects nor V2 were
strictly root phenomena throughout OF, the conditions permitting one
(V-movement) also permitted the other (licensing *pro*), and so we retain
Adams' basic contention that there is a diachronic connection between
these phenomena (although we account for this connection in a different
way).

In Section 3 we move on to Middle French (MidFr), the French of the period 1300–1500. Here we see a considerable erosion of V2, which we take to indicate that a root C no longer obligatorily selects Agr° (cf. 1.4.). We also attempt to document, drawing on Foulet (1935/6), Price (1971) and others, the emergence of a double series of pronouns, whereby the diachronically nominative pronouns become fully atonic, and diachronically oblique pronouns take over the full range of tonic positions, giving the ModFr system of (near) complementary distribution between the two series. We next propose that certain former interrogative left-dislocation structures, thanks to the weakening of V2 and the complementary distribution of the two series of subject pronouns, were reanalyzed as complex inversion. Also, basing our presentation on Hirschbuhler and Junker (1988) and on Vance (1989), we document the rise in occurrence of embedded null subjects and null subjects in non-V2 contexts.

Finally, Section 4 considers the 16th and 17th centuries. We document the last occurrences of simple inversion and propose an analysis of how complex inversion 'ousted' simple inversion, one which relies on our overall framework for treating head-to-head movement, and the Uniqueness Condition on Licensing of 1.5. (119′). Similarly, we document the last occurrences of null subjects, and the loss of V2. Here we briefly discuss the work of Vanelli, *et al.* (1986) and Vanelli (1987), which indicates that Northern Italian dialects and Provençal have undergone a parallel loss of simple inversion and V2, while retaining null subjects. We develop a characterisation of the 'rich agreement' needed for identification null subjects in terms of (6b) that accounts for this difference while treating the loss of V2 and simple inversion in the same way. Finally, we discuss the rise of two other interrogative structures: stylistic inversion (which appears to be the residue of a certain class of OF and MidFr expletive null subjects), the *conjugaison interrogative* of the 17th century, the *ti* interrogative marker of popular French, which represents a further diachronic reanalysis of complex inversion, and the *Wh que* construction.

2.1. INVERSION AND INTERROGATIVES IN OLD FRENCH

In this section we will substantiate and document the claim that OF allowed Nominative-assignment under government. We will first consider the status of interrogatives and then that of declaratives, i.e. of V2 clauses where some element other than the subject is fronted to SpecC′, and the subject remains in SpecAgr′. Our third topic here is the status of certain apparent cases of complex inversion, principally those discussed in Schulze (1888) and Foulet (1921), which we will argue, following Foulet, to be examples of left-dislocation.

Before going any further, one final point should be clarified concerning the parametric change under investigation: our focus is on the loss of Nominative-assignment under government. We are therefore not directly concerned with the question of Nominative-assignment under agreement. Indeed, we will adopt, for concreteness, the hypothesis that OF had a system like that of English in that both modes of Nominative-assignment were available (cf. 1.2.). Straightforward evidence for Nominative-assignment under agreement comes from the existence of subordinate clauses with *que* SV order:

(10) a. Ne creez   ja   glouton ne losengier
         Do not believe now glutton or sycophant

         Que vostre pere n'en   ot   onques un chier
         That your father of-them had never   a   dear (one)
         (*Charroi de Nîmes*, 1. 754–5)

    b. Or dient   et   chantent et   fablent
        Now say (they) and sing (they) and relate (they)

        que li **quens Bougars de Valence faisoit** guere
        that the count B.   de V.   made war

        au conte Garin de Biaucaire
        on count G.   de B.
        (*Aucassin et Nicolette*, II, 1.1–3)

We will see during the course of this chapter that this evidence is not so clear as it appears at first sight. The fact that the clause structure involving Agr-recursion that we will propose in 2.1.2. may have been possible in OF means that Nominative may have been assigned under government by Agr1° to SpecAgr2' in examples like (10). However, the developments which we discuss in 2.3. show clearly that Agr could assign Nominative under agreement at this period (cf. especially 2.3.5.; cf. also 3.4. for related considerations on the history of English). Hence the parametric change that we are primarily concerned with involves moving from a positive setting for both (3a) and (3b) to a negative setting for (3a), while retaining the positive setting for (3b) (or, in terms of 1.2. (52), we are concerned with how French changed from (52b) to (52d)).

2.1.1. *Inversion in OF Interrogatives*

In this section we review the situation concerning inversion in OF interrogatives. Given what we have said about the possibilities of Case-assignment and licensing of null subjects in OF, we expect to find interrogatives with the following configurations:

(11) a. . .[$_{C°}$ V [$_{AgrP}$ NP[−pron] . . .

b. .. [$_{C°}$ V [$_{AgrP}$ *pro* ...

c. .. [$_{C°}$ V [$_{AgrP}$ NP[+ pron] ...

d. .. [$_{C°}$ V [$_{AgrP}$ t ...

In (11a–c), SpecC' may be occupied either by a *wh*-phrase or by the operator Q, giving rise in the former case to a *wh*-question (WHQ) and in the latter to a *yes/no* question (Y/NQ). In (11d), SpecC' must be filled by the *wh*-operator which binds the trace (since we are dealing with matrix clauses, this cannot be an NP-trace as there is no c-commanding A-position for an antecedent), assuming SpecC' is always and only an A'-position (cf. 2.3.1.).

First, we exemplify the structure in (11a). The following are representative examples of WHQ with this configuration:

(12) a. Mes ou   **fu   cele espee   prise** ..?

      But where was that sword taken?

      (*Perceval*, 1. 3640)

b. Deus! que **purrat ço estre**?

    God! what could that be?

    (*Roland*, 1. 334)

(13) a. A quel martire **Sera   cist chevaliers randuz**?

      To what martyr will be this knight   given?

      (*RCharr* 410; Schulze 1888: 203)

b. Dont   **est cist palefroiz venuz**?

    Whence is this palfrey   come?

    (*Mont. Fabl.* III, 38; Schulze ibid.)

c. Dieus! por quoi **fu ma mere   morte**!

    God! why   did my mother die!

    (ibid. III, 159; Schulze ibid.)

In each of these examples, there is what might be taken to be a compound verb form, involving an auxiliary-like element (forms of either *être* 'be' or *pouvoir* 'can') and a non-finite verb-form. The occurrence of the subject in between these two verb forms is a strong indication that the tensed, auxiliary-like verb is in C°, the subject in SpecAgr' and the non-finite verb somewhere in VP.[3] We can thus give the relevant parts of the structure of (12a), for example, as follows (glossing completely over the fact that this example is passive, i.e. we do not indicate the NP-trace occupying object position, or other characteristics of passive constructions, since these are tangential to our discussion here):

(14)

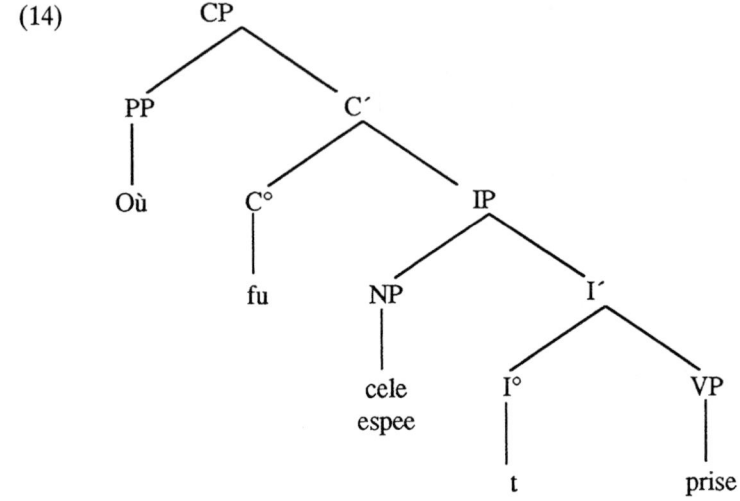

Such a structure is impossible in ModFr. Indeed, the word-for-word translations of all the examples in (12) and (13) are ungrammatical in the modern language. This is then paradigmatic evidence in favour of the kind of parametric change that we have postulated.

Examples of the kind in (12) and (13) are fairly common in the classic texts of the OF period. On the other hand, examples with non-pronominal NP subjects are harder to find in Y/NQ. In addition to (2b), cited from Chrétien de Troyes (12th century) by Price (1971), consider the following examples, taken from Schulze (1888: 202–3):

(15) a.   **Est dont amors infermetés?**
          Is   then love   infirmity?
          (*BChr* 119, 28)

   b.   **Est mon seigneur sain et   haitie?**
        Is   my   lord   well and happy?
        (*MirND* xxxv, 1179)

   c.   **est donc li   rois hermites vostre peres?**
        is then the king hermit   your   father?
        (*Perc* 126)

We have also found the following examples:

(16)a. **est vostre sire ancor levez?**

 is your lord yet   up?

 (*Tristan*, 1. 8021)

 b. **seront leur livre   autel conme je faich?**

 will-be their books such as   I do

 'Will their books be like (i.e.true to) my deeds?'

 (*Merlin*, p. 86)

 c. **Est . . . encore toz mes charroiz entrez?**

 Is . . . yet   all my carriage come in?

 (*Charroi de Nîmes*, 1.1177)

The existence of such examples, which are impossible in the modern language, is further evidence of a parametric change between OF and ModFr.

In the case of the construction in (11b), a clear asymmetry exists between WHQ and Y/NQ. Examples of WHQ are quite common, especially in the 11th and 12th centuries. Here are some examples from *Le Charroi de Nîmes*:

(17) a. Sire niés,   **dont   venez?**

 Lord nephew, whence come (you)?   (1. 32)

 b. Dame, feme, **que quiers?**

 Lady, woman, what want (you)?   (1. 565)

 c. **Por quoi as**   or si   granz sollers de vache . . . ?

 Why   have (you) now such big   leather   shoes . . . ?
 (1. 1329)

Examples of Y/NQ with null subjects are rarer, although not entirely absent. Here are some examples:

(18) a. **plairoit**   vos oïr   un son d'Aucassin . . . ?

 would please (it) you to hear a   song of A . . . ?

 (*Aucassin et Nicolette*, 1. XXXIX, 1. 16)

 b. Rois, **voudroies** le faire issi?

 King, want (you) to do it here?

 (*Tristan*, 1. 1179)

c.   Et **savez**   por coi il   le firent

And know (you) why   they did it?

(*Perceval*, 1. 311)

Again, these sentences are ungrammatical in the modern language. The existence of these examples illustrates the well-formedness of a configuration like (11b) in OF, a configuration no longer tolerated. Our thesis is that the parameter which is responsible for this change from OF to ModFr is the very one which underlies the grammaticality of (12) and (13) in OF and their ungrammaticality in ModFr, namely the parameter in (3).[4,5]

Next we give some examples of the structure in (11c), where the option of an overt pronominal subject is taken. As before, we take WHQ first:

(19) a.   que **vex tu** faire?

what want you to do?

(*Aucassin et Nicolette*, III, 1. 7)

b.   **c'avés**   **vos fait** de   Nicolette ma tresdouce amie . . . ?

what have you done with N.   my very sweet friend?

(ibid., VI, 11. 8–9)

c.   Dont   **estes vos . . . ?**

Whence are   you . . . ?

(*Charroi de Nîmes*, 1. 1121)

(20)a.   Ou   **avez vos** or   cest cuer pris?

Where have you now this heart taken?

b.   U   **ont eles trouvé** jouvent qui   tant lor   dure?

Where have they found youth   which lasts them so long?

(ibid.)

c.   U   **ies tu?**

Where are you?

(Foulet 1921: 246)

Second, Y/NQ:

(21) a.   **Cuide tu,** rois, que ge ne me demente?

Believe you, king, that I   not lament?

(*Charroi de Nîmes*, 1. 93)

b. **conissiés vos** Aucassin . . . ?

know   you A.?

(*Aucassin et Nicolette*, XVLI, 1. 14)

c. enne me **conissieés vos?**

neg me know   you?

'Don't you know me?'

(ibid., XXII, 1. 10)

(22) a. **faites** le vus de gret?

do   it you willingly?

'Do you do it willingly?'

(*Roland*, Gautier (ed.) 2004; Foulet 1921: 244)

b. **As   tu** le duc qui vient vëu?

Have you the duke who comes seen?

(*Ron* III, 7873; Schulze 1888: 207)

c. **Ai   je** dont folie   faite?

Have I then madness made?

(*Ch.* II, 2784; Schulze ibid.)

Since, as we shall see in 2.2.1., nominative pronouns were not clitics in
OF, these sentences could be taken as further evidence of the possibility
of Nominative-assignment under government, since non-clitic pronouns
receive Case in the same way as nonpronominal NPs (although the question is complex, cf. 2.2.2., 2.3.3.).

Finally, the configuration in (11d) is illustrated by the following
examples:

(23) a. E   **ki   serat**   devant mei en l'ansguarde?

And who will be before me in the vanguard?

(*Roland*, 1. 748)

b. . . . **qui   puet** amor **tenir** . . . ?

. . . who can love   hold   (i.e. 'who can hold love?')

(*Tristan*, 1. 573)

c. **Qui a**   ce   fet?

Who has this done?   (i.e. 'who has done this?')

(*Perceval*, 1. 2376)

Here, as usual, the inflected verb occupies C° and *qui* occupies SpecC'.

To the extent that variables, i.e. *wh*-traces, must be Case-marked, the existence of these constructions provides further evidence that Case-marking under government was possible in OF, as the trace must be Case-marked by the verb (i.e. V + I, or V + Agr) in C°. Moreover, these structures exemplify a proper-government configuration typical of a V2 language but no longer possible in French; the trace is properly governed by C° which has the capacity for proper government thanks to its [Agr] feature, the feature also ultimately responsible for V2 (cf. 1.4., 1.5. and the references to Rizzi 1990a given there). In ModFr, such proper government is no longer possible, which accounts in part for the non-extractability of the preverbal subject in complex-inversion structures (**Qui t a-t-il fait cela?*, cf. 1.5.). Accordingly, the string *Qui a fait cela?*, which corresponds to (23c), would be analyzed as follows in ModFr:

(24)   [$_{CP}$ Qui C° [$_{AgrP°}$ t [$_{Agr°}$ a] fait cela]]]

Here the trace in SpecAgr' is head-governed by C°, which takes on the ability to head-govern thanks to Spec-head agreement with *qui* (cf. Rizzi op. cit. for details).

So we find all the structures in (11) in OF (although with certain rather surprising tendential differences in frequency, cf. Notes 4 and 5). None of these configurations is possible in ModFr (note that the strings corresponding to (11c) and (11d) are allowed but, possibly for (11c) and certainly for (11d), the structures corresponding to those strings are different). In every case, this can be attributed to the change in the parameter in (3); the essential fact is that a C° containing a moved verb in ModFr is no longer able to Case-mark, formally license or properly govern an element in SpecAgr'.

2.1.2. Verb Second in OF

It is a well-known fact that OF was a V2 language (Thurneysen 1892, Foulet 1921, 1982, von Wartburg 1934, Price 1971, Vanelli *et al.* 1986, Benincà 1984, 1989, Adams 1987a, b). Since the basic order in VP was VO (although there are a number of examples where various elements, notably past participles, are fronted to a position preceding the inflected verb; cf. (23a—b), Dupuis 1989, Platzack 1990 and below), this means that OF had the basic word-order properties of the modern Scandinavian languages (cf. 1.4.) and Romansch (Haiman 1971, 1974, 1988).

V2 structures are certainly ubiquitous in matrix clauses in the 12th century. The following lines from *Le Charroi de Nimes* (11. 26–31) illustrate this, and show the variety of different elements that could occupy first position:

(25)   **Muetes de chien font**   avec els mener.   (Compl V)
         Troups of dogs   make (they) with them bring.

         Par   Petit Pont sont   en Paris entré.   (PP V)
         By the Petit-Pont are (they) in Paris come.

         Li   cuents Guillelmes fu   molt gentix et   ber: (Subj V)
         The count G.   was very kind and good:

         Sa   venoison fist   a l'ostel   porter.   (Compl V)
         His food   made (he) to the hostel carry.

         En mi   sa   voie   a   Bertran encontré,   (PP V)
         On   his   way   has (he) B.   encountered.

'They had troups of dogs brought along with them. They entered Paris by the Petit-Pont. Count G. was very kind and good: he had his goods carried to the hostel. On his way he met Bertran.'

As this excerpt shows, null subjects are also extremely common in matrix V2 clauses (see 2.2.3.).

The texts we have surveyed clearly illustrate the V2 constraint. The first one hundred matrix declaratives with overt subjects of each text give the following patterns (for *Tristan*, we took the first 115, and for *Aucassin et Nicolette* the first 156):

(26)

	Subj V	Compl V	Adv V	Pred V	V1	V>2
Roland	31%	15%	40%	5%	5%	4%
Charroi de N.	23%	12%	48%	4%	13%	0%
Tristan	30%	7%	55%	2%	3%	3%
Perceval	41%	11%	28%	2%	2%	16%
Aucassin	50%	6%	32%	4%	2%	6%
Merlin	28%	3%	65%	0%	0%	4%

('V>2' in the rightmost column refers to orders where more than one maximal constituent precedes the inflected verb). These data show that the subject had to be analysed as Case-marked under government in 69% of the sentences in *Roland*, 77% of those in *Le Charroi de Nîmes*, 70% of those in *Tristan*, 59% of those in *Perceval*, 48% of those in *Aucassin et Nicolette*, and 72% of those in *Merlin*. Moreover, given the rigidity of the V2 constraint, shown by the generally low proportions of V1 and especially V > 2 sentences (we do not count the order *XP obj-cl V* as V > 2 since object clitics were fully cliticized to V° + Agr° — cf. Adams 1987: 168f., and 2.2.1.), we conclude that the Subj V orders are the result of movement of the subject from SpecAgr' to SpecC'. There is no reason to suppose that acquirers would analyse such examples as involving the subject in SpecAgr′ and the verb in Agr° at this stage in the history of French (but cf. 2.3.1.).

We argued in 1.4., following the proposals in Tomaselli (1989), that V2 correlates with the ability of C° to host a clitic and license a null subject. We will take up these points in 2.2.2. and 2.2.3.

OF also patterns like a typical Germanic V2 language in the classes of apparent V1 structures that it allows. We saw in 1.4. that all the V2 Germanic languages show V1 structures in three contexts: (i) Y/NQ; (ii) conditionals; (iii) 'lively narrative style' (German also shows the phenomenon of 'Pronoun Zap'; we leave this aside here, as, to my knowledge, it does not exist in OF). We documented the various types of OF Y/NQ in the previous subsection, and so will say nothing more about them here. We will now give some examples of V1 conditionals and of lively narrative style. The following is an example of a V1 conditional:

(27)   **Fust** i   li reis, n′i   oüssum damage

        Were here the king, not here had (we) damage

        'If the king were here, we wouldn't suffer any damage'

        (*Roland* 1102; Harris 1978: 240).

This kind of conditional is fairly rare in OF, the variant with *se* ('if') being generally preferred.

As the figures in (26) indicate, *Le Charroi de Nîmes* is relatively rich in V1 sentences. Here are some examples:

(28) a. **Fueillissent** gaut   **reverdissent** li pré

         Bloom   the woods, become green the meadows

         'The woods are blooming, the meadows become green'

         (1.15, also given in Adams 1988a, (26a), p. 14)

   b.   **Tienent**   oiseaus por lor   cors   deporter

         Hold (they) birds   for their bodies to disport

         (1. 26)

   c.   **Voit** le li rois

         Sees him the king

(This construction is also discussed and illustrated in Adams 1988b, Dupuis 1988, Hirschbuhler and Junker 1988, Hirschbuhler 1989 and Vance 1989). We analyse both of these kinds of V1 structures as proposed in 1.4., i.e. as involving a null operator of one kind or another in SpecC′. Note that both (27) and (28c) are examples where the Tobler–Mussafia Law (cf. 1.3.2.) is obeyed; this law bans clitic-first orders, and so forces enclisis where nothing precedes the inflected verb, giving *voit le* in (28c). This phenomenon is characteristic of the OF of this period (cf. Alberton 1990, Benincà 1989, de Kok 1985 and below).

Up to now, we have restricted the discussion to V2 in matrix clauses. As in the V2 Germanic languages, however, we do find cases of embedded V2. Adams (1988a, b, c) points out that V2 is possible in the complements to bridge verbs on the basis of examples like the following (with or without *que*, which could be dropped in OF):

(29) a.   Et   il   respondirent que **de ceste nouvele sont** il   moult

   And they replied that of this   news   are   they very

  lié

  happy

  'And they replied that they were very happy with this news'

  (*Le Mort le Roi Artu*, J. Frappier (ed.), Droz, Genève, 1964, 45)

 b.   Or   voi ge bien, **plains** es   de mautalant

  Now see I   well full   are (you) of bad intentions

  'And now I see clearly that you are full of bad intentions'

  (*Le Charroi de Nîmes*, l. 295)

These examples, and others like them (cf. Adams 1987b, 1988a, b, c, Dupuis 1988, Hirschbuhler and Junker 1988, Vance 1988, 1989: 134f.) show once more that OF has the typical V2 pattern, in that it shares the properties of the V2 Germanic languages (cf. the discussion of (88) in Chapter 1). So we analyse these examples as involving selection of C[+Agr], giving rise to embedded V2. Note that, if embedded V2 is possible in OF, examples like (10), to the extent that they involve bridge verbs, are not evidence for the idea that OF allowed Case-assignment under agreement, as the subject could in principle be in the lower Spec-Agr', Case-marked under government by V + Agr from C°.

However, unlike most Germanic languages, OF also appears to allow V2 structures in embedded *wh*-clauses (null subjects are also possible here, a matter we discuss in more detail in 2.2.4.). This kind of data has been discussed by Dupuis (1989), Hirschbuhler and Junker (1988), Adams (1988a, c) and Vance (1988, 1989).

In fact, there are very few truly unequivocal cases of embedded V2 in non-bridge complements in OF (cf. Dupuis 1989: 147f). Most of the cases that have been cited can and should be handled in other ways. One class of cases involves Italian-style free inversion (cf. 1.5.):

(30) a. celui jor **que vint Nostre Sires** en la cité de Jerusalem

        that day that came Our   Lord into the city of J.

        (Vance 1989, (109), p. 94)

    b. . . . que li soudans de Coine oï   dire que si faitement

        . . . that the sultan of C.   heard tell that so in this way

        avoient fait li Francois

        had   done the French

        (R. de Clari *La Conquête de Constantinople*, P. Laurier (ed.), 1956, Paris, CFMA, Champion, LII, 33; Dupuis 1989, (56), p. 163)

Since OF was a null-subject language, we expect to find free inversion of this type. It was less common than in present-day Italian, however, probably in part because it was frequently disguised by V2 (cf. 2.3.4., 2.4.1.).

Other putative cases of embedded V2 can be treated as instances of Styl-F (cf. 1.4.):

(31)   **quant** il   de   ci   **departiront**

        when they from here will leave

        (Vance 1988, (11), p. 89)

Here, *de ci* has undergone Styl-F. We saw in 1.4. that a precondition for Styl-F is the presence of a subject gap, usually a trace or *pro*. In (31), however, there is a subject pronoun. Platzack (1988: 8) discusses similar examples in Old Swedish, and suggests that the condition on Styl-F is satisfied since the pronoun cliticizes to C, so there is a trace in subject position. In 2.2.2., we will argue that subject pronouns cliticized to C in OF. Hence (31) is parallel to Platzack's Old Swedish cases as a case of Styl-F.

Styl-F could also involve null subjects in OF, as the following examples from Adams (1988a, c) show:

(32) a. . . . je me plaing d'une amor ke [**longuement** ai   servie]

        I weep   of a love which long   have (I) served

        'I weep over a love which I have long served'

        (Colin Muset XI; Foulet 1919/1982: 314; Adams 1988c, (10b), p. 10)

    b. . . . por ce   que [**chevalier** me face]

        in   order that knight   me make (he)

        '. . . so that he'll make me a knight'

(Chrétien de Troyes *Cligés*, A. Micha (ed.), Champion, Paris, 1957, 113; Adams 1988c, (12a), p. 11)

c. Il vaut   grant argent, quant [**latin** parole]

it is worth much money since   Latin speaks

'It is worth a lot of money because it speaks Latin'

(*Fabliaux*, R.C. Johnson and D.D.R. Owen (eds.), Oxford, 1957, 7; Einhorn 1974: 104; Adams 1988c, (12b), p. 11)

Presumably, OF had greater liberty of Styl-F than Old Swedish or present-day Icelandic because null subjects were more freely available. On null subjects in embedded clauses in OF, see 2.2.4.

Still other examples involve participle-fronting of a kind found in a range of conservative Romance varieties (cf. Lema & Rivero 1990b, on Old Spanish; the same construction is found in Rumanian (Lema and Rivero 1989, 1990a), in various Southern Italian dialects and in Sardinian (Jones 1988)). As both Dupuis (1989) and Lema and Rivero (1990b) point out, this rule may in fact be a variant of Styl-F:

(33) a. . . . com vus   **conté fu**

         . . . *as   to-you told   was*

         '. . . as was told to you.'

(Der anglonor. Beuve de Hamtoue, 339, Sk. 26; Hirschbuhler and Junker 1988, (18b), p. 73)

b. Se je a li   **parlé eüsse** . . .

    If I to him talked had . . .

    'If I had talked to him. . .'

(Huon le Roi, *Le Vair Palefroi*, A. Langfors (ed.), Champion, Paris, 1912, 291; Adams 1988c, (29a), p. 25)

Examples of the following sort could be treated as Styl-F of (tonic) pronouns (cf. Adams 1988b, (22a–b), p. 21; 1988c, (21a–b), p. 11):

(34) a. Je voi tel chose don **moi**   poise

         I see such thing which on-me weighs

         'I see a thing which weighs on me'

(Béroul *Le Roman de Tristan*, E. Muret (ed.), Champion, Paris, 1974, 4455)

    b. Quant **lui** plaira

        since him pleases

        'Since it pleases him . . .'

        (*La Queste del Saint Graal*, A. Pauphilet (ed.), Champion, Paris, 1923, 167)

Nevertheless, there is an irreducible residue of examples which seem to be genuine cases of embedded V2 (in non-bridge complements) or of V1:

(35) a. Quant l'ot   **li** **chapelain** escrit

        When it-had the chaplain written

        'When the chaplain had written it'

        (Béroul *Le Roman de Tristan*, E. Muret (ed.), Champion, Paris, 1974, 2649; Adams 1988c, (19a), p. 19)

    b. s'a la   vostre bonté   vousist **mon pere** prendre garde

        if against your good will wanted my father to take precaution

        'if against your good will my father wanted to take precautions'

        (Huon le Roi *Le Vair Palefroi*, A. Langfors (ed.), Champion, Paris, 1912, 378–9; Adams 1988b, (19c), p. 19)

    c. Quant a aus   est **li** **rois** venus, . . .

        When to them is the king come, . . .

        'When the king came to them, . . .'

        (Chrétien de Troyes, *Guillaume d'Angleterre*, M. Wilmotte (ed.), 1962, Paris, CFMA, Champion, 573; Dupuis 1989, (40), p. 148)

If we put the evidence in (35) together with Adams' comment (ibid.: 22) that the order *WH XP Subj V* is not found, and that in fact 'only one constituent shows up between the subordinate Comp and V_I' (ibid.), we are led to the conclusion that V1 and V2 *wh*-complements were possible, although not very common, in OF (cf. Dupuis 1989: 4.1, where a similar conclusion is reached).

    Both Adams and Dupuis analyse this phenomenon along the lines of Santorini's (1988, 1989) and Diesing's (1988, 1990) treatment of V2 in Yiddish (see 1.4.). This analysis relies on the idea that the subject, null or overt, is able to remain in VP at SS, while some other constituent is fronted to SpecI'. Such an analysis will not carry over to OF on our assumptions, however. The discussion of Nominative-assignment under government in 1.2. implies that the subject can only remain in VP at SS if T° is the Nominative assigner, because Agr° does not govern the base position of the subject owing to the intervening T°. We saw in 1.2. that T° may assign Nominative to the DS-position of the subject in French and Italian, giving rise to free (or stylistic) inversion. We have just seen that OF had free inversion. However, free inversion shows that the base position of the VP-internal subject is on the right of the rest of VP, hence Adams' analysis cannot be adopted since it puts the subject on the wrong side of the rest of VP.[6]

As we have seen, many of the examples Adams uses to motivate a Yiddish-style analysis of OF can be handled in other ways. (35) nevertheless shows that there is some motivation for adopting an Agr-recursion analysis of the type Cardinaletti and Roberts (forthcoming) propose for Icelandic (cf. 1.4.). On such a view, OF clauses feature two occurrences of Agr, which we call Agr1 and Agr2, so that the basic structure of clauses is as follows (cf. 1.4. (92)):

(36)

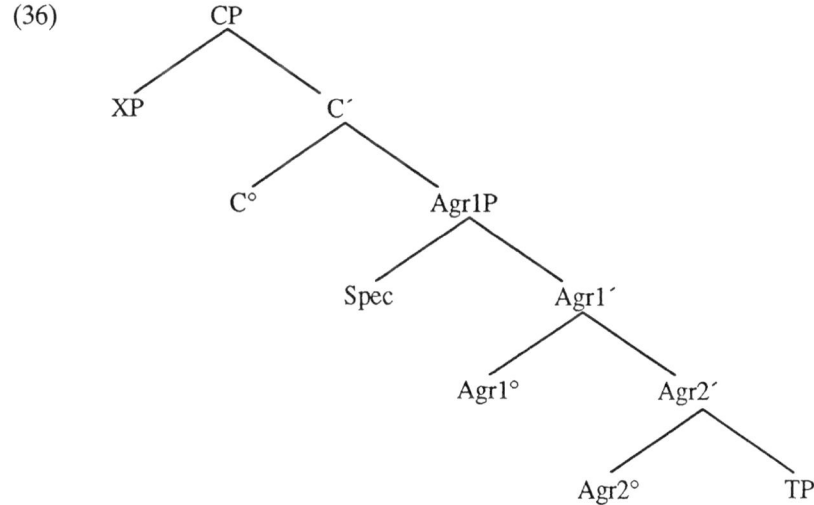

We could then assign the following structure to examples of the sort in (35):

(37)

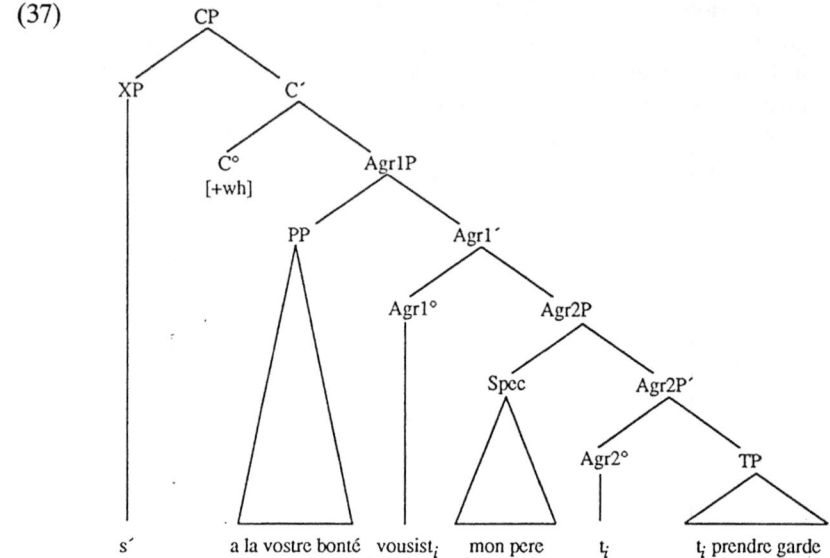

Leaving aside various technical clarifications and assumptions, it is clear
that such an account will work well for generalized embedded V2. Moreover, we will see in 2.2.4. that this structure permits an account of the
distribution of null subjects in subordinate clauses in (certain stages of)
OF. Also, the fact that OF obeyed the Tobler–Mussafia Law (see (27),
(28c)) suggests, if the sketch of this kind of this kind of 'clitic-second'
effect given in 1.3.2. is on the right track, that OF had a clause structure
like that in (37). We defer further discussion of this hypothesis until 2.2.4.,
where we will broach the topic of null subjects in embedded clauses
generally, and the licensing of V1 orders in *wh*-complements of the kind
in (35a).

In this section we have seen that OF patterns like a typical V2 Germanic
language. In fact, OF resembles Icelandic fairly clearly in having Styl-F
(we will see in 3.1. and 3.2.4. that Middle English had Styl-F too), and,
possibly, in allowing somewhat general embedded V2. We suggested that
the 'double Agr' hypothesis might be necessary to account for embedded
V2. We will say more about the application of the double-Agr structure
to OF in 2.2.4.

The central point for our general discussion that emerges from this
section is that OF was a V2 language. This provides further evidence that
Nominative-assignment under government was possible.

2.1.3. *Apparent Complex Inversion in OF*

We have seen that OF allowed simple inversion, a structure which is not allowed with a non-pronominal subject in ModFr. On the other hand, ModFr has the complex inversion structure, described and analysed in 1.5. Thus, examples like (2), which in OF featured simple inversion, would naturally be rendered in ModFr by complex inversion, as follows:[7]

(38) a.   Comment cette lettre fut-elle faite?

    b.   Yvain veut-il donc tuer Gauvain?

In this section we discuss the evidence that complex inversion also existed in OF. We will argue that, despite the existence of strings identical to that in (38b), there are good reasons to think that the complex inversion construction as analysed in 1.5. did not exist, and that strings of the type in (38b) are instances of left dislocation (cf. Adams 1988a: 17, Foulet 1921: 248f).

Examples of the string in (38b), i.e. Y/NQ with initial order *NP V pronoun*, are found throughout the OF period. Schulze (*op. cit.*: 190) gives a number of instances of this, among them the following:

(39) a.   **L'aveirs**   **Carlun est il** appareillez?

         The treasure C.   *is*   *it made ready?*

         'Is C.'s treasure made ready?'

         (*Roland*, l. 643; also cited in Foulet 1921: 249, Price 1971: 266)

    b.   **Iceste guerre dura**   **ele** toudis?

         This   *war*   *will-last it*   *always*

         'Will this war last for ever?'

         (*RCambr.* 5183)

    c.   **Icist preudon Est il**   or   nez   de vostre vile?

         This man   *is*   *he now born in*   *your town?*

         'Was this man born in your town?'

         (*Claris* 18181)

Although one example is found in *Roland*, namely (39a), and a few in Chrétien de Troyes, Schulze points out that this construction is more frequent in the 13th century ((39b) is from a late 12th-century *chanson de geste*, *Raoul de Cambrai*, and (39c) from Montaiglon's collection of 13th-century *fabliaux*), mentioning specifically the *Miracles de Nostre Dame*, a text which is usually thought to date from the end of the 13th or beginning of the 14th century. So there is some indication that this construction was slowly increasing in frequency through the OF period.

In 1.5., following essentially the analysis proposed in Rizzi and Roberts (1989), we analysed the sequence *NP V pronoun* in ModFr Y/NQ in the following way (for simplicity we return to the IP-notation here and in what follows):

(40)

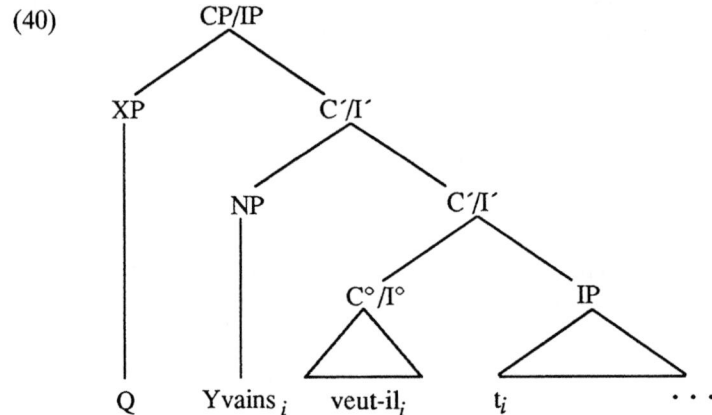

(For the details of this analysis, cf. 1.5., and for the background to the postulation of hybrid categories like CP/IP, cf. 1.3.3.). However, there are a number of reasons which lead us to think that this is probably not the structure of OF examples like those in (39). Instead, the sentences in (39) are best treated as instances of left dislocation; so we assign the structure in (41):

(41)

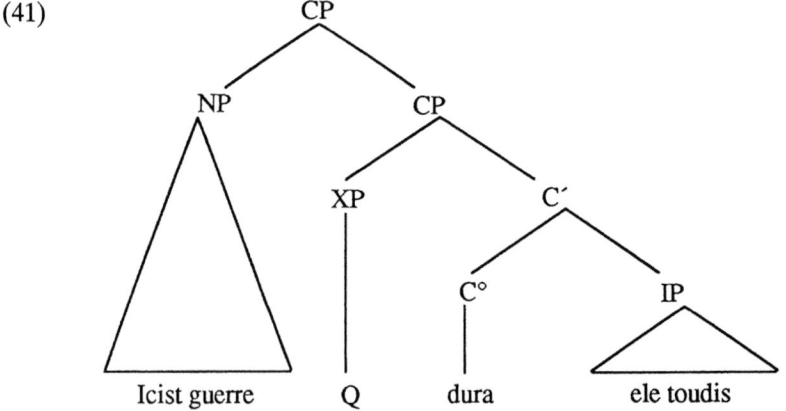

The fundamental difference between these two representations concerns the position and relations of the two candidates for the grammatical function of subject. In OF, as the structure in (41) indicates, the pronoun is the subject in all relevant senses: it occupies subject position (SpecI'), it receives Nominative Case from the inflected verb in C° under government, and it receives the subject's Θ-role.[8] The non-pronominal NP is peripheral to the core syntactic relations in the clause, and does not itself have a grammatical function; instead, it occupies a position adjoined to CP, which we take to be typical of dislocated elements (at least in OF). We assume that its grammatical function is determined by the formation of a composed chain (in the sense of Chomsky 1986b) with the pronominal subject; in this way it is related to the Case and Θ-properties that determine its grammatical function with respect to the clause.

On the other hand, as we argued in 1.5., the non-pronominal NP in a structure like (40) is the subject of the clause in all relevant senses: first, it occupies a position identifiable as subject position (the A-specifier of C'/I'); second, it receives Nominative Case under agreement with the verb in C°/I°; third, it receives the subject Θ-role (recall that this NP is base-generated in the base subject position in VP). The pronominal subject is an expletive element which receives Case by incorporating with C°, but has no Θ-role. We suggested in 1.5. that it owes its presence to the fact it licenses the trace in SpecI' for the ECP.

There are several factors which lead us to favour the analysis in (41) for the OF examples in (39). We will now review them in turn.

First, the OF examples are all Y/NQ. If these examples had the same structure as those in ModFr, we would expect to find, alongside the Y/NQ in (39), WHQ with complex inversion, i.e. examples analogous to (38a) having the order *WH NP V pronoun*. This sequence is not attested in OF. Schulze (op. cit.: 195) says: "I have encountered no trace of the ModFr operation according to which a stressed subject appears between the question-word and the verb."[9,10] This is exactly what we expect: OF was a V2 language, which means that I-to-C movement was triggered by C° having an [Agr] feature. In terms of the typology of incorporation elaborated in 1.3.3., this means that I-to-C did not create the hybrid category C/I in OF, but rather that C remained C after incorporation. Thus there is (aside from the very marginal possibility of topicalization to C', mentioned in Note 11) no position available between that occupied by the *wh*-constituent (SpecC') and that occupied by the inflected verb (C°). Adopting the structure (41) for (39) leaves unexplained the absence of WHQ with complex inversion and is inconsistent with the clearly V2 nature of OF.

Second, the order *NP WH V pronoun* is quite commonly attested. Schulze (op. cit.: 196) gives the following examples, among others:

(42) a. . . . **mi chevalier U   sunt il?**

      my knights   where are   they?

  (*Ch* II, 11650)

b. **La grant amour dont   tu   m'amoies Que peut-elle**
    The great love   with which you loved me   what can it
    estre devenue?
    have become?
    (*MirND* XVIII, 1625)

c. **Vostre proesce qu'est-elle** devenue?
    Your   prowess what is it   become
    (*Am. Am*. 1527)

Such examples must be treated as left-dislocations, since the subject precedes the *wh*-consituent. So the structure in (41) is clearly the appropriate one for these cases, with the *wh*-constituent occupying SpecC' in place of Q. The existence of such examples in the OF corpus, contrasted with the (near) nonexistence of the inverse order of the *wh*-consituent and the subject, leads us to treat the examples in (39) as cases of this structure rather than as cases of complex inversion. In other words, the existence of such left-dislocation structures and the absence of clear instances of complex inversion in WHQ is most simply accounted for if we assume that only the former structure existed. So we assign the structure in (41) to the examples in (39).

Further evidence comes from the null-subject counterparts of examples like those in (38). Since OF allowed null subjects in this kind of configuration (cf. 2.1.1.), we expect to find examples with the order *NP V pro*, as well as, parallel to the left-dislocations just discussed, the order *NP WH V pro*.

Taking the second of these two possibilities first, we find plenty of examples of this type. Schulze (op. cit.: 196) provides the following cases, among others:

(43) a. Et **cele dame,** fet il, **ki**   est?
         And that lady,   said he, who is (she)?
         (Jonckbl. LXXXI)

b. **Guillot, ma fille,   ou**   est?
    G.   my daughter, where is (she)?
    (*MirND* XVIII, 968)

A number of examples of this construction were found in the texts we surveyed, among them the following:

(44) a. **Iche coment** peut   avenir?
         This how   can (it) happen?
         (*Perceval*, l. 2379)

b. **mes chevax Ou**   remanra . . . ?

my   horse   where will-(he)-stay?

(*Perceval*, 1. 6724)

c. Et   **je que**   sai?

And I   what know (I)?

'And what do I know?'

(*Tristan*, 1. 4302)

(Note the dislocated nominative pronoun in (44c), a form no longer possible, cf. 2.2.1.). There is nothing surprising about such examples; structurally, they are to be analysed exactly like those in (42), i.e. in terms of the
structure in (41).

Moreover, there are a large number of examples in which some XP
other than the subject precedes the *wh*-constituent, suggesting that the
kind of left-dislocation that we are arguing that (39) represents was quite
a general strategy in questions (presumably used for emphasis), with no
particular restriction to subjects, unlike complex inversion. Among the
examples we have found with a dislocated XP ≠ the subject are the following:

(45) a. **Cest nostre rei**   por coi lessas   cunfundre?

This our   king why   let (you) overwhelm?

'Why did you let our king be overwhelmed?'

(*Roland*, 1. 2583)

b. **La   teste** por coi n'en   culpastes?

The head why   not-of-them cut-off (you)?

'Why didn't you cut their heads off?'

(*Perceval*, 1. 2342)

c. **Des   chevaliers** que vos diroie?

Of the knights   what you shall-say (I)?

'What shall I say to you about the knights?'

(*Tristan*, 1. 3991)

These examples provide further indirect evidence in favour of a left-
dislocation analysis of (39). The latter examples can then be seen as
instances of a general emphatic construction in questions, which involved
placing the constituent to be emphasised to the left of the *wh*-constituent.
It seems better to treat these cases as left-dislocation than as topicalization, as, since topicalization is a case of *wh*-movement, it should not be

possible to topicalize something past the *wh*-constituent in SpecC′ (cf.
*John, who saw t). Moreover, as we shall see in 2.3.1., topicalization to
CP is in general not allowed. On the other hand, there is no pronominal
'reprise' of the kind one would expect to find if this were 'standard' left-
dislocation. Whatever the precise nature of this emphatic construction,
we should assimilate the subject cases in (42–44) to the cases in (45), and
hence not treat the subject cases as complex inversion (note that treating
examples like (43) and (44) as topicalization poses no problem for head-
government of the subject trace since OF is a V2 language — cf. 1.4. and
2.1.1.).

We observed in 2.1.1. (Notes 4 and 5) that null subjects were rarer in
Y/NQ than in WHQ in the 12th century. This is only a tendency, however,
not an absolute ban. So expect to find at least a few examples of *NP V
pro*, although we expect this order to be rare, as only a subset of Y/NQ
with null subjects can be expected to show left dislocation. Schulze (op.
cit.: 190–1) gives just three such examples:

(46) a. Et **vous** onques puis le **veïstes?**

       And you never after him saw?

       'And you never saw him afterwards?'

       (*Perc Forts* 28037)

    b. Et **cil dene muert** bien ki le mal relenquist?

       And this officer dies well who evil gives up?

       (*Poem. mor.* 331ᵇ)

(46a) (as well as a third example given by Schulze, which we have not
reported since is rather less clear) features another constituent before the
verb. This opens up the possibility of treating this as a case of regular V2
order with topicalization or dislocation of *vous*. Schulze claims he found
no other examples of this order[11] and we have found no others either. So
it seems that the rarity of Y/NQ with null subjects, multiplied by the
comparative infrequency of left dislocation, underlies the near non-existence of these examples.

We can interpret this situation in such a way as to indirectly derive from
it a further argument that the examples in (39) are not true cases of
complex inversion. Recall the UCL of 1.5. (119′), which we repeat here,
explicitly adding the specification that formal licensing, not identification,
is in question:

(47) *Uniqueness Condition on Licensing (UCL)*
     X° cannot formally license:
     (i) two empty categories in a single structure;
     (ii) two A-positions in a single structure.

We saw in 1.5. that there is independent evidence from the cross-linguistic distribution of complex inversion that (47) constrains Case assignment and the licensing of null subjects by the same head. In that case, the examples of *NP V pro* that Schulze found must be examples of left dislocation: if they were analysed as complex inversion, they would fall foul of (47) in the same way as the cases discussed in 1.5. So (47) tells us that these strings are evidence for a left-dislocation analysis of (39) and similar examples in OF.[12]

A fourth consideration which favours a left-dislocation analysis of examples like (39) in OF is the absence of any such sentences where the initial NP is a non-referential quantifier. In each example in (39) the initial NP is definite: this is also true of all the examples given by Schulze. As we pointed out in 1.5., left-dislocated NPs cannot be non-referential quantifiers (cf. 1.5. (102)), a fact which leads us to conclude from the possibility of a preverbal non-referential quantifier in ModFr complex inversion (cf. 1.5. (103)) that these structures are not left dislocations. The absence of non-referential quantifiers in the corresponding OF examples we are interested in here strongly suggests that these constructions are not equivalent to the ModFr case, but instead are left dislocations.

Finally, Foulet (1921) points out that the context of these examples strongly favours a heavily emphatic interpretation. Foulet (pp. 247–8) discusses the order *NP WH V pro*, on the basis of the following examples:

(48) a. Nostre escu   por quoi *furent*   fet?

      Our   *shields why*   *were* (*they*) *made?*

      (Chrétien de Troyes *Cligés*, Foerster (ed.) 1910, 1303)

   b. Mes sa parole que li   coste?

      But his word   what him costs (*it*)?

      (*Renart*, Martin (ed.) 1882, br. I, 782)

Foulet says:[13]

'Nostre escu', 'sa parole', since they bear a fairly strong accent, constitute complete sentences by themselves. One could write '[Et] nostre escu? Por quoi furent fet?', '[Et] sa parole? Que li coste?' This would probably be an exaggeration of the effect of such examples, but at least this punctuation would indicate the general sense in which we should understand this effect.

So we conclude that OF had a left-dislocation construction that involved placing the subject in a position left-adjoined to CP, forming a composed chain with a pronoun (either null or overt) in the normal subject position. This construction was therefore quite distinct from the ModFr complex-inversion construction. However, it is clear that the modern construction evolved from this construction, in a way that we will describe in detail in 2.3.4.

The evidence in this subsection and the preceding two establishes two things: (i) OF allowed Nominative-assignment under government; (ii) complex inversion did not exist in OF. Both of these properties represent differences with ModFr. In 2.3. and 2.4. we will trace how the OF system evolved into the ModFr one. First, however, we need to look at the status of subject pronouns, both null and overt, in more detail. This is the topic of the next section.

2.2. PRONOMINAL SUBJECTS IN OF

In the previous section we saw the evidence that simple inversion around non-pronominal subjects existed in OF, while complex inversion, i.e. the ModFr construction described in 1.5., did not. Here we turn our attention to the status of pronominal subjects in OF, both phonologically overt ones and phonologically null ones. The main questions we will address are: (i) the clitic or non-clitic nature of overt nominative pronouns, and (ii) the distribution and licensing of null subjects. In connection with (i), we will see that overt nominative pronouns are non-clitic in all environments (2.2.1.) except immediate postverbal position (2.2.2.), where the situation is less clear, but indirect evidence suggests that in this position nominative pronouns were clitics (in this we concur with Vance 1989). In connection with (ii), we will see, following Adams (1988a, b, c), Dupuis (1988, 1989), Hirschbuhler (1989) and Hirschbuhler and Junker (1988), but *contra* Adams (1987a, b), that null subjects are possible in many types of embedded clauses at least in some OF texts. There is nevertheless an intimate relation between the licensing of *pro* and verb-movement. We will capture this by retaining the idea that the licensing condition on null subjects depends on government by Agr, adopting and refining the 'double Agr' clause structure introduced in the previous section.

These issues are relevant to the question of how Nominative Case was assigned in OF. The clitichood of nominative pronouns is relevant because clitic pronouns, by incorporating with some head, are able to circumvent restrictions on the usual mechanisms of Case-assignment (this is what allows subject-clitic inversion in ModFr — cf. 1.5.). Hence we must determine at what point nominative pronouns were in principle able to cliticize in the history of French and, more importantly, we need to know when and how the double series of subject pronouns characteristic of ModFr emerged (cf. 2.3.3.). To the extent that null subjects are licensed in contexts of (Nominative) Case-assignment (cf. (6)), the distribution of null subjects gives an insight into the contexts in which Nominative Case-assignment may take place. Given our formulation of (6), this is a one-way implication, in that Case-assignment is in principle possible in contexts where null subjects cannot be licensed, cf. 2.2.3.

2.2.1. *Nominative Pronouns in Non-Postverbal Position*

As we said above, the purpose of this subsection and the next is to discuss the clitichood of nominative pronouns in OF. Before embarking on a discussion of the data, it is important to be clear about what we mean by 'clitichood'. As we briefly mentioned in 1.3.3. and 1.5., we understand cliticization as incorporation by adjunction of one head to another. Cliticization is thus an instance of incorporation of the type illustrated in (72b) of Chapter 1, which we repeat here:

(49)

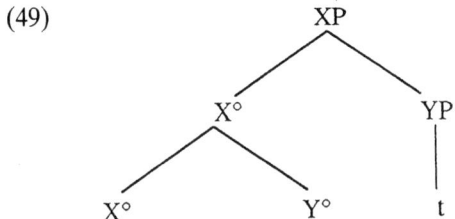

In this configuration, the clitic is $Y°$, and the host of cliticization is $X°$. Order internal to $X°$ is irrelevant; we illustrate with the order in (49) as that is characteristic of subject-enclisis, which will be our main concern in this section. Kayne (1990: 2) proposes that Romance complement clitics are always left-adjoined to a functional head. The characterization of cliticization in (49) says nothing about what allows or forces some elements and not others to incorporate — on this matter for French nominative pronouns see 2.3.3.

Two questions arise concerning the operation of cliticization, understood as in (49). First, does it take place in syntax (the mapping from DS to SS) or in phonology (the mapping from SS to PF)? Second, is it optional or obligatory? Both of these questions are relevant for our investigation of the nature of Nominative-assignment in the history of French. Concerning the first question, since we assume that the requirements of Case theory must be met at SS, cliticization in PF does not interact with Case theory, and so PF clitics receive Case in the same way as non-pronominal NPs (we will modify this supposition in 2.3.3.). Concerning the second question, if an element cliticizes only optionally at SS, this may indicate that it can satisfy Case theory in one of two ways, either by being assigned a Case or by incorporation. On the other hand, obligatory cliticization at SS may indicate that Case-assignment is impossible in the context in question and so incorporation is forced for PF-identification, as is the case for subject clitics in inversion contexts in ModFr (cf. 1.5.). Alternatively, it may indicate that Case-assignment as such is not adequate to guarantee well-formedness of the structure containing the clitic, since the clitic is subject to some further morphosyntactic condition. Something of this sort must be true for non-subject clitics in Romance, and may also be true of ModFr subject clitics — cf. 2.3.3.

A number of factors define the clitic pronouns of ModFr and other Romance languages. If we apply these diagnostics to the nominative pronouns of OF and ModFr, the contrasts between the two stages of the language come out clearly. It emerges that, in all environments except immediately post-verbally, the OF nominative pronouns were not obligatorily clitics.

We now take the diagnostic properties of ModFr clitics one by one (the presentation is inspired by Price 1971: 144f, Kayne 1975, 2.4, and Adams 1987b: 168f):

(i) *ModFr clitics cannot be stressed:*

(50)   *JE vois Jean

        I   see John

OF subject pronouns could be stressed. We can see this from the fact that such pronouns could occur as the initial NP in the proto-complex-inversion structures discussed in 2.1.3. Recall that there we said, following Foulet (1921), that the initial NP in a sequence *NP (WH) V pronoun/pro* was emphatic in the sense that it had its own intonation contour. In that case, the existence of examples like the following suggests strongly that nominative pronouns were able to be stressed in this sense:

(51)   Et **je** que sai?

        And I what know (I)?

        'And what do I know?'

        (*Tristan*, 1. 4302; cf. (43c))

A further indication that the nominative forms could be stressed comes from examples like the following (from Foulet ibid.):

(52) a.   Renars respont: "**Jou** je n'irai"

           R.   answers: "I   I won't go"

           (*Couronnement Renart*, A. Foulet (ed.) 1929, 598)

     b.   Et **jou** je cuit . . .

           And I   I believe . . .

           (ibid. 1616)

These examples indicate that nominative pronouns were able to bear stress in OF, but are no longer able to do so in ModFr. (The spelling *jou* (in other regions *gié* was used) might be significant here; Foulet 1935/6: 312,

1982: 154 implies that it indicates a stressed form of the pronoun, while Price 1971: 145 denies this (at least for *gié*)).

(ii) *ModFr clitics cannot be conjoined:*

(53)   *Je et tu irons à Paris
        I and you will-go to Paris

Contrast this with the following example from *Roland*, cited by Price (1971: 144):

(54)   e **jo** e **vos** i   irum
        and I and you there will-go

Again, there is a clear difference between OF and ModFr here.

(iii) *Subject clitics can only be separated from the verb by other clitics in ModFr:*

(55)   *Il, paraît-il, est malade
        He, seems it, is sick

Again, this was not the case for OF nominative pronouns:

(56) a. et il, a   toz ses oz . . . , s'en ala
         and he, with all his army,   went away
         (Villehardouin; Price (ibid.))

     b. **Ge** autre terre, sire, ne vos demant
         I   other land, sire, not you ask
         (*Charroi de Nîmes*, l. 500; Adams 1987b: 168).

(iv) *ModFr subject pronouns cannot stand alone, for example in elliptical constructions where no verb is present:*

(57)   Qui sera là?   *Je et   tu
        Who will-be there? I and you

Again, this constraint did not hold in OF:

(58) a. et qui i   sera? **jou** et **tu**
         and who there will-be? I   and you
         (Price 1971: 145)

     b. . . . Et **je** ausi
             And I too
         (Adams 1987b: 168)

(v) *Nominative pronouns could be modified in OF*, in the sense that they could at least form compounds with *meïsmes* ('self', ModFr *même*):

(59) a.   Se **je meïsmes** ne li   di . . .
          If I self   not him say . . .
          'If I don't tell him myself . . .'

     b.   Con s'**il**   **duï** ne fussent quë uns
          As if they two not were   but one
          'As if the two of them were one'
          (both examples from Franzén 1939: 20)

This is quite impossible in ModFr; forms such as **ils-mêmes* do not exist.

We can summarize the ModFr situation with the following statement: nominative pronouns must appear adjacent to Agr. This accounts for all the above facts except for the fact that the ModFr nominative pronouns cannot be stressed; to account for this we can add that these pronouns must form a PF unit with Agr, and assume that subparts of a PF unit cannot have their own stress contour. In these terms, the relevant generalization for OF becomes that the nominative pronouns did not obligatorily form a PF unit with Agr (this does not exclude the possibility that nominative pronouns, at least the possibly weaker forms written *je*, were phonologically clitics; however, the evidence is that they were not required to cliticize any particular head, unlike ModFr nominative pronouns).

Two further points are worth making here. First, if OF nominative pronouns were genuine syntactic clitics in the sense defined above, they would not be able to fill the SpecC′ position, and so they would not be able to satisfy the V2 constraint (this point is also made by Adams ibid.). However, it is easy to find examples where a pronominal subject occupies the position preceding the inflected verb, i.e. SpecC′. The following examples were found in the first pages of the *Le Charroi de Nîmes*:

(60) a.   Et **ge irai**   a Looÿs parler
          And I   will-go to L.   to speak
          'And I will go and speak to L'
          (l. 48)

     b.   **Tu es** or   riche et **ge sui** po   proisié
          You are now rich and I   am little valued
          (l. 252, also cited in Adams, ibid.)

c. **Ge fis**   monter dos mile   chevaliers

    I   made go up   two thousand knights

(l. 255)

Although we are unable to draw a clear contrast with ModFr in this case, as ModFr is not V2, this observation indicates at least that preverbal nominative pronouns are not incorporated into C° in OF (at SS). In this respect, nominative pronouns differ from their non-nominative counterparts, which appear to be part of C° (probably, in fact, part of the raised V° + Agr° — cf. Kayne 1989) and hence do not 'count' for V2 (cf. 2.1.2.).

Second, it is often taken that the existence of a double series of pronouns in complementary distribution, one tonic and one atonic, is an indication of the clitichood of the atonic pronouns (cf. Vanelli *et al.* 1986, Adams ibid.). ModFr has exactly this pattern; alongside the nominative pronouns we have been discussing (the series is *je, tu, il/elle, nous, vous, ils/elles*) there is the series of diachronically oblique pronouns (*moi, toi, lui/elle, nous, vous, eux/elles*). In ModFr, the *moi*-series appears in the contexts in (50–59) above:

(61) a. Moi, je vois Jean (cf. (50))
    b. Moi et toi, nous irons à Paris (cf. (53))
    c. Elle, paraît-il, elle est malade (cf. (55))
    d. Qui sera là? Moi et toi (cf. (57))
    e. Eux-mêmes (ils) mangeaient ce qu'ils pouvaient trouver (cf. (59))

And, with the exception of certain rather literary registers where 3rd person forms (*lui/eux*) are possible, only *je*-forms are possible in subject position:

(62)   *Moi vois Jean

    'me' see J.

So the two sets of pronouns are in near-perfect complementary distribution in ModFr. However, as the data in (50–59) show, no such complementary distribution existed in OF, in that the *je*-series appeared where only the *moi*-series is allowed in ModFr. Conversely, however, the *moi*-series could appear in their modern positions (i.e., those in (61)) in OF, at least in the 13th century, according to Foulet (1935/6):[14]

(63) a. . . . que je nes   vuel noient   ocire

    . . . that I not-them want nothing to-kill

    ne   **moi** ne gent   de mon empire

    neither me nor people of my   empire

'that neither I nor my subjects in any way want to kill them'
(Béroul, Muret (ed.) 2nd ed., 1922, 2026; Foulet op. cit.: 264)

b. Sire, dist il, **et   moi et   vos** irons   nos
    Sire, said he, and me and you shall-go we
    'Sire, he said, you and I shall both go'
    (*Couronnement Renart*, A. Foulet (ed.) 1929, 598; Foulet op.
    cit.: 263)

c. . . . dont   vous ne deüssiez avoir hounour **et   vous**
    . . . of which you   shouldn't   have honour and you
    et   ly
    and him
    '. . . for which neither you nor he should have honour'
    (*Galeran* 2977; Foulet op. cit.: 262)

d. . . . s'il   eüst l'ame   et **moy** le corps
    . . . if he had the soul and me   the body
    (*Galeran* 4378; Foulet op. cit.: 260)

e. C'est **moi meïsmes**, car c'est m'ame
    It's   my self,   for it's my soul
    (*Mérangis* 4888; Foulet op. cit.: 33)

Once again, then, it is clear that the OF situation was quite different from that found in ModFr. If the existence of a double series of pronouns in complementary distribution is evidence that the atonic series is a clitic series then OF provides no such evidence, since the two sets of pronouns were not in complementary distribution. We will return to the topic of the oblique pronouns in 2.3.3., when we discuss the emergence of the double series.

How can we formally characterize these differences in terms of the conception of cliticization outlined above? We said above that the basic constraint on nominative pronouns in ModFr is that they must appear string-adjacent to Agr° and they must form a phonological unit with this element. The constraints on these pronouns that we described all indicate that the pronouns are phonologically bound to Agr°, hence they cannot bear separate stress, be separately conjoined, be non-adjacent to Agr°, appear where Agr (or V + Agr) is elided, or form autonomous compounds not involving Agr (*je-même*, etc.). Technically, then, subject clitics must incorporate with Agr° at PF (cf. Kayne 1983). On the other hand, ModFr postverbal clitics incorporate at SS; as we saw in 1.5., this follows from the way in which Nominative-assignment works in ModFr. Preverbal clitics occupy a Case position, while postverbal clitics do not. Nevertheless, both are clitics (although there are general differences between enclisis and proclisis — cf. Benincà and Cinque 1990). What this indicates is that 'clitichood' is a property independent of Case-assignment to positions occupied by clitics. For a proposal, cf. 2.3.3. We can account for the distribution of the tonic pronouns in terms of the assumption that they cannot appear in contexts of structural Case-assignment (with the exception of the literary *Lui a fait cela*).

Let us now compare the above analysis of ModFr with what has to be said about OF. The data we have reviewed for OF indicate that non-postverbal nominative pronouns certainly were not obligatory clitics. Also, unlike ModFr *moi*-forms, they were able to appear in positions of structural Case-assignment. So they were not distinct from other NPs in the relevant respects (rather like English pronouns, as Adams (1987b) observes). It is possible that, at least by the 13th century, they optionally cliticized in PF when adjacent to Agr°. This may explain the growing preference for *moi*-forms in the positions where we find these forms today (cf. (63) and the discussion in Foulet 1935/6). In 2.3.3. we will outline how the *je*-forms were ousted from the positions in (63) in MidFr, i.e. how PF-cliticization to Agr became obligatory.

We have seen that postverbal clitics in ModFr satisfy Case theory in a different way to non-pronominal NPs, and, most important, they are thus able to appear in a relation with Agr which is unavailable for non-pronominal NPs. So, having seen that OF nominative pronouns differed from ModFr ones in not being PF clitics in non-postverbal position, we now turn to the examination of the behaviour of these pronouns in postverbal position. The object of this investigation is to see whether the ModFr requirement on pronouns in this position — syntactic cliticization to C° — held in OF.

2.2.2. *Nominative Pronouns in Postverbal Position*

In this section, we consider the behaviour of nominative pronouns in immediate postverbal positions, i.e. in inversion contexts where the inflected verb has raised to C° and the nominative pronoun is not fronted to SpecC', but remains in SpecI'. We have been assuming the main points of Kayne's (1983) analysis of ModFr, which says that nominative pronouns are syntactic clitics here. Our question is: were they syntactic clitics in this context in OF? We will see that there is fairly direct evidence that they were clitics, and indirect evidence that they were **syntactic** clitics (Dupuis (1989: 119f) also argues that nominative pronouns in immediate postverbal position were enclitic, in part on similar grounds to what follows).

In what follows, we will rely heavily on the discussion in Vance (1989:

70ff). There Vance argues for the following constraint on nominative pronouns in OF:

(64)   Nominative pronouns must appear in SpecI' position

The evidence for this comes from the failure of nominative pronouns to remain in VP in constructions where Nominative Case could be assigned to a VP-internal position. Vance interprets this as evidence that postverbal nominative pronouns were at least PF clitics on C°, a conclusion we agree with and elaborate on.

We saw in 2.1.2. that OF was like Italian in allowing free inversion. Vance (p. 58ff) shows that OF allows direct objects to receive Nominative Case *in situ* in passives and unaccusatives. The evidence is provided by sentences like the following:

(65)a.   ainçois lor   en **fu coverte la vraie semblance**
         rather to-them of-it was covered the true   appearance
         (Vance's (51), p. 67)

     b.   cele nuit **furent servié** et   **ariesié li   compaignon**
         that night were   served and satisfied the companions
         'that night the companions were served and satisfied'
         (Vance's (53), p. 67)

(66) a. tant   **fu** de bone hore **nez li   chevaliers**
         so much was of good hour born the knight
         'the knight had been born at such a fortunate time'
         (Vance's (59), p. 69)

     b. et   lors **s'alerent** seoir **li   chevalier**
         and then went   to-sit the knights
         'and then the knights went to sit down'
         (Vance's (61), p. 69)

(67) a. A ceste espee trere fors de cest perron **ont**   hui
         to this   sword draw out of this rock   have today
         failli des plus proisiez chevaliers de mon ostel
         failed the most worthy knights   of my   household
         'Some of the worthiest knights of my household have failed today to draw this sword out of this rock'
         (Vance's (72), p. 74)

b.   Car a   ceste Queste ne   **doit refuser nus preudoms**

For to this   quest   neg must refuse no man

ne   por mort ne   por vie

neither for death nor for life

'For no man must refuse this quest, either for life or death'

(Vance's (82), p. 76)

(65) gives examples of passives, (66) examples of unaccusatives, and (67) shows cases with transitive and unergative intransitive verbs (although (67a) may be a case of Heavy NP-Shift). In all of these examples, the nominative NP follows a non-tensed verb form, and so this NP cannot be in SpecAgr'. In fact, there is no reason to think that this NP has moved from its DS position inside VP (whether this is a complement position, as in (65) and (66), or the DS subject position, as in (67)). The important point in the present context is that there are no cases of this structure where the VP-internal Nominative NP is a pronoun. It is this observation that leads Vance to formulate the constraint on nominative pronouns in (64).

Further evidence that the distribution of postverbal subject pronouns is constrained along the lines indicated by (64) comes from the interaction of subjects and negative particles, as discussed by Skårup (1975: 51f). OF, unlike ModFr but like Modern Italian, had optional postverbal negative elements which semantically reinforced the sentence-negator *ne*. These elements included *mie* (cf. Italian *mica*) and *pas*. Non-pronominal subjects could follow these elements, but pronominal subjects always preceded them, as the following examples illustrate (Skårup ibid.: 48 shows that other adverbs like *donc* and *or* generally followed this pattern too):

(68)a. Si   n'en   fait   **mie li contes del   saint**

thus neg-of-it makes not the tale   of the holy

Graal mencion

grail   mention

'Thus the tale of the Holy Grail makes no mention of it'

b.   De mon nom, fet il, *ne* puez **tu   mie** savoir

Of my   name, said he, neg can you not know

"You cannot know my name", said he

(Vance's (88, 89), p. 80)

(69)a.   Ha! dame, or   n'i   verroiz **vos pas** vostre chevalier

Ha! lady,   now neg-there will-see you not your   knight

'Ha! lady, now you will not see your knight there'

(*Mort Artu* 40, 15; Hirschbuhler and Junker's (9a), p. 68)

b.   De ceste novele n'est   **pas Tristan** molt liez

Of this   news   neg-is not T.   very happy

'Tristan isn't very happy about this news'

(*Tristan* prose 395, 26; Sk. p. 54; Hirschbuhler and Junker's (9c), p. 68)

Assuming that *mie* and *pas*, like Italian *mica*, English *not*, and ModFr *pas*, occupy SpecT' (cf. 1.1., and recall that we are abstracting away from Pollock's (1989) proposed NegP in this chapter), (68) and (69) show that pronominal subjects must appear at least as high as SpecAgr', while nominal subjects are able to remain in lower positions. Given our assumptions regarding the possible subject positions of Old French (cf. 2.1.2.), it is hard to determine the exact position occupied by the subject in (68a) and (69b). As Dupuis (1989) points out, this contrast is a robust one, and so more should be said. We will return to this question below.

Moreover, in his discussion of OF interrogatives, Moignet (1973: 352) makes the following observation: "the subject pronoun (. . .) regularly follows the inflected verb, from which it can only be separated by personal pronouns or the adverbs *en* and *i.*"[15] This statement is very reminiscent of the conditions on preverbal subject pronouns in ModFr, suggesting that the constraint in (66) is due to the fact that postverbal subject pronouns were clitics in OF. In fact, Vance (p. 81) makes precisely this proposal.

Another argument in favour of Vance's condition on nominative pronouns comes from a consideration of the form of personal pronouns in predicative sentences. The normal form in OF was *ce suis je*, as in the following example:

(70)   ce ne sui je mie

         it not am I not

         'it is not me'

         (*Mérangis* 4377; Foulet 1935/6: 49)

Here the predicate is *ce*, which has moved to SpecC', the verb is in C° and *je* occupies subject position. Starting very early on, the status of *ce* changed in such a way that it was reanalysed as the subject: this can be seen from the occurrence of forms like *c'est vous* in place of *ce estes vous*, i.e. the fact that the verb agrees with *ce* and not with *vous* shows that *ce* is the subject and *vous* is the predicate. Foulet (ibid.: 50) dates this change as taking place in the 13th century.

The striking thing is that we never find forms like *c'est je*. Foulet (1935/6:

43ff), on whose observations this account is based, attributes this to the phonetic weakness of *je*, but this does not seem compatible with the existence (and survival until the modern period) of forms like *vais-je*, *sais-je*. However, after the reanalysis of the position of *ce*, *je*, as the predicate, would occupy some postverbal position other than SpecAgr' (SpecIP in Vance's terms). So we can take the non-existence of these forms as evidence for Vance's constraint.

If this argument can be maintained, it tells us that the gradual cliticiz-ation of nominative pronouns was not simply a matter of a requirement that they appear adjacent to a verb, since in **c'est je*, *je* is adjacent to the verb. Instead, the relevant generalization seems to be that nominative pronouns in postverbal position were required to be governed by Agr, the nominative-assigning head. Without going into the details of the struc-ture of predicative sentences, it is clear that the predicate *je* in *c'est je* is not governed by *est* in C°, since at least Agr° and T° intervene. So this will account for the non-existence of *c'est je*. Note that the natural way to make sense of this requirement is by saying that postverbal pronouns were syntactic clitics; in that case we can see the requirement that the pronoun be governed as an instance of the ECP's requirement that the trace of the incorporated clitic be properly governed. So it is ultimately due to the ECP that, once *ce* was reanalysed as the subject in predicative sentences, *ce suis je* was replaced by *c'est moi*.

We can now restate Vance's constraint (64) as follows:

(71)   Nominative pronouns must form a chain with a position gov-erned by or in Spec-head agreement with Agr° (where Agr° is present).

(71) has the precise effect of requiring nominative pronouns to appear outside VP at SS, and so entails that pronouns cannot appear in the VP-internal 'freely inverted' position (for this reason, it is crucial (71) is formulated in terms of the notion 'chain' rather than the notion 'CHAIN'). The addition in parentheses is intended to cover elliptical cases like (58); here, if Agr is present it governs or agrees with the pronoun, and if it is not present (71) does not apply. (71) is reminiscent of a condition recently proposed by Holmberg (1990) to deal with weak pronouns in some varie-ties of MSc (e.g. Swedish), where the elements in question are free morphemes — and hence not clitics — but are nevertheless restricted in distribution compared to 'full' NPs. Holmberg's condition requires that these elements be 'adjacency-governed' by a functional head (where adjac-ency-government is the combination of minimal c-command by X° and strict adjacency). It may also be appropriate to apply a condition of the type in (71) to 'tonic' pronouns of the *moi*-series in ModFr, as Luigi Rizzi (pers. comm.) has suggested; note that these pronouns cannot appear as

the inverted subject in Styl-Inv (*Le jour où est arrivé lui 'The day where arrived him').

It is possible to relate the constraint in (71) and the PF-cliticization of nominative pronouns in this position to another observation made both by Vance (p. 87) and by Hirschbuhler and Junker (1988: 68), in such a way as to shed light on one kind of V1 order. These authors observe that in matrix V1 sentences definite pronouns do not occur. This suggests, given (71), that the subject is forced to be in VP in these cases, not in SpecAgr', hence the subject cannot be pronominal.[16]

The evidence we have reviewed here indicates that nominative pronouns were subject to the constraint in (71), and that, when in postverbal position, they were required to appear in SpecAgr', a position immediately adjacent to and governed by C°. So they were very close to being clitics in this position. The question is: did these pronouns incorporate from this position into C°? There are three reasons to think that subject pronouns underwent syntactic cliticization from this position: two directly from OF, and one based on cross-linguistic considerations.

The first OF argument comes from contrasts of the type seen in (68) and (69). Pronominal subjects are regularly found adjacent to a preceding inflected verb which occupies C° in inversion contexts, while non-pronominal subjects do not have to be strictly adjacent to the inflected verb when the verb is in C°. One way to account for this is to say (i) that the second negator mie/pas in examples like (68) and (69) is not in SpecT' but in some higher position (contra what we said above after (69)), and (ii) that pronouns cliticize to C° over mie/pas, while non-pronominal NPs do not. In this way we account for the differential positioning of pronominal and non-pronominal subjects in inversion contexts. Of course, this argument depends on treating pronominal subjects in post-verbal position as clitics in OF. (This approach implies that pas has changed position since OF; note that in OF pas was not the main negator, and so was arguably not associated with NegP. We leave the details of this question open, since we are not considering the question of the distribution of NegP in OF).

The second OF argument depends on Styl-F, which we saw in 2.1.2. A condition on Styl-F is the presence of a subject gap (cf. 1.4.). Platzack (1988) points out that Old Swedish allows Styl-F where there is a subject pronoun, and suggests that this is possible to the extent that subject pronouns cliticize to C. OF examples like (31), which we repeat here as (72), show exactly the same thing:

(72)   quant il   de   ci   departiront
        when they from here will leave
        (Vance 1988, (11), p. 89)

So, in order to maintain a view of Styl-F in OF which is coherent with what is known about this operation in Scandinavian languages, we should conclude that subject pronouns cliticized to C in OF.

It is clear from the foregoing that postverbal nominative pronouns had a closer structural relationship to $C°$ than non-postverbal ones (a situation that persists in ModFr, as we have seen). This state of affairs is not unique to French: Haiman (1989: 2.2.) documents a number of Rhaeto-Romansch dialects where subject pronouns cliticize only in inversion contexts (Surmeiran, Puter and Vallader). In fact, Haiman ((38), p. 31) states the following implicational universal:

(73)   If a language has atonic subject pronouns in direct order [i.e. SV order — IGR] it also has them in inverted order.

Both OF and ModFr conform to this statement. But if atonic (i.e. clitic) pronouns resulted only from syntactic cliticization, we would have an immediate explanation for (73) in terms of the c-command component of proper government; only in inverted orders does the host of cliticization c-command the base position of the clitic. This explanation of Haiman's implicational universal suggests that cliticization is fundamentally a syntactic operation, in that it takes place in the syntax whenever it can. We will elaborate the conception of cliticization in 2.3.3. so that this result emerges naturally. So let us tentatively suppose that cliticization is a syntactic operation whenever it can be, i.e. typically in inversion contexts. In that case, the OF cliticization operation we have just seen the evidence for was a syntactic operation.

We conclude that postverbal pronouns were syntactic clitics in OF while preverbal ones were optional PF clitics. This conclusion does not directly entail that postverbal clitics satisfied Case theory in a different way to preverbal clitics and non-pronominal NPs, i.e. by incorporation, not by assignment. We will develop a theory of cliticization in 2.3.3. which will make it clear that the development of the double series of pronouns in MidFr was the factor which unambiguously altered the Case-theoretic status of nominative pronouns, and hence favoured the development of complex inversion. We now turn to the question of null subject pronouns.

2.2.3. Null Subjects in V 2 Contexts

In this section we discuss in detail the facts concerning the distribution of null subjects in OF matrix declarative clauses, i.e. V2 clauses. It is well-known that this is the basic context in which null subjects appear in OF (in the traditional literature, this observation is made by Einhorn 1974, Foulet 1982, Franzen 1939, Wartburg 1946, and in the generative literature by Vanelli, Renzi and Benincà 1986, Benincà 1983, and Adams 1987a, b).

Examples of null subjects in V2 contexts are easy to find in the 12th and 13th century texts. In addition to the extended text given in (26), here are some representative instances from the texts we looked at:

(74) a. Tresqu'en la mer **cunquist**   la tere altaigne
         Until   the sea conquered (he) the land high
         'He conquered the high land all the way to the sea'
         (*Roland*, l. 3)

     b. Aprés **conquist**   Orenge la cité
         After conquered (he) O.   the city
         'Afterwards he conquered the city of Orange'
         (*Le Charroi de Nîmes*, l. 7)

     c. Si   **chaï**   en   grant povreté
         Thus fell (I) into great poverty
         'Thus I fell into great poverty'
         (*Perceval*, l. 441).

     d. Or **fait**   senblant con s'ele plore
         Now makes (she) seem   as if she cries
         'Now she pretends to cry'
         (*Tristan*, l. 8)

     e. por vos **sui**   en prison misse
         for you am (I) in prison put
         'I have been put in prison for you'
         (*Aucassin et Nicolette*, v, 1. 20)

     f. si en **orent**   moult grant **merveille**
         so of-it had (they) very   great wonder
         (*Merlin*, p. 1)

In all these examples, the null subject is licensed under government by the verb which raises to the functional head which governs it:

(75)   ... V + Agr$_i$ [pro [t$_i$ ...

It is usually assumed in the generative literature, e.g. by the authors cited above, that the verb is in C° in (75). We will initially assume this, too, although we will refine this assumption in the next section. It is clear that this situation is in conformity with the licensing condition in (6); *pro* is licensed by Agr in a context in which NP can receive Nominative Case from Agr.

Note that, if we continue to assume that Nominative Case could also be assigned under agreement in OF (cf. the discussion of (10) and (34a–c) above), the one-way implication in (6) becomes important; Agr° could Case-mark SpecAgr' in a configuration of agreement but a null subject could not be licensed in this kind of configuration. Thus, null subjects are licensed in a **subset** of the contexts in which Nominative can be assigned. If null subjects could be licensed under agreement, we would expect, since OF is a V2 language (cf. 2.1.2.), to find *pro* in initial position in matrix clauses, i.e. we would expect to find a fairly large proportion of V1 orders and no asymmetry between root and embedded clauses. Although earlier texts show these features to some extent (cf. 2.2.4.), we suggest that this is evidence for a double-Agr structure of the type discussed in 1.4. and 2.1.2., and that the licensing conditions for *pro* are the same throughout; at the earlier stage *pro* is licensed by the inflected verb in Agr1, later it is licensed by the inflected verb in C (see 2.2.4.). We thus continue to assume that *pro* could only be licensed in government configurations. This is the formal condition on *pro*.

Another issue which is raised by the conditions in (6) is the question of the attribution of grammatical features from Agr° to *pro* (or perhaps from Agr1 to *pro*), i.e. the question of the identification of *pro*'s content. The classic observation (which a theory based on (6) is in part a formalization of) is that canonical null-subject languages like Latin, Spanish or Italian have person/number inflections that are sufficiently differentiated that an overt subject pronoun is not required. In terms of the theory based on (6), we would say that Agr° contains a set of inflectional features that are rich enough to permit the recovery of the content of a null subject, and so *pro* can be identified as long as it is in the relevant structural relation with Agr°.

However, as Foulet (1935/6: 275ff) points out, it is not immediately clear that OF possessed a sufficiently 'rich' set of endings in this sense. In the following discussion of the 'richness' of agreement, we restrict attention to the present tense of verbs of the most widespread conjugation (the *-er* conjugation). We make this move partly for simplicity of exposition, and partly as we think it is a justified idealization; these are by far the most frequent verb forms in the trigger experience, and hence play a major role in determining the status of the agreement system. At the beginning of the OF period, the present-tense conjugation of an *-er* verb was as follows (cf. Vance 1989: 124, where the problems for Jaeggli and Safir 1989's system — see below — that this paradigm raises are also discussed):

(76)   chant, chantes, chante(t), chantons, chantez, chantent

Here, if we count the zero-inflection for 1sg as an ending, there are six distinct person inflections, as in Latin, Spanish or Italian. However, in

spoken OF (according to Foulet, early in this period), these endings were
reduced to the three that we find in ModFr as a result of two processes:
(i) phonetic erosion of final consonants, eliminating 2sg -*s*, 3sg -*t* (the
latter already 'hardly more than a memory' in the 12th century, cf. Foulet
op. cit.: 275) and 3pl -*nt*; (ii) an operation of analogy, which added -*e*
in 1sg. After a very detailed discussion of these developments, Foulet
concludes:[17]

> ... from at least the 12th century on, we had in France the kind of conjugational system
> which we still have today, i.e. a paradigm where the three persons of the singular and the
> third person plural are perceptually identical (ibid.: 292).

So the situation since the 13th century has been one where only 1pl and
2pl have distinct endings, the rest of the paradigm being identical.

A naive interpretation of the above account of the identification of *pro*
would lead one to expect French to cease to be a null-subject language
after these developments, as, intuitively at least, Agr no longer seems rich
enough to permit the recovery of the person/number specification of *pro*.
In fact, however, French remained a null-subject language until the 16th
century, i.e. for approximately three centuries after the restructuring of
the verbal paradigm took place. It is also worth pausing over the second
of these developments: why should analogical pressures lead to the formal
assimilation of one person to others in a null-subject language? Phonological attrition may obscure distinctions in a paradigm; this is a development
whose origins lie outside the morphological system, but analogy within a
paradigm is a purely morphological process. One might, naively, expect
paradigms to be restructured so as to maximize differences among persons
in a null-subject language rather than the converse (such a development
has in fact taken place in the history of Italian, where 1sg -*o* was introduced
into the imperfect tense, obviating the syncretism between 1sg and 3sg
(which remains in Portuguese and Spanish) which results from the loss of
Latin -*m* (1sg) and -*t* (3sg) (Harris 1978: 129)).

These observations lead us to propose a slightly more elaborate system
for identifying null subjects. The 'traditional' intuition concerning richness
of agreement is essentially based on a **functional** notion of 'richness'.
Another kind of 'richness' can also be envisaged, one where the paradigm
simply makes available a slot for agreement affixes; call this **formal** richness (not to be confused with formal licensing; both functional and formal
richness are aspects of content-licensing). In fact, Jaeggli and Safir (1989:
29f) (see also Jaeggli and Hyams 1987) have recently proposed that formal
richness in this sense is what is relevant for licensing null subjects. They
suggest that the notion of 'morphological uniformity' of verb paradigms
determines whether a language allows null subjects or not. Jaeggli and
Safir define Morphological Uniformity as follows:[18]

(77)   An inflectional paradigm P in a language L is morphologically

uniform iff P has either only underived inflectional forms or only derived inflectional forms.
(Jaeggli and Safir's (43), p. 30)

Note that (77) appears to be problematic for the early OF paradigm given in (76) since 1sg had no ending. In fact, OF paradigms (prior to restructuring) were rich, in that the zero ending unambiguously identified 1sg and all the other endings were distinct, but they were not uniform in Jaeggli and Safir's sense. After restructuring, the paradigms were uniform, but not rich. Since French remained a null-subject language independently of restructuring, either type of situation seems to be adequate for licensing the content of *pro*.

What we propose, then, is that there are two ways in which paradigms can be rich enough to permit the identification of the content of *pro*: a functional way and a formal way. Functional richness is compatible with a zero ending for one person in the paradigm, since this clearly will not interfere with the function of uniquely identifying that person. Following the 'traditional' idea about such paradigms, we adopt Rizzi's (1982, Ch. 4) characterization of such paradigms as [+ pron]. We make the following very specific hypothesis about what makes an agreement paradigm [+ pron]:

(78)   A [+ pron] paradigm allows up to one syncretism.

The evidence from uncontroversially null-subject languages like Spanish and Italian indicates that we cannot enforce a rigid one-to-one mapping between endings and null subjects; however, in these languages, when there is more than one sycretism (as in the Italian present subjunctive), an overt subject must be used with at least one of the person forms. This suggests that more than one syncretism is not tolerated.

So a [+ pron] paradigm allows one zero ending and one syncretism to coexist (the zero ending can be the syncretism, giving the possibility of two zero endings if all other persons are distinct). It is clear, then, that pre-13thc. OF paradigms were [+ pron].

Formal richness, on the other hand, simply requires a morphologically uniform paradigm where an agreement slot is available throughout (cf. Note 18 on the difference between this and Jaeggli and Safir's formulation in (77)). So we refer to such paradigms as [+ MU]. In principle, any number of syncretisms are tolerated, but no zero endings (if we allowed zero endings, paradigms like the regular English one would satisfy the condition). This was the situation in OF after restructuring of the verbal paradigms. So, in 12th-century OF, when the 2sg and 3pl endings started to coalesce with 3sg, the paradigm shifted from [+ pron] to [+ MU]. As a related development, 1sg took on a recognizable ending, and thus aligned itself with the rest of the paradigm (this development was caused by purely morphological factors; we do not mean to suggest that conditions on the identification of *pro* affected morphophonemics in a direct way). The introduction of 1sg *-e* was related to the retention of null subjects in the face of the erosion of the paradigms that was taking place in OF (recall that final *-e* was pronounced throughout OF and MidFr). A similar development took place in the imperfect, although here the phonological details are more complex. We will discuss this system of identification of null subjects in more detail in 2.4.3., when we discuss the loss of null subjects in French, which took place in the 16th-century. There we also compare the French developments with those which have taken place in Italian dialects and Provençal as discussed in Vanelli *et al.* (1986), Benincà (1984), Vanelli (1987).

As we saw in 2.0., two properties are correlated with the existence of null subjects in standard work on the null-subject parameter: free inversion and apparent *that*-trace violations. Free inversion was possible in OF, as we saw in 2.1.2. and 2.2.2. It seems that this option was less frequent in OF than in Modern Spanish or Italian; however, V2 may in many cases obscure this kind of inversion, in that the order *XP V subject* could in principle result either from free inversion or from V2, or, in fact, from both operations applying together. Thus an example like (79), also taken from Vance (op. cit., (67), p. 72) could in principle have any one of the structures in (80) (returning to the IP notation for simplicity):

(79)   Lors entra li preudons en sa chapele
        Then entered the man   into his chapel
        'Then the men entered his chapel'

(80) a. $[_{CP}$ lors $[_{C'}$ entra $[_{IP}$ li preudons . . .

     b. $[_{CP}$ lors $[_{C'}$ entra $[_{IP}$ *pro* t $[_{VP}$ t li preudons . . .]]]]

     c. $[_{IP}$ lors $[_{IP}$ *pro* $[_{I'}$ entra $[_{VP}$ t li preudons . . .]]]]

(80a) is a standard V2 structure with the subject in SpecI', i.e. there is no free inversion. (80b) shows the combination of V2 and free inversion (note that such an analysis requires assuming that the PP *en sa chapele* has been extraposed, cf. also (30a)). (80c) represents the structure with free inversion only. We assume that this structure was not available in OF; aside from the fact that it violates the V2 constraint, such a structure requires the possibility of licensing *pro* under agreement, which was otherwise impossible in OF.[19]

In the Introduction to this chapter, we outlined Adams' analysis of the correlation between V2 and null subjects in OF. In the next section, we will review the evidence that null subjects were possible in embedded contexts in OF, and we will see that, although there are instances of this, the essential correlation between V2 and null subjects can be maintained. In that case, it is important to consider Adams' account of this correlation quite closely.

As we said earlier, Adams adds to the licensing conditions on *pro* in (6) a condition on directionality: the directional relation between *pro* and its licensing head must be canonical for the language in question, in the sense that the linear relation between the licensing head and *pro* must be the same as that between the verb and its direct object. This addendum to (6) gives the result that the licensing head can appear only to the left of *pro* in a VO language such as OF. Hence, for *pro* to be licensed, Agr must raise to C. This explains the synchronic and diachronic connection between V2 and null subjects in French; the loss of (V to) Agr to C movement entails the loss of null subjects, as the correct configuration for licensing *pro* can no longer arise.

This account is plausible and appealing for the history of French. However, we encounter empirical problems when we attempt to extend it to other languages. Moreover, internally to the history of French there are some problems, in that the loss of null subjects is not fully explained: why were null subjects not retained in interrogative contexts where Agr to C movement remained (cf. 1.5.)?[20] A second empirical problem concerns the development of a wider range of null subjects in MidFr, as argued for convincingly in Vance (1989). Vance shows that null subjects could be licensed in a configuration of agreement in MidFr. We will discuss and analyse the evidence for this in 2.3.5.; for the moment the thing to note is that such a change in the directional government property of *pro* is not expected under Adams' account, and that, since, on her assumptions, it is necessary to admit that it happened, we expect French to have continued to be a null-subject language to the present day (the latter point can also be made against Vance's account of MidFr). We will propose an analysis in 2.4.3. which does not suffer from these drawbacks, and which relates the history of null subjects in French to other developments in French syntax.

Let us now compare the directionality-based system for licensing null subjects with the one we have proposed, which is essentially based on the parameters of Case-assignment in (3) combined with the licensing condition in (6) alone, i.e. one which is based on the idea that *pro* can be licensed under either government or under agreement. This kind of approach lacks an independent directionality clause, since the notions of government and agreement are configurational rather than linear. A directionality-based account of the type adopted by Adams makes the following typological predictions (where X is the licensing head for *pro*):

(81) a.   VO & X *pro*

    b.   OV & *pro* X

   c. *VO & *pro* X

   d. *OV & X *pro*

OF instantiates the situation in (81a). (81b) would be exemplified by a non-V2 verb-final language with null subjects; an obvious candidate is Latin (other likely cases are Turkish, Japanese and Basque).

What is more important is to consider the cases that the directionality approach rules out. (81c) essentially says that VO languages cannot have a null-subject system where Agr licenses a *pro* in its Specifier. As we saw in 2.0., however, this is the analysis which is most widely adopted for the 'classic' null-subject languages Spanish and Italian. To cope with this problem, Adams proposes that null subjects always appear in the freely inverted position in these languages, so that in fact they instantiate (81a), like OF but in a different configuration. However, Rizzi (1987) gives evidence that null subjects in Italian do not share the properties of inverted subjects and do share the properties of preverbal subjects. The evidence, illustrated in (82) and (83), concerns various kinds of anaphoric relation:

(82) a. [PRO essendo stanco], Gianni è andato via
       'Being tired, G. left'

    b. *[PRO essendo stanco], è andato via Gianni
       'Being tired, left G.'

    c. [PRO essendo stanco], è andato via
       'Being tired, (he) left'

(83)a. Tutti i soldati sono andati via
       'All the soldiers have left'

    b. I soldati sono tutti andati via
       'The soldiers have all left'

    c. Sono andati via tutti i soldati
       'Have left all the soldiers'

    d. *Sono tutti andati via i soldati
       'Have all left the soldiers'

    e. Sono tutti andati via
       '(They) have all left'

The contrast between (82a) and (82b) shows that an inverted subject cannot be construed with the PRO subject of a gerundive adjunct; the natural interpretation of (82c) is therefore that the null subject is in preverbal position, since, if it could occupy only postverbal position, we would expect this example to be ungrammatical. Similarly, (83a–b) show that the quantifier *tutti* can 'float' off a preverbal subject, while (83c–d) show that this floating is not possible for an inverted subject (we mentioned this fact in 1.5.). The grammaticality of (83e), where *tutti* is construed with a null subject, therefore suggests that the null subject is in preverbal position. (82) and (83) provide a strong indication that null subjects in Italian at least can be preverbal. This is in direct contradiction with the prediction of a directionality-based approach in (81c). On the other hand, these data pose no problem for our approach; as we said in the Introduction to this chapter, we assume that in Italian Agr licenses *pro* under agreement, just as it assigns Nominative Case under agreement (cf. 1.5. for further details on the conditions under which *pro* appears in Italian, and 2.4.3. for a further constraint on what kind of Agr can license *pro* under agreement).

Consider finally (81d), which entails that null subjects in SpecAgr' cannot be licensed by C° in verb-final, C-initial languages. Cardinaletti (1989), Dupuis (1988) and Tomaselli (1989) point out that this is possible, under restricted conditions, in many West Germanic varieties, including Standard Dutch and German. As we saw for German in 1.4. (78), C° is the licensing head, and null expletive subjects can appear in SpecAgr'. We repeat the relevant examples here:

(84) a. Mir   wurde *pro* geholfen

      To-me was   helped

      'I was helped'

   b. Hier wurde *pro* getanzt

      Here was   danced

      'There was dancing here'

The restriction to expletive null subjects falls out rather naturally from the idea that C° is the licensing head; since C° does not bear person/number features, it cannot identify the content of anything, therefore it can only license expletives (but cf. Cardinaletti (1990a) for arguments that it can license quasi-arguments, too). The [Agr] feature related to V2 is too weak to license a referential null subject, as it does not show any person/number marking.

The facts in (84) are problematic for a directionality approach, given the idea that C° is the licensing head. (84) appears to perfectly instantiate the schema in (81d). Once again, these data pose no problem for our approach: C° licenses *pro* under government in German. We can see that C° licenses *pro* only under government from the ungrammaticality of the following example (cf. Cardinaletti op. cit.):

(85)   *(Ich glaube daß) *pro* wurde getanzt

     I   believe that (it)   was   danced

We suggested in Note 5 that the UCL of (47) may imply that C is not the licenser of *pro* here; however, the relevant reformulation of either the UCL or of the licensing condition on *pro* in Dutch and German will almost certainly retain the idea that *pro* is licensed under government by (some element in) $C°$ in these languages, so the argument against Adams holds. For one possible reformulation, or reinterpretation, of the UCL, see Note 32 to this chapter.

We conclude from these facts that an approach to the licensing of null subjects of the type advocated here fares at least as well as a directionality-based approach for the OF data, and does rather better when a wider range of Germanic and Romance languages are considered. It is also conceptually preferable, as the licensing of null subjects is synchronically and diachronically tied to the Case parameter in (3).

We next consider one range of facts which is problematic for the proposals in Adams (1987a, b), namely the cases of null subjects in embedded contexts in OF.

2.2.4. *Null Subjects in Embedded Contexts*

Our final topic in the discussion OF concerns the possibility of null subjects in embedded clauses. As we saw in the previous section, the original analysis proposed in Adams (1987a, b) predicted that null subjects were an exclusively (or nearly exclusively, see below) root phenomenon. However, as we shall see, there is evidence (from Adams 1988a, b, c, Dupuis 1988, 1989, Hirschbuhler and Junker 1988, Hirschbuhler 1989 and Vance 1989) that null subjects were possible in a range of embedded clauses, including, most importantly, *wh*-complements.

This topic is relevant for our general discussion as we have attempted to show that the licensing condition for null subjects in (6), linked to the Nominative-assignment parameter in (3), can account for the distribution of null subjects in OF. If this is so, then the change in the parameter in (3) which led to the exclusion of Nominative-assignment under government played a crucial role in the loss of null subjects. If null subjects could appear only in configurations of the type in (75), then there is no problem for our approach, and we expect no null subjects where V2 is impossible. Other things being equal, then, we expect to find null subjects only in those embedded clauses where V2 is possible. To account for null subjects in embedded clauses, we propose an account of the licensing of null subjects in terms of the 'double Agr' clause structure introduced in 2.1.2. The result is that we are able to retain the fundamental link between licensing null subjects and V2 observed by Adams, expressing it in terms of the condition that *pro* is licensed under government in OF. In this way, we can maintain our overall contention that the change in (3) was in large part responsible for the loss of null subjects.

In her earlier work (Adams 1987a, b), Adams claims that V2 and null subjects are possible in the complements to bridge verbs. The class of bridge verbs in question is comparable to the class which in V2 Germanic languages typically allows complements with matrix properties, i.e. epistemic verbs and *verba dicendi* (cf. 1.4.). We saw some examples of this construction in our discussion of embedded V2 in 2.1.2. Some of these examples featured null subjects. We repeat one of them here by way of illustration:

(29) b.   Or   voi ge bien, **plains es**   de mautalant

Now see I   well full   are (you) of bad intentions

'And now I see clearly that you are full of bad intentions.'

(*Le Charroi de Nîmes*, 1. 295)

In this example *que* is not present, suggesting that it is a case of German-style embedded V2 ('conjunctive discourse' — cf. 1.4 (87)). However, *que* was possible in such cases, as the following example (from Dupuis 1988) shows:

(86)   . . . et   disent   que molt   avoient   bien fait

. . . *and say (they) that much had (they) well done*

(R. de Clari *La Conquête de Constantinople*, P. Larnier, 1956, Paris, CFMA, Champion, LII, 9; Dupuis' (12), p. 48)

It appears, then, that OF bridge verbs were optionally either like those of German, or like those of the other Germanic V2 languages (cf. 1.4.).

The embedded sentences in examples like (29) and (86) can clearly be analysed as follows:

(87)

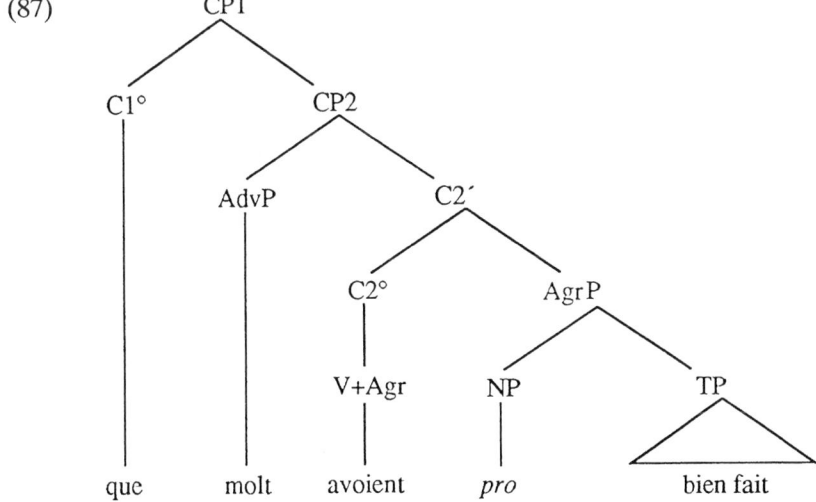

It is clear that the part following *que*, CP2, is a just like a matrix clause, and so the occurrence of V2 orders and null subjects is expected.

However, we said in 1.4. that V2 is typically banned in *wh*-complements in the Germanic V2 languages, except Yiddish and Icelandic. The Yiddish case is rather particular, and we will say no more about it here. We saw in 2.1.2., though, that there is some evidence that OF is rather like Icelandic in that it appears to allow embedded V1 and V2 in non-bridge complements.

The kinds of clauses that interest us thus have V1 and V2 orders with null subjects in *wh*-complements. Adams (1988b, c) gives the following cases (1988c: (9), (11), pp. 10f) (the same examples are given in Hirschbuhler (1990: 36), see below):

(88) a. Je sui le sire a   cui [**volez**   parler]

        I am   the lord to whom wish to speak

        'I am the lord to whom you wish to speak'

        (*Aymeri de Narbonne*, L. Demaison (ed.), Société des Anciens Textes Français, Paris 1887, 4041)

   b. L'espee   dont   [**s'estoit**   ocis]

        the sword by which himself-was killed

        'The sword which he killed himself with'

        (*La Chastelaine de Vergi*, F. Whitehead (ed.), Manchester University Press 1944, 913)

   c. Ainz   que [**m'en aille** en France]

        before that go   to France

        'Before I leave for France'

        (*Aymeri de Narbonne*, L. Demaison (ed.), Société des Anciens Textes Français, Paris 1887, 204)

   d. Quant [**vit** le roi]

        when   sees the king

        'When he sees the king'

        (*Aymeri de Narbonne*, L. Demaison (ed.), Société des Anciens Textes Français, Paris 1887, 702)

In terms of the assumptions made in 1.4., the verb cannot move to a [+wh] C°. There is no reason to assume that the verb is in any position other than Agr° in these examples. But if the verb is in Agr°, where is the null subject, and how is it licensed?

Dupuis (1988, 1989) provides some further examples of the above type

and proposes an interesting solution to the problem they pose. Some of
her examples can be treated as Styl-F, e.g. the following (Dupuis 1988,
(37a–b), p. 54):

(89) a. Por l'esperance qu'an   lui **ont,** . . .
         For the hope   which in him have
         'For the hope which they have in him,'
         (*Ch. lyon* 4013, Tobler: T8, p. 10)

     b. Et   si ne sait   que faire **puisse**
         And so not knows what to-do can
         'And so he doesn't know what he can do'
         (*Guillaume* 528, cited in Moignet 1973: 228)

After a fairly detailed discussion of this type of construction in 12th and
13th century prose and verse texts, Dupuis concludes "In the verse literature of the period, both the order COMP XP ϕ V and the order ϕ V are
possible" (p. 55).[21]

To account for this kind of possibility, Dupuis proposes (p. 57) that $C°$
is the head which formally licenses *pro* in OF, while binding by Agr
identifies its content. For Dupuis, then, the two licensing requirements can
be met by distinct heads. Dupuis then suggests that the formal licensing
requirement is indeed subject to the directionality condition, following
Adams, but that the identification requirement is not.

Dupuis' data and analysis are very interesting. However, there are a
number of problems. First, maintaining the idea that formal licensing is
subject to the directionality condition does not obviously avoid the problems for Adams' system that we raised in the previous section. Second, it
is conceptually undesirable to 'split' the licensing of *pro* in this way; this
represents a serious weakening of Rizzi's system. An analysis in which a
single head can provide both types of licensing would be preferable, since
it is optimal that those heads which a given system designates as capable
of formally licensing *pro* should be those whose grammatical features
identify the content of *pro* (although we shall see in 2.3.5. that a 'split
licensing' analysis of this type is appropriate for the late 15th and early
16th centuries, when null subjects started to become highly restricted in
distribution).

Third, and most important, Hirschbuhler (1990) presents evidence that
the situation in the OF period was more complex than Dupuis' (1988) or
Adams' discussions suggest. Hirschbuhler studies 12th and 13th century
prose and verse, and concludes that there are essentially two systems at
work, according to the nature of the text. One system, which we might
dub the 'conservative' system (our term, not Hirschbuhler's), allows null

subjects in embedded clauses fairly freely. This system is typical of 12th-century prose texts and of both 12th- and 13th-century verse. The examples in (88) above are a case in point; (88a, c–d) are from *Aymeri de Narbonne*, a *chanson de geste* of the first quarter of the 13th century, and (88b) is from *La Chastelaine de Vergi*, a 13th-century poem. In these texts, embedded clauses of basically all types appear to allow null subjects and V1 order. Among many others, Hirschbuhler ((2a–b), (3b), p. 36) gives the following examples from these texts of the order in a relative clause (90a,b) and an adverbial *wh*-clause (these correspond to examples (88a—b, d) above):

(90) a.   Je sui le   sire   a cui [—   **volez** parler]
          I am the knight to whom (you) want to speak
          'I am the knight to whom you want to speak'

   b.   L'espee   dont [—   **s'estoit** ocis]
        The sword of-which (he) self was killed
        'The sword which he killed himself with'

   c.   Quant [— **vit** le   roi] . . .
        When (he) saw the king, . . .
        'When he saw the king, . . .'

Similarly, Hirschbuhler shows that a number of other early texts have the same freedom of V1 orders in embedded contexts (*La Chanson de Roland* (11th century) and *Le Charroi de Nîmes* (12th century)).

On the other hand, 13th-century prose texts (the discussion is based on Vance's (1989) study of the *Queste del Saint Graal* and Dupuis' (1989) study of *La Mort le Roi Artu*), embedded V1 orders with null subjects are limited to two types of rather fixed expressions: *se ne fut . . .* ('if it weren't for') and *quant vint à* ('when the time came for/to'). Call this the 'advanced' system. Here are some representative examples:

(93) a.   se ne **fu**   chiés le Roi Mehaigniée
          if not were 'chez' King M.
          'if it were not at the court of King M.'
          (*La Queste del Saint Graal*, A. Pauphilet (ed.), CFM, Paris, Champion, 16; Hirschsbuhler's (7), p. 39)

   b.   se ne **fust** la grant bonté   qui *est* en vos
        if not were the great goodness which is in you
        'if it weren't for the great goodness in you'
        (*La Mort le Roi Artu*, J. Frappier (ed.), TLF, Genève, Droz, 14, 33; H's (15a), p. 42)

c. quant **vint** a cele hore que . . .

   when came to that time that . . .

   'when the time came that . . .'

   (*La Queste del Saint Graal*, A. Pauphilet (ed.), CFM, Paris, Champion, 82; Hirschbuhler's (9c), p. 39)

d. quant **vint** au   jor que la reïne dut   respondre a

   when came to the day that the queen must answer
   sa fiance
   her fiancé

   'When the day that the queen had to answer her fiancé'

   (*La Mort le Roi Artu*, J. Frappier (ed.), TLF, Genève, Droz, 142, 17; H's (12a), p. 41)

These are clearly cases of expletive null subjects, as are those in (35). Moreover, they seem to represent an unproductive option.

We tentatively suggest, on the basis of Hirschbuhler's data, that the 'double Agr' system was at work in the more conservative texts. So, for instance, we assign the following structure to the embedded clause in (88a):

(92)

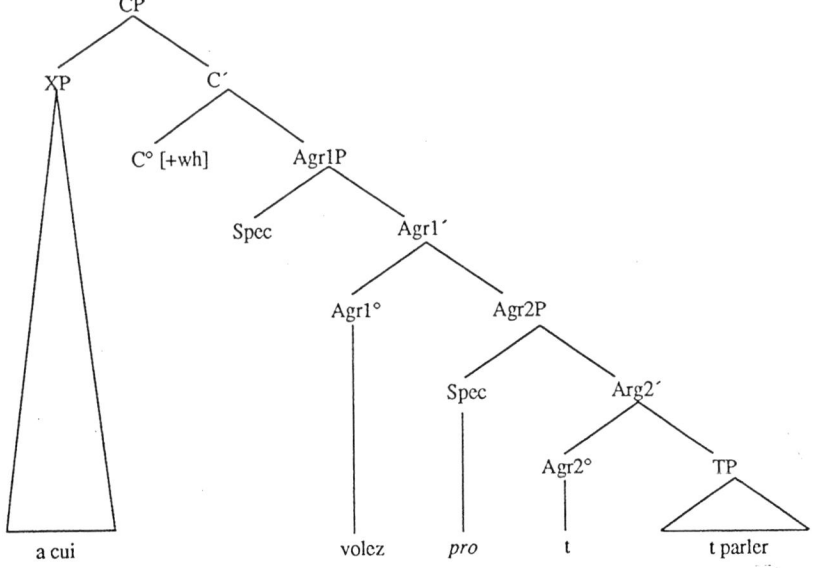

Here the verb appears in Agr1° and licenses the null subject, the *pro* in
SpecAgr2', under government. The verb moves from Agr2 to Agr1 to
license the subject position in SpecAgr2', either by assigning Nominative
or by licensing and identifying a null subject. We assume that SpecAgr1'
is the site of optional topicalization. How can we allow SpecAgr1' to be
empty and still be consistent with the 'Extended Projection Principle' of
1.4. (85)? We do this by assuming that Agr1° does not really contain
agreement features (e.g. an agreement affix), but only Agr2°. So
SpecAgr2' must be filled, but there is no similar requirement on Spec-
Agr1'. The same is true in Icelandic, but not in Northern Italian (cf.
Cardinaletti and Roberts (forthcoming, Section 3)). Languages with very
poor Agr (and presumably only one Agr-projection) like English and MSc
arguably lack content in Agr (cf. 3.1.3.); however, in these languages
there is simply no alternative subject position, and no expletive *pro*,
available.

A system like this may be connected to the Tobler/Mussafia effects, as
we mentioned in 2.1.2. Cardinaletti and Roberts (forthcoming) develop
the account of this phenomenon proposed in 1.3.2.: the basic idea is that
the clitic is in Agr1° and the verb in C° in configurations of enclisis (cf.
Benincà 1989, Alberton 1990). The structure associated with enclisis is
illustrated in (93):

(93)

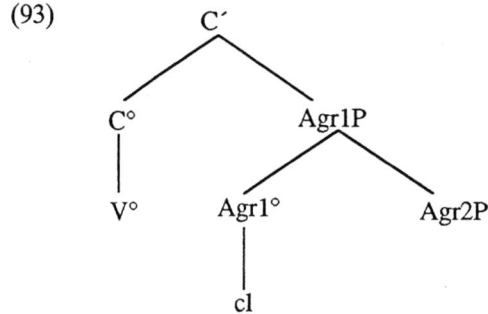

V moves to C as a 'last resort' to avoid the banned clitic-first order (cf.
1.3.2. and Lema and Rivero (1990b) on LHM). C does not morphologically select V (or Agr2) here, hence the movement to C is A'-move-
ment. Moreover, since Agr1° does not select V (or Agr2), V-to-C movement (i.e. Agr2-to-C movement) can 'skip' Agr1° (cf. 1.3.2.). This analysis
might seem to pose a problem for null-subject sentences with enclisis,
since if *pro* occupies SpecAgr2' it is not governed by V, or by a trace of V.
However, we can assume that in such examples the null subject occupies
SpecAgr1', and hence is governed by the inflected verb in C°.

A further complication (pointed out by an anonymous reviewer) arises
from the fact that we have to prevent subject pronouns from appearing

in SpecAgr2' in (92), since the order verb—*pronoun* is not found in embedded clauses. We cannot simply maintain that the pronoun must cliticize to C°, since this, in conjunction with the above proposal for Tobler–Mussafia effects, would give rise to the order *verb—subj. pronoun—obj. pronoun*, while only the order *verb—obj. pronoun—subj. pronoun* is found where an object pronoun is enclitic. To account for this order, we have to say that Agr1° containing the object pronoun cliticizes to C° in the configuration in (92), and the subject pronoun then cliticizes to C° from SpecAgr1'. In this way, we retain the idea that subject pronouns cliticize to C°, even in 'Tobler–Mussafia' constructions where an object pronoun is also enclitic to C°.

Significantly, de Kok (1985: 93) gives early examples of clitic-first orders in Y/NQ in the 13th-century prose texts *La Mort le Roi Artu* and *La Queste del Saint Graal*. This indicates that Tobler–Mussafia effects begin to erode in 13th-century prose. It is in these same texts that Hirschbuhler identifies a change in the distribution of embedded null subjects. Clearly, this correlation needs further investigation.

For the 'innovative' system, where only expletive null subjects were allowed in embedded contexts, the obvious analysis is that the verb in Agr1 was no longer able to license a referential null subject. As just suggested, we think this is because Agr1 was not present at all. This left only C° as a potential licenser here, and so only expletive null subjects were available (other than in complements to bridge verbs, which involve C-recursion, not Agr-recursion) in the 'advanced' OF texts. A limited range of expletive null subjects continued to be possible for a time, as these elements required only formal licensing. Here we find a typical situation where *pro* ceased to be able to be licensed in a given configuration: null subjects are retained in a few isolated and rather fixed cases — cf. the discussion of 17th-century matrix null subjects in 2.4.3.

A clear prediction emerges from these proposals: we should find both V2 and V1 with postverbal subjects in *wh*-complements in the 'conservative' texts, but not in the advanced ones. So our proposals correspond exactly to those in Adams (1987a, b) in that we explicitly link the possibility of V2 order to the possibility of null subjects. This correlation indeed holds for the cases of V1 and V2 order in *wh*-clauses considered in 2.1.2. The examples of embedded V1 and V2 we considered there, (35a–c), are all from verse texts: (35a) is from the 12th-century *Tristan*; (35b), from a 13th-century verse text, *Le Vair Palefroi* by Huon le Roi, and (35c) is from *Guillaume d'Angleterre* by Chrétien de Troyes, usually dated 1165. On the other hand, Vance (1989) concludes her analysis of matrix word order in the *Queste del Saint Graal* by saying "the fronting of an adverb or VP complement and the inversion of subject and verb are prohibited in embedded clauses" (p. 46). She goes on to discuss the possibility of V2 in complements to *que*, adopting an analysis similar to the one we have proposed (cf. 1.4., 2.1.2., and above). Most important, she says: "Subordinate clauses introduced by words such as *quant* 'when', *ou* 'where', *se* 'if', *comment* 'how', and the relatives . . . strictly exclude CVS [i.e. V2— IGR] order" (p. 49).

So we tentatively conclude from these remarks that earlier OF had a 'double Agr' clause structure which effectively hid many root/embedded asymmetries, at least as far as V2 and null subjects were concerned, since the verb was able to move to Agr1 and license a null subject in Agr1 regardless of the overall status of the clause. Actually, Dupuis (1989: 151f) reveals that the situation may be still more complex. Her data confirms Hirschbuhler's division of OF into two periods/registers regarding the distribution of embedded null subjects, but suggests that embedded V2 with overt subjects was lost earlier than embedded null subjects. In the *Quatre Livres du Roi* (Anon: 1170), both embedded V2 with overt subjects and embedded null subjects are found. However, in *Guillaume d'Angleterre* (Chrétien de Troyes: 1165) and *Galeran de Bretagne* (Renard: 1212), embedded null subjects are found, but there are very few cases of embedded V2 with overt subjects. All the cases of embedded null subjects with V2 order can be treated as cases of Styl-F; hence it may be that the system represented by *Guillaume d'Angleterre* and *Galeran de Bretagne* is one with Styl-F, but without generalized embedded V2. As we have suggested elsewhere (cf. 1.4.), Styl-F is connected to the 'double Agr' possibility, but in ways that are not clear. Given the uncertainty surrounding the analysis of Styl-F, we leave open the possibility that *Guillaume d'Angleterre* and *Galeran de Bretagne* represent a third (intermediate) OF system with Styl-F and embedded null subjects, but without generalized embedded V2.

Embedded null subjects are rare in 13th-century prose, as we saw above. We interpret this to mean that Agr1 was no longer a possible landing site for verb-movement, and so referential null subjects became impossible in embedded clauses which did not feature CP-recursion (as did V2, if it was not already impossible). This analysis of the OF situation allows us to maintain that null subjects were always and only licensed under government in OF, which is the central conclusion that we wish to draw here.

The "double agr" analysis we have sketched for conservative OF texts raises two questions. First, we risk losing any account of the root/embedded asymmetry with regard to V2. Second, we need to say something about why and how Agr1P was lost.

Considering the first question first, the existence of such an asymmetry can be shown by comparing the following figures for 49 tensed embedded clauses taken from *La Chanson de Roland* (ll. 1691–1931; ll. 2259–2396) with the figures for matrix V2 given in (26), which we indicate here also:

(94)	Subj V:	28 = 56%	(matrix 31%)
	Compl V:	3 = 6%	(matrix 15%)
	Adv V:	9 = 18%	(matrix 40%)
	V1:	8 = 16%	(matrix 5%)
	V > 2:	1 = 2%	(matrix 4%)
	Pred V:	0 = 0%	(matrix 5%)

The asymmetry is very clear: subjects are twice as frequent in initial position in embedded as in matrix clauses, while complements and adverbs are half as frequent, and V1 orders are three times as frequent.

We can explain these asymmetries in terms of our analysis. Given what we have said so far, SpecAgr1' is a topic position. Now, embedded topicalization is more marked than matrix topicalization, undoubtedly for functional reasons. Suppose that, as in matrix clauses in MidFr (which we discuss in 2.3.1., 2.3.2.), SVO orders could be unmarked in the sense that an initial subject, unlike an initial complement or adverb, was not necessarily interpreted as a semantic topic. Since semantic topicalization is relatively rare in embedded clauses, fronting of the subject is relatively frequent as a functionally neutral way of filling SpecAgr1'. This situation created the possibility of reanalysing SpecAgr1' as a subject position rather than a topic position, which, as we shall see in 2.3.1. and 2.3.2., is what happened in matrix clauses in MidFr. Similarly, the greater frequency of V1 embedded clauses can be attributed to the fact that SpecAgr1' did not need to be filled, combined with the rarity of embedded topics.

The second problem is the loss of Agr1P. We cannot give a full account of this here, but it seems that two, possibly related, factors may be relevant. First, as we mentioned above, the loss of 'Tobler–Mussafia effects', i.e. the innovation of clitic-first orders, appears to correlate with the loss of embedded null subjects and embedded V2. It is unclear whether this is a cause or an effect of the loss of Agr1P, but it is certainly related to it if the idea that Agr1° is the Wackernagel position (cf. 1.3.2, 3.4.) is to be maintained. A second development which may be relevant is the loss of the morphological case system. It is well-known that OF had a morphological case system (which distinguished nominative from non-nominative in NPs headed by (most) masculine nouns). This system was lost between the 12th and the 14th centuries (Foulet 1935/6: 279f; 1982: 32f). Now, as we saw in 1.2., Agr1P (or Agr1°) facilitates Nominative-assignment under government. When Agr1P is lost, this becomes Nominative-assignment under agreement. Suppose, as seems intuitively reasonable, that Nominative-assignment under government is linked to generalized nominative morphology (i.e. nominative morphology not restricted to the pronominal system). One way to think of this is by taking Agr1P to be really NomP, a projection of a head whose sole function is to assign Case (as a result of which it attracts clitics, inflected verbs, etc.). Then, the loss of the morphological case system triggers the loss of Agr1P. This proposal has the virtue of tying the loss of Agr1P to a very well-known development in the history of French. The Germanic languages offer other examples of a possible relation between a morphological case system and Agr1P: German and Icelandic both have both, while English and MSc have neither. Cf. 3.4. for a sketch of some historical developments in English which confirm this view, and largely parallel what we have proposed for 13th-century French.

The above proposals accomplish two things: first, they allow us to retain the idea that verb-raising, either to C° or to Agr1°, was initimately connected with the licensing of referential null subjects; second, although we have proposed a clause structure which allows for V2 orders under any kind of C°, we can maintain the clear preference for SVO orders in embedded clauses.

This concludes our discussion of the OF data. Most important for the sections to come are the following five properties that we have argued to hold of OF:

(95) a.   Simple inversion in interrogatives

b.   V2 (of a type very close to Germanic)

c.   Null subjects

d.   Non-clitic preverbal nominative pronouns

e.   Clitic postverbal nominative pronouns

Moreover, we argued in 2.1.3. that, despite appearances (cf. (39)), OF lacked complex inversion. The properties in (95a–d) all underwent changes during the MidFr period, and were lost in the early 16th century, while complex inversion was introduced around 1450. Our contention is that the loss of (95a–c) was due to the change in the Nominative-assignment parameter in (3), and that the change in (95d) and the related introduction of complex inversion played a causal role in this parametric change. It is now time to see in detail how all this took place.

2.3. DEVELOPMENTS IN MIDDLE FRENCH

The previous sections established that OF had the syntactic properties listed in (95). The purpose of this section is to see in detail the changes that affected these properties during the Middle French period (1300–1500), with particular emphasis on the 15th century. In 2.3.1. and 2.3.2. we discuss the gradual erosion of the V2 constraint. There are two aspects of this: the rise in $V > 2$ orders (2.3.1.), and the growing preference for SVO orders (2.3.2.). We will suggest that, at a certain point, the preponderance of these orders was such that grammars of French were acquired which at least allowed the possibility of matrix AgrP, rather than CP. At this point, then, the technical correlate of V2 (or, at least, of the 'innovative' later V2 system, which can be fully assimilated to German — cf. 2.2.4.), i.e. the obligatory presence of [Agr] in C°, ceased to hold; in effect, French was no longer a V2 language. We concur with other authors (notably Adams 1987b) that V2 was eliminated from French early in the 16th century.

In 2.3.3., we document the development of the double series of subject pronouns and in so doing elaborate on the theoretical status of clitics. This development made possible the change we describe in 2.3.4., the reanalysis of left-dislocation structures of the type discussed in 2.1.3. as complex inversion. Our final topic, in 2.3.5., is the apparent change in the configuration in which null subjects were licensed. Basing our discussion primarily on Hirschbuhler and Junker (1988) and Vance (1989), we will see evidence that MidFr allowed referential null subjects to be licensed in configurations of agreement, in addition to configurations of government.

The net effect of these various changes was a dramatic increase in the environments in which agreement configurations were relevant for Case-assignment and licensing, and a corresponding decrease in the contexts in which these relations were established under government. Consider again the three properties which fall under the Case-assignment parameter of (3), given in (95a–c):

(95) a. Simple inversion in interrogatives

   b. V2

   c. Null subjects

In MidFr, complex inversion emerged as an alternative interrogative structure. Moreover, as Foulet (1921) shows, the (qu)'est-ce que construction became a genuine non-emphatic interrogative at this time. Assuming (postverbal) ce to be a clitic at this period, and adopting the analysis of complex inversion in 1.5., in both of the new structures Nominative-assignment did not take place under government, while it clearly did in the older simple inversion construction. Simple inversion remained grammatical until the early 16th century (cf. 2.4.1.), but from MidFr on there were two alternative constructions available in which the subject NP was Case-marked under agreement rather than under government.

Similarly, the increased preference for SVO orders, and for V > 2 orders (orders where more than one maximal constituent precedes the inflected verb) where the second element was the subject, greatly reduced the occurrences of surface inversion, i.e. of sentences in which the subject had to be analyzed as receiving Case under government. Here, whether

we treat Nominative as being assigned to SpecAgr' under government
with subsequent topicalization of the Case-marked NP to SpecC', or
whether we treat the subject as receiving Case in SpecAgr' under agreement depends on whether root clauses were obligatorily CPs, which is in
turn related to the presence of the [Agr] feature in C°. We will show that
from the 15th century on, root clauses no longer had to be analysed as
CPs.

Finally, Vance's evidence that null subjects were licensed under agreement in MidFr (cf. 2.3.5.) shows that for null subjects, too, agreement
configurations played a more prominent role in MidFr than in OF.

All of these factors — and the interactions among them — contributed
to the change in the Case-assignment parameter in (3), which took place
in the early 16th century, as we shall see in 2.4.

2.3.1. Matrix V > 2 Orders

In our discussion of V2 in OF (2.1.2.), we saw that matrix $V > 2$ orders
were quite uncommon in typical OF texts. This was shown by the figures
in (26). Here we repeat (26) in a rather different form, showing the
relative percentages of non-inverted orders (Subj V), inverted orders (XP
V) and $V > 2$ (and disregarding V1):

(96)		Subj V	XP V	V > 2
	Roland	31%	60%	4%
	Charroi de Nîmes	23%	64%	0%
	Tristan	30%	64%	3%
	Perceval	41%	41%	16%
	Aucassin	50%	43%	6%
	Merlin	28%	68%	4%

Two of the later texts (*Perceval* (late 12th century) and *Aucassin* (13th
century)) show a larger proportion of $V > 2$ orders and a larger proportion
of Subj V orders respectively. Nevertheless, the optimal assumption for
the OF period is that the system was V2, in the sense that C° bore the
feature [Agr].

However, while OF was an essentially V2 language, the MidFr situation
is far less clear. The only obvious conclusion that one can draw from the
data, as many authors have observed (Adams 1987a, b, Vance 1989:
173, Zwanenburg 1978), is that MidFr was a 'transitional period'. Strictly
speaking, of course, any period is a transitional period. Nevertheless, this
often-repeated observation has a clear implication in the present context:
in this period the grammar of French became such that the feature [Agr]
was no longer obligatorily associated with matrix C°. Correspondingly,
matrix declaratives were no longer obligatorily CPs.

A major difference between a V2 system and a non-V2 system is that the CP-level is active in matrix declaratives in the former case, but not in the latter. Also, although little is known in real detail about the syntax of adverbs, it is widely agreed that adverbs adjoin more readily to AgrP than to CP. Contrasts of the following type in English support this:

(97) a. Yesterday John left   (adjunction to AgrP)

   b. *Yesterday no way had he left   (adjunction to CP)

   c. John said yesterday that Bill left

   d. John said that yesterday Bill left

While (97c) is grammatical, it cannot be read such that *yesterday* refers to the time of Bill's leaving. We take this to mean that this element cannot be part of the lower clause, i.e. it cannot be adjoined to the lower CP. On the other hand, (97d) shows that this adverb can adjoin to the lower AgrP.

A similar contrast is found in German:

(98) a. Das Buch hat gestern   Johann gelesen   (adj to AgrP)
         The book has yesterday John   read

   b. *Gestern   Johann hat das Buch gelesen   (adj to CP)
         Yesterday John   has the book read

   c. *Johann sagte gestern   daß Wilhelm weggegangen war
         John   said yesterday that Bill   left   was

   d. Johann sagte daß gestern   Wilhelm weggegangen war
         John   said that yesterday Bill   left   was

German of course has the extra possibility where the adverb appears in SpecC'. Nevertheless, the basic contrast with respect to adjunction to AgrP and CP holds up in both main and embedded clauses.

(97) and (98) show that, for typical sentence adverbs, the order *Adv XP V* is impossible in matrix clauses in V2 languages ((98b)). On the other hand, where XP is the subject, it will be possible in non-V2 languages ((97a)). What we typically find in V2 languages, in fact, is that a few adverbs are able to appear in initial position and be followed by a V2 clause. A well-known example is German *denn* ('so, therefore'):

(99) a. . . . denn Johann hat gestern   das Buch gelesen
         . . . *so   J.   had yesterday the book read*

   b. . . . denn gestern   hat Johann das Buch gelesen
         . . . *so   yesterday had J.   the book read*

The same is true in OF. Vance (p. 155) gives the following list of adverbs which do not trigger V2: *sanz faille* ('without fail'), *neporquant, nequedant, neporec* ('nevertheless'), *certes* ('certainly'), *apres* ('after'), *onques* ('never'), *por Dieu* ('by God'), and *espoir* ('perhaps') (the possibility of left-dislocation in interrogatives, as in the analysis of 'proto-complex-inversion' in 2.3.1., is a further case).

As Vance goes on to demonstrate (p. 157ff), the class of elements able to appear in initial position without triggering inversion enlarges considerably in MidFr. The following are representative of Vance's examples (the first two are taken from the 15th-century text *Jehan de Saintré*, the third from Froissart's *Chroniques* (late 14th century)):

(100) a. Lors la   royne *fist*   Santré appeller

  then the queen made S.   to-call

  'Then the queen had Saintré called'

  (Vance's (15), p. 158)

  b. Et   a ces   parolles le roy **demanda** quelz prieres

  And at these words   the king asked   what requests

  ilz   faisoient

  they made

  (Vance's (31), p. 161)

  c. Apres disner le chevalier me   **dist** . . .

  after   dinner the knight   to-me said . . .

  'After dinner the knight said to me. . .'

  (Vance's (78), p. 185)

To these we add the following from the *Quinze Joyes de Mariage*. (c. 1400) and Alain Chartier's *Quadrilogue Invectif* (1422):

(101) a. Et   voulentiers telles veilles   marieez a jeunes homs

  And willingly   such old (women) married to young men

  sont si jaleuses et   gloutes

  are so jealous and greedy

  (*La Quatorziesme Joye*, l. 91)

  b. Et   jamés une jeune femme ne **seroit** si jaleuse

  And never a   young woman would be so jealous

  (ibid., l. 95)

  c. et   en ce cas la victoire que fist   le vaillant

  and in this case the victory that made the valiant

jouvencel comme vainqueur ne **peut** . . .

young man as victor cannot . . .

'and in this case the victory that the young man made as victor cannot . . .'

(*Quadrilogue Invectif*, ll. 15–6)

These examples are to be contrasted with the following OF examples, where analogous adverbial material triggers V2:

(102) a. Lors **oïrent** ils venir un escroiz de tonoire

    then heard they come a clap of thunder

    'Then they heard a clap of thunder come'

    (Vance's (23), p. 159)

  b. car ainsin **estoit** il ordonne

    for thus was it ordained

    'For thus was it ordained'

    (Vance ibid., (26b))

  c. Et por ce me **merveil** je de ce que vos me dites

    and for this me marvel I of that which you me tell

    'And for this reason I marvel at what you tell me'

    (Vance's (34a), p. 161)

  d. jamais n'**ert** si vailant

    never neg was so valiant

    'Never was there one so valiant'

    (*Vie de St. Alexis*, 2c)

  e. Volontierz **est** oiz qui ment

    willing is eye that lies

    'Willing is the eye that lies'

    (Godefroy (1893), Vol. II, 869)

  f. Apres se **sont** mis au chemin

    after selves are put on road

    'After they went on their way'

    (ibid., Vol VIII, 157)

The differece between OF and MidFr can also be seen from a comparison of the proportion of V > 2 orders in MidFr texts with those found in OF.

We found the following percentages of V > 2 orders in the three MidFr texts we looked at:

(103)   c. 1390, Froissart *Chroniques* (xxv, xxvi): 12% (of 73)
         c. 1400, *Quinze Joyes* (*14esme Joye*, 1–103): 15% (of 40)
         1422, Chartier *Quadrilogue Invectif* (1–127): 11% (of 45)

Comparing these figures with (99), we find that V > 2 is consistently two to three times as frequent here as in OF texts (with the exception of *Perceval*, which seems anomalous in this respect).

The above data indicate that adjunction to a position preceding the preverbal elements was becoming more frequent in the MidFr period, and that a larger class of adverbial elements was able to appear in this kind of position than in OF. We thus consider it as evidence that the V2 constraint was at least less rigid in MidFr than in OF. Children acquiring the French of the first quarter of the 15th century would be exposed to significantly more occurrences of the order *Adv XP V* than the children of one or two centuries previously.

A similar picture emerges if we consider the possibility of topicalizing complements. Again, complements are not generally able to be topicalized to CP, in either V2 or non-V2 languages, while topicalization to AgrP is possible (for English, (104a) is worse than (97b); Tomaselli (1989: 410) suggests that this is due an argument-adjunct asymmetry):[22]

(104) a. *John, no way will I talk to

       b. John, Mary saw yesterday

       c. *Diese Sache gestern   hat Peter erledigt
           This   matter yesterday has P.   taken care of

       d. Ohne   Belohnung hat diese Sache gestern   Peter
           Without reward   has this   matter yesterday P.
           erledigt
           taken care of

       (Schwartz and Vikner 1989, (35), p. 18)

(104c) involves adjunction to CP combined with topicalization to SpecC′, and is ill-formed. (104d) is regular topicalization to SpecC′. In general, then, genuine V2 systems do not allow the order *Complement XP V*, while non-V2 languages allow this order where XP is the subject. (Again, left-dislocation of the type seen in 2.1.3. patterns differently, but this is a different case since (a) the subject does not come second; (b) it is a property of interrogatives. Thus there is no way that these constructions could be taken as AgrPs; instead, once V2 became sufficiently weak, they were analysed as complex inversion — see 2.3.4.).

In her discussion of *complement — XP — V* order, Vance (1989: 184ff) shows that OF only allowed it under very special conditions (leaving aside proto-complex-inversion, essentially where the complement was a sentence). On the other hand, in MidFr this order is found where both direct and indirect objects are fronted, as the following examples (Vance's (81), (82), p. 186) show:

(105) a. De laquelle plaisant nouvelle tous se   **prindrent** a rire

     Of which   pleasant news   all   selves took   to laugh

     'Everyone started laughing at this good news'

   b. le   petit Saintré les yeulz de Madame ne **cessoient**

     the little Saintré the eyes of Madame not stopped

     de regarder

     to watch

     'Madame's eyes did not cease to look at little Saintré'

This is further evidence that the V2 constraint did not hold in full force in MidFr. This kind of data is the more striking since topicalization of complements to SpecC' appears to be quite rare in MidFr. In the texts we looked at (cf. (103)), none were found. Moreover, Brunot (1905, Vol. I: 481) comments that such examples are rare. Although we do not believe that complements could not be topicalised to SpecC', it is clear that MidFr allowed topicalization of complements of the type in (105) alongside topicalization of complements to SpecC'. If so, then in this respect MidFr patterned either like English or like German, as a comparison with (104) shows. So, as far as complement-fronting is concerned, MidFr is an optional V2 language.

Adams (1987b: 184f) discusses the order *XP-subject pronoun-verb* in MidF. She claims that constructions of this type "represent subject pronoun cliticization, not the loss of V2 effects" (ibid.). Her claim is that these constructions appear just when subject pronouns are becoming clitics; hence, the order *XP Subject-Pronoun V* is on her account an instance of V2 with XP in SpecC' and the pronoun in C° (just like the order *XP Object-Pronoun V*). However, the analysis of cliticization that we gave in 2.2.2. rules out such an approach; following essentially Kayne (1983), we assumed there that preverbal clitics are PF clitics, and hence in the sequence *XP Subject-Pronoun V* the subject pronoun occupies SpecC' (at least at SS, cf. 2.3.3.), and so XP occupies an adjoined position.

There is also independent evidence of the type in (100) and (101) that shows that topicalization of adverbs was possible where there was a non-pronominal subject, so we must in any case allow for the possibility of topicalization to the clausal category with the subject preceding the verb.

It has often been claimed that non-pronominal subjects are quite rare with topicalized complements (cf. Adams 1987b: 191, Offord 1971, Price 1961, Vance 1989: 187f). However, the figures in Vance (1990) indicate that topicalization of complements in clauses with nominal subjects is only slightly rarer (a mean of 6.75% over four texts) than the same topicalization with pronominal subjects (a mean of 9.5% over the same four texts); the difference between the two kinds of subjects lies more in the fact that verb-nominal subject order is more frequent than verb-pronominal subject order (presumably because pronominal subjects can also be null).

We have shown that both adverbs and complements could appear in an adjoined position in MidFr more readily than in OF, creating V3 orders. A comparison with the German and English data we have presented suggests that these V3 orders should be interpreted as AgrPs rather than as CPs. If such clauses are AgrPs, a clear prediction emerges: the second element in a V3 structure will always be the subject, since the second position — SpecAgr' — is a subject position and not a topic position. This is in fact the case (cf. Adams 1987b: 193: 'the sequence... (XSVO) is attested, but I have found no instances of [...] (XOVS)"). This is further support for an AgrP-adjunction analysis of the data presented above.

Moreover, this conclusion sheds some light on how a V2 system can begin to erode diachronically, i.e. on what was responsible for the differences between OF and MidFr that we have been observing. The idea is that the possibility of overt expletives in initial position is crucial, since this provides clear evidence to acquirers that the initial position can be an A-position. The basic observation, inspired by Cardinaletti (1989: 10), is that subject-initial orders in V2 languages do not necessarily semantically 'topicalize' or 'lend emphasis to' the subject. This can be clearly seen from the fact that expletive pronouns, which by their very nature cannot bear semantic emphasis, can appear in first position:

(106) a. **Es** wurde t getanzt

   It was   danced

   b. **Es** hat t viel   geregnet

   It has   much rained

   (Cardinaletti ibid.)

Similar sentences are found in OF and MidFr:

(107) a. **Il** est juget que nus les ocirum

   '*It is judged that we will kill them*'

   (*Roland*, 1. 884)

   b. **Il** ne me   chaut

   It not to-me matters

'It doesn't matter to me'

(Einhorn 1974: 123)

    c. **il** i   avoit bien   .xxiiij.M. archiers a   piet

    there were a good 24,000   archers on foot

    (Froissart, *Chroniques*, xxvi, l. 15)

Cardinaletti suggests that SpecC' in German (and presumably in other V2 languages) may in principle be either an A-position or an A'-position. It follows from relativized minimality that when any argument other than the subject is raised to SpecC', this position must count as an A'-position or a structure equivalent to superraising will result due to the formation of an ill-formed A-chain across an A-position specifier (cf. Chapter 1, (58)). On the other hand, when the subject appears in SpecC', this position may in principle count either as an A-position or as an A'-position; the possibility of interpreting it as an A-position means that it is not necessarily associated with a topic interpretation and so expletives can appear there. But if it is an A-position immediately preceding the inflected verb, and if Agr° precedes TP, it becomes possible to reinterpret it as SpecAgr', with the verb in Agr°. In that case, SVO clauses with an expletive or semantically non-topicalized subject are amenable to an analysis as AgrPs, which in turn permits adjunction of adverbial and topicalized material to the pre-subject position. This, we propose, is how the V3 sentences we have been looking at in this section originated: SpecC' functions as an A-position, and is reanalysed as SpecAgr', entailing reanalysis of the matrix CP as AgrP.

    We can also integrate the proposed 'double Agr' structure for OF into this account. Agr1 disappeared as a separate category in the 13th century, a development that we suggested in the previous section may have been related to the loss of morphological case. After the loss of Agr1, C°'s selection property was satisfied by Agr2. Hence, by MidFr, there was only one Agr-projection, the one corresponding to the former Agr2. It may be, however, that the former Agr1 favoured the reanalysis of C as Agr which came later. This would result if, in the OF double-Agr system, clauses with non-topic subjects and expletives in initial position were Agr1Ps, not CPs (cf. 3.4. on Middle English). When Agr1 is lost, these were preferentially reanalysed as AgrPs where possible, with the general consequences for V2 that we just outlined.

    Why are matrix AgrPs not found in the Germanic V2 languages of the present day? For German and Dutch (and all the Continental West Germanic languages) the answer is straightforward. The fact that Agr° is on the right of TP prevents this reanalysis of CPs as AgrPs: in AgrP, the verb is not medial but final, unlike in CP. (We are glossing over the possibility that, in German at least, Agr1 may be present and head-initial as the Wackernagel position — cf. 1.3.2.; in any case the inflected verb never appears in this position in contemporary German and Dutch).

The question is trickier for MSc, since these are basically head-initial languages. Interestingly, V3 sentences of the type considered here are impossible, as the following Swedish example shows (cf. Schwartz and Vikner 1989: 46, (41)):

(108)   *Aldrig Johan vill läsa de   här bökerna
        Never John   will read these here books

As Schwartz and Vikner conclude, this is convincing evidence that SVO clauses are CPs in Swedish. By the same token, the grammaticality of such sentences in MidFr suggests that SVO clauses were at least optionally AgrPs.

Since initial expletives are also possible in MSc (cf. the Danish example in Note 17 of Chapter 1), what forces SVO clauses to be always analyzed as CPs in these languages? The answer lies in the question of V-to-Agr movement. We saw in 1.3. that MSc lacks (visible) V-to-Agr movement but clearly has V-to-C movement. This means that the relative position of sentence negation and other elements such as VP-adverbs with respect to the finite verb will indicate clearly whether the verb is in $C°$ or not. On the other hand, French has always had V-to-Agr movement (see 1.1.), and negation and VP-adverbials could not therefore disambiguate tensed matrix CPs from tensed matrix AgrPs because they cannot tell us whether the verb is in $Agr°$ or in $C°$ (additionally the fact, pointed out by Luc Moritz (pers. comm.), that OF and MidFr lacked obligatory *pas* in negatives may be relevant here).

In this context, the situation in (Modern) Icelandic is very relevant, since this language has V-to-Agr movement (cf. 1.3. (64)), and is head-initial. Here there is evidence that in fact V3 sentences of the MidFr type are possible. The following example (from Thráinsson pers. comm.) shows this:

(109)   Ég bara hef aldrei seð hann
        I just have never seen him

However, Rögnvaldsson and Thráinsson (1990) analyse these as IPs with the adverb in SpecI'. So they propose exactly what we are proposing for MidFr, with the difference that some constituent other than the subject may occupy SpecAgr' (i.e. their SpecI'). This difference follows if Icelandic has the double-Agr clause structure, as following Cardinaletti and Roberts (forthcoming), we suggested in 1. 4. MidFr had lost the double-Agr structure, though, so the V3 sentences had to be analysed as simple AgrPs.

So, in order for CP to be reanalysed as AgrP, three independent properties must hold: (i) the base order must be Agr-VP; (ii) V-to-Agr must be general, at least in tensed clauses; (iii) there must be no Agr1P. Middle English is similar to Middle French in that it certainly had general V-to-Agr raising and Agr-VP order. As is well known, Middle English lost V2 (cf. van Kemenade 1987, van Kemenade and Hulk 1990; in 3.4., we further discuss the loss of V2 in English). Another case where V2 was lost under these conditions was the Medieval Northern Italian dialects; these dialects were essentially like MidFr in the relevant respects; cf. Vanelli, Renzi and Benincà (1986), Vanelli (1987), Benincà (1984, 1989), and 2.4.3. The modern dialects have (almost) all lost V2. However, Romansch appears to have retained V2, despite apparently having all the preconditions for losing it; further research is needed here. Finally, although contemporary MSc is no problem for our proposals the medieval varieties of these languages had V-to-Agr (cf. Platzack 1987, 1988, Holmberg and Platzack 1988, Platzack and Holmberg 1989, and 3.1.3.). However, since they were in general very similar to Modern Icelandic (e.g. in having Styl-F), we can assume that they had an Agr1P with Modern Icelandic properties and, as such, were not amenable to reanalysis of the kind discussed here. In fact, it may be more correct to say that MSc lost Agr2P rather than Agr1P. Cf. 3.1.3., 3.4.

Returning to MidFr, we conclude the following: MidFr SVO clauses could be analysed as AgrPs rather than as CPs. This in turn means that Agr-to-C movement was not obligatory, and so the [Agr] feature was not an obligatory property of [-wh] matrix C°. In other words, MidFr was an optional V2 language (for SVO clauses with expletives and semantically non-topicalized subjects).

In the next section, we pursue this line of investigation by considering the nature and frequency of SVO clauses in MidFr.

2.3.2. *SVO Order, Least Effort and Diachronic Reanalysis*

We concluded in the previous section that it was at least possible for matrix SVO clauses to be analysed as AgrPs in MidFr. We saw that in this respect MidFr differs from the contemporary V2 Germanic languages (except Yiddish, which is a special case, cf. 1.4., and Icelandic). In fact, Travis (1984, 1986) presented an analysis of Germanic V2 which proposed precisely this. Although, in part because of the impossibility of orders like *Adv XP V*, this analysis cannot be maintained for the V2 Germanic languages (cf. Schwartz and Vikner (1989) for a convincing refutation of Travis' position based on data from German and Swedish), this does not mean that no such system could exist. What we are proposing, in effect, is that MidFr instantiates that system. Moreover, we suggest that this is what characterizes the 'mixed' or 'transitional' nature of MidFr: matrix declaratives could be either CP or AgrP.

In this section, we will document the rising frequency of SVO sentences. This is logically independent of the Travis-style analysis of MidFr V2 that we have proposed. A system which allows SVO sentences to be AgrPs does not in itself require that SVO orders become favoured; still less does it require that topicalization should adjoin material to AgrP rather than substituting it in SpecC'. However, we will see that these options were progressively preferred over the former V2 system. We attribute this, not to any principle of grammar as such, but rather to the Least Effort Strategy, which we take to be a principle of acquisition. The effects of the LES are manifested in language change through Diachronic Reanalysis, a relationship between the grammars of successive generations. We introduce the Least Effort Strategy, and suggest how it may act as a sufficient condition for change. Moreover, we distinguish three aspects of syntactic change: Steps, Diachronic Reanalysis and Parametric Change.

We saw in the previous section that the fact that the subject and only the subject occurs in second position in MidFr V3 clauses can be taken as an argument that these clauses are AgrPs, with the initial element adjoined. There is another possibility, however. The analysis of ModFr complex inversion presented in 1.5. appeals to the possibility of C having a double specifier in order to account for the attested order *Wh NP V* in this construction (here too, for reasons deriving from relativized minimality, the NP can only be the subject — cf. 1.5.). What prevents an analysis of the V3 orders just discussed in similar terms, as a kind of 'declarative complex inversion', or 'complex V2'?

The answer is the ECP. To see how this works, let us consider in more detail the interactions of various assumptions we have made up to now. The ECP requires that traces be properly governed, where proper government means government in X' by one of a class of designated X°s (cf. Rizzi 1990a, Ch. 2). Consider the putative 'complex V2' analysis for a V3 sentence:

(110) $[_{CP/AgrP}$ Adv $[_{CP/AgrP}$ NP $[_{C'/Agr'}$ $[_{C°}$ V] $[_{AgrP}$ t . . .

We saw in 1.5. that C°'s [Agr] feature confers on C° the capacity of properly governing subject traces. This is what allows subjects to move to SpecC' in V2 sentences, both in Germanic and in OF. Now, a C° which allows complex inversion, i.e. which licenses two specifier positions, like the one in (110), cannot have the feature [Agr]. Therefore, C° in (110) cannot properly govern the subject trace, and this representation is ruled out by the ECP. So the MidFr V3 examples discussed in the previous section cannot be cases of 'complex V2'. As we saw in 1.5., the subject trace in ModFr complex inversion is properly governed by the subject clitic incorporated into C°.[23] In this way, the ECP interacts with our system of head-to-head movement so as to prevent an analysis of V3 orders as complex V2. This further supports the conclusion of the previous section.

It is frequently commented that SVO orders became favoured in the MidFr period. Marchello-Nizia (1979: 331) gives the following statistics for inverted, non-inverted and null subjects in matrix declaratives for two late 15th-century texts:

(111)	SV	VS	NS
Anon., *Cent Nouvelles Nouvelles* (1466):	60.2%	10%	12%
Anon., *Le Roman de Jehan de Paris* (1495):	60%	10%	30%

(The figures for the *Cent Nouvelles Nouvelles* do not add up to 100%; Marchello-Nizia does not comment on this). These figures should be compared with those for OF texts given in (26) (although the figures are divided along different lines). Marchello-Nizia (ibid.) sums up the discussion of these and other figures concerning inverted and non-inverted word orders in MidFr with the following remark: "In independent and main clauses, it [SV order — IGR] dominates in a proportion varying between 52% and 75% of cases (while in this case, in OF, the proportion is, with some exception, lower than 50%)."[24] It is clear from these figures that SVO order was preferred, but not obligatory, in matrix declaratives in the late 15th century.

Earlier MidFr texts give the same result, and permit us to see the emerging preference for non-inverted orders. Our analysis of three texts from the late 14th and early 15th centuries along the same lines as Marchello-Nizia's analysis of later texts gives the following results:[25]

(112)	SV	VS	NS
Froissart, *Chroniques* (c. 1390)	40%	18%	42%
15 Joyes (*14esme Joye*) (c. 1400)	52.5%	5%	42.5%
Chartier *Quadrilogue* (1422)	51%	7%	42%

The figures in (111) and (112) clearly show a growing preference for SV(O) orders during the MidFr period. At the end of the 14th century, this order appeared 40% of the time; early in the 15th century, it rises to around 50%, and later in the century it is consistently around 60%. This should also be compared with an average of 35% SV orders in the OF texts surveyed in (26).

In terms of our analysis, this means that there was a growing preference for matrix declaratives to be AgrPs, but they could nevertheless still be CPs even in late MidFr. So C° continued to optionally carry the feature [+Agr].

Why were SVO orders preferred at this point? Adams (1987a, b) suggests that SVO V2 systems generally tend to be reanalysed as simple SVO systems, owing to the ambiguity of SVO clauses. Other things being equal, an SVO clause in an SVO V2 language could be taken as a CP or as an AgrP. Adams proposes that the AgrP hypothesis was preferred. There is clearly an element of truth in this account, but we need to spell out why AgrP was preferred. Obviously, the answer is that it represented a simpler structure. We can concretize the notion of simplicity in the following terms:[26]

(113)   *Least Effort Strategy (LES):*

Representations assigned to sentences of the input to acquisition should be such that they contain the set of the shortest possible chains (consistent with (a) principles of grammar, (b) other aspects of the trigger experience).

In other words, (113) requires acquirers to always look for the representation whose chains have, on aggregate, the smallest number of links (this idea is quite close in spirit to the Transparency Principle of Lightfoot 1979). Chomsky (1989) proposed an informal version of (113) as a kind of 'guideline' of UG. We suggest that the Least Effort Strategy should instead be considered as a strategy of acquisition, and, again *contra* Chomsky's suggestion, that it should be stated in terms of syntactic representations along the lines of (113).

In terms of (113), we can see how SVO clauses in a V2 SVO language might be analyzed as AgrPs rather than as CPs. Analysing such clauses as CPs entails positing the following chains (where x indicates a *wh*-trace, which heads an A-chain and forms the tail of an A'-chain):

(114) a. (V, t, t, t) (V-to-T-to-Agr-to-C)

b. (x, t)   (subject raising)

c. (NP, x)   (subject 'topicalization')

The total number of chain positions here is eight. On the other hand, analysing these clauses as AgrPs gives the following chains:

(115) a. (V, t, t)   (V-to-T-to-Agr)

b. (NP, t)   (subject raising)

Here the total number of chain positions is 5. So LES favours the AgrP analysis, all other things being equal. In these terms, we can understand the preference for treating SpecC' as an A-position in the manner outlined in the previous section; this gives the following chains:

(116) a. (V, t, t, t)

b. (NP, t, t) (cyclic subject raising)

This reduces the number of chain positions by one compared with (114), and so is preferred. We may thus expect 'pure' V2 systems where SpecCP is always an A'-position to be reanalysed as systems where SpecCP can be an A-position; see the discussion of Step I below.

It is also clear, as Adams again points out, that all other things are not equal in OV languages like Dutch and German. The final position of Agr° rules the AgrP analysis, and (113), out of contention. In MSc, we can claim that the position of negation, etc., has a similar effect. (On the other hand, it is hard to see how a system goes from a double-Agr system to an obligatory matrix-CP system, although it is compatible with this conception of change to move from a double-Agr system to an obligatory-CP, single-Agr system. This is what happened in 13th-century French, we have suggested).

Now consider a case of topicalization of a direct object. In a V2 system, where the direct object is topicalized to SpecC', we have the following:

(117) a. (V, t, t, t) (cf. (116a)

    b. (NP_i, t) (subject raising)

    c. (NP_j, x) (topicalization)

The total number of chain positions here is eight. On the other hand, topicalization to AgrP gives the following:

(118) a. (V, t, t)   (= (115a))

    b. (NP_i, t) (subject raising)

    c. (NP_j, x) (topicalization)

Since the verb moves one step less in this structure, it is favoured over (117) by LES as it contains seven chain positions instead of eight.

In these terms, we can see how SVO orders came to be preferred during the 13th–15th centuries. The sequence of steps was as follows:

I.   SpecC' analyzed as an A-position. Saving: one chain position (cf. (116) vs. (114)). Result: expletives in this position.

II.   SVO clauses reanalysed as AgrP. Saving: two chain positions (cf. (115) vs. (116)). Result: V3 orders with initial topics and adverbs.

III.   AdvSV and TopSV begin to replace AdvVS and TopVS. Saving: one chain position (cf. (118) vs. (117)). Result: increased frequency of SV.

Step I must have happened at some point in the OF period (arguably with the introduction of the 'innovative' OF system in the 13th century) and seems to have happened in all the V2 Germanic languages (alternatively, the first step may be the loss of Agr1, with the result that in embedded clauses one chain position is lost; this led directly to Step II in the manner outlined in the previous section; on this view Step I has not happened in the V2 Germanic languages). Step II took place early in the MidFr period, probably in the 14th century; we have seen why this change has not taken place in the V2 Germanic languages. Step III took place during the 15th century, it seems.

The steps in the loss of V2 are presented above in such a way that the relations among them can be clearly seen. The result of each step provides the data necessary for the next step to happen; we could consider this to be the necessary condition for the next step. The saving at each step is phrased in terms of the LES, so that we can see why the option made available by the previous step was selected; this is the sufficient condition for each step.

At this point, we should distinguish three notions in the theory of language change. First, there is the notion of "step." The appearance of a new construction, or a significant change in the frequency of a construction, in a set of texts can be thought of as a step. This is also the traditional notion of change; it is an observationally adequate notion in the sense of Chomsky (1964). When a language takes a new step this does not necessarily imply a change in the grammar; for example, passing from Step II to Step III did not involve a change in the grammar of French, as adverbs and topics could adjoin to AgrP at the earlier stage also. In terms of the distinction in Chomsky (1986a: 19f) between I(internal)-language (i.e. the mental object that linguistic theory is an account of) and E(xternal)-language (some set or corpus of sentences), we can think of the notion of Step as the diachronic relation between E-languages.

Second, there is the notion of Diachronic Reanalysis (DR); a given construction has structure S at period P and structure $S' \neq S$ at period P'. This notion is close to Lightfoot's (1979) radical reanalysis, or Andersen's (1973) notion of abductive change. The reanalysis of SVO clauses from CP to AgrP in MidFr (Step II above) is an example of Diachronic Reanalysis. As a notational convention, we will indicate DRs with double arrows. So Step II can be schematized as follows:

(119) a. $[_{CP} NP_i [_{C'} V + Agr_j [_{AgrP} t_i [_{Agr'} t_j \ldots \Rightarrow$

b. $[_{AgrP} NP_i [_{Agr'} V + Agr \ldots$

Formulating some step as a DR amounts to a descriptively adequate account of a change. We can think of DRs as relations between the E-language of one generation (ambiguous trigger experience susceptible of a 'simpler' analysis in the sense defined earlier), and the I-language of a subsequent generation.

The third notion involves genuine explanation, in Chomsky's sense. An explanatory account of language change treats a range of changes in terms of the shift in the value of a single parameter. Just as the traditional synchronic notion of construction is subsumed by the notions of principle and parameter in current theory (cf. the introduction to Heny 1979 on this), we suggest that the traditional diachronic notion of change is subsumed by the idea that a given generation of speakers may set a given parameter of their grammar differently from the setting underlying their parents' production of their trigger experience. None of the steps in (118) instantiate this, but the overall loss of the properties in (95a–c) is a case of this, as we have already suggested and will see in detail in 2.4. Clearly, Parametric Changes are diachronic relations among I-languages. To the extent that the notion of construction is epiphenomenal in current syntactic theory, the notion DR may also prove to be epiphenomenal. All DRs may turn out to be instances of Parametric Change. However, we will continue to use this notion as it has real utility and expository value. It may be that DRs, unlike parameters, have no place in the theory of syntax as such; however, they have a place in the theory of syntactic change (in this respect, too, the notion of DR is close to Lightfoot's 1979 notion of radical reanalysis motivated by the Transparency Principle).

In terms of these ideas, the following postulate of the theory of change emerges rather naturally: structures are eliminated due to parametric changes only. Steps can and frequently do make certain constructions rarer, but they do not eliminate them totally, in the sense that the grammatical system still permits them. DRs act in such a way as to radically reduce the frequency of certain construction-types in the data, but nevertheless the constructions in question are not eliminated; DRs typically result in the innovation of new constructions alongside older ones. With parametric change, however, one or several constructions may be eliminated altogether from the grammar. Parametric changes may eliminate structures which were already obsolescent, but they may also eliminate otherwise perfectly viable structures, or cause them to undergo DR.

The LES is relevant for all three notions of change, since, as we just said, it is the sufficient condition for the move from one step to the next. Therefore, any DR will involve a reduction in the number of chain positions in the structure in question (however, it may entail complications elsewhere in the grammar; we will see in 2.3.5. that the DR in (119) complicated the licensing of null subjects in MidFr). DRs frequently create the conditions for parametric changes, by removing the structural evidence for a given parametric setting. The DR in (119) is a case in point; in (119a), before this DR, Nominative is assigned by V + Agr in $C°$ to the trace in SpecAgr' in a configuration of government. In (119b) Nominative is assigned by V + Agr in $Agr°$ to the subject in SpecAgr' in an agreement configuration. Thus the DR in (119) fed the parametric change we are concerned with, by removing at least one class of sentences that triggered the conservative setting.

Of course, although this view of language change relies quite heavily on the LES, it does not follow that languages (or grammars) are getting simpler. As we just indicated, DRs simplify given constructions, but they may complicate other areas of the grammar. More importantly, parametric changes do not simplify anything; they simply provide a grammar with different properties to the one underlying the production of a given kind of trigger experience, one which is roughly compatible with that trigger experience, but which generates quite different structures elsewhere. To say that after a parametric change a language is simpler than it was the before the parametric change is exactly as false as saying that French is simpler than Latin.

On the other hand, parametric changes interact with DRs in that a parametric change may force a number of DRs. A parametric change leads to a number of simultaneous, or near-simultaneous, DRs, manifested as observed changes, i.e. steps. DRs may in turn feed other parametric changes. It is this possibility of feedback which perpetuates syntactic change.

Returning to the case in point, the steps in (118) and the DR in (119) led to a considerable erosion of the V2 constraint by the end of the MidFr period. However, there was no parametric change before the 16th century. The result of the changes in (118) and (119) was that not all matrix clauses were V2. However, there were still V2 clauses, and in these V2 clauses C° was [+Agr] as before. Given the DR we have just seen, however, the evidence for C[+Agr] (i.e. for V2) is less robust than in former times. In other words, French remained a V2 language after (119) had taken place, but in somewhat reduced circumstances. The only clear V2 declarative sentences were OVS or AdvVS. Moreover, in the next sections we shall show that many (X)VS orders were amenable to analysis as something other than simple inversion. For interrogatives, we will see in 2.3.4. a major case of DR which was directly incompatible with the presence of [+Agr] in C°: the innovation of complex inversion. First, however, we should return to the topic of subject clitics in order to see how developments in this domain also weakened the evidence for Nominative-assignment under government in MidFr.

2.3.3. *The Emergence of a Double Series of Subject Pronouns*

We discussed the properties of OF subject pronouns in 2.2.1. and 2.2.2. What we saw there was that the modern situation of complementary distribution between the atonic *je*-series and the tonic *moi*-series did not obtain in full. In preverbal position, the *je*-series was not obligatorily adjacent to the inflected verb, as in ModFr. Moreover, in early OF, *moi*-forms appear in direct-object position. However, *moi*-forms are never subjects, and so never appear in SpecAgr', while *je*-forms, if they appear

postverbally, must appear in SpecAgr'. So there was complementary distribution between the two series in SpecAgr'. We suggested that *je*-forms
syntactically cliticized from postverbal position, i.e. SpecAgr', onto C°.
We saw in 2.2.2. that OF postverbal subject pronouns should probably be
analysed as syntactic clitics on C°. This is a sufficient, but not a necessary,
condition for them to satisfy Case theory by incorporation rather than by
assignment.

The question that concerns us in this section is: at what point did subject
clitics become **required** to satisfy Case theory by incorporation rather than
by assignment? The answer to this question is clearly relevant to our
investigation of the change in the Case-assignment parameter in (3).

Our contention in this section will be, however, that it took the development of full complementary distribution with the *moi*-series to create the
conditions which meant that the *je*-forms **had** to incorporate in order to
satisfy Case theory.

In order to see how this idea works, it is necessary to sharpen a little
our conception of Case theory and of the nature of clitics. Here we will
propose one or two refinements of the system presented in 1.2.; the ideas
are not necessarily new or original, being based in large part on Baker
(1985, 1988), Everett (1986, 1989), Rizzi and Roberts (1989).

The basic requirement of Case theory is the Case Filter, which we take
to be one aspect of a general PF-identification requirement applying to
both verbal and nominal projections. For the moment, we give just the
subpart of this condition relevant for NPs (see Chapter 3 and Roberts
1985 for discussion and motivation of the 'verb-visibility' requirement):

(120)   Every phonologically realized NP must be associated with the
         Case feature [+F] of some head.

As we pointed out in 1.2, and as the above authors suggest, the association
of an NP with [+F] can take place in one of two ways, either by assignment
or by incorporation. We assume that assignment is in fact a checking
operation (cf. Chomsky 1981, Jaeggli 1982): NPs are lexically inserted
with some Case feature, which at SS is required to match with the Case
feature of some governing or agreeing head. This technical move in itself
has no consequences for the overall view of Case-assignment outlined in
1.2. It does give us a way to characterize the inherent morphosyntactic
difference between clitics and non-clitics, however: we propose that clitics
are exactly those NPs which are lexically inserted without a Case feature.
Therefore, in order to satisfy (120), they (or more precisely the head of
the NP) must incorporate with the head bearing the Case feature. Since
they are not morphologically selected by this head, and the head is not
empty (this is obviously true for lexical heads, and true for Agr in all
Romance languages as well as many others), the incorporation takes place
by adjunction (see (49)). In this way, through the chain formed between

the landing site of incorporation and N°, the Case feature is transmitted to N° and hence to NP. (An intermediate possibility between Case-assignment and incorporation may be (71), appropriately rephrased in terms of Holmberg's (1990) notion of 'adjacency government'; in this case, 'weak' elements presumably have a Case feature and participate in Case-matching, but they require a more constrained syntactic environment for Case-matching than other NPs. This is in fact exactly what Holmberg proposes).

The Case Filter is generally assumed to hold at SS. At first sight, this predicts that all cases of cliticization motivated by (120) in the way we just described have to take place at SS. Moreover, since the ECP applies to traces of syntactic movement, the approach based on (120) predicts that cliticization always takes place from a governed position to the governing head. However, these predictions are too strong, as they rule out PF-cliticization and cliticization taking place in agreement configurations. Most importantly, the analysis of ModFr preverbal subject pronouns that we have been assuming up to now is excluded (or else we have to arbitrarily assume that these pronouns are not true clitics). If we wish to maintain this analysis, or indeed the possibility of PF-cliticization as independent of syntactic cliticization at all, we will have to qualify the above account slightly. At the same time, we would like to account for the obligatory incorporation of subject pronouns with Agr in ModFr in terms of (120).

These results can be achieved if we consider that the Case Filter is really a constraint on the interpretive components of the theory, imposing a visibility requirement which must be satisfied both at PF and at LF. For this reason, it must in general be satisfied at SS; however, we suggest that a representation can be well-formed if it satisfies (120) independently at PF and at LF. Since Case-checking is an operation distinct from the well-formedness requirement in (120), and Case-checking takes place at SS, only elements exempt from Case-matching can satisfy (120) elsewhere than at SS. Clitics are the only elements of this type, so this will only happen with cliticization. We conclude that cliticization is not in itself obliged to take place at or by SS.

At PF, as we have already suggested, the ECP does not hold (or at least it does not hold in the same manner as at other levels). Therefore incorporation from SpecAgr' into Agr° is possible, even though this goes against the c-command condition of the ECP. This is precisely the analysis of ModFr preverbal subject pronouns that we gave in 2.2.1., following Kayne (1983). Where this happens, (120) is satisfied at PF.

However, the ECP certainly holds in full force at LF, so there is no possibility of relaxing the c-command requirement on antecedent-trace relations in this component. Here we can appeal to the proposal common to a number of recent accounts of English *do*-support (cf. 1.3.2., 1.3.3., 3.2.1.) that tensed verbs undergo QR to C in LF. Raising a tensed verb from Agr to C in LF in French means that Agr will be in a position at LF where it (or rather the complex head of which it is a part) c-commands SpecAgr', and cliticization from subject position will be possible without violating the ECP.[27] So it is possible to maintain that ModFr preverbal subject pronouns are incorporated with Agr at both PF and LF, and that in this way (120) is satisfied. And we retain the view that preverbal subject clitics in ModFr are in SpecAgr' at SS.[28]

We now have a clear morphosyntactic notion of clitic which is independent of the theory of incorporation. In these terms, it becomes clear what the diachronic development of a class of clitics must be: the loss of the ability to bear a Case feature. The absence of this feature precludes Case-matching and so requires incorporation, as a function of (120). In OF, then, the pronouns of the je-series had a Case feature; in ModFr they do not have one.[29] The evidence for the loss of the Case feature consists in the disappearance of je-forms from all contexts other than those governed by, or agreeing with, Agr° — contexts from which incorporation into Agr would have been impossible. Call these, for convenience, 'non-Agr' contexts. The earlier appearance of je-forms in non-Agr contexts shows that they had a Case feature (how this feature was matched in some non-Agr contexts, e.g. ellipses, is a more general problem which we will not go into). Hence the disappearance of je-forms from non-Agr contexts is what we are concerned with. When je-forms could no longer appear in non-Agr contexts complementary distribution with moi-forms resulted because, from the OF period on, moi-forms could no longer appear in complement positions. So it is the development of complementary distribution between the two series which provides the evidence that the pronouns were clitics in the Case-theoretic sense defined above.

We saw in 2.1.1. that there were five contexts in which je-forms appear in OF where ModFr requires moi-forms (we repeat a selection of the OF forms which illustrate the differences):

(i) stress:

    (49) a. Et **je** que sai?

          And I what know (I)?

          'And what do I know?'

(ii) coordination:

    (51)   e **jo** e **vos** i   irum

          and I and vos there will-go

(iii) separation from the verb:

(54) a. et **il,** a   toz ses oz . . . , s'en ala
and he, with all his army,   went away

(iv) elliptical constructions:

(56) a. et qui i   sera? **jou et tu**
and who there will-be? I   and you

(v) modification:

(57)   Se **je meïsme** ne li di
if I self   not him said

It is possible to find sentences of this type in Froissart (late 14th century), as the following examples show:

(121) a. Et **je** d'autre part   je sui bien de tous les naviers
And I on the other hand I am well of all   the sailors
(Froissart *Chroniques*, Luce-Raynaud (ed.); Foulet 1935/6: 308)

b. et sarons   liquelz est plus fors en ce pays, ou **je** ou
and (we) will know which is   stronger in this land, I   or
vous
you
(Froissart *Chroniques*; Price 1971: 145)

c. Et **je** Froissars, acteres de ces croniques, fui en Escoce
And I Froissart, author of these chronicles, was in Scotland
(*Chroniques*, xxv, 1. 39)

d. comme il seroit **ilz** meysmes
as   he would be they selves
(Froissart *Chroniques*, Luce-Raynaud (ed.); VIII, 286; Foulet op. cit.: 309)

We conclude that in 1400 the *je*-series still had a Case feature. Vance (1989: 197f) gives similar data from *Jehan de Saintré* (1456), indicating that the Case feature remained a property of these pronouns well into the 15th century.

However, there is widespread agreement that by the 16th century the situation was essentially as in ModFr.[30] Humphreys (1932, cited by Marchello-Nizia ibid.) gives the last occurrence of *je et X* in a literary

text as 1466. Adams (1987b: 188), Marchello-Nizia (op. cit.: 185) and
Moignet (1965: 124) all give the following quotation from the *Donait
françois*, a 15th-century phrase-book for English speakers: "si come en
ceste exemple *Janyn que fais tu?* il doit respondre *que moy?* et non pas
Je? et l'aultre luy doit dire *Voire toy* et non pas *Tu* et ainsi des aultres"
("Just as in this example *Janyn what are you doing?* he ought to reply
What me? and not *I?* and the other ought to say to him *Indeed you* [Obl]
and not *you* [Nom] and so on for the others", translation give by Adams
ibid.). Also, Marchello-Nizia (ibid.) gives evidence that *moi*-forms replaced *je*-forms in elliptical constructions, comparatives (*more than me/I*)
and in emphatic apposition to the subject during the 15th century.

   Since the modern situation of complementary distribution was by and
large in place at the beginning of the 16th century, we conclude, on the
basis of the above reasoning, that the nominative pronouns lost their Case
feature during the 15th century, the loss possibly occurring at different
times for different persons (cf. Brunot, 1905, I: 457, Franzén 1939: 12),
and at different rates in different registers. For these reasons, we cannot
be more precise in our dating than this.

   By early in the 16th century, then, subject pronouns of the *je*-series
obligatorily incorporated with Agr° in order to satisfy (120). In these
terms, the diachronic cliticization of a set of pronouns involves the introduction of a chain: that linking the incorporated N° with the trace inside
the NP. This situation is not, despite initial appearances, in conflict with
the LES as formulated in the previous section, as this is an instance where
a grammatical principle — namely (120) — creates the necessity for a
chain, a situation that we explicitly allowed for in our formulation of the
LES in (113). Once subject pronouns were unable to bear a Case feature,
(120) forced incorporation to take place, thereby complicating the structure in terms of LES in the sense that an extra chain-position was introduced. The LES cannot prevent developments such as the loss of the
ability to bear a Case feature; this in itself has nothing to do with chain-
formation. The loss of the Case feature is presumably related to phonological weakening in some way, although it is not clear exactly how.

   So much for preverbal clitics. We should integrate what we said in
previous sections (notably 2.2.2.) about postverbal clitics with this view
of cliticization. In 2.2.2., we concluded that postverbal subject pronouns
were syntactic clitics on C° in OF. However, we have seen that these
clitics did not lose their Case feature until the 15th century, and so (120)
was not responsible for the formation of the incorporation chain in OF.
Neither can we attribute the incorporation of these pronouns to the fact
that these nominative pronouns were arguably 'weak elements' in
Holmberg's (1990) sense. However, we suggested in 2.2.2 that syntactic
clitic movement is generally preferred over PF cliticization, since syntactic
movement creates a situation in which visibility is satisfied just once at

SS, rather than being independently satisfied at LF and PF. This is the factor which overrides the LES; there is a general pressure for dependencies to be analysed as syntactic movement wherever possible (following Chomsky (1989), there might be a more global notion of 'least effort' behind this; cf. also Pesetsky's (1990) 'Earliness Principle'). In this way, new chains can arise in syntax. To sum up, the change in the pronominal system in the 15th century had the following characteristics:

(122)   Step: Nominative pronouns lose their Case feature.
         Saving: none ((120) overrides the LES).
         Result: complementary distribution of *je-* and *moi-* forms.

We said above that the saving effected by a change amounts to a sufficient condition for that change; in this case, since there was no saving, we must assume that the sufficient condition for the change was some ill-understood aspect of the relation between phonological 'heaviness' and the ability to carry syntactic features like Case. As we will see in the next section, the result of this change was the DR that introduced complex inversion.

The general conclusion of this section is that by the 16th century subject pronouns in French obligatorily incorporated with Agr° in order to satisfy the Case Filter (120). In the next section we will put this together with the other MidFr changes we have been reviewing, in order to see how complex inversion was innovated, through a DR, in the 15th century.

2.3.4. Diachronic Reanalysis in 15th-Century Interrogatives

In this section we will describe the emergence of complex inversion in the 15th century. In 2.1.3 we discussed OF interrogatives with the order *NP V pronoun*, for example (39), which we repeat here:

(39) a.   L'aveirs   Carlun est il appareillez?
          The treasure C.   is it made ready?
          'Is C.'s treasure made ready?'
          (*Roland*, l. 643; also cited in Foulet 1921: 249, Price 1971: 266)

     b.   Iceste guerre dura   ele toudis?
          This   war   will-last it   always
          'Will this war last for ever?'

     c.   Icist preudon Est il   or   nez de vostre vile?
          This man   is   he now born in your   town?
          'Was this man born in your town?'

We argued in 2.1.3. that these structures were left dislocations with the structure in (41), which we also repeat:

(41)

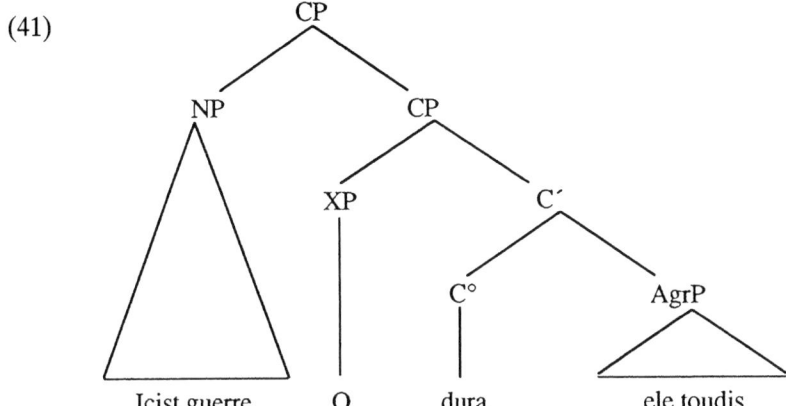

We gave five arguments to prefer this analysis over a complex-inversion analysis. These were (a) the order *NP V pronoun* is found only in Y/NQ, while complex inversion is possible in WHQ, too; (b) the order *NP WH V*, which is clearly a left dislocation, is found in WHQ; (c) in *NP (WH) V*, NP does not have to be a subject, which further supports the idea that *NP (WH) V pronoun* is a left dislocation; (d) NP is always definite in examples like (39); (e) Foulet's observation that these constructions are highly emphatic. So we concluded that (41) was the correct structure for (39).

At some point in the 15th century, the left dislocations with *NP V pronoun* order were reanalysed as complex inversion. So there was a DR which converted (41) into (123) (returning once again to IP-notation for simplicity) (cf. (40)):

(123)

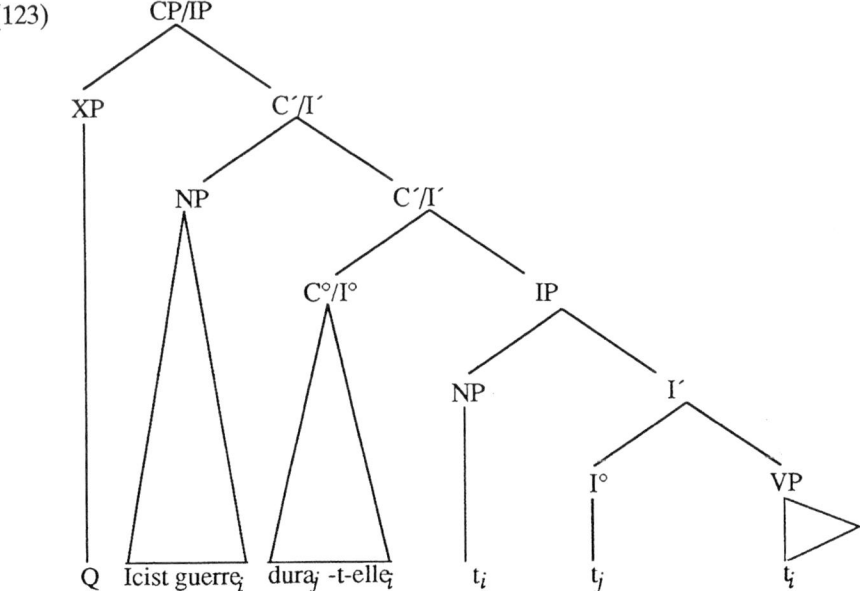

The occurrences of *NP V pron* in the 15th century were, in principle, ambiguous between an analysis of the type in (41) and an analysis of the type in (123). If (123) is the structure, we expect to also find instances of the types of order that were absent in OF and that the left-dislocation analysis excludes. So when the structure in (123) appears, we expect to find at least:

> (124) a. *WH NP V pronoun* orders (cf. argument (a)).
>
> b. *NP V pronoun* with non-referentially quantified NP (cf. argument (d)).
>
> c. A decrease in emphasis (cf. argument (e)).

Arguments (b) and (c) do not really play a role with respect to the DR, because the DR did not eradicate the former left-dislocation construction. Unambiguous cases were still analysed in this way, as they are in ModFr, cf.:[31]

> (125) a. Jean, quand est-ce qu'il arrive?
> *John, when does he arrive?*
>
> b. Pierre, qui l'a vu?
> *Peter, who has seen him?*

We will now examine the status of the properties in (126) in MidFr on the basis of Froissart's *Poésies* (late 14th century), Gréban *La Passion* (1452), Anon. *Les Cent Nouvelles Nouvelles* (1466), Anon. *Jehan de Paris* (1495).

(a) **WH NP V pronoun** *order*. No examples of this sort are found in Froissart. However, there is one clear example of this sort in Gréban:

> (126)   **Comment Cristus** *sera*   **il tel?**
>
> *How   Christ   will-be he such*
>
> 'How will Christ be like that?'
>
> (*La Passion*, l. 19890)

This is a clear case of the order *WH NP V pronoun*.

In *Les Cent Nouvelles Nouvelles* we find the following example, which may be a further instance of this order:

> (127)   et   **comment ce   seroit   il?**
>
> *and how   this would-be it?*
>
> 'and how would this be?'
>
> (XVI: 123)

The analysis of this example depends on the status of *ce*. It seems likely, however, that *ce* here is not the demonstrative pronoun *ce*, but rather a spelling of the reflexive clitic generally written *se*. A footnote in the edition we checked (cf. Appendix for the full reference) glosses this sentence as *et comment ce pourroit il faire?*, which is naturally understood as a case of the medio-reflexive use of *pouvoir* ('to be able to') to express epistemic modality. The sentence then means 'and how could this be?' So (127) is not a clear case of the order we are interested in.

No examples of this sort are found in the shorter text *Jehan de Paris*. The evidence of (126) indicates that the analysis of (123) for *NP V pron* strings was possible by the 1450s, i.e, that complex inversion was introduced by this time.

(b) **NP[-ref] V pronoun**. Again, no examples of this sort were found in Froissart. The first cases come from Gréban, where we find the following:

(128) **Chacun   a   il** ce qu'il faudra?

Each-one has he what it will-need?

'Has everyone got what he needs?' (l. 5233)

Indefinites like *chacun* cannot be left-dislocated in ModFr, but are possible in contexts of complex inversion (cf. the discussion of *personne* in 1.5.):

(129) a.*Chacun   il   est arrivé en retard

Each one, he arrived   late

   b. A quelle heure chacun   arrivera-t-il?

At what   time   each one will-arrive he?

'What time will each one arrive at?'

There are also examples of this sort with NPs which appear to have a generic interpretation:

(130) a. **Messager qui va par les champs**
      doit il point boire par coustume?

'*A messenger who goes through the fields, should he not drink by custom?*'

(l. 6357)

   b. **Gens   d'armes vont ilz**   a la guerre . . .?

Armed men   go   they to war?

'Do armed men go to war?'

(l. 12237)

It is unclear whether these NPs are definite or not; ModFr is of no help here since bare plurals are no longer possible, an article always being required. However, bare plurals are formally indefinite in the sense that they lack a definite article or demonstrative, and so may be further instances of the order that interests us.

Again, *Jehan de Paris* provides no examples of this construction. Nevertheless, the evidence from Gréban shows that in the mid-15th century the two most important syntactic indications of genuine complex inversion were present. We conclude from this that complex inversion was introduced between the period of Froissart and that of Gréban, i.e. between 1400 and 1450.

(c) *Emphasis*. Here we follow the remarks in Foulet (1921: 249f). Foulet points out examples of the following sort, where *NP V Pron* and simple inversion occur side by side:

(131) a. **Ces harnois cy sont ilz** pourrys? . . .
    Sont ces espees vermoulues?

    '*These harnesses here are they rotten?*
    Are these swords worm-eaten?'

    (from Gréban, *La Passion*, ll. 27720, 27723)

   b. **N'est pas ceste robe** assez longue, **mes cheveux** sont ils point longs?

    Isn't this dress long enough, my hair is it not long?

    (*Les Cent Nouvelles Nouvelles*, XCIII, 51)

Foulet comments 'It is clear that in passages of this type the two constructions have the same status. They are no longer distinguished by any nuance of meaning' (ibid.) ('Il est clair que dans des passages de ce genre les deux tournures sont sur le même pied. Aucune nuance de sens ne les sépare plus'). If left dislocations always carry at least some degree of emphasis, this remark indicates that orders of the type *NP V pron* were analysed as something other than left dislocation, i.e. as complex inversion. The evidence that the other reflexes of complex inversion, an indefinite initial NP and the same order in WHQ, were possible by the mid-15th century, strongly suggests that many cases of *NP V pron* order were instances of the structure in (123) rather than of that in (41) at this time (or soon after).

This idea is supported by the fact that the OF constructions which positively supported the left-dislocation analysis of the sequences *NP V Pron* are considerably rarer in the 15th century than in the 12th and 13th (cf. 2.1.3. and Note 31).

NP WH V, which appears in 8 out of 46 WHQ in *Roland*, is found in Froissart's *Poésies*. Buchli (1989: 23) points out the following cases:

(132) a. Et **je**, qu'en   sa   je?

      And I   what-of-it know I?

      'And I what do I know about it?'

      (p. 294; l. 2478, tome I)

    b. Et **le grant seigneur Espensier**,
       Qui de larghece est despensier,
       Que t'a il fait?

       'And the great lord E., who is the dispenser of generosity, what has he done to/for you?'

       (p. 9; ll. 269–71, tome II)

    c. Par son nom ce **rommant**, comment
       L'apellés vous?

       'By its name this romance, what do you call it?'

       (p. 107; ll. 700-1, tome I)

However, Buchli comments (ibid.) that such examples are harder to find in Froissart than in OF.

In Gréban and in the Anonymous *Cent Nouvelles Nouvelles* there are no examples of this order, while in *Jehan de Paris* there is one:

(133)   Et **vous**, a qui estes vous?

       'And you, to whom are you?'
       (i.e. in whose service are you?)

       (p. 35, l. 16)

This example would be fully acceptable also in ModFr. It seems, then, that MidFr, like ModFr and unlike OF, did not frequently make use of left dislocation as device for emphasis in WHQ (although, as in ModFr, the structure is grammatical). If this is true, then the case for analysing *NP V Pron* orders as complex inversion is the stronger.

Similarly, the order *NP V pron* where NP ≠ subject is rarer in MidFr than in OF. Buchli (op. cit.: 17) gives two examples from Froissart's *Poésies*, one of which involves a very heavy initial NP. There are six examples in Gréban, of which the following are typical:

(134) a. **Aultre chose** n'arons   de toy?

      other   thing not-will-(we)-have of you?

      'Will we have nothing more from you?'

      (l. 14446)

b. **en ce manoir** vous   fault il rien?

in this manor to-you needs it nothing?

'You need nothing more in this manor?'

(l. 729)

There is one possible example of this sort in the Anonymous *Cent Nou-*
velles Nouvelles (XXXVI, 69), which may in fact be an instance of declarative (V2) order. The comparative rarity of such examples in MidFr is
significant in the light of the above remarks.

Against this background of the general rarity of left-dislocations in
interrogatives, it is also significant that the proportion of interrogatives
with the order *NP V Pron* increases during the 15th century. The figures
are as follows, for the texts we looked at:

(135)   Froissart, *Poésies:*   0%
         Gréban, *Passion:*   1%
         CNN: 2.5%
         Jehan de Paris: 7%

Since there is no increase whatsoever in left-dislocation in WHQ or of
dislocation of non-subjects in Y/NQ, it seems clear that these figures
record a rise in complex inversion rather than a rise in left-dislocation of
subjects in Y/NQ.

The above considerations lead to the conclusion that the DR in (123)
had taken place by the second half of the 15th century. Complex inversion
thus exists from this time on in the grammar of French. The necessary
conditions for this DR were two. First, the weakening of V2 at this period
(cf. 2.3.1., 2.3.2.). This meant that C° no longer obligatorily bore the
feature [Agr], and so unselected incorporation of Agr into C was possible,
giving rise to two specifier positions. Second, the cliticization of subject
pronouns, in the sense that they lost capacity to bear a Case feature (as
described in the previous section) forced an incorporation analysis of post-
C° subject pronouns, leaving open the possibility of Agr in C° assigning
Nominative Case to its specifier in a configuration of agreement.

The sufficient condition for this DR was the reduction in the number
of chain-positions that it led to. This can be seen if we compare (41) with
(125) in terms of the chains involved:

(136) a. (41):   (V, t, t, t)   —V-raising

                  (pronoun, t)   —subject-raising

                  (NP)   —dislocated NP

                  ((NP), (pronoun, t)) —left dislocation

b. (125): (V, t, t, t)   −V-raising

          (NP, pronoun, t, t)   − subject-raising

We count the composed chain of left-dislocation as a two-member chain (each subchain being a member), and then separately count the members of each subchain. This gives a total of nine chain-positions in (136a). In (136b), there are eight chain-positions. So we see how the DR was motivated by the LES, and permitted by the other changes that were taking place in the 15th century that were discussed in the preceding sections. (This is also an argument for defining the LES in terms of chain-positions rather than traces or nodes; if the LES is defined in terms of chain-positions, then left-dislocation is seen as costly. Such a result is correct to the extent dislocated structures are frequently reanalysed as non-dislocated, as here).

We must now address the converse question: what was the status of simple inversion at this period? Taking WHQ first, of the various cases of *WH V NP* (NP ≠ pronoun) that we find in the 15th century, we should distinguish various subclasses. This is due, above all, to the possibility of free inversion (which later developed into stylistic inversion, cf. 2.4.4.1.). In matrix clauses, free inversion differs from simple inversion in that the subject NP appears inside VP on the right periphery, with an expletive *pro* in subject position. The two structures can be schematized as in (137):

(137)   Free inv: $[_{CP}$ WH C $[_{AgrP}$ *pro* . . . V+Agr $[_{VP}$ t . . . NP$]]]$

         Simple inv: $[_{CP}$ WH V $[_{AgrP}$ NP . . . .$]]$

In ModFr Styl-Inv, V does not raise to C; we assume that this was equally the case in earlier stages of the language in embedded clauses. For matrix clauses, we assume that V raised to C at least for as long as V2 remained operative, and so the situation in the 15th century is unclear. We abstract away from the question of the position of the verb in what follows; in fact it is extremely difficult both for the linguist and for the contemporary acquirer of French to decide whether V is in Agr or in C in free inversion constructions at this period, as the only thing separating the two positions is a necessarily null subject (see also 2.4.1.).

A very large number of sentences in the texts we have surveyed are ambiguous with respect to the two structures in (137). Any sentence of the general form *WH V NP* with an intransitive verb in a simple tense could be analysed either as in (137a) or as in (137b). Unsurprisingly, there is a good number of such cases. Here are some examples:

(138) a. ou **est** ton frere Abel?

       'where is your brother Abel?'

      (Gréban, *Passion*, l. 1168)

   b. Dont   vous **vient** ce mal?

      Whence to-you comes this evil?

      'Where does this evil come to you from?'

      (*CNN*, XX, 120)

   c. Et qui **est** ce Jehan de Paris?

      '*And who is this J. de P.?*'

      (*JdeP*, p. 46, l. 11)

Alongside these are, on the one hand, unambiguous cases of Styl-Inv, where the subject follows both elements of a compound tense, of the following type:

  (139) a. qu'**est ja**   **devenu** cil par qui   ce bien m'est venu?

        what is already become he by whom this good to-me is come?

        'What has the person by whom this good came to me become*?*'

        (Gréban, *La Passion*, l. 12446)

    b. Mes d'ou   **sont sailli** si en haste tels vivres . . .?

      But from where are come so quickly such provisions?

      'But where did such provisions come from so quickly?'

      (ibid., l. 12953)

And, on the other hand, there are unambiguous cases of simple inversion where the subject NP intervenes between the two elements of a compound tense as in (140a), or is otherwise unambiguously outside VP, as in (140b):

  (140) a. par quelle voye nous **est Lazaron eschapés?**

        by which way us   is L.   escaped?

        'Which way did Lazarus escape from us?'

        (ibid., l. 15100)

    b. Et ne m'a   **le medicin point ordonné** de regime?

      And not me-has the doctor   not   ordered of diet?

      'And hasn't the doctor ordered me on a diet?'

      (*CNN*: 26826)

The ambiguity of the forms in (138) introduces a significant element of indeterminacy into the trigger experience for simple inversion. By the mid/late 15th century, the only clear trigger for this construction had to involve a transitive verb (without movement of the object) or a compound tense. Also, the subject must be a non-pronominal NP; subject pronouns do not trigger simple inversion (and subject pronouns are by far the most common subjects of interrogatives in the texts we looked at). Thus, very common questions like (141–143) were all indeterminate with respect to simple inversion:

(141)   Que veut Jean?
         What wants John?

(142)   Où   va Jean?
         Where goes John?

(143)   Qu'as-tu   fait?
         What have you done?

We are thus beginning to see to what extent simple inversion was becoming 'opaque' in the trigger experience.

Since the subsequent development in the 16th century featured the retention of free inversion and the total loss of simple inversion, it seems that, although we have no synchronic means of deciding which of the structures in (137) is the correct one for the ambiguous examples like (138), at some point in the second half of the 15th century these examples began to be consistently treated as free inversion. This was another DR, which we schematize for (138b) in (144):

(144) a. $[_{CP}$ Dont$_j$ $[_{C°}$ vous + vient$]_i$ $[_{IP}$ ce mal$_k$ $[_{VP}$ t$_i$ t$_k$] t$_j$]
         $\Rightarrow$

      b. $[_{CP}$ Dont$_j$ C° $[_{IP}$ *pro* $[_{I°}$ vous + vient$]_i$ $[_{VP}$ t$_i$ ce mal] t$_j$]

Assuming that the subject is in its VP-internal base position in free inversion then at least one chain-position is saved in (144b) compared to the simple inversion structure in (144a).[32] When the parametric change took place in the early 16th century, these examples had to be treated as free inversion as the change in the mode of Nominative-assignment meant that Case theory precluded treating them as instances of the structure in (137b).

We conclude that simple inversion was on the decline in the second half of the 15th century. However, it was nevertheless possible; sentences which unambiguously had the structure (137b), e.g. (140), are still attested. No structure was eliminated at this point, but two important structures changed their status. In other words, no parametric change had yet taken place affecting the interrogative system, although up to two relevant DRs had.

Turning now to Y/NQ, we find that this construction was possible in the 15th century (unlike its 'successor' Styl-Inv, cf. 1.5, 2.4.4.1.):

(145)   **Sont pendus** ces   deux maleureux   compagnons?

Are hung   these two   unfortunate companions?

'Have these two unfortunate companions been hung?'

(*Passion*, l. 25066)

(cf. Foulet 1982: 233 for evidence that this was also the case in OF).

So we are faced with a similar situation in the case of Y/NQ as with
WHQ. A number of examples of the following kind could be analysed as
either Styl-Inv or as simple inversion in 15th-century French:

(146) a. Viendra   encores Jehan de Paris?

Will-come again   J. de P.?

'Will J. de P. come again?'

(*JdeP*, p. 61, l. 2)

b. se   fait   ainsi le   depart   de nous deux?

self does thus the departure of us   two?

'Does our departure take place like this?'

(*Passion*, l. 25364)

However, there do not seem to be as many ambiguous cases as there are
with WHQ. Y/NQ with unambiguous simple inversion decrease steadily
through the 15th century. In *Jehan de Paris* we find none at all. While
this should not be taken as indicating that the structure was impossible
by 1495, it nevertheless clearly shows the increasing rarity of this construction. *Jehan de Paris* does in fact contain one ambiguous example, namely
(146a). Here too, then, we see that simple inversion is on the decline.

In this section we have seen evidence that matrix interrogatives with
the order *NP V pron* were reanalysed in the first half of the 15th century:
formerly they had the structure in (41), after the DR they had the
structure in (123). Second, we saw evidence for a second DR during the
15th century, the one in (144) that converted many former cases of simple
inversion into cases of free inversion.

We conclude that complex inversion was introduced in the 15th century,
almost, but not quite, at the expense of simple inversion. Once again, it
is worth stressing that simple inversion nevertheless remained grammatical; we will explain both its fall from favour and its loss in 2.4.1.

The consequences of the development of complex inversion are (i)
that a class of constructions in which Nominative was as assigned under
government — namely, simple inversions — was made considerably more
infrequent and opaque, and (ii) that complex inversion, being exclusive
with V2 owing to the nature of Comp and the ECP (see 2.3.2.), provided
evidence to acquirers that French did not have a V2 system. The evidence

for V2 being already rather weak, the development of complex inversion constituted an important step away from a V2 system.

The DRs discussed in this section fed the parametric change in the Case system that took place in the early 16th century. Before moving on to the 16th century, however, we must briefly consider the status of null subjects in the 15th century.

2.3.5. *Null Subjects in Non-V2 Contexts*

In 2.2.3. and 2.2.4. we analysed OF null subjects. We saw that null subjects were licensed under government by Agr, and that V-raising was therefore necessary to license them (in this respect, our analysis coincides with Adams' 1987a, b). In 2.2.4., we suggested that certain cases of embedded null subjects were licensed in SpecAgr2' by a verb raised to Agr1° in early OF (12th-century texts generally and 13th-century verse). This possibility no longer existed in later OF, at least for referential null subjects, as Hirschbuhler (1990) shows. In later OF, referential null subjects could be licensed only in contexts where V raises to C°, i.e. in the classic V2 contexts: matrix clauses and complements to bridge verbs. The unavailability of Agr1° as a landing site for V-movement in embedded clauses is presumably due to the disappearance of this projection in the 13th century, as we suggested in 2.2.4. By the beginning of the MidFr period Agr was reduced to just one projection. So, at this period, null subjects were formally licensed under government by the single Agr°. It is for this reason that they were available only in the classic V2 contexts. This, with the further (but rather limited) possibility of expletive null subjects in some types of embedded clauses, was the situation in the 13th-century prose romance *La Queste du Saint Graal*, as reported both by Vance (1989) and Hirschbuhler (1990). See 2.2.3. and 2.2.4.

Content-licensing of null subjects was possible because the agreement paradigm was formally rich in the sense in which we defined this term in 2.2.4. Typical paradigms were morphologically uniform (cf. 2.2.3. (78)); every person had an affix. Agr was [+MU] but not [+pron], however, because there was a good deal of syncretism (in the present tense of *-er* verbs, four persons out of six had the same ending).

In MidFr null subjects underwent a major development, as recent work by Hirschbuhler and Junker (1988), Vance (1989) and Hirschbuhler (1991) has shown. The class of syntactic contexts in which null subjects were possible enlarged. The optimal analysis for this, in terms of the framework of assumptions that we have adopted here, is that it became possible to license null subjects in contexts of agreement. The importance of this development for our general concerns is, first, that it is a further case where an agreement configuration takes on some of the functional load formerly carried by a government configuration and, second, the increase

in the contexts in which null subjects could be licensed made certain
aspects of the trigger experience much more opaque than previously.
Hence the trigger experience was weighted a little more against setting
the Case-assignment parameter in (3) in such a way that Agr° assigned
Case under government.

We will now report Vance's and Hirschbuhler's data (the data in Hirschbuhler 1991 is basically a refinement of what that in Hirschbuhler and
Junker 1988, and so we report only the more recent paper). Vance discusses *Le Petit Jehan de Saintré* (*Saintré*, 1456), and Hirschbuhler Vigneulles' *Cent Nouvelles Nouvelles* (1505–1515). (Vigneulles' *Cent Nouvelles
Nouvelles* should not be confused with the anonymous *Cent Nouvelles
Nouvelles* of 1466, which was one of our sources in the previous section).

According to Vance (1989: 149f), MidFr allows referential null subjects
in three contexts where OF did not allow them: matrix V1 clauses, embedded V1 clauses (both 'conjunctional', i.e. introduced by bridge verbs, and
not) and embedded V2 contexts. Moreover, she argues that apparent
matrix V2 clauses with null subjects may be further instances of preverbal
null subjects, given the general weakening of V2 (cf. 2.3.1.). We will now
consider these cases one by one, bringing in elements from the discussion
in Hirschbuhler where necessary. In general, we will simply summarize
the authors' data and commentary, recasting their observations in terms
of our general assumptions where necessary.

a) *Matrix V1.* The frequency of matrix V1 orders increases in MidFr.
This is especially clear if comparison is made with an 'innovative' OF text,
such as *La Queste del Saint Graal*, which is the object of Vance's study
of OF. On the basis of a 700-line sample, this order is six times as frequent
in the 15th-century *Le Petit Jehan de Saintré* as in the *Graal* (Vance (1988),
Table IV, p. 151). The following are representative examples, taken from
de Kok (1985: 309):

(147) a. Et   me   dist l'on depuis . . .
         And to-me says one since . . .
         'And people have told me ever since . . .'
         (Anon., *CNN*, Tome I, T. Wright (ed.), Paris, P. Jennet, 1858,
         95)

      b. Se **appensa** de faire   ung amy   qui a
         Refl thought of making a   friend who to
         son besoing la   secourrait
         her need   her would-help

'She thought of making a friend who would help her in her need'

(*Nouvelles Françaises inédites du quinzième siècle*, E. Langlois (ed.), Paris, Champion, 1908, 15: 19)

There are two reasons to distinguish these cases of MidFr V1 from the cases of V1 of the type found in early OF texts (cf. 2.1.2.). First, OF V1 died out in the 13th century (i.e. it was a feature of 'conservative' rather than of 'innovative' OF texts). Second, OF V1 obeyed the Tobler/Mussafia Law, as we saw in 2.1.2. However, as the clitic-first order in (147b) shows, this law is not obeyed in MidFr (cf. de Kok 1985: 308f). We interpret this as indicating that the structure of MidFr V1 examples is quite different from that of the OF examples. For these reasons, examples like (149) should be analysed either as in (148a) or as in (148b):

(148) a. $[_{CP}$ *pro* $[_{C'}$ V AgrP]]

    b. $[_{AgrP}$ *pro* $[_{Agr'}$ V TP]]

The question is then one of choosing between AgrP and CP. In either case, we are forced to regard these as cases where the null subject is licensed under agreement. The considerations concerning the progressive loss of V2 that we raised in 2.3.2. strongly favour an AgrP-analysis. That is, to the extent that matrix SVO clauses could be AgrPs, sentences like those in (148) should also be treated as AgrPs. Note that null subjects are in no sense emphatic or semantically salient, so it seems clear that *pro* here cannot be treated as occupying an A'-position. We conclude, with Vance (but for different reasons), that these are instances of AgrPs. This conclusion entails that the null subject is licensed under agreement with Agr°.

Further evidence for this comes from examples of the following type, with a topicalized constituent and a null subject (Vance's (67), (68) p. 173):

(149) a. Apres mes trés humbles et tresobeissans recommandacions, pour obeir a voz prieres qui me sont entiers comandemens, **me suis** delicté a vous faire quatre beaus traictiez

    '*After my very humble and very obedient recommendations, in order to obey your wishes which are entirely commandments to me, (I) took great delight in making you four fine stories*'

    b. A ces dures et si cruelles parolles, ne **pensa** pas mains que d'estre mort

    '*At such harsh and cruel words, (he) thought no less than to be dead*'

Again, following the argument in 2.3.1. that AgrP-adjunction is in general preferred over CP-adjunction, these examples should be treated as AgrPs. If these are AgrPs, the null subjects must be in SpecAgr', licensed under agreement by Agr.

b) *Embedded V 1*. The increase in embedded V1 between the *Graal* and *Saintré*, as reported by Vance, is even more striking. As we have seen (cf. 2.2.4. (91)), embedded null subjects are restricted to two or three contexts where the null subject is expletive in the *Graal*. On the other hand, in *Saintré*, null subjects are found in a variety of embedded contexts, including *wh*-complements. This is illustrated by the following examples (Vance 1989: 150):

(150) a. Mais que **soions**   en la chambre, nous rirons

More that (we) are in the room,   we   will-laugh

'As soon as we are in the room, we will laugh'

b. Madame, je feroie tout ce   que   me **vouldriés** commander

Madame, I will-do all   that which me (you) wish to-command

'Madame, I will do all that you would command me'

If there is only one Agr-projection, as we are assuming in general for MidFr, and if CP-recursion is ruled out in these kinds of complements (cf. 1.4.), then these examples must have the structure in (151), where the null subject is licensed under agreement by Agr:

(151) $[_{CP} \ldots$ que $[_{AgrP} \text{ pro } [_{Agr'} \text{ V + Agr} \ldots]]]$

So this is a further example of the increased possibilities of MidFr null subjects.

Both Vance and Hirschbuhler point out that in these contexts the distribution of null subjects is skewed according to person. There is a clear preponderance of 3sg and 2pl null subjects: in *Saintré* 30% of subordinate null subjects are 3sg and 40% 2pl (Vance ibid.: Table V, 219); in Vigneulles' *CNN* 35.5% are 3sg and 43% 2pl (Hirschbuhler op. cit.: 77). The preponderance of 3sg null subjects is presumably attributable to the overall preponderance of 3sg subjects, whether overt or not, in any narrative text. However, the frequency of 2pl is more surprising. We concur with both Vance and Hirschbuhler in attributing this to the phonological 'richness' of 2pl morphology (usually written *-ez, -es, -és* and pronounced /e(z)/ or /e(s)/; the final consonant was probably not pronounced in non-liaison contexts in popular speech in the 15th century (Brunot 1905, Vol. I: 494)). This greater phonological prominence more readily permitted recovery of the features of the null subject. In a system where the content of null subjects is licensed by the systematic presence of an agreement affix, it is unsurprising that the phonologically more distinct affixes should show a statistical preference of this kind for licensing null subjects. We will return to this point directly.

Another factor seems to play a role in licensing these null subjects, one discussed in detail for CNN by Hirschbuhler. Embedded null subjects are clearly preferred in clauses where $C°$ is [+wh] (although Hirschbuhler also points out some complications to this statement, for example that [+wh] *que* in $C°$ does not appear to be able to license *pro* — we have nothing to add to Hirschbuhler's discussion of these points). It is striking that $C°$ [+wh] licenses an expletive null subject in ModFr, in Styl-Inv constructions. It seems natural to treat this phenomenon as a contributory factor in the development of Styl-Inv, a matter we take up in 2.4.4.1., where we will suggest an account of how the ModFr restriction to expletive null subjects in Styl-Inv contexts came about.

For the MidFr situation, it is tempting to treat the preference for null subjects in $C°$ [+wh] complements as a statistical tendency. However, this preference interacts with the preference for 2pl null subjects in a way which suggests that the situation is more complex. Hirschbuhler points out that in non-V2, non-*wh* complements almost the only referential null subjects are 2pl (see Table 1, given in 2.4.3.). Thus, in Vigneulles, the configurations in (152a–c) are found with embedded null subjects, but not that in (152d):

(152) a. [$_{CP}$ $C°$ [+wh] [$_{AgrP}$ *pro* . . .

     b. [$_{CP}$ $C°$ [$_{CP}$ XP V [$_{AgrP}$ *pro* . . .

     c. [$_{CP}$ $C°$ [$_{AgrP}$ *pro* {[2pl], [−ref]} . . .

     d. [$_{CP}$ $C°$ [$_{AgrP}$ *pro* [¬2pl], [+ref] . . .

In Vance's data, a clear tendency in the same direction is apparent (if we count 1pl null subjects as having similar possibilities to 2pl ones). Moreover, there are no clear examples in *Saintré* of the configuration in (152d); Vance's Table V (p. 219) gives three cases of 3pl null subjects, but since they all involve bridge verbs, these are instances of (152b). There is also the following example with a 1sg null subject (although *se* ('if') could be treated as [+wh] here, in which case this example would be an instance of (152a)):

(153)   et se n'**eusse**   esté bien tost secorue, . . .

        and if not-had (I) been well soon rescued, . . .

        'and if I hadn't been rescued immediately, . . .'

        (Vance's (167), p. 239)

Thus there are no clear cases of (152d) in *Saintré*.

The facts reported by Hirschbuhler suggest that an account along the lines of that proposed by Dupuis (1988) for OF may in fact be correct for MidFr. We earlier rejected Dupuis' analysis of OF on the grounds that it represented an unnecessary weakening of Rizzi's theory of null subjects by splitting formal licensing from identification (cf. (6)). Such a move significantly complicates our proposed parametrization of null-subject languages, since it is unclear which part of the licensing condition should be parametrized. Moreover, such a move would predict the existence of eight different types of null-subject language, and there is no cross-linguistic evidence for this. However, ascribing formal licensing and identification of *pro* to different heads as intrinsic properties of those heads is compatible with Rizzi's idea that a single head licenses a null subject, as long as the heads are combined when licensing takes place at SS. So we propose, for this stage of French, that Agr° had the features which identified *pro*'s content, while C° was the formal licenser. These two heads thus had to combine to meet both parts of the licensing condition in (6). Thus, we expect that just at the time that regular Agr-to-C movement, i.e. V2, is being lost, the null-subject system is destabilized. In fact, the data in (147–153) force us to say that, at least for a transitional period, Agr° was able to both formally license and identify a null subject **if C° was absent**. If C° was present, however, only 2pl Agr° had this capacity.

So we propose the following account of the array of data in (152). C°, when present, is the formal licenser for null subjects. It can only license referential null subjects when it hosts Agr° or when it bears the [+wh] feature. Equally, when C° is present Agr° can identify *pro* but not formally license it, unless it is 2pl. 2pl agreement is able to both formally license and content-license null subjects under any conditions, whether C° is present or not. In this sense, [2pl] is the pendant in the agreement system of [+wh] in the C-system. When C° is absent (or perhaps inert in the way it is at SS in declarative non-V2 clauses), Agr° can formally license and identify any person. This captures the facts of Vigneulles' *CNN* and of *Saintré*.

The system just described seems rather strange, and might be considered to be purely an artefact of the texts in question. However, Poletto (forthcoming) arrives at a remarkably similar analysis of Renaissance Veneto. As we shall see in 2.4.3., Medieval Veneto shows a relationship between V2 and null subjects which is very close to the OF one (see 2.4.3. for examples and references). At the Renaissance period, V2 was decaying, and null subjects appear either where C° is [+wh] or with particular persons of the verb (in this instance 1Sg and 1Pl). In combination with what we have just seen, Poletto's data and analysis suggest that systems of this sort arise where the productive licensing and identification of null subjects by the Agr°/C° combination that V2 creates breaks down, owing to the weakening of V2. Systems like this seem genuinely transitional, in that both in Veneto and in French they were followed by the complete loss of null subjects (null subjects have subsequently been reintroduced in Veneto — see 2.4.3.).

This approach to licensing *pro* entails that (6a), the general statement of formal licensing, should be altered in the following way:

(6a′)   If X° licenses *pro* in configuration Y, then X° either **dominates** or **is** a potential Case-marker of *pro*'s position in Y.

So, since C° is not a Case-assigner, C° must contain Agr° in order to license *pro*.

This approach to null subjects is a slight modification of the version of Rizzi's approach that we proposed in 2.0. However, it retains an account the central fact about the OF system: the necessary connection between null subjects, Case assignment and V2 in OF. The case where C° or C° [+wh] licenses a null subject does not fall under either (6a′) or the earlier (6a). This exception is not limited to MidF and Renaissance Veneto; it is also relevant for ModF Styl-Inv and, if the analysis proposed in 1.5. is correct, for free inversion in Italian interrogatives. Clearly, our approach implies that some property unconnected to Case-assignment allows C° to license null subjects, although we will not speculate here as to what this might be (see also Notes 12 and 14 of Chapter 3).

Putting these complexities aside, the important point for our purposes is that any Agr was able to identify *pro* under agreement, since the verbal paradigm was [+MU]. Moreover, in matrix AgrPs where the C-system is not activated any Agr is able to formally license *pro*. So, Agr consistently plays a role in licensing null subjects in a configuration of agreement.

c) *Embedded V2*. The cases that are of interest here involve the fronting of some constituent in a *wh*-complement. The fact that the complements in question are *wh*-complements means that they are not V2 complements, i.e. the verb is not raised to C° here (cf. 1.4.). Rather, they are cases of topicalization by adjunction to AgrP of the kind discussed in 2.3.1. Although we only discuss cases of *wh*-complements, i.e. cases where a CP-recursion analysis like (152b) is ruled out, it should be clear that cases which are in principle amenable to a CP-recursion analysis could be analysed in this way, once topicalization to AgrP became possible (although such a move would call into question the generalizations that we made on the basis of (152), since it would allow null subjects in the context (152d) in embedded clauses).

Here is an example of a null subject in a seemingly 'V2' complement with [+wh] C° from Vance ((134), p. 227), and one from Hirschbuhler ((20), p. 76):

(154) a. Madame, qui de ces   parolles estoit si aise
Madame, who of these words   was   so happy

que plus ne **pouoit**
that more not could

'Madame, who was so happy that she couldn't be happier . . .'

   b. tant   fist   par ses journées que en brief temps **vint**
   so-much (he) did in   his days   that in short time (he) came

   'he rode so hard by day that in a short time he came'

   (Vigneulles *CNN* 081010)

This order is very common in relatives; note the close similarity to Styl-F of the type discussed for OF in 2.1.2. We nevertheless treat these examples as involving adjunction to AgrP, since Styl-F proper is associated with other properties of OF, and may be somehow linked to the Agr-recursion structure. Here is an example with a relative clause (also from Hirschbuhler op. cit.):

(155)   compte-moi . . . comment celle faute   que envers
   tell me . . .   how   this wrong that towards

   moi   a   commis
   me (he) has done

   'tell me . . . how this wrong that he has done to me'

   (Vigneulles *CNN* 094044)

The embedded clauses in these examples have the following structure:

(156) $[_{CP}\ C°\ [+wh]\ [_{AgrP}\ XP\ [_{AgrP}\ pro\ [_{Agr'}\ V + Agr\ .\ .\ .]]]]$

The null subject is licensed by C° [+wh] in the manner described above.

d) *Matrix V 2.* The remarks just made open up the possibility that even matrix clauses with V2 order are instances of null subjects licensed under agreement (cf. again 2.3.1.). Therefore, it becomes possible, in principle, to consider examples of the 'classic' OF null-subject configuration, that found in matrix V2 clauses, as instances where the null subject is licensed under agreement. Here it becomes clear to what extent the greater MidFr liberty of distribution of null subjects destabilized the former system.

Vance provides circumstantial evidence that some clauses of this type should be analysed as being AgrPs with an adjoined constituent and a preverbal *pro*. The idea is to infer the position of *pro* from the possible positions of overt subject pronouns. One such case is the following (Vance's (100), p. 206):

(157)   Et quant Saintré fut prest pour monter a cheval, **print** congié
         de son hoste et de pluseurs autres

         '*And when Saintré was ready to get on his horse, (he) took leave
         of his host and of several others*'

If an overt subject appears in such a sentence in *Saintré*, it is always
preverbal. This suggests that the CP (*quant Saintré* . . .) here is adjoined
to AgrP, and that the clause is an AgrP with the null subject in SpecAgr'
licensed by Agr under agreement. It is clear that the density of cases of
null subjects licensed under agreement in matrix V2 clauses depends on
the status of V2 at this point. If matrix clauses were no longer analysed
as V2, then we are forced to consider that null subjects are licensed (by
Agr°) under agreement here.

In conclusion, both Vance and Hirschbuhler give convincing evidence
that MidFr allowed null subjects in contexts where they were not allowed
in (late) OF: in initial position in matrix clauses and in subordinate clauses.
In a sense, this is a surprising development; a simple comparison of OF,
a null-subject language, with ModFr, a non-null-subject language, might
lead to the expectation that MidFr would be a weak null-subject language
in some sense, perhaps in just allowing expletive null subjects. Moreover,
as we saw in 2.2.3., the agreement system of MidFr was fairly poor, but
in essence neither significantly poorer nor significantly richer than that of
OF and at least early ModFr.[33] Nevertheless, we find a clear increase in
the number of syntactic contexts in which null subjects are possible.

This change in the distribution of null subjects has to be treated as a
change in the licensing conditions for *pro*. It is also related to the ongoing
demise of V2. Following Vance (1989), we propose that the connection
with the loss of V2 is that null subjects were previously possible in
SpecAgr' in matrix clauses with the order *XP V pro* and when these
clauses started to be analysed as AgrPs, **null subjects remained possible
in this position**. But now the position of the null subject relative to the
inflected verb (i.e. to Agr°) had changed, since the position of the inflected
verb had changed. This is because the DR in (119) changes *XP V pro* into
XP pro V, with XP adjoined to AgrP in the new structure. Hence, the
licensing condition for *pro* had to change since it formerly depended on
the combination of Agr° and C° that we find in V2. As we saw above
Agr° and C° continue to interact in complex ways when the C-system is
activated. But when the C-system is not activated Agr simply licenses a
null subject under agreement. This is a case where a DR which simplified
the grammar from the point of view of reducing the number of positions
in chains (cf. the discussion (119) in 2.3.2.) complicated the grammar in
another respect, as it is clear that the new licensing conditions for *pro*
were more complex than the old ones.

We want to maintain that the licensing conditions changed minimally.

One way to say this would be to alter the view put forward in 2.2. and maintain that C° was **always** the formal licenser of null subjects (or at least from the time of the loss of Agr1P, cf. 2.2.4.). Formal licensing and identification were nevertheless effected by the same head, i.e. the C + Agr resulting from Agr-to-C movement. By the late 15th century, however, Agr-to-C movement was waning in frequency, for the reasons we have seen in the earlier sections, and so the formal licensing and identification properties were associated with heads that did not combine at SS, with the complex results we have seen here. In this system, Agr identifies *pro* under agreement, a fact which further weakens V2 and creates more pressure for the parametric change in the Case-assignment system that came later. As we mentioned above, the system described here was short-lived, and seems genuinely transitional. We will return in 2.4.3. to the question of how null subjects were finally lost from French (*modulo* Styl-Inv).

To repeat, the importance of the developments discussed in this section for our general account of the history of French is (i) that agreement relations became important for a further class of constructions in which government relations had formerly played a crucial role, and (ii) that the increased distribution of null subjects rendered the former V2 system more opaque. For acquirers of French c1500, there was much less evidence for simple inversion — whether declarative or interrogative — than there had been c1400.

2.3.6. *Conclusion*

This concludes our discussion of MidFr. The results of this discussion emerge most clearly if we briefly reconsider the major properties of interest in OF, which we summarized in (95):

(95) a.   Simple inversion in interrogatives

   b.   V2 (of a type very close to Germanic)

   c.   Null subjects

   d.   Non-clitic preverbal nominative pronouns

   e.   Clitic postverbal nominative pronouns

None of these properties of OF disappears in MidFr, but they all change status. Simple inversion in interrogatives is rivalled both by complex inversion and by free inversion, thanks to the DRs discussed in 2.3.4. V2 erodes significantly, to the point where matrix SVO clauses can be AgrP (thanks to another DR, cf. 2.3.2.), matrix XSVO clauses are fairly common, and must be treated as AgrPs (2.3.1.), and matrix V2 clauses with null subjects are also possibly XSVO clauses with a preverbal null subject

(2.3.5.). Moreover, SVO starts to become the clearly predominant main-clause order (2.3.2.). The distribution of null subjects widens between OF and MidFr, as outlined above. This too can be seen as a reflex of the DR which reanalysed matrix SVO clauses as AgrP rather than CP. Also, nominative pronouns are reduced in distribution so that full complementary distribution with tonic, diachronically oblique pronouns emerges. In 2.3.3., we took this development as indicating that the status of the atonic nominative pronouns changes in that they become fully clitic pronouns in the sense of not having a Case feature. Therefore they must always incorporate for visibility, preferably by SS.

As we have said, each of the OF constructions in (95a–c) was evidence for, and depended on, the possibility of Nominative Case being assigned in configurations of government. That these constructions did not disappear in MidFr (they were all still grammatical in 1500 − cf. the data from Vigneulles' *Cent Nouvelles Nouvelles* in 2.4.1.) shows that the parameter determining Nominative assignment in (3) did not change before 1500. However, owing to the DRs that we have discussed, the evidence available to the acquirer of French in 1500 that this parameter was set for government was considerably impoverished in comparison with that available to the acquirer in 1300. Simple inversion in interrogatives was rivalled by complex inversion, a construction in which Nominative is assigned by agreement. The reanalysis of SVO clauses as AgrP rather than CP meant that a large class of instances of Nominative-assignment under government was replaced by evidence of assignment under agreement; the associated increase in the overall proportion of SVO clauses decreased the evidence in favour of a government-based system still further. The possibility of licensing null subjects under agreement had exactly the same effect, and the clitic nature of nominative pronouns (i.e. their lack of a Case feature) contributed still further to the same process.

The constructions in (95a–c) were all lost or obsolescent by 1600 and are (with the exception of expletive null subjects in Styl-Inv) totally impossible in contemporary French. The topic of the next section is the examination of the parametric change which explains the disappearance of these constructions.

2.4. THE SIXTEENTH CENTURY AND AFTER

This section is primarily concerned with the parametric change that took place in the 16th century. Our claim is that the parameter governing the assignment of Nominative Case changed at this time, in such a way that the option of Nominative-assignment under government was excluded. This led to the elimination from the grammar of French of the three constructions in (97a–c): simple inversion, V2 and null subjects. In the subsections below, we will discuss the loss of each of these constructions in turn.

First, however, a word on the relation between parametric changes of this kind and the current conception of a 'parameter-setting' account of language acquisition (Chomsky 1981, Hyams 1985, Lightfoot 1989).

It is difficult to see how parametric changes can be fully explained in terms of properties of the trigger experience alone (except perhaps in cases of massive bilingualism, etc., which was not the situation in 16th-century France (or 16th-century England; cf. Chapter 3)). In the case of a change like the one in question, it is not enough to simply claim that the relevant trigger experience simply became defective or ambiguous at a certain point; French had retained fully productive simple inversion/V2 constructions for several centuries (and note that null subjects survived the restructuring and apparent 'impoverishment' of the agreement system in the 12th/13th centuries — cf. 2.2.3.) and so for a number of generations the trigger experience concerning the modes of Nominative-assignment was fully adequate. Although the defectiveness of the trigger experience is obviously relevant, in that it is clear that the factors discussed in the previous section reduced the density of the evidence for Nominative-assignment under government and thereby played a causal role in the parametric change, the question is always begged to some degree: why should the trigger experience change non-randomly unless the grammar underlying it has changed? This line of investigation leads to the possibility of an unproductive regression if we attempt to account for changes in the grammar solely in terms of defective trigger experience.

Moreover, since one of the major contentions of generative grammar is that language acquisition is vastly underdetermined by the data to which acquirers are exposed, and since it is widely assumed that syntactic changes are rooted in the acquisition process, it seems strange to assume that syntactic changes are caused by defective trigger experience. Instead, we will propose, very much in the spirit of Lightfoot (1979), that there are strategies of acquisition which interact with the trigger experience in such a way as to give rise to syntactic changes.

We propose that there are two such strategies: one is the Least Effort Strategy, introduced in 2.3.2. (115). The other is essentially the Subset Principle of Berwick (1985). We have already discussed the role played by the LES in language change, and so we will say no more about it here. We give the following informal statement of the Subset Principle:

(158)   Acquirers choose the smallest grammar compatible with the trigger experience.

Here 'smallest' means 'capable of generating the smallest set of grammatical sentence-types'. Thus where the trigger experience is compatible with two grammars G_1 and G_2, where G_1 generates the set of sentence-types

$\{P_1 \ldots P_n\}$ and G_2 the set $\{P_1 \ldots P_m\}$ and $n > m$, G_2 is to be preferred. 'Preferred' in this context means 'assumed in the absence of data to the contrary'. So for an acquirer to posit G_1 in the situation just sketched, s/he would need direct positive evidence, i.e. would need to hear some sentence-type unambiguously generated by G_1 but not by G_2.

We interpret (158) as applying to parameter-setting. As we mentioned in the introduction to this chapter, it is possible to think of parameters as yes/no questions, and, at least for purposes of exposition, formulate the questions in such a way that a 'yes' answer permits a certain class of structures which a 'no' answer excludes.[34] In that case, (158) means, quite simply, that 'no' is the default answer; for a 'yes' answer, unambiguous positive data is needed. So let us now reconsider our formulation of the Nominative-assignment parameter given in (3) (cf. also 1.2. (50)):

(3) a.   Agr° assigns Nominative under government? Yes/no.
    b.   Agr° assigns Nominative under agreement? Yes/no.

The interaction of the Subset Principle with a set of parametric choices like that in (3) should be clear; choosing the 'yes' option for both (3a) and (3b) should be dispreferred by acquirers in the sense that positive, unambiguous trigger experience will be needed to fix the parameter in this way. Now we can begin to see what must have happened in the late 15th/early 16th century leading up to the change in (3a): the crucial data giving a 'yes' answer for (3a) become amenable to some other analysis, and so this option is no longer selected, with the result that the structures that depend on this setting are lost.[35]

With these remarks on the relationship of the trigger experience to parameter-setting in mind, we can now turn to the discussion of our parameter change. The discussion centres around the loss of various constructions, in part since we have claimed that this is the clearest sign of a parametric change and in part since we are concerned with the move from a 'superset grammar' to a 'subset grammar'.

2.4.1. *The Loss of Simple Inversion*

The first change to discuss is the loss of the order *(WH) V NP[-pron] X* in questions. In our discussion of the development of complex inversion in the 15th century in 2.3.4. we saw that, if the fairly large number of examples which are ambiguous between simple inversion and free inversion are analysed as free inversion, simple inversion undergoes a fairly clear decline in the 15th century. This decline can be attributed to the emergence of two alternative interrogative constructions: complex inversion and *(qu)'est-ce que*. We discussed the origin of the former construction in detail in 2.3.4. Concerning the latter, Foulet (1921: 251ff) shows that it largely lost its former emphatic force (in OF it was most likely akin

to English '(wh) is it that') and became an alternative interrogative form
in the 15th century, a development that Foulet links to the cliticization of
ce.

In purely quantitative terms, then, we expect simple inversion to be
less frequent given the emergence of these alternatives. However, it is not
excluded in the 15th century, as the sentences in (140), which we repeat
here, show:

(140) a. par quelle voye nous **est Lazaron** eschapés?

       by which way us   is L.   escaped?

       'Which way did Lazarus escape from us?'

    b. Que **voelt ceste parolle** dire?

       What wants this word   to-say?

       'What does this word mean?'

In percentage terms, a mean 4.125% of matrix interrogatives in the 15th-
century texts we looked at were unambiguous cases of simple inversion of
this type.

In the 16th century, however, simple inversion disappears. Foulet (ibid.:
250) claims that it is no longer found in Rabelais (1530s). He does,
however, give the following example from Calvin's *Insitution de la Religion
Chrétienne* (1536):

(159)   **Ignoroit l'ancienne Eglise** quelle compagnie Jesus Christ eust
      admise à sa Cene?

      *'Ignored the old Church what company J.C. would have admit-
      ted to his Last Supper?'*

Foulet suggests, however, that this is a consciously archaic usage at this
point. Our examination of Vigneulles' *Cent Nouvelles Nouvelles* (1505–
15), excerpts from Rabelais (*Gargantua* and *Pantagruel*), Volume One of
the *Institution de la Réligion Chrétienne* and du Bellay's *Deffence et
Illustration de la Langue Françoyse* (1549) revealed just one clear case of
simple inversion. This is the following:

(160)   Pourquoi **sont nos heures** en temps de moisson et de vedanges
      courtes?

      *'Why are our hours at the time of harvest and grape-harvest
      short?'*

      (Rabelais, *Gargantua*, Ch. 27, l. 46)

(This suggests that Foulet's statement concerning Rabelais was not entirely accurate). Similarly, we find no examples of this sort in the 17th-
century text we checked: d'Aubigné's *Lettres* (1583–1630).

However, there are a number of examples which are in principle ambiguous between free inversion and simple inversion (i.e., between the two structures in (137)). These are cases of *WH V NP* orders with an intransitive verb (or with a transitive verb and an extracted object) in a non-compound tense, i.e. examples of the type in (161):

(161) a. que **fera**   donc le   **paouvre pécheur** ...?

   what will-do then the poor   sinner ...?

   'What will the poor sinner do then?'

   (Calvin, *Inst.*, p. 173)

   b. mais où **sont voz oyes**?

   '*but where are your geese?*'

   (Vigneulles, *CNN*, XIX: 14)

   c. Quel **est l'espoir de son étude**?

   '*What is the hope of his study?*'

   (Rabelais, *Gargantua*, Prologue: 1. 61)

We also find quite unambiguous examples of free inversion in these texts, of the following kind:

(162) a. Pourquoy donc **sont couronnez les fidèles**?

   Why   then are   crowned   the faithful?

   'Why are the faithful crowned then?'

   (Calvin, *Inst.*, p. 170)

   b. Mais de   où   deable **peut venir cecy**?

   But from where devil   can come this?

   'But where the devil can this come from?'

   (Vigneulles, *CNN*, XX: 105)

   c. Pourquoy doncques **ont   voyaigé les Anciens Grecz** ...?

   Why   then   have travelled the Ancient Greeks ...?

   'Why then did the ancient Greeks travel ...?

   (du Bellay, *Deffence*, I: x)

Since we find almost no unambiguous examples of simple inversion the decision to treat ambiguous examples of the type in (161) as free inversion seems justified (just as we would treat analogous examples in present-day French as free inversion, i.e. Styl-Inv). When the parameter changed, these sentences had to be reanalysed as free inversion.

As in earlier periods, we also find instances of free inversion in Y/NQ.

This construction is not very common, however; we found two examples
in Rabelais and one in Vigneulles:

(163) a. Ne **périrait**   **le noble art d'imprimerie**?

       Would-not-perish the noble art of printing?

       'Wouldn't the noble art of printing perish?'

       (Rabelais, *Pantagruel, Tiers Livre*, Ch. 51, 1. 10)

    b. **t'est venue ceste doleur** ainsi soudaine comme tu   dis?

       you-is come this   pain   so   suddenly as   you say?

       'Did this pain come to you as suddenly as you say?'

       (Vigneulles, *CNN*, XCIII: 74)

Foulet (op. cit.: 251) quotes the following lines from d'Aubigné's *Tra-giques* (completed in 1589, published in 1616), noting that this is a very
stylistically marked context (these are the last lines of a prayer):

(164)   Ne **partiront** jamais du throsne où tu sieds
       Et la Mort et l'Enfer qui dorment à tes pieds?

       '*Will go never from the throne where you sit,*
       Death and Hell which sleep at your feet?'

This construction is prescribed against from the 17th century on (Brunot
1905, Vol III: 670). See 2.4.4.1. on the loss of this and its retention in *wh*
(and other) contexts, giving rise to ModFr Styl-Inv.

We can conclude from this discussion that simple inversion was elimin-ated from the grammar of French in the first quarter of the 16th century,
surviving as a literary option into the 1530s (the time of the Calvin and
Rabelais texts), but completely gone by the second half of the century.

What caused this structure to die out at this point? It is clearly not
adequate to attribute this simply to the competition of other interrogative
constructions like complex inversion and (*qu'*) *est-ce que*. Moreover, these
new alternatives are more complex, both in an obvious intuitive sense
and in terms of the number of chain-positions they require, than simple
inversion. As we have said, we attribute the elimination of this construc-tion to Case theory; once the Nominative-assignment parameter changed
(i.e. once the negative option of (3a) was chosen), there was no way for
an NP in SpecAgr' to receive Case if Agr-to-C raising had taken place.
This approach is clearly of greater explanatory value than appeal to a
notion of competition.

The question now becomes: what led to the change of the Nominative-assignment parameter at this point? We suggest that this was indirectly
due to the development of complex inversion and the erosion of V2, 15th-century developments that we described at length in 2.3. It may be enough

to postulate that the erosion of V2 interacted with the Subset Principle and the LES in such a way as to eliminate Nominative-assignment under government (especially given the evidence from Northern Italian dialects that a similar change has taken place apparently independently of complex inversion — see 2.4.3.). However, we will briefly speculate in how the introduction of complex inversion may have destabilized the older system still further.

In interrogatives in a typical V2 language like OF or Modern German, there are two reasons for Agr° to move to C°: the necessity of realizing C°'s [+wh]-feature, and fact that C° morphologically selects Agr°. In such a system, then, the C° of a matrix interrogative is [+wh, +Agr]. However, in a system where V2 is eroding, C° no longer obligatorily morphologically selects Agr°, hence the trigger for obligatory movement to C° must be the [+wh] feature, as in English (cf. 1.4.). So Agr-to-C movement in interrogatives does not provide evidence to acquirers that C° is [+Agr], and there is no independent general requirement for C° to be [+Agr]. Moreover, the existence of complex inversion shows acquirers that [+wh] C° **cannot** be [+Agr] (cf. 2.3.4. on why complex inversion and V2 are incompatible). So [+wh] C° was consistently analysed as [-Agr]. This meant that any matrix interrogative C° could in principle have a double specifier; again, the existence of complex inversion showed that this option was in fact exploited by the grammar (complex inversion was permitted for the reasons connected with cliticization that we discussed in 1.5.).

In this situation, acquirers would naturally attempt to generalize the 'double-specifier' structure to all matrix interrogatives, including simple inversion. So suppose that simple inversion was assigned the double-specifier structure like complex inversion:[36]

(165) $[_{CP/AgrP}$ Q $[_{C'/Agr'}$ *pro* $[_{C'/Agr'}$ V +Agr . . .

This was a possible analysis of simple inversion from the time of the introduction of complex inversion (presumably in the second half of the 15th century). In this structure, the Uniqueness Condition on Licensing (47) (cf. also (119') of 1.5.) is violated owing to the presence of *pro* in the second (A−) Spec of C'/Agr'. In (165), C° must license Q and Agr° must Case-mark the subject; therefore neither of them is able to license *pro* without violating (47). The alternative is to assume either that C° is [+wh, +Agr] here; this would give a 'single-specifier' structure, but as we have seen it is an assumption with no positive motivation, and real counterevidence elsewhere. The result is that, while not strictly ungrammatical, there is no natural way to integrate simple-inversion structures into a system which had developed complex inversion and was losing V2. Another way of putting this may be to say that simple inversion became highly marked with respect to the rest of the system after complex inversion had been introduced.

So we claim that soon after the introduction of complex inversion, simple inversion became 'opaque' in that it was either assigned a structure at the C-level which was quite distinct from that of other typical matrix interrogatives (in having a single pre-C° specifier) or, if it had two pre-C° specifiers, it was ruled out by (47). This was what led to simple inversion being largely replaced by the alternative interrogative structures. Due to its opacity simple inversion was not an active part of the trigger experience, and so it did not block the change in the Nominative-assignment parameter (which the Subset Principle and general strategies of parameter-setting discussed earlier favoured).

Other cases of inversion are not rendered opaque in this way, however. In subject-clitic inversion, Agr° does not Case-mark the clitic and so is able to (formally) license *pro*. Note that, given what we said about null subjects in 2.3.5., this *pro* could be referential, giving a kind of null-subject complex-inversion structure. We cannot assume that this is the modern structure in subject-clitic inversion, since Styl-Inv, which also involves an expletive *pro*, is incompatible with this operation – cf. Kayne (1983), Rizzi and Roberts (1989), 1.5. The double-specifier structure was eliminated from subject-clitic inversion when null subjects were eliminated in contexts where they were licensed under agreement – cf. 2.4.3. (This conclusion depends on the interpretation of (47) we arrived at in Note 32, where we concluded that (47i) applies to individual components of complex heads, while (47ii) applies to complex heads taken as a whole).

As things stand, we expect that *WH V NP[-pron] X* may have remained possible after *V NP X* disappeared, since in this construction there was the possibility of C° licensing *pro*. Brunot gives some evidence (1905, III: 670) that this may have been the case:

(166) a. Pourquoy n'**auront pas ces pauvres aveuglez** usé de mesme liberté?

      'Why would have not these poor blind (people) used the same freedom?'

      (1619, Fornier *Discours Académiques de l'origine de l'âme*)

   b. De quelle attaque plus cruelle **pouvoit la fortune** blesser mon contentement?
      'From what attack more cruel could fortune wound my happiness?

      (1621, Nervèze *Amours Diverses*)

If *pas* is in a position higher than the subject here (cf. the suggestion we made regarding (68) and (69) in 2.2.2.), then (168a) could be a case of simple inversion. On the other hand, we could take the position of *pas* to be as in ModF, in which case this example would not involve simple inversion, but would instead be a case of free inversion combined with extraposition of the category headed by the participle. (166b) is also problematic, but a similar analysis to the second alternative proposed for (166a) may be tenable here, although we have no direct evidence for it. Or again, we might treat this example as an isolated survival of simple inversion (in a literary context). In any case, examples of this type, Brunot (ibid.) implies, are rare; there are none in the 16th-century texts we looked at.

The evidence indicates, then, that there is no significant difference between WHQ and Y/NQ regarding the disappearance of simple inversion. Let us see why. The structure that we are concerned with is the following:

(167)

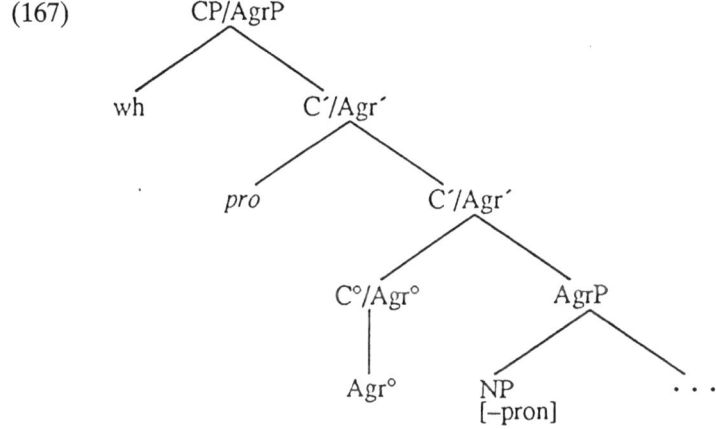

We need to see why C°/Agr° cannot license *pro* here. The answer is clear: this head cannot simultaneously Case-mark NP, and formally license *pro* (cf. the discussion of comparable Italian examples in 1.5., where the positions of *pro* and NP are reversed). These elements are both in A-positions, and one of them is overt, so (47ii) applies (i.e. the part of (47) that applies to complex heads taken as a whole).

Evidence for this rather intricate system comes from a noteworthy gap in the data from this period. There are no Y/NQ with null subjects (we saw in footnotes 4 and 5 that this construction was already rare in OF). Thus structures of the following type are excluded:

(168)   *$[_{CP/AgrP}$ Q $[_{C'/Agr'}$ *pro* $[_{C'/Agr'}$ C°/Agr° $[_{AgrP}$ *pro* . . .

(47) blocks this structure; Agr/C must formally license the *pro* in SpecAgr' and so cannot license the one in SpecAgr'/C', or vice versa. So this structure is banned (it exists in Gréban, where we found the first instances of complex inversion; however, we can assume that the double-specifier structure was not fully generalized in interrogatives at that point).

On the other hand, we find a few cases of null subjects in WHQ in Rabelais and in Vigneulles:

(169) a. **Que** vous en **semble**?

   What to-you of-it seems?

   'How does it seem to you?'

   (Vigneulles, CNN, LIX: 109)

   b. **Que** n'**avés**   aussi bien soufflé les *Kyriez* . . . ?

   Why not-have (you) as   well played the Kyrie . . . ?

   'Why didn't play the *Kyrie* as well as . . . ?'

   (Vigneulles, *CNN*, LXI: 193)

   c. **Comment** vous va?

   How   you goes?

   'How is it going?'

   (Vigneulles, *CNN*, XCIX: 315)

   d. Cela, **que signifie**?

   That what means?

   'What does that mean?'

   (Rabelais, *Pantagruel*, *Tiers Livre*, Ch. 47, l. 3)

In all these cases the null subject is expletive, except in (169b), where it is 2pl. How does Agr°/C° license the two 'null subjects'? A possible solution is that these examples do not involve Agr-to-C movement, but are instead cases of free inversion (or, rather stylistic inversion, since they are comparable on this view to examples like (210) of 2.4.4.1.) with the inflected verb in Agr°. In that case, Agr° licenses the single occurrence of *pro* in SpecAgr' under agreement. Support for this comes from the fact that the null subjects that we find here correspond to those found in (152c) (see 2.3.5.).

Finally, the Uniqueness Condition on Licensing (47) is confirmed by the absence of examples of complex inversion with null subjects. This structure is ruled out for the same reason as in Northern Italian dialects and in Standard Italian (cf. 1.5.): C°/Agr° cannot both Case-mark a preceding NP and license a following *pro*.

In this section, we have covered the central topic of this chapter, giving an account of the loss of simple inversion in interrogatives. To summarize, simple inversion was ruled out by the change in the value of the Nominative-assignment parameter. This came about since the presence of complex inversion led to simple inversion being analysed in a way that was suffi-

ciently 'marked' or 'opaque' as to make it inactive in the trigger experience, permitting the change in the parameter (to which we suggested that
acquirers are predisposed by the Subset Principle). Our assumptions about
licensing *pro*, and in particular the Uniqueness Condition on Licensing,
play a major role here. To the extent that this account works, these
assumptions are justified.

In the next sections, we will try to show how the other constructions of
(95) were lost as a result of the change in the Nominative-assignment
parameter, in an attempt to show that our proposal has genuine explanatory value.

2.4.2. *The Loss of V2*

In 2.3.1. and 2.3.2. we discussed the erosion of V2 in MidFr. Our conclusion was that MidFr was an optional V2 language, in the sense that $C°$
optionally carried the feature [+Agr], giving the effect of optional Agr-
to-C raising in matrix clauses and certain classes of embedded clauses (cf.
1.4. for discussion of the class of V2 clauses). We suggested an account
of the transition from obligatory to optional V2 in 2.3.2. which was based
essentially on the LES. Here we will document and analyse the further
transition from optional to impossible V2, a transition which took place
in the 16th century.

The examples in (170) illustrate our claim about the history of French:

(170) a. Hier   a   Jean mangé

       Yesterday has John eaten

   b. Hier   Jean a   mangé

       Yesterday John has eaten

(170b) was impossible in OF, since Agr-to-C movement was obligatory in
matrix clauses owing to the presence of the [+Agr] feature in $C°$ (cf. 1.4.,
2.1.2.) and adverb-adjunction to CP is in general impossible (cf. 2.3.1.).
(170b) was possible due to (a) the possibility of XP-movement to SpecC';
(b) Agr-to-C movement; (c) Nominative-Case assignment under government.

In MidFr, as we saw in 2.3.1. and 2.3.2., (170b) becomes possible, while
(170a) remains possible. We interpreted the appearance of sentences like
(170b) as evidence that Agr-to-C raising was no longer obligatory; however, the continued appearance of sentences like (170a) shows that this
movement was nevertheless possible, and also shows that Nominative-
assignment under government was still possible. In ModFr, (170a) is impossible, since Nominative-assignment under government is impossible,
and since $C°$ can no longer carry the [+Agr] feature. What we wish to
propose here is that $C°$ became unable to carry the [+Agr] feature pre-

cisely because the Nominative-assignment parameter changed. Thus the change in the Nominative-assignment parameter is not responsible for the **decline** in V2, as that began much earlier, but is responsible for the **elimination** of V2; this is consistent with our overall view of syntactic change, in that the elimination of structures is associated with parametric changes, but changes in frequency and status (e.g. optional vs. obligatory V2) of structures may be the consequence of lower-level factors, typically DRs.

We find that the two developments discussed in 2.3.1. and 2.3.2. (increasing frequency of $V > 2$ orders and of SVO orders) continue in the 16th century, to the point where V2 is eliminated in all but a rather restricted class of cases, involving a restricted class of adverbs (*ainsi* ('thus'), *peut-être* ('perhaps') and others; see below).

We now consider the relevant developments one by one.

a) $V > 2$ *orders*. In 2.3.1. we saw that this order increased in frequency between OF and MidFr. The mean frequency of $V > 2$ in the OF texts listed in (96) is 5.5% (3.4% if the anomalous-seeming *Perceval* is disregarded); in the MidFr texts reported in (103) it is 12.6%. The mean frequency in Vigneulles, Calvin and du Bellay is 19% (in matrix declaratives with overt subjects). The majority of these examples have adverbs in initial position, although there are a number of examples with complements in initial position, e.g. the following:

(171) a. mais **d'une chose** je vous prie

'*but of one thing I beg you*'

(Vigneulles, *CNN*, II: 46)

b. **A ces choses** ilz repugnent

'*At these things they are repelled*'

(Calvin, *Inst.*, p. 13)

In terms of the reasoning based on the dispreference for CP-adjunction presented in 2.3.1., the increasing frequency of $V > 2$ order shows an increasing frequency of matrix clauses where the verb is in Agr°, rather than C°. This in turn means that C° more rarely had the feature [+Agr], and so, formally speaking, less matrix declaratives were V2 clauses.

b) *SVO orders*. The really striking development in the 16th century is the fixation of SVO order. Over the three texts, this order is found in a mean 71% of matrix declaratives, rising to 79% in Calvin. Still more striking, we find the following figures for SV (i.e. SVO and $V > 2$ together), VS (clear cases of V2 clauses, where a non-subject occupies initial position) and null-subjects:

(172)		SV	VS	NS
	Vigneulles, *CNN* (1505–15)	60%	11%	29%
	Calvin, *Inst.* (1530s)	89%	2%	9%
	du Bellay, *Deffence* (1549)	84%	9%	7%

These figures should be compared with those for the 15th century that we gave in (111) (from Marchello-Nizia 1979) and (112). We repeat (112) here for convenience:

(112)		SV	VS	NS
	Froissart, *Chroniques* (c. 1390)	40%	18%	42%
	15 Joyes (*14esme Joye*) (c. 1400)	52.5%	5%	42.5%
	Chartier, *Quadrilogue* (1422)	51%	7%	42%

The mean figures for the 15th century and the 16th century are given in (173):

(173)		SV	VS	NS
	15th century:	48%	10%	42%
	16th century:	77%	3%	15%

These figures should be compared with a mean of 35% SV orders and 61.5% VS orders in the OF texts surveyed in (26). We can see from these figures that a major change occurred between the early 15th century and the early 16th century. It would certainly be reasonable to say that by the mid-16th century, or perhaps, given the figures from Calvin in (172), the 1530s, French was basically no longer a V2 language (on the remaining VS orders, see below). In this, we concur with the standard view; for example, Adams (1987b: 202) says "Although the V2 construction remained an occasional option to writers of the sixteenth century, it is clear that one can no longer speak of a V2 constraint."

The disappearance of V2 in the early 16th century is due to the loss of the [+Agr] feature on $C°$. This feature was already optional and reducing in overall frequency; however, the change in the value of the Nominative-assignment parameter meant that the appearance of this feature on $C°$ was disfavoured to the point where V2 was (almost) totally eliminated. After the change in the parameter, there were only two ways in which this feature could appear on $C°$, trigger Agr-to-C movement and give rise to a well-formed structure: (i) if the subject moved to the pre-$C°$ position, or (ii) if the subject was a pronoun (and therefore able to incorporate with $C°$).

The first case gives rise to SV orders, which, thanks to the LES, are interpreted by the next generation as AgrPs. Therefore, although well-formed, this structure was at best purely transitional. The second case is more interesting, and in fact sheds some light on the remaining VS examples in the 16th-century texts. We can divide these cases into those where the subject is a pronoun and those where it is not, further dividing the latter into possible and impossible free inversion. In that case, the following picture emerges:

(174)		pronoun	unambig NP	ambig NP
	Vigneulles	$8/35 \approx 23\%$	$14/35 \approx 40\%$	$13/35 \approx 37\%$
	Calvin	$3/3 = 100\%$	0	0
	du Bellay	$11/14 \approx 78\%$	$1/14 \approx 8\%$	$2/14 \approx 14\%$

For Calvin and du Bellay, the situation is clear; V2 may have remained possible, but only where the subject was pronominal (or, in the case of free inversion, expletive *pro*). This data is therefore fully consistent with the proposal that the Nominative-assignment parameter had changed to its modern setting for these writers. (Note that this does not mean that we must take these clauses to be genuinely V2, in the sense that C° has the feature [+Agr]; there may be some other factor triggering Agr-to-C movement here, as we will suggest directly).

For Vigneulles, however, the situation is less clear. There is an irreducible residue of 14 examples from our sample that it is either implausible or impossible to treat in any way other than as cases of simple inversion. These are cases where the subject appears between the verb and a participle or a complement. The following are representative examples:

(175) a. par ces   conditions devantdictes **eust**

    by   these conditions above-said   had

    Symonnat l'absoluçon

    S.   absolution

    'S. had absolution by the above-mentioned conditions'

    (II: 3)

   b. Or **avoit nostre curé** à ce jour là priez des aultres prebtres

    'Now had our vicar on that day asked the other priests . . .'

    (II: 14)

   c. et   ne **fut sa penitence** acomplie . . .

    and not was his penitence finished

    'and his penitence was not finished . . .'

    (II: 59)

This type of case makes up roughly 5% of our total sample. Although it may be possible to treat some of these examples in other ways, we tentatively conclude that Vigneulles' system must have allowed Nominative-assignment under government. This conclusion does not conflict with anything we saw in the previous section; moreover, it is consistent with the fact that there are no examples of complex inversion in Vigneulles, while 9% of matrix interrogatives in Calvin feature this construction and 5% of those in du Bellay. What this suggests is that Vigneulles' text is representative of the old system, while Calvin and du Bellay (and Rabelais) are representatives of the modern system. We implicitly took Vigneulles as a representative of the old system in 2.3.5., when we reported Hirschbuhler's (1988) data on null subjects in this text. In the next section, we will see further evidence that confirms this idea.[37]

A similar picture emerges from the discussion of the position of the subject in Brunot (1905, Vol. II: 479f, Vol. III: 663f). Of the examples he gives of postverbal subjects (Vol. III: 480), a good number involve pronouns, and of those with nonpronominal NPs, several are clearly cases of free inversion, since the subject follows the participle, and only one seems to be a plausible case of simple inversion, viz.:

(176)   Alors **descendit Gymnast** de   son cheval

          Then got-down G.   from his horse

          'Then G. got off his horse'

          (Rabelais, *Gargantua*, Ch. 42, vol. I, 157)

Similarly, as Brunot points out, the statements of contemporary (or near-contemporary) commentators are revealing. Brunot comments that Maupas' (1607) praise of this construction as 'elegant' and 'to be used gracefully' ('de s'en servir avec grâce') indicates that it was probably of purely literary use by this period.

Another point emerges clearly from Brunot's report of the discussions of 17th-century grammarians (Maupas, writing at the beginning of the 17th century, Oudin, writing between 1632 and 1656, Malherbe (early 17th century) and Vaugelas (mid-17th century)). In their attempts to fix literary usage, these grammarians discussed which adverbs and conjunctions required the inversion of the verb and a pronominal subject. These included 'concessive' conjunctions, some of which (e.g. *aussi* ('also'), *peut-être* ('perhaps')) still optionally trigger inversion in present-day French, others which rarely do so nowadays (*encore* ('still')), and still others which no longer exist (*pource* ('so, because')). The particle *si*, a semantically neutral clause-introducer which was very common in V2 clauses in OF and MidFr, triggers pronoun inversion until its disappearance. There was disagreement and hesitation over other cases, e.g. *or* ('now') and *et* ('and'), neither of which can trigger inversion in present-day French.

The importance of these observations for our purposes is that they show that inversion was no longer triggered by a general property of C°, but rather by the presence of a definable class of elements in SpecC' (even if the exact membership of this class is subject to variation). This means that C° no longer bore the feature [+Agr] under any conditions by the 17th century (whether or not it was residually capable of doing so immediately after the parameter change, provided that either the subject moved to SpecC' or a pronoun appeared in SpecAgr'), and so French was no longer in any sense a V2 language. Presumably, on analogy with Rizzi's (1990b) treatment of other cases of 'residual V2', these adverbs trigger the presence of some feature on C° through Spec-head agreement, which in turn triggers Agr-to-C raising, much as in interrogatives (the precise nature of this feature is not very clear and need not concern us, although it is probably 'modal' in some general sense).

Moreover, the fact that the 17th-century discussion concerns subject-pronoun inversion only, and not inversion with non-pronominals, shows that the ModFr restriction on the subject was in place in the 17th century. This is, of course, consistent with our account of the parameter change.

A further prediction emerges from this. If the inversion following these adverbs in the 17th century was genuinely like that in present-day French in that it was impossible around a non-pronominal subject, we expect, other things being equal, to find complex inversion here too. This is certainly possible in present-day French:

(177)   Peut-être **Jean a-t-il** parlé
         '*Perhaps John has spoken*'

Examples like this provide the final confirmation that V-to-Agr movement here does not involve C° with the feature [+Agr], owing to the incompatibility of C[+Agr] with complex inversion (cf. 2.3.2.). Unfortunately, Brunot does not give any 16th or 17th century examples of this kind of construction, and we were unable to trace its development using any other source.

Brunot (ibid.: 670f) also mentions other constructions that disappeared in the early 17th century. These are 'optative inversion' and Aux-to-Comp:

(178) a. **Vueille ton voyage** estre si prospere, que je le desire!
         '*Would (that) your journey be as prosperous as I desire (it)!*

      b. **Ayant ce bon homme** fait tout son possible, . . .
         '*Having this good man done everything he could, . . .*'

These both seem to be fairly clear cases of constructions where Nominative is assigned from C° under government. Optative inversion, i.e. V1 order with a subjunctive verb, is similar to that found in various Germanic languages (cf. 1.4., 2.1.2.).

Optative inversion around a non-pronominal NP disappears, at the latest, early in the 17th century. Certain frozen expressions remain in literary ModFr; Brunot cites *Fassent les Dieux* 'Do (subj) the Gods' ('may the Gods do it'), which in any case could be an instance of free inversion, but the construction was probably no longer productive after the early 17th century. Brunot seems to suggest, however, that it survived longer where a pronoun was inverted, giving the following example:

(179)   **Fusse-je** aussi heureux que vous, . . .
          'Were I as happy as you, . . .'

This seems to be an example of the modern possibility of subject-clitic inversion in conditionals (in normal current usage, the conditional is used in place of the imperfect subjunctive: *serais-je* . . . 'should I be . . .'). So, if we make allowances for the independent decline of the imperfect subjunctive, conditionals show a development analogous to that of interrogatives with respect to inversion. Thus, it may be possible to consider the loss of this rather more marginal construction as an effect of the parameter change. The fact that this construction was apparently lost about a century after the likely date of the parameter change may be due to its comparative rarity and its stylistic status. We see the effects of the parameter change much more immediately in matrix interrogatives and declaratives as these are much more common and stylistically neutral sentence-types.

The construction in (178b), being limited to the gerundive forms of the aspectual auxiliaries *avoir* and *être*, seems very similar to the Italian Aux-to-Comp construction of Rizzi (1982), which we saw in 1.2. involves raising to C°. In 1.2., we analysed this construction as involving Case-assignment under government by T° in C°, arguing that T° maintains this capacity when not incorporated with Agr° (and, even then, can assign Nominative to positions it governs from its base position by the Government Transparency Corollary). If this analysis is correct, the loss of Aux-to-Comp in 17th-century cannot fall directly under our parameter, which explicitly concerns only Agr°'s Nominative-assigning capacity. We cannot extend our claim and say that French lost Nominative-assignment under government completely, because the subject retained (and retains to the present) the ability to receive Nominative in its base-position from T°, along the lines proposed in 1.2. So we must say that the disappearance of (178b) is due to the independent loss of the T-to-C rule in French (itself an instance of LHM in the sense of the discussion of Lema and Rivero in 1.3.2.). In forthcoming work, I relate this to the change in the Nominative-assignment parameter in terms of the idea that once finite Agr ceased to license null subjects, non-finite Agr lost the capacity to head-govern a trace of Long Head Movement in T° (cf. the discussion of LHM and head government in 1.3.2., 1.3.3.). This can account for the loss of Aux-to-C, the loss of infinitive — *pas* order (cf. 1.3.3. (76)) and the loss of clitic-climbing (cf. Kayne 1989a); all of these developments took place within a century of the change in the Nominative parameter.

We have now seen two major effects of the change in the Nominative-assignment parameter. Simple inversion in questions was lost, and V2,

already on the decline, was eliminated. These constructions in fact seem to
have disappeared rather suddenly. This is a natural correlate of parametric
change, although clearly many factors can intervene to 'cushion' the effects
of a parametric change in a speech community and particularly in the texts
of a given period: dialect differences, stylistic differences, and above all
the conservative influence of a literary standard. It may be no accident
that the changes we are considering are relatively visible in the texts of
the period precisely because the French of the 16th century had yet to
develop a full-fledged set of literary norms (this in fact happened in the
17th century, and the norms were clearly fixed according to the 'modern'
grammatical system). In any case, the changes that we have considered
up to now are clearly discernable if one compares, for example, Calvin
with Vigneulles. The fact that we can account for the manifest syntactic
differences between these two systems in terms a single minimal underlying grammatical difference is strong evidence for our approach.

2.4.3. *The Loss of Null Subjects*

We have now seen evidence from the loss of simple inversion and the loss
of V2 that the Nominative-assignment parameter changed in the early
16th century. In this section, we will consider the implications that the
parameter change had for null subjects. We will see that the direct effect of
the parameter change was to dramatically reduce the number of contexts in
which a null subject could be licensed. Moreover, we will elaborate on
the theory of the relation between morphological agreement and the
identification of *pro* proposed in 2.2.3., in a way that allows us to see that
the indirect result of the parameter change was that referential null subjects were entirely lost, except for a small residue. We also compare the
historical developments in French with those in certain Italian dialects and
Occitan, as discussed by Benincà (1983), Vanelli *et al.* (1986) and Vanelli
(1987).

In 2.2.3. and 2.2.4. we argued that, thanks to the double-Agr clause
structure of OF, it is possible to maintain that null subjects (of all kinds)
appeared only in contexts where they were governed by Agr. This captures
the basic correlation between null subjects and V2 in OF, and allows for
certain occurrences of null subjects in embedded clauses. In 2.3.5., we
reviewed the evidence from MidFr of Hirschbuhler (1991) and Vance
(1988, 1989), which indicates that null subjects were additionally able to
be licensed in configurations of agreement at this period. Taking Vigneulles' *CNN* as a late example of the old system, the discussion in 2.3.5.(based
on Hirschbuhler 1991) showed null subjects could appear in the following
contexts before the parameter change:

Table 1. Distribution of null subjects (NS)[a]

	1	2	3	31[b]	ce	Person 4	5	6	Tot	%
Main clauses	127	14	927	415	28	28	53	300	1894	79
Subord. cl.	7	6	127	208	–	7	127	31	510	21
	134	20	1054	623	28	35	180	331	2405	100

[a] From Hirschbuhler (1991).
[b] Person 31 = impersonal 'il'.

(180) a. $[_{CP}$ XP $[_{C'}$ C° + Agr° $[_{AgrP}$ *pro* . . .

   b. $[_{AgrP}$ *pro* $[_{Agr'}$ Agr° . . .

   c. $[_{CP}$ C° $[+wh]$ $[_{AgrP}$ *pro* $[_{Agr'}$ (Agr°) . . .

   d. $[_{CP}$ C° $[-wh]$ $[_{AgrP}$ *pro* $[_{Agr'}$ Agr°[2pl] . . .

The asymmetry in the persons of embedded null subjects is illustrated in Table 1, from Hirschbuhler (1991).

We will now consider the effect of the parametric change on (180a), licensing under government, and (180b), licensing under agreement, in turn. We will briefly discuss the other configurations, and return to them in 2.4.4.1. On the theoretical level, the effect of Case-assignment parameters on null subjects is always indirect, being mediated by the licensing condition (6a′), given in 2.3.5.

(180a); Licensing under government. This is the classic context for null subjects in French, being the basic configuration of OF (cf. 2.2.3.). According to the proposals in 2.3.5., in this configuration *pro* is formally licensed under government by C°, and identified by Agr° in the manner proposed in 2.2.3. (6a′) requires this to be a configuration in which Case can be assigned to *pro*'s position, SpecAgr′. This was of course possible until the parameter change, and impossible afterwards. So this is the context where the parameter change directly resulted in the elimination of null subjects.

In Vigneulles we find a number of examples of null subjects in this configuration:

(181) a. car **de   mes membres ne   me**   **povoie**   encor bien aidier
       for with my   limbs   not myself could (I) still   well help
       'for I still could not well do things with my limbs'
       (*CNN*, Prologue: 22)

b. **Sy desfermerent** le coffre, . . .

   so opened (they) the trunk, . . .

   'So they opened the trunk, . . .'

   (*CNN*, V: 107)

Just over half (51/92 ≈ 56%) of the null subjects in the Prologue and first five Nouvelles of the *CNN* are of this type. 40 (i.e. 80%) of these are referential, and so Agr° is both the formal licenser and the identifier for *pro*. Since null subjects make up 29% of the total of positive declaratives in this sample (cf. (173)), this means that null subjects licensed by Agr° in a configuration of government make up roughly 15% of this total, and referential null subjects roughly 12%. This is clear evidence that the grammar of Vigneulles represents the old system.

In Calvin, on the other hand, we find just four examples of this kind in the first 25 pages of the *Institution de la Religion Chrétienne*, two of which are expletives (one of which in fact is instance of a null subject that is frozen as such in present-day French: *tant s'en faut* ('far from it')). The other examples are both 1sg, although this is probably due to the nature of the text:

(182) a. Et **premièrement l'ay**   mis en latin

   And first   it have (I) put in Latin

   'And first I wrote it in Latin' (p. 4)

   b. Et **principalement vouloye**, par ce mien labeur, servir à noz François

   'And principally wanted (I), by this my labour, to be of use to our Frenchmen (p. 7)

Treating these as genuine cases of the configuration in (180a), they make up 4/15 (≈27%) of the null subjects in this sample, and therefore roughly 2% of the total number of declarative sentences. This is the same as the figure for VS orders in this text (cf. (173)). As in the case of VS orders, however, it is also possible to analyse these examples in a manner consistent with the new system by treating them as cases of (180b) (the same is possible, but less plausible, for the examples in Vigneulles; in particular, *si/sy* in (181b) seems to be best analysed as only appearing in SpecC').[38] We conclude from this that the distribution of null subjects in Calvin follows the new system, since there is no unambiguous evidence that null subjects are licensed under government, and this in turn supports the idea that null subjects are also affected by the change in the Nominative-assignment parameter in the early 16th century.

In du Bellay, we find just two clear cases of null subjects in a configuration like (180a), both of which are expletives:

(183) a. Encore moins **doit**   avoir lieu,   de ce que . . .

    Still   less   should (it) take place, that . . .

    (Ch. II)

    b. Vray **est**   que . . .

    True is (it) that . . .

    (Ch. X)

These examples constitute about 2% of the total number of matrix declaratives. Moreover, (183a), like (182), does not have to be analysed as an instance of (180a) rather than (180b). (183b), on the other hand, is more likely to have the structure in (180a), since the predicate is fronted. However, since the subject is expletive it does not require identification, and there is the possibility that C° is able to formally license it (see 2.3.5. and below). Alternatively, there is the possibility that this was a fixed expression at this period. In any case, the distribution of null subjects in du Bellay is clearly consistent with the new system in which null subjects cannot appear in (180a).

The above paragraphs show that, if we treat Vigneulles as having the old system, null subjects practically ceased to exist in the context which depended on the possibility of Case-assignment under government.

(180b): Licensing under agreement. The possibility of licensing null subjects under agreement, as in (180b), emerged in the MidFr period, as we saw in 2.3.5. We do not predict that the change in the Nominative-assignment parameter had any effect at all on this null-subject configuration. However, the data shows that this kind of case also became significantly rarer after the early 16th century, suggesting that the parametric change also affected this context.

In our sample of Vigneulles, 41 ($\approx$44%) null subjects appear in this configuration, all but four of them referential (with no discernable bias in favour of 2pl). This is roughly 14% of the total number of matrix declaratives. In Calvin, we find 11 examples of this type ($\approx$7% of the total), of which 8 are expletive. In du Bellay, we find 8 ($\approx$4%), of which two are expletive (both appearing in the modern frozen construction *tant s'en faut*). So the overall picture is similar to that in government contexts.

We can relate this development to the loss of null subjects in government contexts, and thus to the change in the Nominative-assignment parameter, if we make the following claim about the ways in which null subjects are licensed:

(184)   If Agr° formally licenses *pro* only under agreement, then Agr° must be [+pron].

This claim has a certain naturalness, since it states basically that genuinely rich Agr (in the sense defined in (79)) is needed if null subjects are licensed only in structural configurations of agreement. On the other hand, morphologically uniform ([+MU]) Agr (cf. the discussion of Jaeggli and Safir 1989 in 2.2.3.) must be able to formally license *pro* in a configuration other than agreement (i.e. under government), or there must be another formal licenser for Agr° to combine with for a (referential) *pro* to be well-formed (e.g. C°). These two possibilities for Agr° are not exclusive; in 2.3.5., we saw that in MidF, which had [+MU] Agr, Agr° could combine with C° (although, owing to the weakening of V2, this was weaker than formerly) or it could license *pro* under agreement. In fact, it was in MidFr that the possibility of licensing under agreement emerged, along with various other complications that we discussed in 2.3.5. As long as null subjects could be licensed under government as well, (184) allows French to remain a null-subject language (as the figures in (111) and (112) show). Once the Nominative-assignment parameter changed, however, (184) prevented null subjects from being licensed under agreement, given that Agr was formally rich. Hence, null subjects largely disappeared from agreement contexts as well.

We saw in 2.2.3. that verbal paradigms were restructured in 12th/13th-century French, giving rise to an Agr that was [+MU] but not [+pron]. One might expect a concomitant change in the distribution of null subjects, but in fact (184) allows even [+pron] Agr to fail to license *pro* — the evidence from 'conservative' OF appears to show too many restrictions on null subjects for us to say that [+pron] Agr licensed *pro* purely under agreement, as in that case we should have a system just like Modern Italian. In even the earliest OF texts overt expletives can be found, which strongly implies that the null-subject system was already more restricted than that of Modern Italian.

Interesting support for (184) comes from the history of other Romance varieties that have undergone developments rather similar to French: Occitan, Northern Italian dialects (Veneto, Milanese, Piedmontese and Friulian) and Fiorentino (this presentation is based on Benincà 1989, Poletto forthcoming, Vanelli *et al.* 1986 (henceforth VRB) and Vanelli 1987). The medieval forms (12th–14th centuries) of these varieties show traits parallel to OF: V2 orders (at least to some extent, although the precise details differ from one variety to the next, cf. Benincà 1984, 1989), simple inversion in interrogatives, and null subjects in matrix contexts only. We illustrate with examples from Veneto (in the (a)-examples) (*Lio Mazor*; where there are no examples this is because sentences of the relevant type were unavailable to me); Milanese (*Le opere volgari di Bonvesin de la Riva; Bonv.*) and Piedmontese (*Sermoni Subalpini*) in the (b)-examples, and Fiorentino (the (c)-examples):

(185) *V 2 Orders*

a. e   cosi **vogà eli** fina ala   punta del   canal
and thus rowed he up   to the end   of the canal
'and so he rowed up to the end of the canal'
(*Lio Mazor* 21r, 24; Benincà 1986: 6)

b. Bon   vin **fa**   l'uga   negra
Good wine makes the grape black
'Dark grapes make good wine'
(*Bonv.* 36, 205; VRB's (6), p. 166)

c. Ciò **tenne** il   re   a grande meraviglia
That held   the king in great   marvel
'The king considered that a great marvel'
(*Nov.* 64, 14; VRB ibid.)

(186) *Aux S V Orders*

b. desot **eren li   tapit   estendù**
below were the carpets laid out
(*Serm. sub.* 5, 18; VRB's (12), p. 168)

c. poi **fu   Azolino preso** in battaglia
then was A.   taken in battle
(*Nov.* 135, 16; VRB ibid.)

(187) *Matrix Null Subjects*

a. lo pan . . **dè**   *pro* per   la boca a Madalena
the bread gave (I)   through the mouth to M.
'I gave the bread to M.'s mouth'
(*Lio Mazor* 14 r, 17; Benincà 1984: 7)

b. De lu **farev**   *pro* svengianza
Of him will-make   you revenge
'You will avenge yourselves of him'
(*Bonv.*, 39, 287; VRB's (7), p. 166)

c. Si li   **livrerò**   *pro* d'uccidere
So them will-deliver (I)   to kill

'So I will deliver them up to be killed'

(Lucca 147; VRB ibid.)

(188) *Lack of Embedded Null Subjects*

a.   **el** dis *ch'***el** me pagarave   quando **el** vorave

he said that he me would-pay when   he wanted

'He said he'd pay me when he wanted to'

(*Lio Mazor* 2 t, 3; Benincà 1984: 6)

b.   e **ela** lor   a   dit que **ela** i   metrà un drap vermeil

and she them has said that she there will-put a   red   sheet

'and she told them that she would put a red sheet there'

(*Serm. Sub*. III, 54–5; Vanelli 1987: 10)

c.   Madonna, **io** v'ho   onorata quant'i'ho   potuto

Madonna, I you-have honoured as-much-as-I-have been able

'Madonna, I have honoured you as much as I could'

(*Nov*. 101, 15; VRB's (4), p. 165)

(185) clearly does not show on its own that these are V2 varieties; cf.
Vanelli *et al.* (1986), Vanelli (1987), Benincà (1984, 1989) for further
discussion. These examples, along with (186), show that these languages
allowed Nominative-assignment under government. Similarly, (187) and
(188), taken together, indicate that the basic pattern of null subjects was
as in OF. In each of the examples in (188), the (second) subordinate
clause contains a subject which is coreferential with the subject of the
previous clause, and which is nevertheless overt (cf. the OF example in
(8b) for a further instance). This is highly marginal in languages where
null subjects are free to appear in embedded clauses, as the following
Standard Italian example illustrates (the effect is clearer, and independent
of focus, in adverbial clauses of the type illustrated):

(189)   ??Il professore$_i$ ha parlato dopo che lui$_i$ è arrivato
         '*The teacher spoke after he arrived*'

The evidence in (185–188) indicates that Nominative Case could be assigned under government in these languages at this period.

Neither Vanelli *et al.* (1986) nor Vanelli (1987) discuss simple inversion
in interrogatives, but the evidence in (187) and (188) leads us to expect
it to exist. Indirect evidence for its existence comes from the fact that
these languages all had tonic subject pronouns (cf. VRB's (2), p. 164),
like OF (cf. 2.2.1.) combined with subject-pronoun inversion, and from
interrogatives with a null subject. Cf.:

(190) a. me **voj-tu** dar la taverna?

to-me want-you to-give the tavern?

'Do you want to give the tavern to me?'

b. **Creis tu** zo que dit lo Vangeli?

Believe you that which says the gospel?

(*Serm. Sub.* 1, 117; VRB's (8), p. 167)

c. non **ài tue** vercognnia?

not have you shame?

'Have you no shame?'

(Lucca 19; VRB ibid.)

(191) b. E **perquè est** *pro* apelaa noit?

And why is (it) called night?

(*Serm. Sub.* 2, 36; VRB's (9), p. 167)

c. **Avetemi** *pro* rinvenuto lo mio mantello?

Have-me (you) found the my coat?

'Have you found my coat?'

(Lucca 1356; VRB ibid.)

Benincà (pers. comm.) has also provided the following Piedmontese examples, which indicate that the subject received Case from the verb in C° in interrogatives:

(192) a. Perché **dist nostre Seignor** aquesta parola?

Why says our Lord this word?

'Why does our lord say this word?'

(Piedmontese, *Sermoni Subalpini*, ca. 1200)

b. Cum **po zo** eser que home seit animal . . . ?

'How can this be that man be animal . . . ?

(ibid.)

It emerges that these languages were parallel with OF in the relevant respects, and so we conclude from the above evidence that they allowed Agr° to assign Nominative under government.

In the modern languages, this is no longer the case. (193) illustrates the situation in Modern Veneto (Cecilia Poletto, pers. comm.):

(193) a.***Ga Nane fato** 'sto guaio?

Has John made this thing?

b. **Galo**   magnà?

   Has-he eaten?

c. Ieri   Nane ga magnà un pomo

   Yesterday J.   has eaten   an apple

d. ??La mama$_i$ la te   ga visto dopo che ela$_i$ la ze rivà

   Mother   she you has seen after that she is arrived

   'Mother saw you after she arrived'

(193a) shows that simple inversion around a non-pronominal NP is impossible, while (193b) illustrates the possibility of subject-clitic inversion. (193c) is intended to show that Veneto is not a V2 language. In all these respects, then, Veneto has undergone a parallel evolution to French.

However, Modern Veneto is a null-subject language, as (193d) shows. This example shows that Modern Veneto is parallel to Standard Italian (cf. (189)) with respect to the distribution of null subjects; null subjects are possible in embedded contexts, and in fact preferred where the referent of the pronoun is the same as in preceding discourse (the obligatory subject clitic *la* here is a marker of agreement, not a subject pronoun — see Note 40). Here, the parallel breaks down. However, we can explain this difference between Veneto and French in terms of (184), since the agreement paradigm of Veneto is [+pron]. The modern paradigm is as follows (Poletto, pers. comm.):

(194)   magno, te magni, el magna, magnemo, magnè, i magna

Veneto Agr is clearly [+pron] in the sense defined in (78) since it distinguishes five out of six forms.[39]

Modern Fiorentino is similar to Veneto, cf. Brandi and Cordin (1989: 113) (we use WHQ as Y/NQ do not involve inversion, cf. Brandi and Cordin, Note 15):

(195) a.***Icché ha Gianni** preparato?

   What has John   prepared?

b. **Icché ha-egli** preparato?

   What has he prepared?

c. Ieri   la Carla l'ha telefonato

   Yesterday Carla   has telephoned

d. (=(189))

Fiorentino also has a functionally rich Agr° (cf. Brandi and Cordin ibid.). So the same account will hold as for Veneto. Modern Piedmontese shows exactly the same traits as Veneto and Fiorentino in these respects (Raffa-ella Zanuttini, pers. comm.).

The evidence that we have reviewed strongly favours our account of the developments in French in terms of a single parameter change. It appears that we can maintain that the same parameter changed in the history of a number of other Romance languages, with the difference that the latter languages, having a [+pron] Agr° retained, in fact generalized, null subjects after the parameter change, while French lost them. This latter difference is due to the principle in (184).

We will see below that some varieties of contemporary *français popu-laire* appear to be developing 'Northern-Italian'-style subject-clitic systems (cf. Note 39 on subject clitics in Northern Italian dialects), where the subject clitic functions as a kind of agreement marker. Exactly this change may well have happened in some Northern Italian dialects. Poletto (1991) argues that Renaissance Veneto was a defective null-subject lan-guage in ways that are remarkably similar to what we saw in 2.3.5. on MidFr in that null subjects are only productive in certain persons, unless the null subject is expletive or C° is [+wh]. This system was followed by the loss of null subjects altogether, although they have subsequently been reintroduced via a reanalysis of the clitic system. In any case, the contem-porary dialects are consistent with (184) in having [+pron] Agr and Nomi-native-assignment only under agreement. If they (or at least one of them) lost null subjects with the loss of Nominative-assignment under govern-ment, then we expect that at the time this happened the agreement para-digms were rather 'poor', i.e. like French rather than like Italian. Accord-ing to Poletto (forthcoming), there is evidence that this was the case, at least in Veneto. Conversely, a dialect with 'rich', Italian-like agreement paradigms at the time of the change in the Nominative parameter would generalize null subjects. This may have happened in Fiorentino.

In fact, the parallelism between French and the other languages is so close that it suggests that the Nominative parameter may have changed in a parallel way. If this is so, we would be led to look for complex inversion in these dialects at least at some point in their development (although we know that it is ruled out in the modern languages by the Uniqueness Condition on Licensing, since they are null-subject languages, cf. 1.5.).

Two factors are relevant to the discussion of complex inversion synch-ronically and diachronically in Northern Italian dialects. First, are the subject clitics NPs or functional heads of some kind? Vanelli (1987) and Poletto (forthcoming) show that subject clitics in the dialects in the Re-naissance period were similar to those in ModFr, and unlike those in the present-day dialects in the relevant respects. In particular, they were in complementary distribution with the subject (ibid.: 19), while in many modern dialects (e.g. Fiorentino, as (195c) shows), they are required in all sentences even when the subject is present. Even in those dialects where this is not the case (e.g. Veneto, according to Poletto 1990b), the distribution of subject clitics is not like that of the subject NP, as it is in ModFr (*modulo* inversion, of course), while it was at an earlier stage (cf. again Poletto forthcoming). Moreover, the clitic could be left out of a second conjunct in a coordination. Cf. the following well-known contrast between ModFr and Modern Veneto (cf. Rizzi 1986b for discussion):

(196) a. Il chante et danse.
          '*He sings and dances*'

     b. *El canta e bala

The existence of such genuine (i.e. NP) subject clitics increases the expectation that complex inversion existed.

The second factor concerns expletive clitics. If such clitics were possible, then complex inversion should have been possible, other things being equal (cf. 1.5.). However, we have no data on this matter at present. Both Poletto (forthcoming) and Vanelli (1987) discuss null expletive subjects. Poletto gives the following example of an overt expletive subject clitic in Renaissance Veneto:

(197)   L'è   stà   suspeso   le prediche al signor Geronimo
         It has been suspended the preaching to Sr.   G.
         'Preaching to Sr. G. has been suspended'

So we are led, all other things being equal, to expect complex inversion in the Renaissance dialects. However, we have not been able to determine whether this expectation is borne out or not. Of course, the possibility exists that the same parameter changed in the same way but that the change in its value was triggered by different factors in the dialects as compared to French. In any case, the fact that the Nominative parameter can account for the striking diachronic parallels in a unified way favours our overall account of the history of French.

It also seems clear that the Italian dialects have undergone a further development that is responsible for the difference with (Standard) French: the subject clitics have become 'true' clitics, i.e. elements base-generated in Agr, which license a null subject. As soon as this takes place, complex inversion is ruled out by the UCL (unless the language retains a series of French-style subject clitics alongside those generated under Agr°, as I argue to be the case for Valdôtain in Roberts 1990, cf. Chapter 1, Note 25). It is possible that certain varieties of French have undergone this development: Sandfeld (1970), for example, claims that examples like *Chacun il a sa chimère* 'Everyone he has his chimera', with a quantified NP and subject clitic, are possible in Picard French (cited in Vanelli 1987:

33; compare this with the discussion of *chacun* in Standard French in 2.3.4.). We expect such varieties of French to lack complex inversion.

Returning to the history of French, we conclude that the loss of null subjects both in (180a) and in (180b) was due to the change in the Nominative-assignment parameter. In order to explain how the configuration in (180b) was eliminated, we appealed to (184). We have seen evidence from similar changes in other Romance varieties in favour of (184).

This account carries over to (180d); even the phonologically heavy 2pl agreement was prevented from formally licensing *pro* by (184) after the parameter change. However, if we suppose that Agr had uniformly lost its capacity to formally license due to the parameter change, but that 2pl retained, for a while, the capacity of identifying *pro*, we explain one class of contexts in which null subjects were still allowed in the early 17th century (according to Maupas 1607, cited in Brunot 1905, Vol. III: 477, Note 2). Maupas says:[40]

We also often omit the first and second persons plural, also in the continuation of a sentence, and after the conjunctions *et, aussi, que, aussi que . . .*

Maupas gives the following examples:

(198) a. J'ay receu   les lettres que   m'**avez**   envoyees

      I've received the letters that (you) to-me have sent

   b. Vous voyez qu'**avons**   soin de vous

      You see   that (we) have care for you

We can suppose that C° acted as the formal licenser here. Notice that, since the verb has not raised to C°, *pro*'s position here is in accordance with (6a'), as it can be Case-marked in this configuration.

A second context Maupas mentions is where inversion is triggered by some element of the type discussed in the previous section, roughly speaking 'concessive' conjunctions, as well as *et* and *si*. Here are Maupas' examples, as cited by Brunot (ibid.):

(199) a. Vous m'avez bien conseillé, et vous **croyrai** une autre fois.

      You have advised me well, and you (I) will-believe another time

   b. Il vous respecte et si vous   **servira**   bien

      He you respects and so you(he) will-serve well

This appears to be a case where the residual inversion context continues to license a null subject. As far as we can tell, this was not a productive possibility by the mid-17th century, when only fixed expressions like *non feray* ('I will not do it') and *si feray* ('I will do it (so)') remained.

A third context where null subjects survived for a time is not explicitly mentioned by Maupas, but can be illustrated from his discussion:

(200)   Rarement advient que ces   pronoms nominatifs

         Rarely   happens that these nominative pronouns

         soient obmis

         be   omitted

Expletive null subjects remained possible into the 17th century, as this example shows. Here, we take it that $C°$ formally licenses *pro*, and no identification of *pro*'s content is necessary.

This possibility was not very productive, however; Brunot (ibid.: 481) suggests that it was basically limited to 'ready-made expressions' ('des expressions qui peuvent être considérées comme toutes faites') like *semble* ('seems'), *faut* ('is necessary'), *y a* ('is/are') (see Brunot's Note 2 for a full list of the contexts where null expletives are found). It seems that $C°$ needed a feature in order to be able to formally license *pro*. This is the context in (180c), which we discuss in 2.4.4.1., since it is associated with the development of Styl-Inv.

To return to (180), the parameter change directly rules out (180a); null subjects disappear from this configuration essentially at the same time as simple inversion and V2 disappear. The parameter change indirectly rules out (180b), via postulate (184); again the chronological evidence supports this idea. We saw that (184) plays an important role in accounting for similarities and differences between French and the Northern Italian dialects. The configuration in (180d) remains for a time after the parameter change, since $C°$ [−wh] seems to be a formal licenser for the remainder of the 16th century, and 2pl agreement retains the capacity to identify *pro* for a while. Also, environments where subject-clitic inversion remained possible allowed null subjects until the early 17th century. The configuration in (180c) never completely disappears; it is the origin of ModFr Styl-Inv; as we shall see in 2.4.4.1.

2.4.4. *Other Interrogative Structures*

The preceding sections document and discuss the various overt changes that we attribute to the underlying change in the Nominative-assignment parameter. In this section, we turn our attention to other developments in French interrogatives, most of which took place in the 17th century. These developments are all related to the Nominative parameter in one way or another.

2.4.4.1. *The Origin of Stylistic Inversion*

We adopt the basic elements of the analysis of the ModFr Styl-Inv construction given by Pollock (1986). According to this analysis, Styl-Inv is in fact the French counterpart of the Italian 'free inversion' construction, with an expletive null subject in SpecAgr' and the subject in postverbal position.[41] So the structure of (201a) is (201b):

(201) a. Où est allé Jean?

     'Where has gone John?

  b. [$_{CP}$ où [$_{AgrP}$ *pro* [$_{Agr'}$ est allé Jean]]]

The contrast between embedded questions and embedded declaratives shows *pro* depends on C°'s [+wh] feature for licensing:

(202) a. Je me demande où est allé Jean

     'I wonder where went John?'

     (Kayne and Pollock 1978, (2a), p. 595)

  b. *Marie pense qu'a crié Pierre.

     'Mary thinks that has shouted Peter'

     (ibid., (9a), p. 597),

Styl-Inv is also possible in certain subjunctive contexts:[42]

(203)   Je veux que parte   Paul

       I want that leave(subj.) Paul

       'I want Paul to leave'

       (ibid., (40a), p. 608)

There are also cases of genuine impersonal *pro*, i.e. where it is not in relation with a postverbal subject:

(204) a. ? Quand sera   procédé au

      When   will (it) be proceeded to the

     réexamen   du problème?

     reeaxamination of the problem?

     (Kayne and Pollock 1978, (64b), p. 615)

  b. Je veux que   soit procédé au   réexamen

     I want that (it) be proceeded to the reexamination

de cette question

of this question

(ibid., (62a), p. 614)

Leaving aside a number of details (cf. Kayne and Pollock op. cit., Pollock op cit.), we can conclude that Styl-Inv represents a residual case of free inversion with an expletive *pro* in subject position. This *pro* is licensed by C° [+wh] or, apparently, C° [+subj]. As we mentioned earlier (cf. 1.5.) Styl-Inv in Y/NQ can be ruled out by the UCL, permitting us to retain the view that C° in Y/NQ is [+wh].

So Styl-Inv is a case of the configuration in (180c), except that *pro* cannot be referential; there is no possibility of 2pl here (contrast (199a)):

(205) a. *Les lettres que *pro*   m'avez envoyées
         the letters that (you) have sent me

      b. *Je me demande qu' *pro*   allons faire
         I wonder   what (we) will   do

Our account of the history of French null subjects allows for this development, if we simply maintain that C° is, under appropriate conditions (i.e. when it has the appropriate feature) able to formally license *pro* under government (which we need in any case in order to account for certain aspects of the distribution of null subjects from the 15th to the 17th centuries; cf. 2.3.5., 2.4.3.). Since C° is unable to identify *pro*, the null subject in question cannot be referential. As we saw in 2.4.3., the change in the Nominative-assignment parameter meant that all other cases of null subjects were lost, since they depended on Agr for either formal licensing or identification or both. However, the one kind of null subject which depended only on C° was unaffected, and so remained; in this sense Styl-Inv is a diachronic relic of the former null-subject system.

Two remarks are in order concerning this account. First, we might expect that the last kind of referential null subject to be lost in French was 2pl *pro* governed by C° [+wh]. This expectation arises because we know that C° [+wh] was and is a formal licenser, and 2pl agreement was able to identify *pro* more readily than other persons (cf. the remark quoted from Maupas (1607) at the end of the previous section). There is some evidence that this is true. One case of the 17th-century prescription against null subjects (Garasse 1622, cited by Brunot 1905, III: 77) explicitly mentions the use of constructions like *le jour que vinstes* ('the day that (you) came'), *ce que fistes* ('what (you) did') by a late 16th-century author (Etienne Pasquier).

Second, we have suggested that Styl-Inv, i.e. free inversion, was formerly possible in Y/NQ. The possibility of interpreting interrogatives of the type *V NP* as free inversion, rather than as simple inversion, played a role in our discussion of the loss of simple inversion (cf. 2.3.4., 2.4.1.). This construction was already rare in the early 16th century, as we saw in 2.4.1. Later in the 16th century, or early in the 17th, it disappears. Here is a late example (from Desportes (late 16th century)):

(206)   **Viendra** jamais le jour qui   doit finir ma peine?

Will-come never the day which must end my pain?

'Will the day when my pain ends never come?'

(Brunot 1905, vol. III: 670)

Cf. also (163) and (164). We can link the presence, and subsequent disappearance, of this construction to the other developments that we have seen. Until the change in the Nominative parameter, the expletive *pro* in subject position was licensed by Agr° under government, or, in MidFr, under agreement (cf. Note 32). After the parameter change, Agr° was unable to license *pro*, but C° [+wh] took over this function in certain contexts (as we saw above and in 2.3.5.). However, C° [+wh] could not take over this function in Y/NQ, given the Uniqueness Condition on Licensing, which prevents C° from simultaneously licensing a null subject and identifying the interrogative operator Q. Hence, after a period where a few examples are found, free/stylistic inversion becomes impossible in Y/NQ.

There is clearly much more to be said about the development of Styl-Inv, particularly concerning the subjunctive contexts, and the contexts in Note 42. We leave open the question whether this is a post-17th century innovation, extending the class of C°'s which are able to license *pro*, or whether these contexts have consistently allowed null subjects since the beginnings of ModFr. The purpose of this subsection was to suggest that the modern construction is a relic of the formerly much more generalized possibility of null subjects; this is the one context which survived the general elimination of *pro* in 16th and 17th-century French.

2.4.4.2. *'Conjugaison interrogative'*

Another property of interrogatives that was introduced in the 17th century is worth mentioning here. This is the 'interrogative conjugation': the use of special verb-endings, at least for 1sg present, in inversion contexts. In place of forms like *romps-je* ('break I'), pronounced then as now /rõž/, forms written *rompé-je*, and pronounced /rõpež/ appear. According to Brunot (1905, V: 721), this usage was widespread in Parisian French in the 17th century. Various spellings were used (*aimé-je, perdez-je, préten-dai-je*), all of which indicate that /e/ appeared in between the last conso-nant of the verb and the initial consonant of *je*. Though in origin due to a phonological or phonetic difficulty, we can see that this was more than a low-level vowel-epenthesis rule from the existence of *allé-je* for *vais-je* ('go I?') (Foulet 1921: 297). Moreover, the vowel is not the reflex of /ə/ in closed syilables, which is open /ɛ/ (cf. Dell 1973, Anderson 1982). This construction was never accepted as part of literary French, forms in *est-ce que* being prescribed instead (e.g. by Vaugelas 1647, cf. Brunot ibid., Foulet ibid.).

Similarly 3sg epenthetic *-t-* could be considered a marker of interrogative conjugation. It is clearly not underlyingly part of the verb ending, as it never shows up in liaison contexts: **il a /t/ ouvert la porte* (vs. *ils ont* (=/t/) *ouvert la porte*). Neither is it motivated by a phonological constraint: a sequence of vowels of the type in **a il* is allowed in French. Moreover, this /t/ appears in contexts where there is already another /t/ in the verb root, giving rise to the realization of /ə/ for syllable-structure reasons: *habite-t-il*, pronounced in careful speech /abitətil/. So it is unlikely that this /t/ is inserted for purely phonological reasons.

These remarks suggest that at this period C° [+wh] had (and perhaps still has) a morphological reflex under certain conditions. The precise conditions seem to be connected to cliticization, since, at least in contemporary French, the 3sg /t/ cannot appear unless there is a clitic present (**Qu'a-t-acheté Jean?* 'What has bought John?'). These morphological changes might be related to C°'s continued ability to formally license a null subject after these had disappeared from all other contexts. So it is conceivable that this development is related to Styl-Inv in ModFr.

2.4.4.3. *Ti*

Finally, we should mention a construction which has never been part of literary French, but which is widespread in non-standard French: the use of the particle *ti* as an interrogative marker in Y/NQ. Foulet (op. cit.: 268ff) provides a long account of both the origins and distribution of this element. He gives the following examples of its occurrence (in non-standard Parisian French of the early 20th century):

(207) a. Elle t'écrit   **ti** souvent?
          She you-writes TI often?
          'Does she write to you often?'

     b. Il   habite **ti** Lyon?
          He lives   TI Lyon?
          'Does he live in Lyon?'

c. On t'a   **ti** demandé ton adresse?
   One you-has TI asked   your address?
   'Did they ask you for your address?'

d. Tu les   avais **ti** vus?
   You them had   TI seen?
   'Had you seen them?'

e. Ça   marche **ti** pas?
   That works   TI not?
   'Doesn't it work?'

These examples give us a fairly clear picture of the basic properties of *ti*.
(207c–e) all show that, although diachronically derived from epenthetic
/t/ and inverted *il* (see below), *ti* does not agree in person or number. In
fact, there is no synchronic reason to consider *ti* a pronoun at all, and at
least one good reason to consider it not to be a pronoun. If *ti* were a
pronoun, it would have to satisfy Case theory, presumably by incorporation with Agr°. However, in an example like (207b), the preverbal clitic
il must also satisfy Case theory by incorporation with Agr°. Rizzi and
Roberts (1989), following Kayne (1983), propose that Agr° cannot license
two clitics by incorporation, in order to account for the ungrammaticality
of the Standard French equivalent of (207b):

(208)   *Il habite-t-il Lyon?

The grammaticality of (207b) in a dialect which allows *ti* indicates that
only one clitic needs to be identified; clearly this is preverbal *il*. Hence *ti*
is not in need of morphological identification, and so not part of the
pronominal system.

   The examples in (207) give an indication of the structural position *ti*
occupies. Following Pollock (1989) (cf. 1.1.), we take *souvent* ('often') to
be left-adjoined to VP, so (207a) shows that *ti* is outside VP, and to the
right of the position occupied by the inflected verb and object clitics, i.e.
Agr°. (207b, c, d) confirm this, showing that it precedes the direct object,
and intervenes between the auxiliary and the participle. (207e) shows that
it precedes *pas*, which we have assumed to be in SpecT' (cf. 1.1.). Hence
it must be right-adjoined to Agr°.[43]

   We can relate this to the account of the origin of *ti* given by Foulet (cf.
also Noonan 1989). Foulet suggests that *ti* emerges in the late 16th century,
as a consequence of (a) the general insertion of epenthetic /t/ after 3sg
verbs in inversion contexts (cf. the above remarks on this phenomenon),
even though orthographic forms like *a il* remain for a while, and (b) the
truncation of final /l/, general then as now in normal speech. These two

factors gave rise to the pronounciation V + *ti* in the 3sg masculine, the most common form of the verb. The 3pl masculine also frequently gave rise to V + *ti*, although here the /t/ was probably part of the verbal ending.[44] Foulet suggests that under these conditions, *ti* was reanalysed as a marker of interrogation. This probably took place in the late 16th century.

In our terms, we can propose the following DR, which creates the *ti*-construction out of complex inversion:

(209) a.

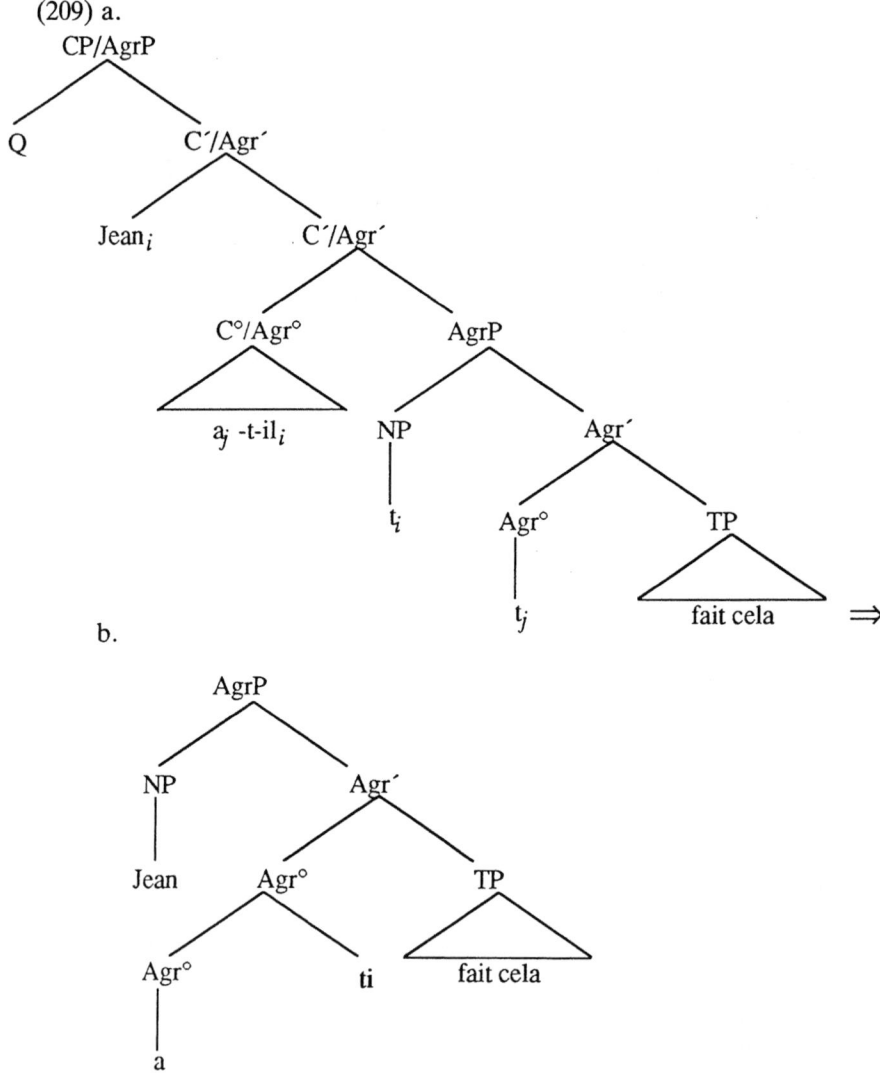

It is clear that this DR gave rise to a simpler construction in terms of LES. The respective chain-positions in the two structures in (209) are as follows ((209a) is equivalent to (136b) of 2.3.4.):

(210) a. (209a): (V, t, t, t)   — V-raising
                  (NP, pronoun, t, t) — subject-raising

      b. (209b): (V, t, t)   — V-raising
                  (NP, t)   — subject-raising

(209b) has five chain positions, as compared to eight in (209a). So the LES very strongly favoured this reanalysis.

It is unclear whether complex inversion was a precondition for the development of the *ti*-construction; it could have come directly from the left-dislocation structure of the type in (41) from which complex inversion developed, via a DR which converted (41) into (209b) (saving four chain positions). It is probable that it came from complex inversion, because we could not otherwise explain the existence of complex inversion; how could this construction have developed from the *ti*-construction? There is of course the possibility that both developed more or less simultaneously from the left-dislocation construction, but then, other things being equal, we would expect complex inversion to be eliminated in favour of the *ti*-construction, i.e. for all cases of complex inversion to be reanalysed as *ti*-constructions. Although this is a plausible account of what happened in nonstandard French, other considerations weigh against it.

The relative chronology favours the idea that *ti* developed from complex inversion; we have seen that complex inversion was introduced in the 15th century, while *ti* appears in the late 16th century.

Foulet gives an interesting argument that *ti* was introduced at this time. Since *ti* has been prescribed against in the literary language, it is hard to know when it came into non-standard use. However, *t-il* was written in one context where it could not have been a pronoun: with *voilà* ('there is/are'). This element is almost certainly a defective verb; it accepts object clitics, e.g. *le voilà* ('there he/it is'), and is clearly derived diachronically from the imperative of *voir* ('see') plus the locative *là* ('there'). However, it cannot appear with a subject pronoun: *je/tu/il voilà*. Nevertheless, from the 16th century on, it appears in questions with orthographic variants of *-t-il*. Brunot (1905, III: 289) gives the following example (from Sorel, *Le Berger Extravagant*, 1639):

(211)   **Ne voila t'il pas** ce que l'on void . . . ?

         'Isn't this what one sees . . . ?'

Foulet suggests, quite plausibly, that this *t'il* is really *ti*. If so, then we have evidence for the existence of *ti* in the early 17th century.

The later appearance of *ti* is also supported by the total absence of null subjects with this element. We never find examples like the following:

(212)   *(Moi) ai   ti dit   ca?
        (Me) (I) have TI said that?
        'Did I say that?'

If *ti* was introduced in the 16th century, after the parameter change, null subjects were already obsolescent (cf. 2.4.3.), and so (212) would never have appeared for simple chronological reasons. The fact that we never find (212) suggests that *ti* indeed appeared after the parameter change, and so after complex inversion. The overwhelming likelihood is then that *ti* originated as a reanalysis of complex inversion in the manner indicated in (209).

This conclusion raises an intriguing question: why did (41) not develop directly into the *ti*-construction? There does not seem to be any purely formal reason that this should not have happened; no syntactic condition would have been violated. The fact that this apparently did not happen should instead be accounted for in terms of the theory of change. We tentatively suggest that DRs are always minimal, in that they reduce structure as little as possible. Given this idea (which of course should be spelled out more rigourously), we would expect (41) to pass through a stage like complex inversion before being reanalysed as *ti*.

2.4.4.4. *Qui que*

The development of the *ti* construction was important, because it meant that Agr was no longer raised to C in Y/NQ in at least one variety of French. The appearance in the 15th and 16th centuries of the *qui que* type of interrogative in non-standard French (Foulet 1921: 272) had the same consequences for WHQ. Foulet (1982) makes the interesting suggestion that this construction derived from free relatives. In fact, interrogatives commonly develop from free relatives (cf. Portuguese *o que* ('what')). We can represent this development as a DR of the following type (where coindexation indicates *wh*-movement, i.e. in (213a) *que* moves, in (213b) *qui* moves):

(213) a.

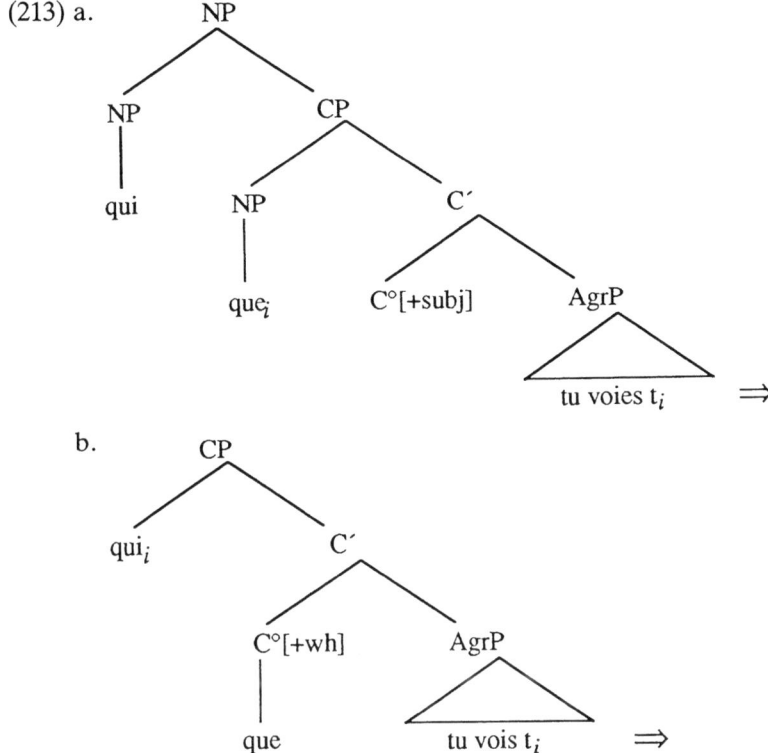

b.

This is a typical DR, at least in that it involves the elimination of structure. Depending on the general analysis one adopts of relatives, it may also involve reduction in the number of chain positions, since *que* arguably forms a chain with *qui* in the relative structure, but does not do so in the interrogative.

In any case, this development is clearly related to the reanalysis of *que* as a member of C° in relatives, and to its cliticization (which probably also took place around this time). Obviously much more should be said about this, but what is important for us is that the development of this kind of interrogative meant that Agr-to-C movement was no longer obligatory in WHQ. Putting this together with the *ti* construction, it emerges that non-standard French no longer had obligatory Agr-to-C movement in interrogatives of any kind from the late 16th century on (and, in fact, inversion probably quickly became impossible in non-standard varieties; this is hard to determine, however, owing to the strong influence of the standard literary language).

The result is that there is a variety of French without inversion. This development is by no means unique to French; Poletto (1990b) shows how different dialects of North-Eastern Italy are minimally distinguished in terms of the status of inversion in interrogatives, with Veneziano show-ing, like *français populaire*, none at all. A precisely parallel range of variation is found in the subdialects of Valdôtain (Roberts forthcoming). Also, the history of Portuguese, and to some extent the synchronic differ-ences between European and Brazilian Portuguese, show the same dia-chronic move away from inversion; cf. Rossi (1990) (the Portuguese facts show that this development is independent of subject clitics, as Portuguese has never had subject clitics; on the other hand, 14th-century Portuguese has many V2 properties, as shown by Mattos e Silva 1989, Ribeiro 1990). Poletto (1990b) formulates the differences among Veneto dialects in terms of Rizzi's (1990b) *wh*-criterion, by postulating a parametric choice of [+wh] base-generated in C°, or [+wh] base-generated in I° (or, equiva-lently, T° — see above). Intuitively, this parameter should be related to V2, since both crucially involve features of C°; how exactly to capture this intuition in unclear, however, and we will leave it as an open question.

2.5. CONCLUSION

In this chapter we have discussed in considerable detail the historical development of French interrogatives between roughly 1050 and 1650. We have tried to show that this development is of some theoretical and empirical interest. Our emphasis has been on one change in particular: the loss of simple inversion in the early 16th century. We proposed that this loss was the reflex of a change in the value of the parameter of Nominative-Case assignment; due to the change in this parameter, simple inversion was ruled out by Case theory.

This core idea has consequences in various directions. First, we have shown that the Nominative-assignment parameter is responsible for more than just the simple-inversion construction: the possibility of V2 depends on the setting of this parameter, and the possibility of null subjects in a language with a relatively impoverished agreement system (one which is only formally rich, in having an agreement affix for every person, but with much syncretism among these affixes) also depends on this. The history of French provides excellent evidence that these properties are connected along the lines we have proposed, since we then have a maximally simple account of the (near-) simultaneous disappearance of all three construc-tions.

Second, the parameter is justified cross-linguistically. A number of other Romance varieties in Northern Italy and Southern France have undergone an almost exactly parallel evolution, as the work of Renzi, Vanelli and Benincà, individually and collectively, has shown. The evolution differs from that of French, however, in that these languages currently have null subjects. The historical parallels between French and these other lan-guages are worthy of much more attention than we have been able to pay to them here. In particular, the role of subject clitics and of complex inversion needs to be clarified; in this respect, Franco-Provençal dialects are highly relevant, since at least Valdôtain has both Northern-Italian-style subject clitics and complex inversion. To the extent that texts are available, diachronic work on Franco-Provençal could make a major contribution here. Similarly, the Renaissance Italian dialects require very detailed investigation. The similarities between French and Northern Italian dialects extend to another important area that we have only touched upon here: that of clitic-climbing. French lost clitic-climbing in the 17th century (cf. Rochette 1988, Martineau 1990), and in most Northern Italian dialects this phenomenon is at least highly restricted (cf. Benincà 1984, Giupponi 1989, Kayne 1989a Note 9, and the references given there).

Third, the discussion of the change in Nominative-assignment led us to look very carefully at the dynamics of syntactic change. At least for purposes of exposition, we find the three-way distinction between steps, DRs and parametric change useful, and we suspect that these distinctions may be of real value in the elaboration of a theory of syntactic change. These notions allowed us to see how parameter changes result from a kind of conspiracy of Diachronic Reanalyses, creating a situation where there is no genuine evidence for a given parametric setting in the trigger experience; all the evidence being either gone, disguised or more readily analysable as something else (in a sense that can be defined in terms of LES). Our historical account has also been relevant for the theory of parameters. We have made a proposal regarding the format for parameters, and, in 2.4.1., we saw how certain notions from learnability theory (Berwick's 1985 Subset Theory and Clark's 1990 notion of 'shifting') may have played an important role in the changes French has undergone. Demonstrating these points is a real challenge for work in diachronic syntax, but, if the challenge is met, work on diachrony can make a unique contribution to the overall goals of generative theory.

Finally, we have been led to make assumptions about acquisition strategies. Here we have said little that is new; we have just applied some old ideas (least effort and the Subset Principle) to new data and, in the case of the Least Effort Strategy, in a slightly novel way. This is another area where diachronic work can be of quite general importance. So, I hope that the foregoing pages have made a contribution in one or more of the following domains: the diachronic syntax of French and other Romance languages; the theory of Case, of *pro* and of head-to-head movement; the ways in which constructions can be lost; the ways in which parameters change diachronically, and the ways in which parameters are set in the course of acquisition.

NOTES

[1] We cite OF (and MidFr) examples taken from secondary sources by giving the page reference to the secondary source, along with as full a reference as possible to the text itself and, where relevant, the date of the text. Examples taken from Schulze (1888) are, however, cited using Schulze's own abbreviation for the name of the text. Examples taken from primary sources will be cited with an abbreviation of the title followed by page and/or line references. Again the date will be included where relevant. Full references to primary texts are provided in the Appendix at the end of the book.

[2] As just suggested, English is probably completely lacking in licensing heads, and so neither condition in (6) can be fulfilled (although cf. Hoekstra and Roberts 1990 for the suggestion that *pro* is found in English, but is licensed under rather different conditions to those under consideration here). The situation in ModFr is more complex — cf. 2.4.4.1.

[3] The exact complementation properties of verbs like *être* and particularly *pouvoir* in OF are not our concern here, although they are of some interest for diachronic syntax, as there is evidence that *pouvoir* and other modal verbs were restructuring verbs in OF roughly in the sense that their Modern Italian counterparts are (cf. Rizzi 1982); on restructuring in OF, see Pearce (1990).

[4] All the examples in (18) have a 2pl subject. The majority of examples of this type have either 2sg or 2pl subjects: all the examples in *Merlin*, all the examples in *Tristan*, and 5 out of 8 examples in *Perceval*. This cannot simply be attributed to the fact that questions, at least in dialogue (which, given the nature of the texts, almost all the examples we are concerned with are taken from) have a tendency to be second person, as a comparison with the null subjects in WHQ in our texts shows: in *Roland*, out of 17 null subjects in WHQ, 3 are 1sg, 4 2sg, 3 3sg (all expletive), 4 1pl, 4 2pl and none 3pl; in *Perceval* we find, out of 36 such null subjects, 1 1sg, 5 2sg, 23 3sg, no 1pl, 6 2pl and 1 3pl; in *Tristan*, out of 20 such null subjects 5 are 1sg, 3 2sg, 5 3sg, 2 1pl, 2 2 pl, 3 3pl; in *Merlin* of the six null subjects of this kind, 2 are 1sg, 1 is 1pl and 3 are 2pl. There is thus no clear preference for any particular person in WHQ (unless maybe for 3sg, which is undoubtedly due to the fairly large proportion of expletive null subjects), while in Y/NQ there is a clear preference for second person. Here again, then, there appears to be an asymmetry between the two types of question. Schulze (1888: 189) discusses this issue, and concludes that there are null subjects in OF Y/NQ. The evidence we have collected indicates an asymmetry between WHQ and Y/NQ, at least for 12th-century texts, with the percentage of null subjects in the latter consistently much lower than in the former. See Note 5.

[5] The following tables compare the proportion of WHQ with null subjects in various 12th and 13th century texts with the proportion of Y/NQ (the calculations are my own, with only approximate percentages; 'overt subject' means overt **pronominal** subject; the percentages do not add up to 100% due to the presence of nonpronominal subjects):

(i)   *Tristan* (12th century)

	WHQ	Y/NQ
Total:	52	17
Null subject:	$20 \approx 39\%$	$4 \approx 25\%$
Overt subject:	$18 \approx 35\%$	$11 \approx 70\%$

(ii)   *Perceval* (12th century)

Total:	112	38
Null subject:	$36 \approx 32\%$	$8 \approx 20\%$
Overt subject:	$31 \approx 28\%$	$24 \approx 60\%$

(iii)   *Le Charroi de Nîmes* (12th century)

Total:	30	10
Null subject:	$18 = 60\%$	$0 = 0\%$

     Overt subject: 6 = 20%   4 = 40%

(iv) *Aucassin et Nicolette* (13th century)
    Total: 35   9
    Null subject: 3 ≈ 9%   1 ≈ 11%
    Overt subject: 20 ≈ 60% 7 ≈ 80%

(v) *Merlin* (13th century)
    (approx. half of Vol. 1 of the Société des Anciens Textes Français edition, to
    p. 142)
    Total: 74   76
    Null subject: 6 ≈ 9%   5 ≈ 8%
    Overt subject: 58 ≈ 76% 64 ≈ 84%

These figures show a clear asymmetry in the occurrence of null subjects in the two types of questions in 12th-century texts, with null subjects dispreferred in Y/NQ but no particular preference emerging in WHQ.

It may be that some version of the Uniqueness Condition on Licensing (1.5. (119′)) is relevant here. In Y/NQ C° must both license the empty element Q in SpecC′ and the null subject in SpecAgr′. This can be ruled out by 1.5. (119′ii), which states that a single head cannot license two empty categories in a single structure. This means that Y/NQ with a null subject should always be ruled out. That this prediction is too strong is shown by the grammaticality of (vi):

(vi) Wird getanzt?

    Was danced?

    'Was there dancing?'

What this suggests is that (vi) may involve licensing *pro* by something other than C°, *contra* the proposals made in 1.4. and the references given there. This is true even if we allow parts of complex heads to count separately for part (i) of the UCL, but only whole heads to count for part (ii), as suggested in Note 32 below. See also Chapter 3, Note 8.

We must nevertheless explain the possibility of 2nd person null subjects that we find in these examples (cf. Note 4). Perhaps pragmatic factors are able to override this condition. We leave this matter open, noting that the basic asymmetry between WHQ and Y/NQ may provide support for the UCL, but that the attested examples are problematic for it as it stands.

[6] For more discussion of generalized embedded V2 in Germanic, see 1.4. and the references given there. For a detailed account of the diachronic development of embedded V2 in Yiddish, see Santorini (1990).

[7] This is not the only way of rendering (2) in ModFr; one could alternatively use the *est-ce que* construction (or *wh-in-situ* without inversion, cf. 1.5.). However, leaving aside questions of stylistic choice, (38) are certainly grammatical sentences of ModFr which are equivalent in meaning to the OF sentences in (2).

[8] Actually, we will see in 2.2.2 that there is evidence that nominative pronouns in postverbal position cliticized to C° in OF. If cliticization already took place in the syntax, as we will suggest that it did, then it would not be correct to say that the clitic receives Nominative Case under government from the inflected verb in C°, but rather that, as in ModFr, it is morphologically identified by incorporation with C°. This does not directly affect the point under discussion, however.

[9] My translation. The original reads: "Von dem nfrz. Verfahren, dem gemäss ein betontes Subjekt zwischen Fragewort und Verbum tritt, ist mir in der alten Sprache keine Spur begegnet." Presumably, Schulze refers to the subject as stressed in this context in implied contrast with the atonic nature of the postverbal clitic.

[10] Schulze does in fact mention just one example of this type:

(i)   **Ou   ci   deable ont il**   tant de jent   pris
        Where these devils   have they so many people taken
        'Where have these devils taken so many people?'

The example is from a late 12th century *chanson de geste*, *La Mort de Garin de Loherain*, l. 1178. It is not clear what conclusions to draw from an isolated example of this type. Since we are aware of no other instances of this order before the mid-15th century (cf. 2.3.4.), we will simply note the occurrence of this example, and tentatively treat it as a case of topicalization to C', rather than as a genuine instance of the structure in (40). This decision seems to be justified by the weight of other evidence from the history of French; treating structures like (40) as emerging only in the 15th century seems to give the most coherent general picture of the developments we are concerned with, as the overall argument of this chapter is intended to show.

[11] 'Ausser [the three examples given — IGR] ist mir in Originalwerken kein Beispiel dafür begegnet, dass im Fall der absoluten Voranstellung eines Subjekts das personalpronominale im Fragesatze selbst nicht ausgedruckt ware,' i.e. 'Besides [the three examples just given] I have found no example in the original texts in which in the case of absolute preposing of a subject the personal pronoun in the interrogative sentence itself was not expressed.'

[12] Cf. 1.5. for an account of Y/NQ in Germanic. The conclusion in the text appears to contradict what we said in Note 5 about the comparative rarity of Y/NQ with null subjects. Notice, though, that the discussion there depended on (47i) while the argument in the text depends on (47ii). This implies that (47i) is the 'weaker' version of this principle, perhaps in the way we suggested in Note 5 by allowing components of a complex head to license separately, which (47ii) does not do, given the discussion of Italian in 1.5. At this point, one might wonder if (47), as we have formulated it, is really a single principle.

[13] My translation. The original reads:

'Nostre escu', 'sa parole' portant un accent assez fort constituent à eux tout seuls des phrases complètes. On pourrait imprimer '[Et] nostre escu? Por quoi furent fet?' '[Et] sa parole? Que li coste?' Ce serait probablement exagerer l'effet obtenu, mais cette ponctuation indiquerait au moins dans quel sens il faut chercher cet effet.

We take it that the exaggeration consists in isolating the initial NPs totally from the clauses. A left-dislocation treatment of the sort we are advocating, however, seems correct, in that it is natural to suppose that a concurrent effect of this structure is that the dislocated element has its own intonation contour. This seems to be the basic thrust of Foulet's remark.

[14] Speaking of the possibility in (59b), Foulet says: "It is probably possible to find examples of the modern construction in the 12th century, and in any case they are not rare in the 13th and 14th centuries." ("Il est probable qu'on trouverait déjà des exemples du tour moderne au XIIe siècle, et en tout cas ils ne sont pas rares au XIIIe et au XIVe siècle"). The forms *moi meïsmes*, etc., instead of *je-meïsmes* are less clearly attested in OF (cf. Foulet op. cit.: 33, particularly Note 1).

[15] My translation. The original reads "le pronom sujet (. . .) suit régulièrement le verbe personnel, dont il ne peut être séparé que par des pronoms personnels conjoints ou les adverbes *en* et *i*".

[16] The absence of such a ban on pronouns in Icelandic V1 sentences (cf. Sigurðsson 1985) indicates simply that Icelandic subject pronouns are not subject to the constraint in (71), and so can stay in the 'inverted' (i.e. VP-internal) position.

[17] My translation. The original reads "dès le XIIe siècle au moins, on connaissait en France le type de conjugaison qui est le nôtre, c'est-a-dire un paradigme où les trois personnes du singulier et la troisième personne du pluriel sont identiques pour l'oreille."

[18] In fact, Jaeggli and Safir's proposal allows null subjects also in the case where the paradigm

systematically does not have an agreement slot. We disregard this proposal, as it is intended to allow for the kind of 'prodrop' found in Oriental languages; however, MSc is clearly problematic, since these languages have no agreement affixes and do not allow null subjects, cf. 1.3.2. Jaeggli and Safir (Note 17) suggest that the null-subject parameter should be stated as a one-way implication (if null subjects, then morphological uniformity) in order to allow for MSc. In that case, the potential counterexample of OF is very important, as it threatens to undermine precisely this implication.

[19] The possibility of analysing this kind of example, and interrogatives with the order *WH V NP* as involving free inversion only will play an important role in our discussion of MidFr and 16th-century French in 2.3. and 2.4.

[20] Adams (1987b: 71) says it was, on the basis of an analysis of complex inversion which takes SpecAgr' to be filled by *pro* in this construction. This assumption is very problematic, as there is then no account for the absence of complex inversion in either Standard Italian or the Northern Italian dialects. As we saw in 1.5. the UCL accounts for these facts, but we must then assume that subject clitics incorporate in complex inversion in French (and in Valdôtain, cf. Chapter 1, Note 25), so that SpecAgr' is occupied by a trace, not by *pro*. Recall that the possibility of *pro* incorporating with $C°$ is excluded on the grounds of structure preservation: *pro* is always and only a maximal projection, and so it cannot adjoin to a head.

[21] 'Dans la littérature en vers de l'époque, tant l'ordre COMP XP φ V que l'ordre φ V sont possibles.'

[22] Vance gives some examples which must be interpreted as topicalization to CP (Vance's (52), (53), p. 169):

> (i) a. et vraiment ainsi fut il
> *and truly   thus was it*
> 'and truly it was so'
>
> b. [qui fut] seur ne fut il pas
> *who (it) was sure neg was he not*
> 'He wasn't sure who it was'

She points out that this appears to be a MidFr innovation. Although these examples mean that we cannot take V > 2 order as a foolproof indication of the absence V-to-C movement, the existence of sentences of this type shows another respect in which MidFr is unlike a typical V2 language. Following the Least Effort Strategy — to be introduced in 2.3.2. — we nevertheless continue to regard XSV sentences as AgrPs, in the absence of clear indications otherwise. Note that left-dislocation (or perhaps topicalization) of the type discussed in 2.1.3. would be unambiguous adjunction to CP in these terms, since this is an interrogative structure.

[23] Complex V2 with a postverbal clitic, e.g. *Hier Jean a-t-il fait cela* can be ruled out in terms of the elaborated theory of head-to-head movement of Rizzi and Roberts (1989) and 1.3. To derive such a sentence Agr must move to C. Now, C is either [+Agr], as in a V2 system, or not, as in a non-V2 system. If C is [+Agr], the movement will not create the extra Specifier position at the C-level, and so the string will be analysed as CP-adjunction and therefore ruled out. We assume, following the remarks on residual V2 in 1.4., that V will not move freely to a [−Agr, −wh] C in a non-V2 system. For this reason, declarative complex inversion in French is not a general possibility. However, it is possible with the inversion-triggering modal adverbs of French, e.g. *Peut-être Jean a-t-il fait cela* ('Perhaps John has done that'). Note that we cannot take this string to be an AgrP, since in that case *il* would have to cliticize from SpecT', and we are assuming that SpecT' is an A'-position (cf. 1.2.). This shows that these adverbs are not residual V2 elements in the sense of

introducing a [+Agr] feature on C°. Instead they are like *wh*-operators, and must somehow be parasitic on the *wh*-criterion. Cf. 2.4.2.

[24] My translation. The original reads: "en indépendante ou principale, il domine dans une proportion variante entre 52% and 75% des cas (alors que dans ce cas, en ancien français, la proportion est, sauf exception, inférieure à 50%)."

[25] There are many more null subjects and, in the last two texts, less cases of inversion, than in the texts surveyed by Marchello-Nizia in (111). In the case of Froissart, this is in part attributable to the very high frequency of sentences with the order *et V*, many of them with null subjects. This feature of MidFr syntax has been often commented on: cf. Marchello-Nizia (ibid.), Vance (op. cit.: 208–9). Independently of this, we expect that for all three texts our survey will yield proportionately more null subjects and less cases of inversion, since we count cases of free inversion as examples of null subjects, while, although Marchello-Nizia does not comment on this, it is safe to assume that she does not distinguish free inversion from simple inversion. So an example like (i) is case of a null subject for us:

(i)   Par ceste maniere **fut puniz   Aurelius**
             In   this   manner was punished Aurelius
             'Aurelius was punished in this way'
             (*QI*, l. 31)

Moreover, certain examples are ambiguous, e.g. (ii):

(ii)   et   les   portoient li   sires de Sees, li   sires de Ferrieres
             and them carried   the lord of Sees, the lord of Ferrieres
             'And the lord of See and the lord of Ferrière carried them'
             (Froissart, ibid., l. 74)

We counted such cases as (simple) inversions (see 2.3.4. and 2.4.1. for more on the role that this kind of ambiguity played in MidFr).

[26] The following is a more formal statement of (113):

> For a given input D,
> Let the set of syntactic representations associated with D be $R = (r_1 \ldots r_n)$ where each r_k contains the set C of chain-positions $(c_1 \ldots c_n)$.
> Let Φ be a partial ordering on R.
> If $i < j$ in Φ, then
> (i) the sum of chain positions (i.e. the cardinality of C) in r_i < the sum of chain positions in r_j;
> (ii) no condition of UG is violated in r_i;
> (iii) D is consistent with r_i.

De Vincenzi (1989) proposes a Minimal Chain Principle as a constraint on adult parsing operations, a principle which imposes exactly the same constraint as our LES (and, like our LES, is not taken to be a grammatical principle). It is entirely likely that our LES is simply the child's version of de Vincenzi's principle.

[27] The relevant parts of the resulting LF-representation will look like this:

(i)

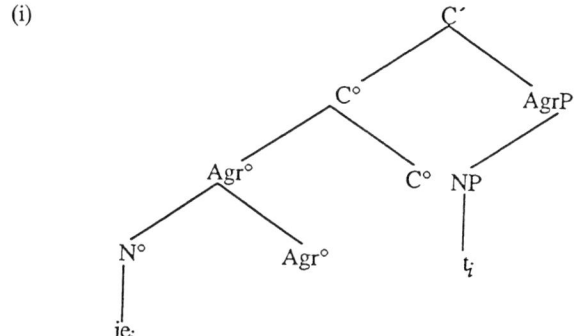

Since nodes to which other categories are adjoined are not genuine projections, but only segments of projections, neither Agr° nor C° here block c-command. Hence the trace is properly bound, in accordance with the ECP.
[28] However, it should be noted that the LF-incorporation idea just outlined takes away the force of Kayne's (1983) ECP-based argument that subject cliticization is a uniquely PF-phenomenon in French; it would be in fact possible to treat it as SS cliticization, with the trace 'saved' at LF by Agr-to-C movement, rather like the trace of Agr in English if an affix-hopping analysis of English agreement along the lines proposed in 3.2.1. is correct. We remain agnostic as to which is the better analysis of ModFr, although it may be necessary to keep Kayne's basic approach in order to account for the differences between French subject clitics and those in Northern Italian dialects discussed in Rizzi (1986b), Brandi and Cordin (1989); cf. also Burzio (1986) for an independent argument that preverbal subject pronouns are not syntactic clitics in ModF.
[29] We can sum up the overall differences between the OF system and the ModFr one in feature terms as follows:

OF: *moi* [−Nom]: *je* [+Nom]; *me* [−Case]
ModFR: *moi* [+Obl]; *je* [−Case]; *me* [−Case]

This indicates, correctly, that accusative pronouns were already clitics in OF (although they did not have exactly the same distribution as in ModFr; cf. the discussion of the Tobler/Mussafia Law in 2.1.2., 2.2.4.), and that *moi*-forms could appear as complements but not in contexts of Nominative-assignment (cf. 2.2.1.). The specification of ModFr *moi*-forms as oblique will account for their inability to appear in contexts of structural Case assignment. The specification [−Case] is used for exposition; it presumably is not a real feature.
    A further point should be made here: if neither *je* nor *me* have Case features in ModFr, what distinguishes them? To answer this, we adopt the proposal in Borer (1984) (which our proposal is conceptually very close to anyway) that clitics are in fact the spell-outs of Case features of heads. So, attaching a pronoun to Agr° yields *je*; attaching it to V° yields *me*, etc. It is worth pointing out that this approach will not work for clitics that occupy the Wackernagel position of the kind found in German, where the clitic's morphological case properties cannot be deduced from the nature of the head the clitic attaches to. This may be a dimension along which clitics should be typologized, a matter we will not go into here.
[30] Brunot (1905, II: 414–5) gives the following examples from the early 16th century, however:

(i) a.   i'espere qu'il et ses deux compagnons satisferont a vostre desir
         '*I hope that he and his two companions will satisfy your desire*'
         (1523)

    b.   ie (combien que indigne) y fuz appelé

'*I (how unworthy) was called there*'
(1534, Rabelais, *Gargantua*)

[31] The version of (25b) without the pronoun is impossible in ModFr:

(i)   *Pierre, qui a   vu?
           Peter, who has seen?

Although this, like its English counterpart, can be explained in terms of relativized minimality, simple topicalizations are also impossible in ModFr:

(ii)   *Pierre, Jean a   vu
           Peter, John has seen

The evidence in 2.1.3. indicates either that topicalization was possible in OF, or that dislocation with a null pronominal was. We consider the loss of this possibility to be an independent development from the ones we are considering here, and will not discuss it further.
For discussion of the development of obligatory *reprise pronominale* in French, cf. Priestley
(1955). Kroch (1989) gives a statistical analysis of Priestley's data which shows a real correlation between the development of obligatory *reprise pronominale* and the loss of V2. We
have no account of this correlation as it applies to non-subjects; for subjects, obligatory
reprise relates to V2 since no trace can be head-governed by C° in SpecAgr' once C° loses
the V2 property — cf. 1.4., 1.5. Cf. also 2.3.1. on the status of the proto-complex-inversion
of 2.1.3. as topicalization or left-dislocation, and the general nature of CP-adjunction.

[32] It is unclear whether Agr-to-C is immediately lost. In (144b), which corresponds to the
contemporary Styl-Inv structure, we have indicated that Agr does not move to C. However,
the continued existence of free/Styl-inv in Y/NQ (cf. (145)) into the 16th century (cf. 2.4.1.,
2.4.4.1) suggests that, in the 16th century — i.e. after the parameter change — V is in Agr
and Agr licenses expletive *pro*. When Agr finally loses the capacity to license expletive *pro*
later in the 16th century, C takes over this role and the UCL then rules out examples like
(145). Prior to the parameter change, V + Agr could be in C, with Agr licensing *pro* and C
licensing Q (cf. the construal of (47) in Notes 5 and 12). Cf. also the discussion of (169) in
2.4.1. Independent evidence that Agr moved to C in at least some cases where it no longer
does — questions on the subject — comes from examples like the following (from Vigneulles'
CNN):

(i)   Que vous plaist, monseigneur?
           What you pleases, . . . ?
           'What would you like, . . . '?

Friedemann (1989) argues that *que* obligatorily triggers Agr-to-C movement (since it is a
clitic; it is reasonable to assume that this element was already a clitic in the 15th-century as
all of the ModFr clitics were clitics at this point — cf. 2.2.1.). In that case, (i) is straightforward evidence of Agr-to-C movement, supporting the idea that in free/styl-inv, Agr-to-C
movement was at least possible at this point. (i) is also evidence that C° retained the capacity
to head-govern a subject trace in Vigneulles (cf. 1.4., 1.5., 2.1.1.); this is consistent with
everything else we have seen concerning Vigneulles (cf. 2.4.2., 2.4.3.). Agr-to-C movement
with non-subject *que* is still possible, on Friedemann's analysis, given (ii):

(ii)   Qu'a   fait Jean?
           What has done John?
           'What has John done?'

As expected, (ii) is impossible in embedded contexts:

(iii)   *Je me demande qu'a fait   Jean
             I   *wonder*   *what done J.*

[33] There is the tricky question of pronouncing /ə/, the ending for all persons except 1pl and 2pl in the most productive conjugation. According to standard accounts (e.g. Brunot 1905, Tome II: 244f), final /ə/ ceased to be pronounced by and large in Standard French around 1600. One might conclude that at that point, which coincides with the beginning of the ModFr period, French verbal paradigms became morphologically non-uniform. However, these endings are still pronounced in many regional varieties of French with no obvious effect on the distribution of null subjects, and, moreover, there is good evidence that the optimal phonological analysis of /ə/ (in the generative tradition — cf. Martinet 1974 for a different approach) entails that it is underlyingly present in these forms in all varieties of French (cf. Dell 1973, Anderson 1982). Also, we will suggest an account of the triggering of V-to-Agr movement in 3.1.3. which will require us to posit that French verb-paradigms are morphologically uniform, so there must be an underlying affix for all persons. We conclude that /ə/ is present in the SS representation of MidFr and ModFr verbs.

[34] This formulation is adopted largely for clarity of exposition. However, the basic idea that Subset Principle is relevant for parameter-setting, in the sense that the only possible parametric choices are those consistent with the 'smallest' resulting grammar, permits some simplifications of the formal theory of parameters. Parameters are frequently assumed to be exclusive binary choices, as in (3). However, nothing in the trigger experience relevant to the fixation of a parameter can ever tell the acquirer that the choice of parameter settings is exclusive; this aspect of the task of parameter-fixing must come from elsewhere. In fact, the Subset Principle plays just this role, while also relativizing the exclusivity of the choice to the trigger experience. So we do not need to stipulate constraints on the form of parametric choices allowed by UG: whether they are necessarily binary or not, whether they are necessarily exclusive or not, etc. The possible forms of parameters can be left relatively open, without posing serious problems for the theory of acquisition. Nevertheless, we continue to present parametric choices as in the text for the sake of clarity. The issues touched on in this Note are discussed in greater detail and with greater rigour in Clark (1990).

[35] In fact, a language which chooses Y for both (3a) and (3b) is a 'shifted language' in the sense of Clark (1990). A shifted language can be formally defined as follows (this is a simplified version of the definition given by Clark (ibid.)):

(i) *Shifting*
Two parameters, x_i and x_j, cause a *shift* at values $x_i(1)$ and $x_j(1)$ just in case:

(a) $(x_1 \ldots x_i(1) \ldots x_j(0) \ldots x_n) \not\subset (x_1 \ldots x_i(0) \ldots x_j(1) \ldots x_n)$
(b) $(x_1 \ldots x_i(0) \ldots x_j(1) \ldots x_n) \not\subset (x_1 \ldots x_i(1) \ldots x_j(0) \ldots x_n)$
(c) $(x_1 \ldots x_i(1) \ldots x_j(0) \ldots x_n) \subset (x_1 \ldots x_i(1) \ldots x_j(1) \ldots x_n)$
(d) $(x_1 \ldots x_i(0) \ldots x_j(1) \ldots x_n) \subset (x_1 \ldots x_i(1) \ldots x_j(1) \ldots x_n)$

Clark argues that such systems are dispreferred. Our point is just that strong positive evidence is needed for such a system, of a type absent from French by 1500 for the reasons we have seen.

[36] This was another DR, presumably. It is not in violation of the LES because, despite appearing to complicate the structure, it in fact adds no chain positions (assuming that the expletive *pro* is completely "inert" with respect to the θ-structure of the clause).

[37] We do not mean to suggest by this that the grammar of French changed between the time of the *CNN* and the time of the *Institution de la Religion Chrestienne*, i.e. in the 1520s. This would be the naïve conclusion to draw. Many other factors should be taken into account: the fact that the authors are from different regions (Calvin from Picardie, Vigneulles from Lorraine) and that the texts are quite different in style and purpose. However, these texts do appear to almost minimally represent different systems, and given that Calvin was forty

years younger than Vigneulles we are justified in saying that Vigneulles is a late representative of the old system and Calvin an early representative of the new.

[38] In fact, if *et* is treated as adjoined to AgrP or CP, rather than as outside it as we have implicitly been assuming, then this analysis would be forced, as (182a–b) would be cases of V3 order. Evidence that *et* could be analysed as CP-internal, in fact as in SpecC′, is provided by the fact that it sporadically triggered subject-pronoun inversion in the 17th century, as we saw in the previous section. Making this assumption would reduce the number of V1 examples in Calvin (see below), but increase the number of V3 cases in the way we just saw, not altering the picture significantly with respect to (180a).

[39] As in many N. Italian dialects, the subject clitics here are obligatory. They are best analysed as manifestations of Agr° also — cf. Brandi and Cordin (1989), Renzi and Vanelli (1983), Rizzi (1986b), as well as Poletto (1990b) for details on Veneto. Whether or not the clitic should be counted in general as part of the paradigm for the determination of the nature of morphological richness, Veneto is clearly functionally rich. The same is true of Fiorentino, as we will see directly. On the diachronic analysis of these subject clitics, see Vanelli (1987), Poletto (forthcoming) and the brief remarks below.

[40] "Plus nous obmettons souvent la premiere et seconde personnes pluriéres, aussi en suite de propos, et apres les conjonctions . . ."

[41] Following what we have been assuming about free inversion in Italian and OF/MidFr, we assume that the subject is in its base position in VP*. On Case-assignment to the postverbal NP, cf. 1.2.

[42] As well as in other contexts: sentences introduced by *ne . . . que*, and certain V2-like structures with an initial PP:

(i)   Ne seront executés que trois innocents
        Not will-be executed but three innocents
        'Only three innocent people will be executed'
        (Pollock 1986, (40a), p. 226)

(ii)   Dans cette prison ont été executés deux innocents
        In   this prison have been executed two innocents
        'Only two innocent people will be executed'
        'Two innocent people have been executed in this prison'
        (ibid., (41a)).

Despite a superficial similarity to V2 in simple tenses, Styl-Inv triggered by an initial PP does not involve Agr-to-C movement and topicalization of PP to SpecC′, but rather V remains in Agr and the PP adjoins to AgrP, with the subject inside VP*. This can be seen in (ii), where the subject follows the participles; the truly V2 order, with the subject intervening between the auxiliary and the first participle, is impossible:

(iii)   *Dans cette prison ont deux innocents été executés

It is important to note that Kayne and Pollock (1978) originally analysed Styl-Inv as involving rightward NP-movement. Pollock (1986) retains this analysis for some cases, while positing an expletive *pro* for others, e.g. the impersonal passive cases. We have glossed over this distinction in the text for the sake of expository simplicity. In any case, it is likely that the ModFr rightward-movement instances of Styl-Inv originate diachronically in a residue of former null-subject constructions, so the account of the origin of Styl-Inv in the text can be retained even if many cases of contemporary Styl-Inv feature a trace, not a *pro* in subject position.

    Cf. also Deprez (1989, 1990) on the typology of Styl-Inv and related constructions (and a rather different analysis to that assumed here).

[43] In Chapter 3 we will adopt the NegP hypothesis, which will make it possible to assume that *pas* occupies a position lower than T°. This leads to the conclusion that *ti* is in T°. In terms of this idea, we can suppose that *ti* is the realization of T°'s [+wh] feature (cf. 3.2.1. and Rizzi 1990b for the idea that [+wh] is a feature of T°). In these terms we can account for the fact that *ti* is impossible in WHQ and in embedded Y/NQ in terms of a more general ban on the occurrence of two 'yes/no' [+wh] features in the clause (cf. the fact that *whether* does not undergo absorption in the sense of Higginbotham and May 1981):

(i)   *Comment tu   as   **ti**   fait?
          How   you have TI done?
          'How did you manage?'

(ii)   *Je me demande si   elle a   **ti**   dit   ca
          I wonder   whether she has TI said that

For a discussion of *ti*-like elements in Valdôtain, see Roberts (forthcoming).

[44] The orthographic final 's' (or 'z') of the 3pl masculine *ils* was probably not pronounced at this period, as the historically motivated form of this pronoun is *il* (since the OF nominative pl. masculine has a zero-ending). This 's' was added in the spelling in the 14th century, but was probably never generally pronounced. Its pronounciation in liaison contexts in present-day speech ('ils ont parlé' /i zō parle/) is a spelling pronounciation. Cf. Foulet (1935/6: 283).

CHAPTER 3

THE ENGLISH AUXILIARY SYSTEM

3.0. INTRODUCTION

In this chapter, we turn our attention to the history of English. As in Chapter 2, our concern is primarily with the history of inversion and interrogative constructions as it is manifested in the development of the Modern English auxiliary system. Since the auxiliary system is the central issue, we will also be concerned with a topic that did not arise in our discussion of French: the lexico-semantic characterization of auxiliaries.

We will discuss three related developments in the history of the auxiliary system:

    (1) a.   Verb-raising: the emergence of the Modern English distinction between auxiliaries and main verbs with respect to movement to Agr (cf. 1.1., 1.3.3.).

       b.   The history of *do*-insertion.

       c.   The development of a class of syntactically distinct and morphologically defective modals.

Providing an account of these developments amounts to giving a history of a large part of the auxiliary system, although we will have little to say about the history of the periphrastic perfect, progressive and passive constructions (note that these constructions are more common cross-linguistically than modal auxiliaries and *do*-insertion).

The basic fact concerning verb-raising was mentioned in 1.1.: in Modern English (NE, i.e. English from the second half of the 17th century on; see Note 1 on the conventionally assumed historical periods of English) inversion of non-auxiliary verbs is impossible:

    (2) a.   *Left John/he?

       b.   Must John/he leave?

In this respect, English differs from all the Romance languages and all the other West Germanic languages (cf. 1.1.).

As is well-known, earlier stages of English patterned with the rest of West Germanic in this respect:[1]

    (3) a.   **Sleppstow,**   man?

          Sleepst thou, man?

b. **Se** ye not how his herte is endurid . . .?

See you not how his heart hardened . . .?

(1407, published in 1530: Anon., *The Examinacion of Master William Thorpe*, 44; Gray 1985: 13).

c. **Wilt thow**   ony thinge with hym?

Will you (do you want) anything   with him?

(Visser, §559; Roberts op. cit.: 23)

It is clear from these examples that ME allowed non-auxiliary verbs to raise to C° (this was also possible in non-declarative sentences throughout ME, to the extent that ME was a V2 language; cf. 3.4.).

Moreover, inflected main verbs preceded clausal *not* until the ENE period, as the following examples show (cf. also (3b)):

(4) a. My wyfe **rose nott**

My wife did not get up

(Mossé 1968, cited in Roberts 1985a: 23).

b. it **serveth not**

it doesn't serve (it's no use)

(1513: Anon., *The Battle of Flodden*, *l*.46; Gray 1985: 9)

This possibility is, of course, ruled out in NE. Abstracting away from the 'split-Infl' structure for the moment, we can describe this difference between ME and NE by saying that in ME verbs could move to Infl, something which is impossible in NE (cf. 1.3.3.). This account extends naturally to the possibility of moving main verbs to C in ME, illustrated in (3). Assuming that inversion in interrogatives is always movement of $I_{[+Wh]}$ (cf. 1.4.) to C, the possibility of this kind of inversion in ME then reduces to the possibility of movement to I (as pointed out in 1.1.; note that, as we formulate it here, this conclusion holds independently of the possibility of Long Head Movement of the type discussed in 1.3.2.). The continued possibility of subject-aux inversion in NE (illustrated with a modal in (2b)) is then an indication either that auxiliaries are base-generated in I, or that they are more readily able to move than main verbs (cf. 1.3.3. and below).

In Section 3.1., we will take up again the analysis of the distinction between auxiliaries and main verbs proposed in 1.3.3., and propose an account of how this split emerged historically. We will propose that the loss of main-verb raising is correlated with the (near-) loss of agreement paradigms. In this context, recent work by Platzack (1986, 1987) and Platzack and Holmberg (1989) on similar developments in the history of MSc is very relevant, as well as the data from Faroese discussed in Barnes

(1987, 1989). We will provide an explicit characterization of the relation between agreement paradigms and verb-raising, based on ideas in Roberts (1985), Platzack (1986, 1987), Holmberg and Platzack (1988), Platzack and Holmberg (1989) and Pollock (1989); this characterization dovetails with the proposals we made in Chapter 2 (2.2.3. and 2.4.3.) for the ways in which different kinds of Agr license null subjects, giving a picture of a range of parameters involving Agr in the Germanic and Romance languages.

Concerning (1b), the central question is the status and distribution of the dummy verb *do*. In NE, the essential points of the distribution of this verb are captured by Chomsky's (1957) rule of *do*-support: *do* must be inserted into a negated or inverted I just where no other auxiliary is present. Where there is no inversion or negation and no other auxiliary, the material in I moves down to V (in Chomsky 1957, this operation is called Affix-Hopping; we refer to it as T/Agr-Lowering):

(5) a.   He left   (Obligatory Affix-Hopping).

    b.   He didn't leave   (Obligatory *do*-insertion)
          Did he leave?

    c.   *He not left   (Illicit Affix-Hopping)

    d.   *He did leave   (Illicit *do*-insertion)

In (5d), *do* is ungrammatical if unstressed. If *do* is pronounced with emphatic stress, the example becomes grammatical: *He DID leave*. Still following Chomsky (1957), we treat the contrastive stress as the realization of a constituent which blocks Affix-Hopping, on a par with negation. The same is also true of other positive-polarity items like *so* and *too*, when they occupy the same position as *not* (cf. Klima 1964, Pollock 1989).

On the other hand, many commentators have observed that late ME and ENE allowed 'free' *do*-insertion in unemphatic contexts like (5d) (cf. Barber 1976, Ellegård 1953, Jespersen *MEG*, V: 429, Visser 1963–73, *OED* (DO, I.B.iii, 25a)). This can be mostly clearly seen in poetry, where the meter tells us whether *do* is in a stressed position or not. The following examples from Shakespeare illustrate the construction:

(6) a.   Thus cónscience **does** make cówards of us áll

          (*Hamlet*, II, i, 83)

    b.   Rough wínds **do** sháke the dárling búds of Máy

          (Sonnet xxviii, l. 3)

In these examples, *do* cannot be stressed (the stressed syllables are indicated with acute accents). So these are cases of (5d), a construction we refer to henceforth as 'free *do*-insertion'. In 3.2.3. and 3.2.4., we will discuss this construction in detail, providing an account of its rise and fall, and of how *do*-insertion came to be restricted to exactly those contexts where it is obligatory, as shown in (5).

In 3.3., we take up the question of the development of a syntactically distinct class of modal auxiliaries. NE modal auxiliaries differ distributionally from main verbs in two principal ways. First, negation and inversion constructions show that modals occupy I:

(7) a.　John must do his homework and so **must** I

　　b.　**Will** you say that again?

(8) a.　I **cannot** judge this question

　　b.　You **shouldn't** say things like that

In these respects, NE modals clearly differ in distribution from NE main verbs. Moreover, NE modals are in complementary distribution with *do* and with overt tense/agreement marking, a classical indication that they occupy the same position as these elements (cf. below and 3.3.). Second, modals fail to appear in nonfinite forms and never appear with direct objects. This is illustrated by the following ungrammatical sentences:[2,3]

(9)　a.　*I **shall can** answer

　　b.　*The dogs are quiet, not **maying** bark

　　c.　*If I had **would**, I had **could** done it

(10) a.　*She **could** a lot about that

　　b.　*John **shall** me a penny

　　c.　*Will you castles and kingdoms?

On the basis of these differences with main verbs, we suggest, as a preliminary hypothesis, that NE modals are inserted in [+ finite] I.

Regarding the ability to appear in I, the NE modals do not differ from their ME predecessors:

(11) a.　A blynde man **kan nat** juggen wel in hewis

　　　　A blind   man cannot judge   well in colours

　　　　(1387: Chaucer, *Troilus* 2, 21, Roberts ibid.)

　　b.　. . . so **mote** they nedes go home on fote

　　　　. . . *so must they needs go home on foot*

　　　　(Visser, §1694; Roberts ibid.: 22)

On the other hand, in ME, (some) modals are found in non-finite forms:

(12) a. I **shall not konne** answere

       I shall not be able to answer

       (1386: Chaucer *CT*, B, in Visser §1649, Roberts ibid.)

    b. They are doumbe dogges, not **mowende** berken

       They are dumb dogs, not being able to bark

       (c1380: Wyclif, *Prov.* 7, 11; Visser § 1684)

    c. if he **had wolde**

       if he had wanted to

       (1525 Ld. Berners, *Froiss.* II, 402, Visser § 1687, Roberts ibid.)

As (12a) indicates, the possibility of non-finite modals means we find sequences of modals in ME. We take the facts in (11) and (12) as an indication that ME modals had the properties of main verbs, and as such were generated in V° (cf. Lightfoot 1979: Ch. 2). (Note also the fact that *not* precedes the modal in (12a), a further indication that the modal is in VP).

Moreover, some modals retained the capacity to take a direct object until ENE, a clear indication that they could be generated under V° (cf. Lightfoot op. cit.):

(13) a. She **koude** much of   wandrynge by the weye

       She knew much about wandering by the way

       (Chaucer; Lightfoot (op. cit.: 99))

    b. euerych bakere of þe town . . . **shal** to þe clerke of

       Every baker of the town . . . owes the clerk of

       þe town a peny

       the town a penny

       (a1400: Usages of Winchester (Engeroff), p. 64; Visser § 549)

    c. **Wultu**   kastles and kinedomes

       Wilt thou (do you want) castles and kingdoms

       (c1225: *Ancr. R.* 389: Visser, § 559)

As originally argued by Lightfoot (1979), the fact that modals lost the properties in (12) and (13) by or during the ENE period suggests a kind of 'categorial reanalysis'. In Roberts (1985), I suggested that this reanalysis was related to the fact that modals lost the capacity to assign Θ-roles and were reanalysed as functional heads. We will take up this idea in 3.3. in terms of the following two questions: (i) How and why did this categorial split take place (3.3.1.)? (ii) Why did a similar split not take place in MSc, languages which, with respect to the loss of agreement and V-to-I, have undergone an apparently parallel development to English (3.3.2.)? That MSc modals are not a separate category is shown by the fact that they occur in non-finite forms, as the following Danish examples show (Vikner pers. comm.):

(14) a.   Jeg **skal ikke kunne** sige det

   I   shall not can   say that (cf. (12a), (9a))

  b.   . . . hvis jeg **havde villet**

   . . . if   I   had   would (cf. (12c), (9c))

(On the other hand, MSc modals show some interesting restrictions: cf. Vikner 1988 and 3.3.2.).

Concerning the first question, in 3.3.1. we briefly recapitulate and re-work the accounts in Lightfoot (1979) and Roberts (1985) of the development of the NE modals, showing that the notion of Diachronic Reanalysis introduced in 2.3.2. is relevant here. For the second question, in 3.3.2. we will suggest that MSc differs from NE in retaining T^{-1}, as shown by the presence of infinitival morphology in these languages. We will also suggest that the T^{-1} parameter underlies two other distinctions between NE and MSc: the existence of a *for NP to VP* construction in NE but not MSc (cf. 3.1.2.), and the absence of a *'faire-par'*-type causative construction in NE but not MSc (cf. also Guasti 1990).

NE aspectual auxiliaries differ from the modals in having non-tensed forms (the same verbs have main-verb uses, but here they are not aspectual auxiliaries — cf. Chapter 1, Note 13):[4]

(15) a.   To have left too late is a shame

  b.   To be feared is better than to be loved

  c.   To be running is worse than to be sleeping

(16) a.   Having left, John was relieved

  b.   Being feared, Nick is very pleased with himself

However, the aspectuals also undergo inversion and negation obligatorily, and *do*-support is impossible (in their aspectual uses):

(17) a.   Have you finished your homework?
      *Do you have finished your homework?

  b.   Were you arrested last night?
      *Did you be arrested last night?

  c.   Are you running for president?
      *Do you be running for president?

We take the aspectual auxiliaries to be V°s heading their own VPs (cf. Ross 1969). In 3.2.1., we will account for their incompatibility with *do*-support in terms of a condition on the assignment of 'verbal Case' (cf. Fabb 1984, Roberts 1985, Zagona 1982, 1989 and *infra*).[5]

Although the three developments in (1) are clearly interrelated, it is not clear that they represent a genuine underlying parametric change, or whether we are instead dealing with a series of mutually reinforcing DRs. However, if the postulate that only parametric changes can lead to the elimination of structures is to be maintained (cf. 2.3.2.), then we must say that this is a parametric change, as sentences like (2a) were once grammatical and no longer are.

Accordingly, we propose the following parameter:

(18)   For X°, is there X^{-1}?   Yes/no

If there is no X^{-1}, there is no possibility of X hosting selected incorporation, and so any incorporation which involves substitution with X° is free incorporation. The subcase of (18) which interests us is that where X = I. As with the parameters discussed in Chapter Two, acquirers are predisposed by the Subset Principle to set (18) negatively. Clearly, the positive evidence needed for a positive setting of this parameter is the existence of bound morphemes of category X; more precisely, as the facts of the history of English and Scandinavian show, and as we shall see in 3.1.3., what is needed is an **inflectional paradigm** of category X. Thus the loss of I^{-1} is related to the well-known attrition of inflectional endings which took place throughout the ME period. By the ENE period, these endings had reduced to the point where no coherent verbal-inflection paradigm remained, and so I^{-1} was no longer postulated by acquirers.

Returning to the 'split-Infl' system, (18) means that NE has neither Agr^{-1} nor T^{-1}. Clearly, English retains a rather limited class of inflectional morphemes that are exponents of categories of tense and agreement: 3sg present -*s* and past -*ed*. We assume that these inflectional morphemes are inserted in Agr° and T° respectively rather than Agr^{-1} and T^{-1}. This implies a more elaborated view of the relation between phonological and syntactic inflection than the one we have implicitly been adopting until now. What we are suggesting is that the proposed X^{-1} level of syntactic structure does not exhaust the traditional notion of bound morpheme. We maintain that if a formative is of category X^{-1}, it is a bound morpheme, but that if a formative is a bound morpheme it is not necessarily an X^{-1}. Elements like -*s* and -*ed* are bound morphemes at the X° level; they are inflections with a different status to standard inflections, because, as we shall see in 3.1., they are inflections without a paradigm (another candidate class of X° bound morphemes is the class of clitics, although we will not elaborate on that point here).

If (18) is set negatively for T and Agr three things follow. First, the negative setting of (18) prevents Θ-assigning verbs from raising to T and Agr, in terms of the analysis proposed in 1.3.3. of verb-raising in English; we will take this point up in detail in 3.1.

Second, lexical insertion of free morphemes into Agr° and T° becomes possible. It is a striking fact that no other Romance or West Germanic language contains any free morpheme (i.e. a clear case of an X°) which can plausibly be regarded as inserted in these positions (although cf. Note 24 for comments on Giusti's 1989 claim that German *zu* is inserted in Infl, and Beukema and den Dikken 1989's idea that *zu* and Dutch *te* are in Agr). This is because of the parameter in (18); in these languages, lexical insertion into Agr° and T° is impossible, because Agr^{-1} and T^{-1} are always generated. There is no lexical insertion into Agr° and T° for the same reason that there is never lexical insertion at the X'- or XP-levels.[6] In NE, on the other hand, there are numerous words which are good candidates for membership of these categories: the modal auxiliaries, *to* and *do*. We will discuss *to* in 3.1.2., taking up Lightfoot's (1979: 186ff) account of the development of English infinitives. In 3.2. we discuss the development of dummy *do*, and 3.3. we discuss the modals. These are all inserted in T°. The X° member of Agr is 3sg -*s* (on the content of non-3sg Agr°, cf. 3.1.).

Third, given the discussion of free substitution of one head into another head-position in 1.3.3., we expect to find evidence of a second specifier position for Agr (or Agr/T) after Agr^{-1} is lost (cf. examples (74) and (75) in 1.3.3.). Ellegård (1953) studied the occurrence of V — *never* as opposed to *never* — V in detail. This study shows that the order *never* — V was possible long before the loss of main-verb raising to Agr, i.e. from the ME period on.

However, several factors interfere so as to make this prediction hard to test. First, as we shall see, ME had a Stylistic-Fronting rule (cf. 1.4., 3.1.1.) which placed adverbial material in front of the first tensed verb, a position practically indistinguishable from the new specifier position. Second, independently of the operation of Stylistic Fronting, it seems that we must allow for a pre-tensed-verb adverb position in ME; cf. 3.1.1. Third, since Agr-lowering will not create a new specifier position, the position should only be available when an auxiliary is present. For these reasons, the effects of the introduction of the new specifier position are imperceptible, and so we will have less to say about this consequence of the parametric change than about the others. (Cf. 3.2.3., 3.2.4. and Vikner (1990: 2.5.2.) for more on the loss of Stylistic Fronting, and its relation to V-to-Agr movement).

In a brief concluding section, 3.4., we will relate these developments to the well-known general loss of inflectional morphology in English. In terms of the proposed parameter (18), it seems possible to conclude that NE is a syntactically isolating language in the domain of functional categories, i.e. for X° a functional head, NE has no X^{-1}. In this section we will also briefly take up the question of the loss of V2 in English, basing our account largely on the one in van Kemenade (1987). The purpose of this is to briefly indicate the similarities and differences between the loss of V2 in English and the loss of V2 in French, as discussed in 2.3.1., 2.3.2., 2.4.2.

3.1. VERB-RAISING AND THE STATUS OF Agr

In this section we consider the evidence that main verbs raised to Agr in tensed clauses in earlier stages of English. In 3.1.1., we exemplify in detail the various constructions in question. In 3.1.2., we analyse the loss of V-to-Agr in terms of the loss of Agr^{-1}, and its consequences in terms of the theory of head-to-head movement of 1.3. In 3.1.3., we compare the development of English with that of MSc basing our discussion on the Swedish data in Platzack (1986, 1987) and Platzack and Holmberg (1989), Danish data provided by Vikner (1990, pers. comm.) and Faroese data from Barnes (1987, 1989). In this section we arrive at a characterization of the notion of inflectional paradigm which is closely related to Jaeggli and Safir's (1989) notion of morphological uniformity. Since we adopted and adapted the idea of morphological uniformity in our discussion of the theory of null subjects in Chapter 2 (cf. 2.2.3. and 2.4.3.), this move makes an interesting connection between null subjects and V-to-Agr movement and allows us to set up a system of parameters for Agr that covers all of Germanic and Romance.

3.1.1. *Evidence for V-to-Agr in ME and ENE*

As we saw in the introduction to this chapter, there are two main kinds of evidence that tensed main verbs moved to Agr in ME and ENE: (i) tensed main verbs appear in C; and (ii) tensed main verbs precede clausal negation. We now consider these constructions in turn, and then consider other evidence that main verbs raised to Agr, applying the tests in Emonds (1978) and Pollock (1989).

(*i*) *Inversion.* Agr raised to C in a variety of contexts in ME and ENE: interrogatives, conditionals and V2 declaratives (cf. 1.4. on Agr-to-C movement in Germanic in general, and van Kemenade 1987, van Kemenade and Hulk 1990, Lightfoot 1990, Weerman 1989, Platzack 1990 and 3.4. on V2 in the history of English). In all of these contexts, it was possible for a main verb to appear in C. This is illustrated in (19):

(19) a. **Seis thou** noght hir that sittis the besyde?
Seest thou not   her that sits   thee beside?

(1420s: James I, *Kingis Quair*, 173; Gray 1985: 76)

b. What **menythe** this pryste?
What means this priest?

(1466–7: Anon., from J. Gairdner (ed.), 1876, *The Historical Collections of a London Citizen*; Gray 1985: 11)

c. Than **longen folk** to goon on pilgrimages
Then long people to go on pilgrimages

(c1387: Chaucer, *C.T.*, *Prologue*, 1)

d. **Ples** yt yow to wet that . . .
Please it you to know that . . .

(1468: Letter from John Paston III to Margaret Paston; Gray 1985: 39)

The following riddles provide further exemplification of the possibility of inverting main verbs:

(20) a. Which parte of a sergeaunte **love ye** best towarde you?
Which part of a sergeant love you best towards you?

b. Why **dryve men** dogges out of the chyrche?
Why drive men dogs out of the church?

c. Why **come dogges** so often to the churche?
Why come dogs so often to the church?

d. Wherfore **set they** upon chyrche steples more a cocke
Why set they upon church steeples more (often) a cock

than a henne
than a hen?

e. What tyme in the yere **bereth a gose** moost feders?
What time of the year bears a goose most feathers?

(c1511 *The Demaundes Joyous*, Wardroper (ed.), 1971; Gray 1985: 369).

Each of the examples in (19) and (20) therefore has the following partial representation:

(21)

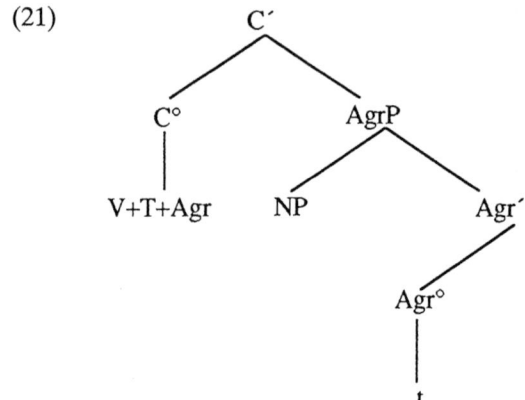

Here, V + T + Agr is in fact an abbreviation for the following structure:

(22)

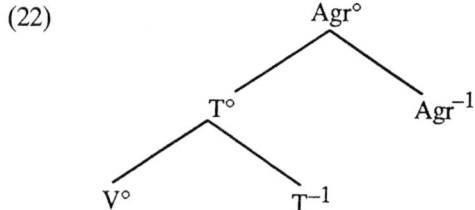

Moreover, in V2 examples like (19c), C^{-1} is also present.

However, it is not the case that apparently 'modern' cases of question-formation do not exist. Examples are found with modals (cf. (3c) and 3.3.) and aspectuals (although the aspectuals probably had a different status in ME, cf. Jespersen 1938, Traugott 1972), and, most importantly, with *do*. Cf., for example, the following riddle, from the same source as those in (20):

(23)   Why **doth** an oxe or a cowe lye?

Why does an ox   or a cow   lie down?

We will see in 3.2. that such sentences are not evidence that the system at this point was as in NE, since in ME and ENE *do* has a different status.

We conclude that main verbs raised via Agr to C in ME and ENE. Although we have seen direct raising from T to C to be possible (cf. 1.3.2.), it is clear from the morphology that when the main verb appears in examples like (19) and (20) it has passed through Agr, as is typical for V-to-C movement in Germanic languages.

It is hard to date precisely the disappearance of main-verb raising in interrogatives. A simple look at the texts would indicate that V still raised to C well after the 16th century. Fortunately, however, we are able to look at the data in a more refined way. Kroch (1989), on the basis of a sophisticated quantitative analysis of data provided in Ellegård (1953), shows that there is a statistically significant change in the occurrence of *do* at Ellegard's Period 7, i.e. 1550–75. Kroch interprets this quantitative change as indicating that 'a major reanalysis of the English auxiliary system' took place at this point. More specifically, Kroch suggests that it is at this point that V-to-I raising for main verbs is lost from the grammar. Putting Kroch's interpretation in our terms, we take the period 1550–1575 as an initial approximation for the date of the loss of Agr^{-1}, and consequent loss of V-to-Agr movement, and hence of V-to-C movement.

As noted above, we still find many examples where the main verb raises to C in interrogatives after this time. However, we can allow that the remainder of the 16th century is a transitional period, where both grammars (the one with main-verb raising and the one without) underlie the behaviour of the speech community. For the 17th century, there is some evidence that interrogatives where the main verb raises were not really part of colloquial speech. Jespersen (*MEG*, VI: 502) says:

In the post-Elizabethan period [i.e. after 1601 — IGR] questions without *do* are not at all rare, chiefly in more or less conscious archaic diction [there follows a page of examples, nearly all from poetic texts — IGR]

We attribute the continued occurrence of main-verb raising to extra-grammatical factors. The influence of Shakespeare (who was born in 1564, and arguably had control of both systems) and of the Authorized Version of The Bible (published in 1611 and full of examples of this kind, possibly for stylistic reasons) on all subsequent literary English is very strong, and so contributes to a possibly artificial maintenance of main-verb raising.

A brief investigation of Milton's poetry confirms this idea: in the *Miscellaneous Poems, Sonnets, Psalms* and the first nine books of *Paradise Lost*, covering the period from 1629 to 1667 and all written in a self-consciously high literary style, just 6% of interrogatives involve *do*-support, while 20% feature raising of a main verb (of the rest, 61% have another auxiliary, i.e. a modal, *have* or *be*, and 11% are *wh*-questions on the subject without inversion). However, we cannot claim that main-verb raising was still possible in normal usage in the 1660s, since, as we shall see in 3.2.4., the contracted form of *not*, *n't*, appears in writing at this time, but we find no case at any point (in Standard English) of *n't* attached to a main verb (e.g. *known't, sayn't*, etc.; this was pointed out by Plank 1984), a possibility that is predicted if verb-raising and *n't* coexisted. We conclude that Milton's poetry is an instance of 17th-century 'high style' which retained main-verb raising. By the latter part of the 17th century, however, this style was not even part of normal literary usage. From the 17th century on, examples of main-verb inversion can still be found, but we can treat them as archaisms often intended to consciously echo Biblical or Shakespearean usage.

We conclude that cases of Agr-to-C raising involving main verbs show that main verbs raised to Agr throughout ME and ENE. From the late 16th century onwards, this system was replaced by a system without Agr-to-C raising. The textual evidence for the grammatical change is blurred by extra-grammatical factors connected with literary style.

(*ii*) *Negation.* The situation regarding negation is similar to that found with interrogatives, as the remarks in the introduction indicate (and as Kroch's quantitative analysis shows). We retain for the time being the assumption that *not* was, in the periods in question, analogous in distribution to the negative elements of other Modern Germanic languages (*nicht, niet, ikke, inte,* etc.), as well as ModFr *pas*. That is, we assume that *not* appeared in SpecT' (cf. 1.1.; we will modify this assumption in 3.2. when integrate NegP into our system). In this position, *not* intervenes between the base position of the verb and Agr, as the following partial representation indicates:[7]

(24)

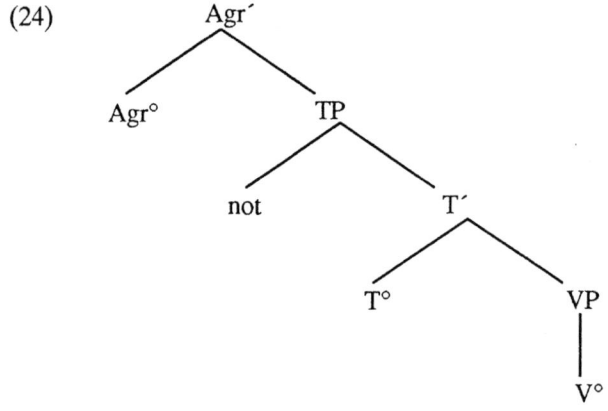

In these terms, occurrences of the order V — *not* must be interpreted as resulting from V-to-Agr movement. Data like (4) and the following examples thus show that main verbs raised to Agr in ME and ENE:

(25) a. Wepyng and teres **counforteth not** dissolute laghers

      Weeping and tears comfort   not dissolute laughers

      (1400–50: N. Love *The Myrour of the Blessyd Lyf of Jesu Christ*; Gray 1985: 97)

  b. Bycause they **come not** up and offre

      Because they come not up and offer

      (answer to (20b))

  c. they were ful soore adredde and **wist**   **not** what it was

     they were full sore afraid   and knew not what it was

     (1438: Anon.: *The Gilte Legende*; Gray 1985: 103)

The structure of examples of this kind is as in (26):

(26)

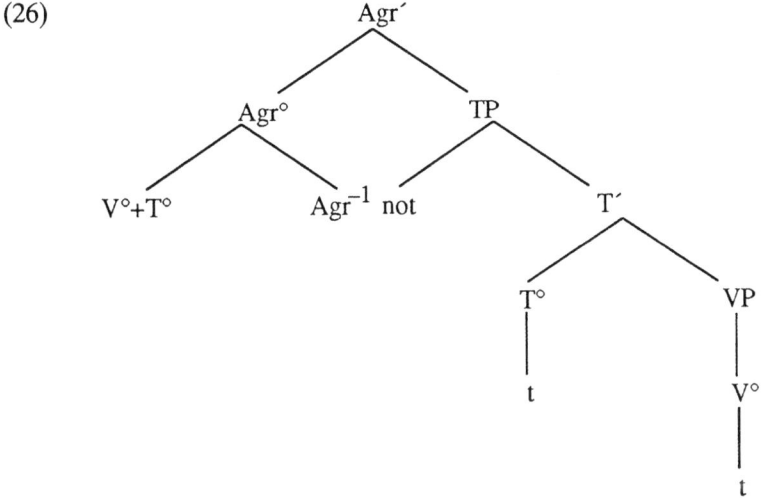

As in the case of Agr-to-C movement discussed above, we also find cases of negation which appear to follow the NE pattern, i.e. where *do* precedes *not* and the infinitival main verb follows. Visser (1963–73: 1529, § 1438) observes that this construction is only found after c1400. Here are some of the 15th-century examples he gives:

(27) a. I pray god . . . that my symple wryttyng **doo yow nott**

      I pray God . . . that my simple writing   do you not

      dyspleyse

      displease

      (14 . .: Beauty of his Mistress; Visser ibid.)

   b. the mony . . . is so little that it **doth not** suffice

      the money . . . is so little that it does not suffice

      (1417: Ellis, Orig. Lett. UU, I, p. 61; Visser ibid.)

   c. If   he be sinnful, I **doe not** know

      If (whether) he be sinful, I do not know

      (c1460: Chester Myst. Pl. (EETS) 237, 193; Visser ibid.)

Note also the following negative question with *do*:

(28)   Why **did** we **not** perysche?

Why did we not perish?

(1492: Anon., from Singer (ed.) *Cat. Alchem. Manuscripts*;
Gray 1985: 143)

Here, as in the parallel inversion cases exemplified in (23), *do* should be
treated as a raising verb, raising to Agr in the manner schematized in
(26), or an NE-style auxiliary inserted in T but without the NE restrictions
on which contexts it can be inserted in. See 3.2. for discussion of these
alternatives.

Finally, there are a few examples of what we might call the 'MSc' order
not − inflected V in the 15th and 16th centuries, and into the early 17th
century:

(29) a.   Thairwith he **nocht growit**

At this   he not   shrank (i.e. in fear)

(c1448: Richard Holland *The Buke of the Howlat*, 7; Gray 1985:
152)

b.   y so **not presuppose**

I so not presuppose

(1450s?: Pecock *Repressor of Overmuch Blaming*; Gray 1985:
124)

c.   Or if there were, it **not belongs** to you

(1600: Shakespeare *2 Henry IV*, IV, i, 98; in Battistella and
Lobeck 1988: 33)

d.   Safe on this ground we **not fear** today to tempt your laughter
by our rustic play

(1637: Ben Jonson *Sad Shepherd*, Prologue 37; in Kroch 1989)

On the subject of this construction, Visser (§ 1440, p. 1532) says:

Before 1500 this type is only sporadically met with, but after 1500 its currency increases and
it becomes pretty common in Shakespeare's time.

We will propose an account of the later, Shakespearean examples in
3.2.4., when we consider the origins of *do*-support. We will suggest that
the earlier examples are cases of Stylistic-Fronting of *not* (cf. 1.4., 2.1.2.
and below).

We conclude that examples like (25), with the structure in (26), indicate
clearly that main verbs raised to Agr in ME and ENE. This construction
largely died out in the latter half of the 17th century, judging from the
figures in Ellegård (1953). In 1600 *do* appeared in roughly 30% of nega-

tives; this figure increased slowly until the mid-late 17th century, and then climbed steeply to over 80% by 1700. However, unlike in interrogatives, an independent factor may influence these figures: the status of negation itself and its role in triggering *do*-insertion (Ellegård's figures are based solely on *do*-insertion, not on verb-raising, and, given the possibility of the MSc order illustrated in (29), we cannot take the absence of *do* to imply the presence of verb-raising). Kroch (1989) in fact argues, again on the basis of a quantitative treatment of Ellegård's data, that the real syntactic change in negation contexts took place in the same period as that affecting inversion contexts: in 1550–1575. The continued occurrences of main verb − *not* orders in the 17th century are due in part to the factors which preserved main-verb movement to C (see above), and in part to the different status of the negative element *not* at this period, a matter we will go into in 3.2.4. Moreover, Jespersen points out (*MEG* VI: 428) that certain V − *not* orders remained quite common through the 17th and 18th centuries, notably *say not* and *know not*. These can perhaps be treated as fixed expressions (Jespersen notes that 'to know' anomalously allows a diachronically conservative negation in other languages, e.g. French *je ne sais*; presumably 'I dunno' has a strong tendency to become a fixed expression).

(*iii*) *Other elements*: *Adverbs and Floated Quantifiers*. As we saw in 1.1., a further diagnostic for V-to-Agr movement concerns the relative position of the inflected verb and certain kinds of adverbs and floated quantifiers (FQs). In NE, as we saw, the only possible order is FQ/Adv − V. In ME and ENE, however, we find the opposite order, as the following examples indicate:

(30) a.   In doleful wise they **ended both** their days
           (1589: Marlowe *The Jew of Malta*, III, iii, 21).

     b.   The Turks . . . **made anone** redy a grete ordonnaunce

           The Turks prepared soon a large number of weapons

           (c1482: Kaye *The Delectable Newsse of the Glorious Victorye of the Rhodyans agaynest the Turkes*; Gray 1985: 23)

We continue to assume that floated quantifiers and adverbs of the relevant type are left-adjoined to VP (cf. 1.1. (26)), and so V follows this position and Agr precedes it. Given these assumptions, examples like (30) provide clear evidence that V raises to Agr.

Similarly, Ellegård's (1953) data concerning the relative orders of *never* and the inflected verb, and Kroch's (1989) reanalysis of it, show a steady increase in *never* − V orders at the expense of V − *never* orders. In Ellegård's Period 2 (1425–1475), two-thirds of the examples involve V −

never orders; by 1600 less than 10% of the relevant examples have this order. Moreover, the decrease in V — *never* order proceeds at the same rate as the increase in *do*-insertion in questions and negatives, supporting the contention that these are reflexes of a single underlying change.

However, on the basis of data from Tatlock and Kennedy's (1927) Chaucer concordance and Kottler and Markman's (1966) concordance to five late ME poems, Kroch estimates that even in ME 16% of examples had *never* — V order. Kroch's example of this possibility is the following:

(31) For many   are that **never** kane halde the
      For many (there) are that never can hold the

      ordyre of lufe
      ordure of love

      (c14: Rolle *The Bee and the Stork* 20-1 (Mossé 1968))

This example can be treated as Stylistic Fronting (cf 1.4., 2.1.2.), since it contains a subject gap. On this analysis, *never* is preposed to the preverbal position. Platzack (1990) cites examples like the following as evidence of the possibility of Stylistic-Fronting in ME:

(32) that ladyes . . . might se Who that **beste** were of dede
      that ladies . . . might see who   best were of deed

There is nevertheless a residue of examples which are not amenable to treatment as Stylistic Fronting, e.g. the following (from the same 1482 text as (30b)):

(33) But oure Crysten   folk **anone herde** . . .
      But our   Christian folk soon   heard . . .

The fact that there is no subject gap precludes a treatment in terms of Stylistic Fronting. It is unclear whether we should treat this as a case where the adverb occupies a higher position (which would have to be adjoined to Agr'), or as a rather early case where V does not raise. In any case, this sort of example shows that we cannot take the development of Adv — V orders to be uniquely the result of the change in V-to-Agr movement, even taking into account the effects of ME Styl-F. We have to leave open the possibility that some adverbs were already base-generated in pre-Agr position in ME. We will see in 3.2.4. that the preverbal adverbs play a role in the development of Agr-lowering.

Despite these complications, it is clear that the general increase in Adv — V orders that Ellegård and Kroch report is consistent with the prediction that the loss of Agr^{-1} makes available an extra pre-Agr specifier position (cf. 1.3., 3.0. for the discussion of the theoretical background to this prediction).

On the basis of the evidence reviewed above, we conclude that ME and ENE up to 1550–1575 allowed, and in fact required, V to move to Agr in all tensed clauses. We now analyse this construction in terms of the theory of head-to-head movement.

3.1.2. *Triggering V-Movement*

As we saw in 1.3.3., there are three types of head-to-head movement. Leaving aside the adjunction option (cf. 1.3.3. (72c)), there are two varieties of substitution of one head into another: selected substitution and free substitution. Adapting these possibilities to the case where the host is I and the incorporated element V, we have the following cases (cf. 1.3.3. (72); we conflate T and Agr for ease of exposition):

(34) a.

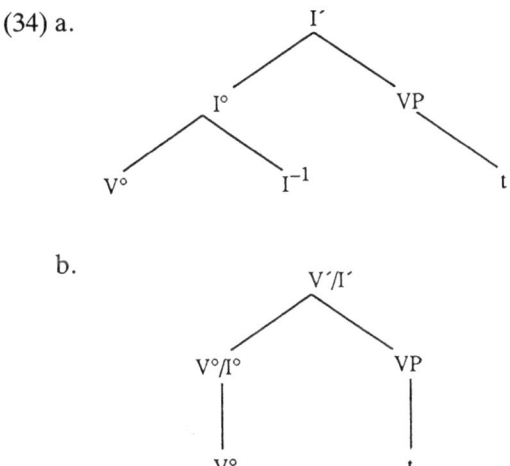

b.

We argued in 1.3.3. that NE has the option in (34b). In this way, we can understand the NE ban on V-to-I where V is a Θ-assigning verb. Free substitution of V into I creates a hybrid category V/I. Where V is a Θ-assigner, this amounts to creating a new Θ-assigning position in the course of the derivation, something which the Θ-criterion and the Projection Principle conspire to rule out (the Projection Principle requires that the new predicate's Θ-roles be assigned, but prevents the creation of new argument positions to which these Θ-roles must be assigned according to the dictates of the Θ-criterion — cf. 1.3.3.). So we account for the NE situation by saying that I does not select V, i.e. there is no I^{-1}. This permits raising of non-Θ-assigning verbs, i.e. auxiliaries, as is clearly correct (although we are assuming that only aspectuals are base-generated in V; cf. 3.2.1. on the precise NE status of *do* and 3.3. on the NE modals). A separate question is why auxiliaries are **required** to raise in NE; we suspect that this is connected to their morphological irregularity — cf.

Note 5 for discussion. Given the ME and ENE data reviewed above, we are led to the conclusion that V-to-I movement at these periods was of the kind in (34a), i.e. that I^{-1} was present and triggered incorporation of V by its morphological selection feature.

The question now becomes: what caused the loss of I^{-1}? Recasting this question in terms of the split-Infl system, we need to find evidence for the demise of both Agr^{-1} and T^{-1}. We first address the question of the loss of Agr^{-1}. Here an obvious answer suggests itself, one which again is proposed in 1.3.3., and, in slightly different terms, both in Pollock (1989) and in Roberts (1985). The idea can be stated as follows:

(35)   'Rich' agreement is a manifestation of Agr^{-1}.

We can attempt to quantify the relevant notion of richness in terms of the same criteria that we used in the discussion of the identification of the content of null subjects (cf. 2.0., 2.2.3., 2.4.3.), although this of course does not mean that identifying null subjects and triggering verb-movement are in any sense the same thing, only that they may depend on similar types of morphological cue. We will in fact propose an explicit connection between the two in the next subsection.

So the proposal is that there must be a certain morphological content to the agreement paradigms in order for Agr^{-1} to be postulated by acquirers. If the agreement paradigm is too feeble, in a sense we will try to make clearer, acquirers will not postulate Agr^{-1} and an NE-style situation will emerge. We can also assume, given the general proposals that we put forward in 2.3.2. for how syntactic change works, that the conditions of acquisition — the Least Effort Strategy and the Subset Principle — together create a situation in which positive evidence is needed for Agr^{-1}.

In the next subsection, we will try to characterize this positive evidence on the basis of comparative data. For the moment, it is enough to note the changes that took place in the (present-tense) agreement paradigms during ME and ENE. Given what we have said so far, we are led to the assumption that these morphological changes so weakened the positive evidence for Agr^{-1} that it was no longer 'found' by acquirers.

Mossé (1968) gives the following paradigms for the present tense of weak verbs in ME (cf. also Jespersen *MEG*, VI: 16):

(36)   1sg: sing**e**
         2sg: sing**est**
         3sg: sing**eth** (south)/sing**es** (north)
         1,2,3pl: sing**en** (midland)/sing**eth** (south)/sing**es** (north)

This system must have been adequate to establish the presence of Agr^{-1}. The paradigm is morphologically uniform in Jaeggli and Safir's sense (cf. 2.2.3. (79)): there is an agreement ending in every person in the paradigm. The East Midland dialect (that used by Chaucer, for example) has four distinct inflectional forms, while the Southern and Northern dialects have three. The paradigms are not [+pron] in the sense defined in 2.2.3. (78), however, since they have more than one syncretism. In any case, there is no doubt as to the richness of these paradigms in terms of the criteria for rich morphology that we elaborated in our earlier discussions of null subjects.[8]

Owing to phonological erosion, these endings were gradually lost. Gray (1985: 495f) gives the following paradigms for London-area English c1400 and c1500:

(37) | *1400* | *1500* |
|---|---|
| cast(**e**) | cast |
| cast**est** | cast**est** |
| cast**eth** | cast**eth** |
| cast**e(n)** | cast(e) |
| cast**e(n)** | cast(e) |
| cast**e(n)** | cast(e) |

So the 1sg ending was eliminated, and the plural ending was somewhat weakened. Jespersen (ibid.) gives *I fall, he falleth, we fall* (he discusses the 2sg elsewhere) as the 16th-century paradigm. Early in the 16th century, the plural marking disappears; St. Thomas More (1478–1535) does not seem to use plural endings, if the following examples are representative:

(38) a. folke which to be excellent in one thing **set** al othir aside
         (Gray 1985: 408)

   b. Ye **build** the tower of Babilon in the corner of the prison
       (Gray 1985: 414)

No examples of plural endings are found later in the writings of later 16th-century authors. The following remark from Jespersen (ibid.: 339) seems to sum up the 16th-century situation accurately:

Isolated survivals of final *n* in verbal forms are found in archaic language in Spenser, in *killen* in Gower's speech in [possibly Shakespeare's — IGR] Per II 19; the sailor Ben in Congreve's Love f. Love 248: *sayn*.

These are certainly archaisms in Shakespeare and Congreve (the latter wrote in the late 17th century). Barber (1976: 243) corroborates this, saying that ME plural ending *-en* in London English was essentially lost by 1500. The following lines from Spenser's *Shepherd's Calendar* (1579) feature this ending as a conscious archaism to suggest rustic speech:

(39)   You **deemen**, the Spring is come attonce
        You **thinken** to be Lordes of the yeare

There are two examples of this ending in Shakespeare: the one from

Pericles mentioned in the above quotation from Jespersen, and one example from *A Midsummer Night's Dream*, spoken by a 'rustic' character (cf. Barber 1976: 245). Barber concludes (ibid.) that "the normal and overwhelmingly predominant form of the present plural during our period [1500–1700] is the uninflected one, the base form."

Similarly, Palsgrave's (1530) French grammar gives no 1sg or plural endings (for English verbs), but quite systematically has 2sg *-est* and 3sg *-eth*. So we conclude that the 1sg ending had been lost before 1500 and that the plural endings disappeared at some point very close to that date. The following quotation, from Ben Jonson's (1637) *English Grammar*, supports this conclusion:

> In former times, till about [1509–1547], they [the plural inflections] were wont to be formed by adding *en* thus *loven, sayen, complainen*. But now (whatsoever is the cause) it has growne quite out of use, and that other so generally prevailed, that I dare not presume to set it a-fotte againe. (Ben Jonson *English Grammar*, 1637 (Waite (ed.) 1909, cited in Roberts 1985a: 43, Note 13)).

The *-en* ending was characteristic of the East Midland dialect of ME, which included London English. As (33) shows, the plural ending in the North was *-es* and in the South it was *-eth*. We defer discussion of the Northern situation until the next section, owing to certain complications. As for the Southern one, Barber (1976: 242) says "The old Southern *-eth* plural appears sporadically throughout the 16th century . . . Elyot [a text from 1531 — IGR] normally has the base form, but occasionally *-eth*." He gives the following example from Elyot (1531: *The Boke Named the Gouernour*):

(40)   for the pannes and pottes **garnisseth** wel the ketchyn the bedde-
          stestars and pillowes **besemeth** nat the halle no more than car-
          pettes and kusshynes **becometh** the stables.

However, this ending is rarely found later in the 16th century, for example in Spenser.

Still leaving aside the Northern situation, we conclude that, certainly by 1550, the English agreement paradigm was no longer [+MU] in the sense defined in 2.2.3., since four persons out of six had zero-endings.[9]

In theoretical terms, the loss of Agr^{-1} has three consequences. First, V-to-Agr raising, although still available, is no longer the result of morphological selection, and so, for the reasons discussed above and in 1.3.3., no Θ-assigning verb can undergo it (on T^{-1}, see below). The second consequence of the loss of Agr^{-1} is that lexical insertion into Agr° of an X°, i.e. a free morpheme, becomes possible. We will see later (cf. 3.2.3., 3.3.1.) that modals and *do* underwent a DR in the 16th century such that they were reanalysed as base-generated in T°. No lexical item was reanalysed as base-generated in Agr°, though. Nevertheless, the prediction is relevant to the development of the English auxiliary system since the remaining affixes of the inflectional paradigm — (e)st and (e)s — became Agr° once Agr^{-1} was lost. Because of this, affix-hopping of these endings became a structure-preserving operation. In a system where affixes are Agr^{-1}, affix hopping is impossible since the adjunction of Agr^{-1} to V° is ruled out by the Structure Preservation Condition (which we construe as banning the adjunction of X^n to Y^m, where n ≠ m). We will comment further on this in 3.2.4.

The third consequence concerns the development of a preverbal adverb position. As we saw in the previous section, although such a position may already have been available in ME, preverbal adverbs increase in frequency during the 16th century. The crucial evidence in favour of our prediction concerns adverbs preceding the auxiliary; however, Ellegård's data, which we reported in the previous section, unfortunately does not distinguish this case from the others. Because of this, we will leave this point aside, noting that the available data is certainly consistent with our prediction.

A further morphologically free functional head emerges around this time: the infinitive marker to. It seems most natural, on conceptual as well as empirical grounds (cf. the fact that it may follow not, as in Not to like pizza is a sin), to treat this element as a member of T° in NE. This suggests that, at about the same time as Agr^{-1} was lost, T^{-1} was also lost. Although this is not the place for a full-fledged account of the history of English infinitives, it is fairly clear from the account proposed in Lightfoot (1979: 186ff) that three related developments took place in infinitives in the 16th century, all of which corroborate the idea that T^{-1} was lost and to started to be inserted in T°. These developments are:

(41) a. The development of the modern for NP to VP construction

   b. The loss of the infinitival affix

   c. The loss of nominal properties of the infinitive

We will now briefly discuss each of these developments in turn.

In ME, as is well-known, for and to could occur adjacent to each other (as in a number of NE dialects; cf. Carroll 1983 on Ottawa Valley English, Chomsky and Lasnik 1977 on Ozark English and Henry 1988 on Belfast English), giving examples like:

(42) a. (I) for to go is necessary

   b. It is good for to go

   c. It grieves me for to go

       (Lightfoot ibid.: 187)

We can treat such examples in one of two ways: either we posit a compound complementizer *for to* (which was in fact frequently written as one word, as in *That wol not auntre forto winne* 'That will not venture to win' (c1390, Gower, *C A* 4, 339; Visser § 1194)), or we consider *to* to be a complementizer (on a par with some treatments of Romance elements like French *à*, Italian *a*, e.g. Cinque 1991; cf. also Kayne 1990: 20) and *for* to be a preposition with a sentential (or nominal) complement. Evidence for the former analysis comes from cases where *for to* are preceded by another preposition, e.g. *after for to speke* (Lightfoot, p. 192). Evidence for the latter comes from the generally more nominal nature of ME infinitives (in many respects they were closer to NE gerunds, cf. Lightfoot's discussion). These two analyses may not in fact be incompatible, and we will certainly not try to choose between them here.

The possibility of a nominative NP preceding *for* as shown in (42a) is a problem for both of the analyses just considered. Such examples are not common, and it may be best to treat them as a sporadic reanalysis of the compound *forto* complementizer as an infinitival marker. This approach resolves the question of the position of the Nominative subject in (42a) (it is SpecAgr'), but not the problem of how it receives Nominative Case. The important point is that both of the above analyses treat *to* as an element in C, rather than in T. Cases like (43), where *to* cooccurs with infinitival morphology, further support this view:

(43)   Ne herte hath noon **to stonden** at deffense
        Neg heart has none to stand   at defence
        'None has the heart to stand in defence'
        (c1400, Hoccleve *The Letter of Cupid*, 295; Gray 1985: 49)

Here *to* is in C, and *-en* is in T.

According to Lightfoot, examples of the following sort appear in the 16th century:

(44) a.   For us to go is necessary

     b.   There is nothing to do but for him to marry Amanda

     c.   What would be better than for you to go?

Lightfoot gives other cases which appeared earlier (in the late 14th and early 15th centuries), but, as he himself notes (p. 196), the sequence *for* NP in these cases can be treated as a benefactive complement with prepositional *for*:

(45) a.   It is necessary to/for a man (for) to go

     b.   I'm afraid for them to see it

We take examples of the kind in (44) as an unequivocal indication that *for* is in C and *to* is in T. Further support for this comes from the fact that (*NP*) *for to V* orders disappear in the 16th century: of 838 examples of ME infinitives given in Visser (§ 2061–2082), 138 ($\approx$ 15.5%) are cases of *for to*, while only 20 of 881 examples of ENE infinitives are of this type ($\approx$ 2%), and these are almost all from the early 16th century. If (44) is an indication that *for* is in C, and *for* is able to govern the subject, then orders like (42) are ruled out since the PRO subject of infinitives cannot be governed (this is the PRO theorem of Chomsky 1981, Ch. 3). The rather swift disappearance of this order (in the standard language) is thus further evidence for the 'modern' situation in infinitives, with *for* in C and *to* in T. So we concur with Lightfoot's conclusion that the modern order emerged in the 16th century. Visser's data confirms this; there are no clear cases of *for NP to VP* order in the ME examples, while there is a small number of ENE cases.

Turning next to (41b), the infinitival ending -*e(n)* disappeared at about the same time as the -*e(n)* plural marking in East Midlands English, i.e. at about the beginning of the 16th century. Lightfoot (p. 192) says it had disappeared by the mid-16th century, and Gray (1985: 493ff) says that -*en* had weakened to a purely orthographic -*e* by the end of the 15th century. As we have already mentioned, this ending cooccurred with *to* (cf. (43)). It also occurred alone, as the following examples show:

(46) a.   Nat can we **seen** . . .

      Not can we see . . .

      'We cannot see . . .'

      (c1400, Hoccleve *The Letter of Cupid*, 289; Gray 1985: 49)

The disappearance of this ending left T° available for lexical insertion of *to* into T°. It is a significant fact about the history of modals that, while they occurred with the instantiation of T° in ME, as in (46a), they cannot cooccur with *to* in NE (with the exception of *ought*). This is consistent with the 16th-century DR for modals that we discuss in 3.3.1.

Moreover, it is significant that the infinitival affix is completely obsolete at the time examples like (44) appear. In ENE, there are no cases either of *for to* or of *for NP to VP* where the verb carries the infinitive affix. There are a few ME cases of *for to* with infinitive affix (18/838 $\approx$ 2%), but no clear case of *for NP to VP* of this kind (there is one ambiguous case from Chaucer, cf. Visser § 2064, *pray*). The loss of this affix was a precondition for the appearance of (42) since in these cases *to* occupies T°.

This account tells us why it was possible for *to* to occupy T°, but not why it was necessary; nor does it tell us why the complementizer *for* can assign Accusative Case to the subject. These are matters which become clearer when we consider the categorial properties of infinitives, (41c).

Lightfoot's main concern in his discussion of the development of infinitives is with (41c). He proposes that ME infinitives were nominal, while NE infinitives are sentential (in terms of the theoretical assumptions in Lightfoot (1979), 'sentential' meant being a VP; for us, however, 'sentential' means AgrP). In Lightfoot's account, this change, which was caused by an increasingly non-NP-like distribution of the infinitives, had several consequences: *inter alia* the development of (44), the obsolescence of (42), and the loss of the infinitive affix. We have accounted for these changes in other terms, and so we do not need to appeal to the categorial change to explain them. Another change which Lightfoot explains in terms of the category change is the NE inability of *to* — VP to be preceded by a preposition; in ME, sequences like *without to* V, *through to* V, etc., are found, although rather rarely after the 16th century (cf. Visser § 976, Mustanoja 1960: 540). This can be taken as an indication of a change in categorial status from 'nominal' to 'sentential' infinitives, and helps us to understand the development of *for NP to VP* sequences of the type in (44) on the assumption that *for*, unlike *without*, *through*, etc., was semantically empty enough and phonologically light enough to be reanalysed as a complementizer. So the reanalysis of infinitives as sentential is a precondition for the construction in (44). Hence, for us what is important is that, if infinitives were nominal at some earlier stage, they must have become sentential by, at the latest, the time that *to* was analysed as a member of T and the *for NP to VP* construction emerged. Whether this change was simultaneous with the reanalysis of *to* or not is a matter we leave open.

Although we cannot begin to do full justice to the topic of the history of English infinitives here, the above remarks suffice to show that T^{-1} was lost in the 16th century. The infinitival affix was lost by the beginning of that century, and *to* was analysed as a member of that position while *for* became a complementizer. This development is remarkable from a comparative point of view, in that nothing of the kind has taken place in other Romance or Germanic languages, including MSc (although Welsh has a kind of *for NP to VP* construction, cf. (6a) of Chapter 1). We will discuss more consequences of this difference between NE and MSc in 3.3.2.

We have shown in this section that English lost both Agr^{-1} and T^{-1} in the 16th century. These developments had the consequences for V-movement that we discussed above. Moreover, they made possible the lexical insertion of free morphemes into these functional-head positions. Infinitival *to* is clearly inserted in $T°$, and we will see in 3.2.1. that *do* and the modals are best analysed in the same way.

3.1.3. *The Determination of Agr^{-1}*

In this section, we will attempt to clarify on the basis of comparative evidence, largely from the Scandinavian languages, how rich a verbal agreement paradigm is required for Agr^{-1} to be posited. What we will see is that number agreement appears to be the determining factor (cf. Platzack and Holmberg 1989, who propose essentially the same thing in rather different terms). In a series of recent papers, Platzack (1986, 1987) (cf. also Holmberg and Platzack 1988, Platzack and Holmberg 1989) has shown that Swedish has undergone a development which parallels what we saw for English in the preceding subsections. The discussion of Swedish and the other Scandinavian languages centres around subordinate-clause word order, since these languages have retained V-to-C raising in main clauses as a reflex of V2 (cf. 1.3.2., and 3.3.2., 3.4. on the relations between this fact and certain divergent developments between English and MSc). Platzack (1987) shows that, if we compare Modern Swedish (NSw, post-1526) and Old Swedish (OSw, pre-1526) with respect to the order of the inflected verb and negation in subordinate clauses, we find that OSw has the order V — Neg, while NSw has Neg — V:

(47) a. . . . at Gudz ord **kan ey** vara j honom (OSw)

  . . . att Guds ord **inte kan** vara i honom (NSw)

  . . . *that God's word can not/not can be in him*

Thus OSw patterns like Icelandic (cf. 1.3.2. (64)). The obvious interpretation of this is that OSw had V-to-Agr raising, while NSw does not have it.

Platzack goes on to establish a correlation between the loss of agreement inflection and the loss of V-to-Agr movement. According to Bergman (1968), at an early period (Classic or Older OSw: 1225–1375), Swedish had a paradigm very similar to that of Old Norse or Modern Icelandic (see below for the Icelandic paradigm), with distinct person endings in the plural. In Younger OSw (1375–1526), the distinct plural endings were collapsed, but the plural/singular distinction remained. This distinction was gradually lost during the Older NSW period (1526–1732). What Platzack (1987: 9f) shows is that V-to-Agr movement was also gradually lost, starting just before 1500. By the late 17th century the modern order was clearly predominant (V — Neg order occurs in a median 24% of cases in the 17th century, as against 36% in 1570–1600 and 80% in 1480–1530; cf. Platzack's (op. cit.: 10) Table 1). It seems possible to conclude, then, that V-to-Agr movement was lost during the Younger NSw period, just when the singular/plural distinction was being lost in the agreement paradigm.

A similar development seems to have taken place in the history of Danish.[10] Here too, the rather rich Old Norse paradigm was levelled into one which distinguished number but not person. In Danish, this development took place earlier than in Swedish; according to Karker (1974: 25), it had taken place by 1400. There are also some indications that the number distinction was lost very early (Karker 1974: 26, Mikkelsen 1911: 463); according to Skautrup (1948–53: I, 273–4), this may have happened by 1350 in some areas of Denmark. Examples without V-to-Agr raising are found from the 15th century on, cf.:

(48) a.   . . . ter som mand **engælund ma**   kommæ pooæ hafuet

     . . . *if   one   not   may come   on   sea-the*

     '. . . if one cannot get there by sea'

b.   . . . saa ath the **jckæ sælwæ kundhe** tidh   komme

     . . . *so   that they not   self   could   in-time(?) come*

     . . . so that they themselves could not come in time'
     (both examples from *Mandevilles reise*, 15th-century translation; Mikkelsen 1911: 636)

On the other hand, V-to-Agr movement certainly seems to persist until the 17th or even 18th century, according to Falk and Torp (1900: 302). However, we can treat the later examples as being due to literary conservativism. In general, the picture that emerges for the history of Danish parallels that of the history of Swedish, with the difference that Danish has been consistently roughly a century 'ahead' of Swedish.

Certain MSc dialects are also relevant here. Platzack (1987) and Platzack and Holmberg (1989) discuss Älvdalsmålet, a conservative dialect spoken in Dalecarlia, Central Sweden. In this dialect, according to Platzack "no personal agreement is found in the singular, both present tense plural and past tense plural have different forms for the persons" (ibid.: 11), and the order Verb — Neg is found:

(49) a.   an-fa chlais'n   **uis   int** ed

     he pretends that-he knows not it

b.   um du **for int** gart ita ia   firi brado

     if   you get not done this before breakfast

     (Platzack's (31a–b), p. 11)

So this seems to be a further case where number agreement plays a crucial role.

Another Scandinavian language which is relevant to this question is Faroese (Lockwood 1955, Barnes 1987, 1989, Vikner 1990). Faroese has the following verbal inflection paradigm, which is very similar to medieval MSc:

(50)   kasta ('to throw'):
        kasti, kastar, kastar, kasta, kasta, kasta

Here we see person distinctions in the singular, while the plural is identical with the infinitive. Strikingly, contemporary Faroese seems to lack V-to-Agr movement (although some literary registers seem to accept it, cf. Barnes 1989 for discussion):

(51)   Har   vóru nógv fólk,   eg **ikki kendi/*kendi ikki**
        There were many people I   not   knew/knew   not

Similarly, the Norwegian dialect of Hallingdalen discussed in Trosterud (1989) has plural forms (in the present tense) that are identical to the infinitive and lacks V-to-Agr:

(52)   e kasta, me kastæ ('*I throw*; *we throw*')
        (cf. Trosterud's (3), p. 88)

(53) a.   at   me **ikke kjøpæ**
          that we not buy

It appears, then, that Hallingdalen is in relevant respects like Faroese. Putting together Faroese, Hallingdalen and Älvdalsmålet, it appears that it is plural agreement which is related to V-to-Agr movement. Älvdalsmålet has overt plural agreement and V-to-Agr, while Faroese and Hallingdalen lack both. This is also consistent with what we saw above concerning the development of Danish and Swedish.

One further variety should be considered before we attempt to draw a conclusion. This is the English of Northern England and Scotland of the 14th to 16th centuries. As we saw in the previous section, the paradigm here was rather different to the Midland and Southern dialects in that both 2sg and 3sg present were marked -(e)s, as were all persons in the plural. Moreover, at least in the 15th-century language, 1sg was also marked -(e)s. However, in all persons of the plural and the 1sg, the ending was in complementary distribution with a pronominal subject, i.e. if the pronoun was present (and adjacent to the verb) no ending appeared. This situation is illustrated by the following examples:

(54) a.   Nathing of lufe I **knaw,** Bot **kepis** my scheip
          Nothing of love I know, but keep my sheep

          (late c15: Robert Henryson, *Robene and Makyne* 10–11; in Gray 1985: 281)

b. Thai **gat** to reste and **slepis** as   ony swyne

   They went to rest and sleep like any swine

   (c1480s: Anon. *The Talis of the Fyve Bestis* 216; in Gray 1985: 158)

c. They **cum** an' teake them — the burds **cums** an' pæcks them.

   (Jespersen, *MEG*, III: 15)

We will return to this striking phenomenon in 3.2.4. For the moment, what is important is that a paradigm of this type nevertheless gave rise to V-to-Agr movement, as examples of the following type show:

(55) a. quhy **syng ye   nocht,** for schame!

   why sing you not   for shame!

   (c1480s: Anon. *The Unicornis Tale*, 227; Gray ibid.)

b. quhen he **trespassit nocht**

   when   he trespassed not

   (ibid.)

We are now in a position to give a synopsis of the relation between V-to-Agr movement and the nature of the (present-tense) verbal inflection. In (56), we give a number of typical paradigms from well-known languages where the status of V-to-Agr is not in doubt (as indicated by 'yes' or 'no' for each language):

(56)

German	*Icelandic*	*French*	*Danish*	*NE*
yes:	yes	yes:	no:	no:
werfe	kasta	jette	kaster	throw
wirf**st**	kast**ar**	jett**es**	kaster	(throw**est**)
wir**ft**	kast**ar**	jette	kaster	throw**s**
werf**en**	kös**tum**	jet**ons**	kaster	throw
wer**ft**	kasti**ð**	jet**ez**	kaster	throw
werf**en**	kast**a**	jett**ent**	kaster	throw

Here the correlation with 'richness' of morphology seems evident, as Platzack and Holmberg (1989) noted. The following summary of the comparative Scandinavian and historical English data that we have been considering refines the picture somewhat (here and in (56) the Swedish situation is identical to that in Danish; the only difference is that Danish lost verbal inflection and V-to-Agr earlier than Swedish, so what we say about 15th-century Danish here is valid for 16th-century Swedish):

(57)   *Faroese*   *Eng (c1400)Eng (c1500)Scots (c15) Danish (c15)*

no:	yes:	yes:	yes:	no:
kasti	cast(**e**)	cast	cast(**is**)*	kaster
kastar	cast**est**	cast**est**	cast**is**	kaster
kastar	cast**eth**	cast**eth**	cast**is**	kaster
kasta	cast**e(n)**	cast(**e**)	cast(**is**)*	kaste
kasta	cast**e(n)**	cast(**e**)	cast(**is**)*	kaste
kasta	cast**e(n)**	cast(**e**)	cast(**is**)*	kaste

(The asterisk next to the Scots forms indicates that the ending in question appeared only where there was no pronominal subject; the English forms are based on the London (i.e. East Midland) dialect).

On the basis of these forms we can posit the following inductive generalization:

(58) Agr^{-1} is postulated only if there's overt distinct morphological plural marking.

Here, 'distinct' means 'distinct from the singular form(s)'. Perhaps (58) could be given more perspicuously as (58′):

(58′) Agr^{-1} is postulated only if there is overt, equipollent marking for [Number = ±Pl].

(Here 'equipollent' is meant in the Prague-School sense of 'equivalently marked'; i.e. an equipollent opposition is one where both values of a given feature are marked). (58′) states clearly that both sides of the number opposition have to be marked, while there is no requirement for the plural endings to be distinct among themselves, although that would imply that at least some of the endings were overt. We can see that this criterion is satisfied in all the languages in (56) which have V-to-Agr movement: Icelandic, German and French.[11] Similarly, this requirement fails in both NE and Danish. In NE, there is no morphology in the plural; the plural forms are identical with the infinitival, bare-stem form of the verb. Therefore Agr^{-1} is not determined. In Modern Danish (and Swedish and Norwegian), the plural forms are morphologically marked, but this marking is not distinct from the singular marking (we will see in 3.3.2. that this is a tense-marking, i.e. T^{-1}). So, once again, Agr^{-1} is not determined.

Turning now to the less well-known cases in (57), we see that Faroese is in the relevant respects just like NE: the plural agreement is non-overt (although distinct from the singular in all persons, unlike in NE), and so Agr^{-1} is not determined, and there is no V-to-Agr movement. The same is true of Hallingdalen, as we mentioned above. Note that this means that the agreement affixes of the singular must move down in Faroese by means of a form of Agr-lowering (in non-V2 clauses; we assume that T^{-1} is present in Faroese, as in other Scandinavian languages — cf. 3.3.2. — and so $[_T \, V \, T^{-1}]$ can raise to Agr and on to C in V2 clauses). The absence of any phenomenon of *do*-support in Faroese implies that the negative element is not a head (cf. Vikner (1990, 2.4.) for discussion, and 3.2.3. and Kroch (1989) on the non-head status of *not* in 16th-century English).

Regarding the history of English, (58) accounts for the historical correlation between the loss of plural marking on verbs c1500, and the loss of V-to-Agr movement later in the 16th century, a correlation that we established in the preceding sections. Similarly, following Platzack and Holmberg (1989), we can relate the loss of V-to-Agr in the history of MSc to the weakening of agreement; by the time the languages had the agreement paradigm in (57) (15th-century Danish and 16th-century Swedish), V-to-Agr was being lost.

What we said about English holds fairly straightforwardly for the Southern and Midland dialects, but the situation in Scots is clearly more complex, given the alternation of the -(e)s ending and the pronoun here. If we treat the ending as part of the paradigm, we have a situation like that of Modern MSc, and so we do not expect to find V-to-Agr; if we treat the ending as something else, and so consider the 1sg and plural forms to be bare stems identical with the infinitive we have a situation like NE or Faroese, and so again we expect no V-to-Agr. However, the evidence from 15th-century Scots in (55) suggests that V-to-Agr existed. Notice though that (58) is formulated as a one-way conditional, and so it allows Agr^{-1} to exist in the absence of the relevant morphology. (58) should really be taken as a statement of the direct, positive morphological evidence which induces acquirers to posit Agr^{-1}; it says nothing about the status of Agr^{-1} in the absence of this direct morphological evidence. Other things being equal, the Least Effort Strategy will favour the abandonment of V-to-Agr as this will 'economise' on the chain-positions formed by V-movement (cf. the discussion of this condition in 2.3.2.), but it is also the case that the trigger experience must be such that there is no independent evidence for V-to-Agr. It is possible that Scots had no Agr^{-1} but that the strange behaviour of the ending provided motivation for V-to-Agr, perhaps in that the ending acted as a clitic attracting V in the 1Sg and Pl. In any case, (58) is stated so that the absence of the relevant agreement morphology is not strictly incompatible with V-to-Agr movement. This move is motivated in part by the Scots data (unless the cliticization suggestion just made can hold up), and by the need for some flexibility in dealing with the 'transitional' periods of English, Danish and Swedish. Moreover, Platzack and Holmberg (1989) report that Kronoby, a Swedish dialect spoken in Finland, combines an absence of agreement inflection with V-to-Agr, illustrated by systematic V — neg order:

(59)   He va bra et   an **tsöfft int bosen**
        It   was good that he bought not the-book
        (Platzack and Holmberg 1989: 74)

This situation is allowed by (58), but not the converse. So what (58) is incompatible with is a situation where there is overt, distinct plural agreement and no V-to-Agr.

It is important to stress that (58) is purely an inductive generalization over a range of cross-linguistic data, and not a principle of grammar. The module of grammar which determines the distribution of Agr^{-1} is X-bar theory; (58) can be taken as a preliminary statement of the major aspect of the trigger experience which determines whether this level of structure is postulated by acquirers. Another way to think of (58), as we intimated in the introduction to this chapter, is as a step towards a definition of a paradigm. Agr^{-1} is the position in which the elements determining an agreement paradigm appear, and once the morphological distinctions carried by the paradigm become sufficiently blurred or reduced, the syntactic position which carries those distinctions may disappear. Looked at in these terms, the crucial reference to number morphology in (58) may be due to the fact that the singular/plural distinction is the major morphological distinction in the paradigm; without clear marking of this distinction, there is no paradigm. The fate of English 3sg -*s* (and Faroese 1sg -*i*, 2sg/3sg -*ar*) is to be an affix without a paradigm.

(58) is rather close, especially if we take the view just sketched, to a grammatical principle that we have discussed elsewhere: Jaeggli and Safir's (1989) Morphological Uniformity Condition (cf. 2.2.3. (77)), which we repeat here for convenience:

(60)   An inflectional paradigm P in a language L is morphologically uniform iff P has either only underived inflectional forms or only derived inflectional forms. (Jaeggli and Safir's (43), p. 30).

Jaeggli and Safir propose that Morphological Uniformity is a necessary condition for the presence of expletive null subjects, as we saw in 2.2.3. There, on the basis of data from Old French, we proposed a rather different approach to licensing null subjects: we suggested that Morphological Uniformity constitutes one kind of 'richness' that permits the identification of null subjects, which we referred to as formal richness, or [+MU], (using Jaeggli and Safir's notion in a slightly different way to Jaeggli and Safir themselves — cf. Chapter 2, Note 18). A paradigm is [+MU] if it has a visible agreement slot in all persons: any number of syncretisms is tolerated, but no zero-endings. This definition means that there are paradigms which are paradigms in the sense of (58), but which are [−MU]. Dutch is a possible case, since the 1sg ending is null, and there are syncretisms in the paradigm (cf. Jaeggli and Safir 1989: 40, n. 19).

The above discussion suggests a way to unify this notion with (58), in terms of the properties of Agr^{-1}. Given the hypothesized Agr^{-1}, morphological uniformity is naturally construed as a property of this position, and formal licensing as a relation between Agr^{-1} and *pro* (this idea generalizes in a natural way to capture the connection between V2 and the possibility of C-licensed expletive null subjects discussed in 1.4.; in this case C^{-1} would be the licenser for *pro*).[12,13] So we take one basic way in which *pro* can be formally licensed to be for it to be governed by Agr^{-1}. One identification condition on referential *pro* is that the Agr^{-1} that governs it be [+MU], where Morphological Uniformity is defined as in (60). As we saw in 2.2.3. and 2.4.3., this gives the correct result for OF and for medieval Northern Italian dialects (and the evidence from MidFr based on Vance 1989 and Hirschbuhler 1991 that we discussed in 2.3.5. indicates that *pro* can also be licensed by agreement with a morphologically uniform ([+MU]) Agr^{-1}). However, in order for Agr^{-1} to be postulated at all, there must be overt, equipollent evidence of number agreement, as we saw above. Thus we arrive at a picture of the relation between null subjects and V-to-Agr movement in terms of a clear (and highly falsifiable) quantification of the different degress of 'richness' of agreement that are required for V-to-Agr movement and for null subjects.

The other basic way in which *pro* can be licensed is by being in an agreement configuration with a [+pron] $Agr°$. This is the situation found in classic null-subject languages like Italian and Spanish. We defined a [+pron] paradigm in 2.2.3. as a paradigm with up to one syncretism and one zero-ending. This characterizes the paradigms of Italian, Spanish, early OF (cf. 2.2.3.) and a number of contemporary Northern Italian dialects (cf. 2.4.3.). As we pointed out in 2.2.3., we can think of a [+pron] Agr^{-1} as a 'pronominal' Agr^{-1} (cf. Rizzi 1982, Ch. 4), since it has the pronoun-like property of distinguishing (almost) every person in the paradigm. Thus [+pron] Agr marks person features in a (near) equipollent way. Note that pronominal Agr^{-1} also implies V-to-Agr, given (58).

Italian (and probably Spanish) is a system in which Nominative Case cannot be assigned under government (cf. 1.2.). Thus, following (6a′), the [+pron] $Agr°$ can only license *pro* in an agreement configuration. This does not imply that [+pron] $Agr°$ is incompatible with licensing under government, however (indeed there is some evidence that earlier stages of these languages had such a system). Now, in order to account for the loss of null subjects in all contexts after the Nominative parameter had changed in 16th-century French, both those where they were licensed under government and those where they were licensed under agreement, we strengthened the idea that [+pron] Agr° does not depend on government configurations to the following proposal (see 2.4.3., (186)):

(61)   If Agr° formally licenses *pro* only in configurations of agreement, then Agr° must be [+pron].

Although (61) remains somewhat stipulative, reformulating the notion of pronominal Agr in terms of Agr^{-1} allows us to see what may underlie it. The peculiarity of a MidFr-type system (discussed in 2.3.5.) can now be summed up as follows:

(62)   If *pro* is formally licensed under agreement by a $[-pron]$ X^{-1}, then *pro* can be formally licensed under government by $[-pron]$ X^{-1}.

The only $[-pron]$ Agr^{-1} capable of identifying *pro* is $[+MU]$. In this way, we see how the null subjects which were licensed under agreement in MidFr were in a sense parasitic on the possibility of being licensed in the government context. What (62) says is that this parasitic relation is generally true for $[-pron, +MU]$ agreement (and recall that Poletto (forthcoming) provides support for this from Renaissance Veneto). Thus, when null subjects could no longer be licensed (and were therefore not identified) in contexts of government, they were excluded also in contexts of agreement, as we saw in 2.4.3. (62) does not apply to Italian or Spanish, since in these systems *pro* is licensed by a $[+pron]$ Agr^{-1}. In fact, for $[+pron]$ Agr, the canonical configuration is agreement.

The preceding paragraphs show that we are able to integrate the theory of null subjects proposed in Chapter 2 with the theory of V-to-Agr movement put forward here. A clear implicational statement emerges from this discussion:

(63)   If a language has null subjects, then it has V-to-Agr movement.

(The same prediction is noted in Roberts 1985a: 33, Note 10). This is so since the same category is at work in both cases: Agr^{-1}. The presence of Agr^{-1} is sufficient for V-to-Agr movement and necessary for null subjects, subject to the further conditions we have discussed. Hence null-subject languages must have V-to-Agr.

This prediction appears to be correct for all the Romance null-subject languages; all the Romance languages that have been studied carefully appear to have V-to-Agr movement (although the Iberian languages pose a number of problems of analysis that we cannot go into here; for Rumanian, Motapanyane (1991) adopts the 'double-Agr' structure, and shows that main verbs move to the lower Agr) and so all the Romance null-subject languages have V-to-Agr movement. Within Germanic, the languages which manifest limited null-subject properties (principally German and Icelandic; cf. 1.4., 1.5. and 2.2.2., as well as ME, cf. Note 8 above) have V-to-Agr. Among the languages lacking V-to-Agr movement, NE and MSc have no null-subject phenomena at all, and so here too the correlation holds up. At first sight, however, Faroese appears to be a counterexample, since, according to Barnes (1989) expletive null subjects are allowed:

(64)   Nú   regnar (tað)

         Now rains   (it)

         'It's raining now'

         (Barnes 1989: 11–12, (2a), (3a))

A natural move here is to relate the possibility of the null expletive to the V2 nature of Faroese, and say that it is a consequence of properties of C^{-1}.[14] However, it is striking that Faroese, unlike Icelandic, allows the expletive to be optionally phonologically realized. Cf. Vikner (1990: 2.5.2.) for an interesting suggestion based on considerations similar to those raised here. Vikner's proposal (following Barnes 1987) regarding the optionality of *tað* is that Faroese is changing from an Icelandic-type situation, where V-to-Agr and null expletives are possible, to an MSc-style situation, where neither are possible. So we can retain the correlation in (63) and say that, to the extent that Faroese allows V-to-Agr, it allows null expletives in V2 contexts (perhaps because the combination of C^{-1} and weak Agr can license expletive *pro* here — cf. the discussion of OF in 2.3.5.).[15]

To sum up, we have proposed here and in Chapter Two the following parameters of Agr (a precursor of (65) is the set of Infl-parameters proposed in Travis 1984, Chapter 5):

(65)a.   **Agr^{-1}?** Trigger: overt distinct number morphology, cf. (58).
                 Consequence: V-to-Agr (in tensed clauses).

         Yes: Romance, Continental West Germanic, Icelandic, OE, ME, OMSc.

         No: NE, MSC (except for Älvdalsmålet and Kronoby), Faroese.

    b.   **Agr^{-1} [+MU]?**   Trigger: an overt (not necessarily distinct) person morphology in all persons, cf. (60). Consequence: referential null subjects licensed under agreement (Case system permitting), and, if under agreement, government (Case system permitting).

         Yes: Later OF, MidFr.

No:	Germanic, early OF, (other Romance languages are [+MU] but also [+pron], see (c)).

c. **Agr^{-1} [+pron]?**   Trigger: distinct person agreement morphology (up to one syncretism), cf. 2.2.2. (80). Consequence: referential null subjects wherever Agr can assign Nominative.

Yes: Early OF, Standard Italian, Spanish, Portuguese.

No: Post-c13 French, Germanic.

The parameters are stated here in such a way that a "yes" value gives a bigger grammar in terms of the Subset Principle, cf. the discussion in 2.4.

Clearly, (65) is rather tentative in some respects. In particular, it is likely that some medieval or Renaissance Northern Italian dialects pattern with later OF and MidFr (cf. Poletto (forthcoming), 2.4.3.). Similarly, we expect that some very conservative Germanic varieties will pattern like Modern Italian, Spanish, etc. This seems to be true of Old Norse, for example (Vikner 1990: 2.5.2.). In any case, (62) illustrates how our proposals regarding parametric options for the internal structure of Agr fit together, how this structure interacts with other parts of the grammar, and how these options are triggered (and so, by implication, how they may change diachronically). As we mentioned above, these proposals are also eminently falsifiable.

This concludes our discussion of the loss of V-to-Agr in English. We have seen that ME clearly had this rule, and that it was lost in the latter part of the 16th century. This loss was a major factor in the development of the NE auxiliary system, since it gave rise to a situation in which auxiliaries are clearly syntactically distinguished from main verbs, as they continue to raise to Agr. We showed, on the basis of a detailed look at the status of plural endings in the 16th century, that there is a real correlation between the loss of V-to-Agr and the loss of verbal agreement morphology, particularly the plural endings. This correlation is not limited to English, but extends to those Scandinavian languages which have lost V-to-Agr. We developed a system of parametric values for Agr^{-1} which puts these properties together with those responsible for various kinds of null subjects.

It is clear that these developments were a major contributory factor in the development of the NE auxiliary system. However, this is not the whole story. It is now time to discuss the properties of some of the auxiliary elements themselves, starting with the cross-linguistically most unusual NE phenomenon of all: *do*-support.

3.2. DO-INSERTION

In this section we will discuss the history of the dummy verb *do* in English. The section is divided into four subparts. In 3.2.1. we provide an analysis of the distribution of *do* in contemporary English. This analysis shares two central ideas with a number of other proposals that have made recently (Chomsky 1989, Jaeggli and Hyams 1989, Pollock 1989, Rizzi 1990a; but cf. Ouhalla 1990 for a different approach): the idea that Agr° is downgraded to V° at SS, and the related idea that V+Agr raises in LF to "save" the unbound trace, with *do* inserted exactly when this operation fails for some reason and SS Agr-lowering is consequently blocked.

In 3.2.2. we consider the status of *do* in ME. Here, basing our discussion on Ellegård (1953), Visser (1963–73) and Denison (1985, forthcoming), we show that *do* at this time was rather like NE *get* or *have*. It had a small-clause complement whose subject could either be an overt NP or an empty category. When it is an overt NP, *do* acts as an Exceptional Case-marking (ECM) verb, and is clearly causative in meaning; this is ECM *do*. When the lower subject is empty, there are two possibilities: either *do* is causative and the lower subject is an empty pronominal of some kind, or *do* is a raising verb (possibly with a rather weak aspectual meaning) and the lower subject is a trace. The causative *do* with an empty complement subject we call 'FP *do*' (owing to the superficial similarity with the French *faire-par* construction, although we do not wish to insist on any parallel analysis).

In 3.2.3., we analyse the free *do*-insertion of ENE (as exemplified in (6)); we treat this as a reanalysis of the raising *do* as optionally base-generated in T° and raising to Agr°. This reanalysis exactly parallels the one which took place with modals at the same time (cf. 3.3.1.). Where *do* is not base-generated, V° nevertheless continues to raise, as we saw in 3.1.1. By the beginning of ENE, the agreement system had undergone the changes discussed in 3.1., making the morphological trigger for Agr^{-1} opaque. As a result of this, *do* starts to function as a semantically empty PF-identifier of V (on PF-identification of verbs, see 3.2.1.). On the basis of the Kroch/Ellegård data (cf. 3.1.1.), around 1575 the remaining agreement affixes -(*e*)*st* and -(*e*)*th*/(*e*)*s* are reanalysed as Agr° and begin to undergo lowering. In 3.2.4., we will show how this lowering was introduced (by a DR of the former Stylistic-Fronting option). Moreover, we show that the restriction of *do* to its present contexts can be seen as a consequence of the introduction of Agr-lowering, if we assume the following constraint on DS:

(66)   DS lexical insertion is always optional

Once V-to-Agr was lost, *do*-insertion was obligatory in at least some contexts (initially interrogatives, as we shall see in 3.2.4.). It follows from

(66) that if a given lexical item is obligatorily lexically inserted, it cannot be inserted at DS. We further assume that post-DS lexical insertion does not take place unless there is no other means of arriving at a well-formed structure: this is essentially a version of Chomsky's (1989) least-effort guideline, where the notion of a language-particular rule is subsumed under the notion of lexical insertion. Hence, once *do* is obligatorily inserted in one context, it takes on its NE property of being a 'last-resort' element, which can be inserted only where it needs to be (see 3.2.1.); this is in fact the only sense in which something can be obligatory, in current theory. (66) is a very natural constraint to impose on DS representations, since this level is supposed to represent substantive lexical and thematic information (cf. Chomsky 1981, Ch. 2); we thus do not expect any DS property to be formally obligatory (independently of the effects of the θ-criterion and the Projection Principle). Conversely, any element which is obligatorily inserted cannot have any substantive lexical or thematic content. This is of course true of contemporary *do*, and, as we shall see, the loss of intrinsic content was an important step in the history of *do*.

Strong empirical support for (66) comes from the observation in Kroch (1989) that the occurrence of *do* in positive declaratives starts to decrease just at the time that Agr^{-1} is lost, i.e. at Ellegård's Period 7 (1550–1575), while interrogative *do* continues to increase in frequency (on negative *do*, cf. 3.2.4.). Our account thus explains the following puzzle noted by Kroch:

Why the competition [between *do*-insertion and affix-hopping — IGR] should begin only when V to I raising is lost is at present unclear and represents an important unresolved issue in our interpretation of the history of the affirmative declarative context.

Because of (66), then, the loss of V-to-Agr led to the modern ban on 'free' *do*-support, i.e. *do*-support in contexts where Agr/T-lowering can give a well-formed LF representation.

The Agr^{-1} parameter that we motivated in the previous section plays a major role in our discussion, since it is the absence of this element combined with the retention of agreement markers which leads to the possibility of Agr-lowering. As we mentioned in 3.1., once the affixes are reanalysed as $Agr°$ they are able to lower to $V°$ without violating the structure-preservation condition on adjunction. Moreover, they are required to lower by the fact that main verbs can no longer raise to Agr (see 1.3.3. and 3.1.1. on this) and by the fact that they are bound morphemes (although it would perhaps be more appropriate to think of them as clitics than as affixes).

In addition, a new strand enters the discussion here. Since we are dealing with the development of an auxiliary, we must make some proposals concerning the nature and distribution of auxiliaries generally. Our basic proposal, in line with Roberts (1985) and Pollock (1989), is that auxiliaries are verbal elements which assign no Θ-roles (cf. 1.3., and Note

13 of Chapter 1). In consequence, when V-to-Agr is lost, they may cease to be (unequivocally) verbal and become functional heads, since the Projection Principle does not require them to be in V° if they have no arguments, and the Least Effort Strategy will, other things being equal, favour an analysis in which they are base-generated in T or Agr rather than raised there. In 3.2.3., we will see how these ideas apply to *do*. In 3.3.1., we consider the more complex case of the modal auxiliaries.

3.2.1. *Do-Support in NE*

In this section we present a purely synchronic analysis of the contemporary phenomenon of *do*-support. As we mentioned above, our analysis is very much in the spirit of the recent proposals of Chomsky (1989), Pollock (1989), Jaeggli and Hyams (1989) and Rizzi (1990a). Nevertheless, it differs from all of those analyses on some points (while relying crucially on the idea of Agr/T-lowering at SS, followed by LF raising, unlike the approach advocated in Ouhalla 1990).

As a preliminary point, we have to make explicit the requirement that verbs, like NPs, must be PF-identified (cf. Baker 1985, Fabb 1984, Roberts 1985, Weerman 1989, Zagona 1982, 1989):

(67)   Every verb must be associated with some inflectional feature
         of a governing head.

(67) is the analogue in the verbal system of the Case Filter on NPs (cf. 2.3.3. (122)) (and corresponds to the V-visibility requirement of Roberts 1985a: 29). Certain differences with the Case Filter come out automatically from the fact that (67) applies to heads while the Case Filter applies to NPs. For example, (67) is always and only satisfied by government, since no head can be in a structural agreement relation with another head (cf. 1.2.). Hence the kind of parametric choice that is relevant for Case-assignment to NPs, and that formed the subject matter of Chapter 2, does not arise in the verbal domain.

In Continental West Germanic and Romance, where Agr^{-1} and T^{-1} are both present, (67) is satisfied by incorporation of the verb with T (we assume that this takes place in both finite and non-finite clauses — cf. 1.3.3. for discussion of French and Belletti 1990 on Italian). As we saw in 3.1.1., this was also the usual situation in ME. In NE, however, this is not possible for main verbs, as 3.1. showed. Therefore, one of two other possibilities is taken: (i) V satisfies (67) simply by being governed by some lexical head; (ii) T° downgrades to V. Both of these options are taken in different circumstances in NE.

The first option depends on the nature of the head which governs V. Aspectual auxiliaries satisfy (67) for V (they also trigger the attachment of participial affixes *-ing* and *-en*; we will leave aside the question whether affix-hopping forms participles in the manner described in Chomsky 1957 here). Arguably, causative and perception verbs with 'naked infinitive' complements also satisfy (67) for a V they govern (cf. Guasti 1989). In these cases, then, the head which makes V_i° visible is V_j°. T° satisfies (67) by governing V° when it contains a free morpheme (otherwise, it is inert for government, like some kinds of C°) so the presence of *to*, *do* or a modal (or the trace of one of these items, by the Government Transparency Corollary, cf. 1.3.) allows V to satisfy (67).

Downgrading of T° and Agr° to V is another way to satisfy (67). We assume that both heads must downgrade, as information from both is necessary in order to determine the phonological form (if any) of the inflection (cf. Johnson 1990 for an account of the conditions determining the phonological realization of English verbal inflection). Downgrading creates the SS chain (t, t, Agr/T/V); Nominative Case is assigned by the first link of this chain, $[_{Agr^\circ}$ t], under agreement with SpecAgr'.

We said above that *do* is inserted in T°. Suppose that this is a last resort strategy (cf. Chomsky 1989) in the sense that it is obligatory insertion of a lexical item after D-structure. Now, assuming that English allows both Agr/T-lowering and post-DS *do*-insertion, the paradigm to be explained for declaratives is the following:

(68) a. He left   (Obligatory Agr/T-lowering)

   b. He didn't leave   (Obligatory *do*-insertion)

   c. *He not left   (Illicit Agr/T-lowering)

   d. *He did leave   (Illicit *do*-insertion)

   e. *He do left   (*Do*-insertion and Agr/T-lowering)

In positive declaratives like (68a), Agr and T lower to V. This operation creates traces that are not c-commanded by their antecedents, giving rise to potential ECP violations (cf. 1.3. on the ECP and head-to-head movement). The representation is saved at LF, however, since in the mapping to this level of representation V raises to C. This gives rise to the well-formed chain (V, t, t, t). We take this LF-movement to be an instance of Quantifier Raising, the version of move-α which adjoins operators to positions which permit their scope to be structurally determined (cf. May 1977, 1985)). The element which must be raised is T; since T is adjoined to V at SS, the whole V raises to C at LF. From C, V antecedent-governs the traces in Agr°, T° and V°. We must assume that this case of QR is cyclic, moving V through T, but skipping Agr, in order to both satisfy RM and avoid improper movement (A'-to-A-to-A' movement, i.e. T-to-Agr-to-C). The operator-variable relation established by this operation holds between V and the trace in the base position of V in VP. The structure corresponding to (68a) is thus (68a'):

(68a′) SS:

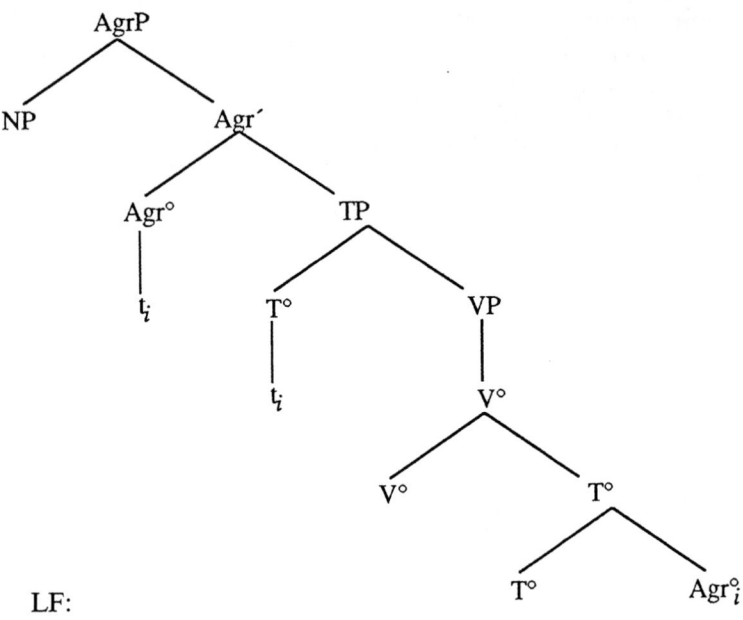

LF:

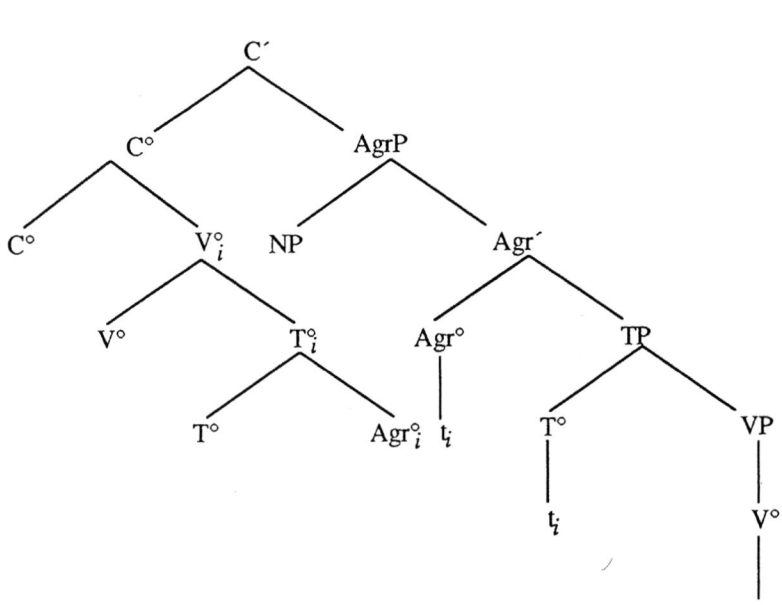

Next, consider why *do*-support is obligatory in negatives: (68b) vs. (68c). We can give an account of this in terms of the idea put forward in 1.3.2. that relativized minimality applies in full at the $X°$-level, i.e. in exactly the selective manner in which it applies at the XP-level (cf. 1.3.2. (58′) for the relevant definitions). For this, we have to explicitly adopt the NegP hypothesis proposed by Pollock (1989). Following Belletti (1990), Moritz (1989), we assume NegP is generated as the complement of AgrP and takes TP as its complement, giving the following structure:

(69)

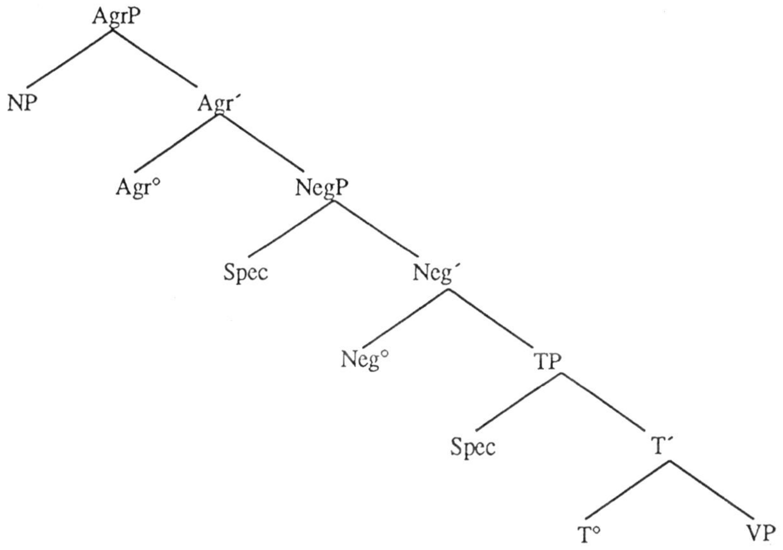

Also following Moritz (1989), we revise our earlier assumption that *not* is in SpecT′ and assume instead that negation is realized either by *not* in SpecNeg′ or by *n't* in Neg°; for a more detailed proposal for the relation between *n't* and *not*, cf. Note 21. In this way, Neg° blocks antecedent-government of head-traces inside its c-command domain from A′-head-positions outside its c-command domain (cf. the definitions given in 1.3.2. (58′)), and thus blocks QR from V to C (or, more precisely, the step from T to C) across negation. Schematically, we have (68c′):

(68c′)

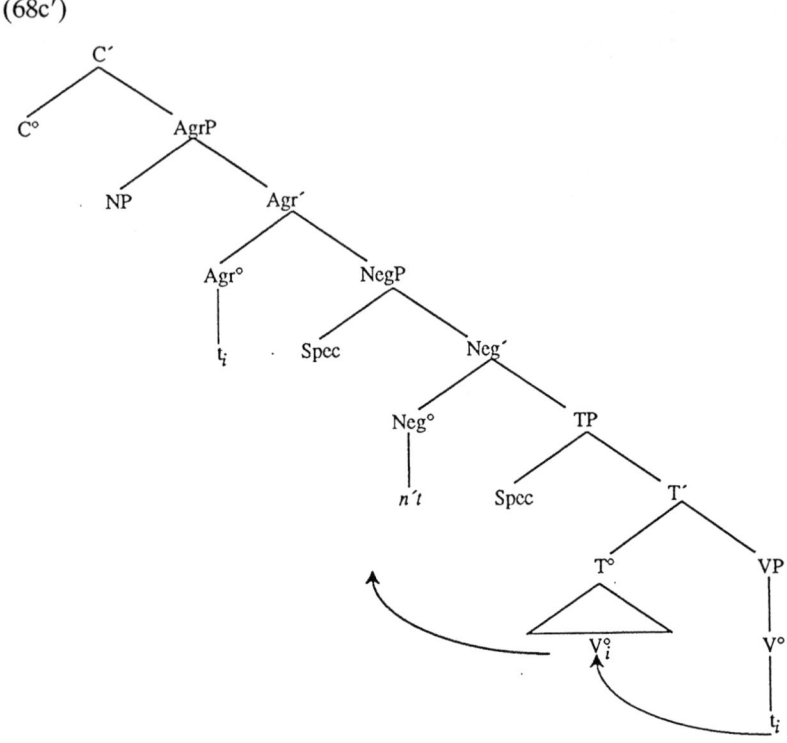

On the other hand, if the verb does not raise, the traces of downgrading
in Agr and T, or at least the one in Agr, will remain unbound. Thus,
there is no way to arrive at a well-formed structure if Agr and T are
lowered across Neg° (or across certain positive polarity elements, like *so*,
too and emphasis, as is well-known; this suggests that we should speak of
a PolarityP, rather than NegP). This situation is illustrated in (68c′). So,
do is inserted in T and raises to Agr (picking up *-s* if Agr is 3sg), T and
Agr do not lower and V stays *in situ*, PF-identified by the trace of *do*. In
this way, the ECP is not violated by QR of T to C.[16] The illustrative
examples in (68) have 3sg verbs, so that the effects of affix-hopping are
visible. However, the fact that *do*-support is obligatory in all persons tells
us that it is not simply 3sg Agr, or the 3sg affix, which must be attached
to V. This is consistent with the view that *do*-support is triggered by a
requirement on V of the type in (67), rather than some affixation requirement on Agr. As we mentioned in 1.3.3., for this account to work LF-

excorporation must be banned. Otherwise V could adjoin to Neg° and then excorporate from it, which would make S-structures like (68c) possible.

The most difficult case for any account of *do*-support to handle is (68d); why is 'free' *do*-support not allowed? We provided the basic answer to this question in the discussion following (66) above. The answer has two parts: (i) no element can be obligatorily lexically inserted in DS; (ii) post-DS lexical insertion is a 'last-resort' option. Given these two ideas, in a positive declarative Agr/T-lowering takes precedence over *do*-insertion as a means of satisfying (67). More generally, Agr/T-lowering takes place wherever this can lead to a well-formed LF. This analysis is very close to, and to some extent inspired by, Chomsky's (1989) theory of 'last-resort' language-particular operations, or Pesetsky's (1990) proposed level of Language-Particular (LP-) structure. However, we differ from Chomsky in that the language-particular nature of *do*-insertion does not determine its 'last-resort' nature (aside from the trivial point that *do*-insertion is a language-particular rule since *do* is a language-particular morpheme); in fact, the peculiarities of NE *do*-insertion derive from the fact that *do* has no content, combined with the fact that NE has affix-hopping. And we differ from Pesetsky in considering that *do*-insertion feeds other syntactic operations, notably movement to C (Pesetsky is led to claim that there is no I-to-C movement in English interrogatives, a conclusion which is highly problematic given the strictly root nature of this phenomenon — cf. 1.3.3., 1.5.).

Finally, (68e) is ruled out because the verb is redundantly PF-identified, once by *do* governing it and once by Agr attaching to it. As with other forms of PF-identification, for example nominal Case, there is a general ban on 'over-identification'; in general, identifying features are in a bi-unique relation to their identifiees (cf. 1.5.). This biuniqueness requirement is violated in (68e). The result is that *do* is inserted just where Agr/T are non-lexical (containing just features) and not lowered.

Do-support is obligatory in questions to the extent questions always involve T-to-Agr-to-C movement to satisfy the *wh*-criterion, since [+wh] is base-generated on T° (cf. 1.4.). If T° moves to C° without insertion of some auxiliary, V fails to be PF-identified. Agr/T-lowering alone is excluded, since the *wh*-criterion applies at SS. Agr/T-lowering followed by raising of V/Agr/T to C at SS is more difficult to exclude. A reviewer suggests that, since V/Agr/T-raising is an instance of QR, this operation is prevented from applying at SS by whatever principle bans QR at SS.[17]

Do-insertion is not blocked by T/Agr-lowering. If both operations take place, however, we arrive at the following:

(70)   *Do John left?

This example is ruled out because V is once again redundantly PF-ident-ified, as in (68e) (the trace of *do* PF-identifies V by the Government

Transparency Corollary (cf. 1.3.), and the tense morphology PF-identifies
V by incorporating with it). To avoid this result, *do* must be inserted
before T/Agr-lowering can take place. However, as we mentioned above,
this cannot happen if Agr/T-lowering can lead to a well-formed derivation,
due to the 'cost' of post-DS lexical insertion.

The above assumptions about the NE auxiliary system are necessary in
order to understand the account we will give of how the system developed
diachronically. Our proposal is that the loss of Agr^{-1} and T^{-1} led to the
development of this system because it allowed certain elements (*do*, *to*
and the modals) to be reanalysed as functional heads, and because it
required main verbs to be PF-identified in some way other than by V-
to-Agr raising. In questions, the only way to resolve the contradictory
requirements of the *wh*-criterion and (67) was to insert a dummy verb in
T. This idea depends on the prior existence of a verb able to play such a
'dummy' role, a matter which we now turn to.

3.2.2. *Do in ME*

The question of the origin of the auxiliary *do* has been much discussed in
traditional studies of the historical syntax of English. Here we will briefly
discuss two well-known proposals, before going on to give a partially
original analysis of the different types of ME *do*.

In semantic terms, there were two kinds of *do* in ME: a causative and
a non-causative (possibly perfective) *do*. In syntactic terms, there were
also two kinds of *do*, one with an overt subject in its complement, and
one without. The two classes overlap to give the three types of *do* we will
now discuss: Exceptional Case-Marking (ECM) *do* is causative with an
overt complement subject; FP *do* (the name is intended to underline the
superficial similiarity with the Romance '*faire-par*' construction; whether
the similarity goes deeper is a matter we leave aside) is causative with an
empty complement subject, and raising *do* is non-causative with an empty
complement subject. We will discuss and illustrate each of these kinds of
do in what follows, showing that all three *do*'s are types of verbs that are
not unusual cross-linguistically. There is clearly nothing unprecedented
from a comparative point of view with regard to the first two kinds of *do*;
we will show also that the raising *do* is found in other West Germanic
varieties. Moreover, raising *do* seems to be the ergative counterpart of
ECM *do*. Two points are of central importance for the subsequent diachronic developments: first, none of these forms were auxiliaries in ME;
second, FP *do* was frequently equivocal with raising *do*. We will return
to these points in 3.2.3.

The two most influential views on the origins of *do* are those of Visser
(1963–73) and Ellegård (1953). Visser proposes that 'periphrastic *do*'
derives from what he calls 'anticipative' *do*, where *do* is a pro-form for a

verb (or VP) which follows. The following example (from Denison 1985: 50) illustrates the kind of anticipative *do* which, according to Visser, was amenable to reanalysis as an auxiliary:

(71)   And so thei **dede** bothe deseiue ladies and gentilwomen,

And so they did   both   deceive ladies and gentlewomen

and bere forthe diuerse languages on hem

and bear forth   diverse languages on them

(c1450 *Knt. Tour-L*. 2.24; Visser § 1413)

Visser's idea is that *do* was interpreted as an auxiliary instead of as a pro-form, with cases like (71) being the kind of equivocal example that allowed the auxiliary *do* to develop.

Denison (1985, forthcoming) criticizes this account on empirical grounds. He points out that clear cases of "anticipative" *do* are simply not sufficiently frequent in OE and ME for it to be a plausible source for ENE construction. Indeed, many of Visser's examples probably do not show what Visser intended them to show, and are not clear cases of anticipative *do* (cf. Denison 1985: 50–1, Mitchell 1985). We concur with Denison's view, and reject Visser's account.

Ellegård (1953) claims that the auxiliary *do* is derived from the ME causative *do*, due to the fact that the causative *do* with an empty complement subject (what we are calling 'FP *do*') was often equivocal with a 'periphrastic *do*' (which we equate with raising *do*; but Ellegård considers periphrastic *do* an auxiliary since he did not distinguish raising verbs from auxiliaries). As both Visser and Denison point out, Ellegård's account is too strong in predicting a development essentially from ECM *do* to FP *do* to periphrastic *do*, a development for which there is no good evidence.

Denison himself proposes a weaker variant of Ellegård's account, which can be summarized in his own words as follows (1985: 57):

I regard a kind of periphrastic DO as coming into being in the thirteenth century or a little earlier, but not in OE. This DO + infinitive had a two-clause, causative structure, and DO was not an auxiliary verb . . . . The construction probably contained a notion of perfectivity or the like in its meaning. Later there was a syntactic re-analysis into a one-clause structure, motivated by the analogy of the modals and the loss of the parallel causative constructions, and probably involving the loss of perfective value.

This account is quite close to what we will propose, particularly in the idea that there is a reanalysis of a two-clause structure into a one-clause one which is related to the change that affected the modals. More specifically, we follow Denison (and a weak interpretation of Ellegård) in saying that the auxiliary developed by a reanalysis (a DR, in our terms) affecting *do* with an empty complement subject. We also follow both Denison and Ellegård's idea that a semantic equivocation between raising *do* and FP *do* facilitated this reanalysis. Also, we agree that the DR very probably led to *do* losing its semantic content (cf. 3.2.3.). We will also suggest something that none of the above authors take into consideration: that the loss of infinitival morphology and the development of *to* as an infinitival marker triggered the reanalysis.

We now discuss the three types of ME *do* in turn.

a) ECM do. ECM *do* is relatively peripheral to our account of the development of the auxiliary. However, it is relevant in that it provides unequivocal evidence for a causative *do* in ME, and clear evidence for a non-auxiliary *do*.

The following are examples of ECM *do* from the ME period:

(72) a. Sche **dede him etyn &   drynkyn**

      She did   him eat   and drink

      (Ellegård 193, 293/7)

   b. thanne he **dide the clerk of the council seek** it

      then   he did the clerk of the council seek it

      (15c, *Paston Letters*, no. 432; Stein 1989: 4)

   c. The kyng . . . **ded his officeres arestin** . . . his uncil

      the king . . . did his officers arrest . . . his uncle

      (1460: *Capgrave, Chron.* 264; *OED*, DO I.B, III, 22a)

In these examples, the subject of the complement of *do* is overtly present, and so there is no possibility of interpreting *do* as a raising verb. The following example has the same property, and the causative reading is all the more clear from the French translation (which is supplied by the author, as the text is a kind of French phrase-book):

(73)   Nowe **doo me have** a good chambre
      Or me faites avoir ungne bonne chambre

      (1497: *A Lytell Treatyse for to Lerne Englysshe and Frensshe*; Gray 1985: 275)

These sentences, then, are equivalent to NE sentences like (74):

(74) a. She made him eat and drink

   b. He had the clerk of the council look for it

   c. The king had his officers arrest his uncle

   d. Now let me have a nice room

We assume that ECM *do* was a main verb with a small-clause complement.

Given what we said in 3.1.2. regarding the status of the infinitival affix as T^{-1}, examples like (72a, c) where the infinitival affix is present indicate that this complement was at least TP. If we maintain that SpecT' is an A'-position (cf. 1.2.), then, in order for the lower subject to be in an A-position, we have to say that the complement is an AgrP here (like other ECM complements).

ECM *do* was not an auxiliary in the sense that we understand the notion of auxiliary: ECM *do* clearly assigned the Θ-role 'Causer' to its subject, and another Θ-role ('Event Caused' or something of the sort) to its complement. Moreover, there are clear cases of infinitival and participial ECM *do*:

(75) a.   He leet the feeste of his Natiuitee **Doon cryen**

      He let the feast of his nativity do   cry

      (c1386, Chaucer, *Squire's Tale*, 38; *OED* 1.B, III, 23)

    b.   Another thing was **doon** ther **write**

      Another thing was done there write

      (1366, Chaucer, *Rom. Rose*, 413)

From these examples we can see that ECM *do* had a distribution different from, for example, NE modals. Cases like (75b) where ECM *do* is passivized also show that the complement subject is assigned Case by *do*, and so is moved to a derived position when *do* is passivised.

In conclusion, ECM *do* was a main verb comparable to NE *make* or *let* with a clausal complement, probably AgrP. This *do* unambiguously assigned Case to the subject of its complement and assigned a Θ-role both to the complement and to its subject. There were other verbs in ME which had these properties: *make* and *let*, which have retained them, and *gar*, cognate with Swedish *göra* and Danish *gjöre*, which is now obsolete:

(76)   þis mustart shal . . . **gar þin eien to rene**

      This mustard shall   make thy eyes to run

      (c1300 *Dame Siriz* (ed. McKnight, ME Humorous Tales); Visser § 1220)

Evidence for the equivalence of these verbs, and so further support for the causative nature of ECM *do*, is provided by the variation in different ms. of a 14th-century ME poem, *Cursor Mundi* (*The Cursor of the World*). There are four extant mss. of this poem, and in three of them the causative verb of the following line is different (for details of which verb occurs in which ms., cf. Visser § 1212):

(77)   siþen he **did/gert/made** þam all oute driue

        since he caused   *them all outdrive (i.e. to be driven out)*

        (EETS 1874: 92)

ECM *do* disappears in the 16th century, cf. Visser (§ 1212). We will see
below that FP constructions generally disappeared in the 16th century.
However, this clearly does not tell us the whole story regarding *do*, since
it is clear that ECM constructions with causative verbs like *make* and *let*
(which in ME also appeared in 'FP' contexts) survived. But we do not
find examples like (78) in NE:

(78)   *He did John clean the car

This is because *do* lost its capacity to take an AgrP complement when it
became an auxiliary. The other causative verbs retained this property,
since they did not become auxiliaries.

b) 'FP' do: FP *do* is the case of *do* with a non-overt complement subject
and a causative reading. As mentioned above, we use the term "FP" to
recall the superficially similar Romance constructions with *faire* and its
cognates (although we do not wish to imply that the similarity is necessarily
more than superficial). Examples of this type are hard to distinguish
formally from raising *do*, but the following seem to be good cases:

(79) a. He is innocent And can not write, nor **hath done**

         He is innocent and cannot write, nor has done

         writen, the certaynte of the dayes and tymes thereof

         write,   the certainty of the days and times of it

         (1461–2: *Pl & Memorand*, London Guildhall Records
         (*MMED*) A 86, m. 4; Visser § 1212)

     b. they shall putt or **done putt** in any certaine place

         they shall put or do   put in any certain   place

         (c1475 *Gregory's Chronicle*, p. 145; Visser ibid.: cited in Rob-
         erts 1985a: 44)

FP *do* does not appear to differ notably from ECM *do* in its distribution
or in the nature of its complement. We thus assume that it has a small-
clause complement and assigns a Θ-role both to this category and to its
subject; hence FP *do* is a main verb. FP *do* also had non-finite forms, as
the participle in (79a) and the infinitive in (79b) show.

    Since the complement subject is an empty category, examples of the
kind in (79) are formally ambiguous between FP and raising *do*. This

ambiguity, which, as we saw, is at the heart of both Ellegård's and Denison's accounts of the origin of periphrastic *do*, extends to the interpretation when the complement subject is naturally interpreted as coreferential with the matrix subject of FP *do*. If the context, or the lexical content of the sentence, indicate that the lower subject is not coreferential with the matrix subject, then we have a plausible case of FP *do*. In (79), as pointed out in Roberts (1985), the coordination of verbs without *do* followed by verbs with *do* suggests (although does not categorically require) a disjoint interpretation for the subject of *do* and the lower subject.

As we mentioned above, there were other causative verbs in ME — *gar*, *let* and *make* — all of which appeared in FP constructions:

(80) a. Sum . . . saide þam   thoughte it best to **gerre**

      Some   said   them (*i.e. they*) *thought   it best to make*

      smyte of his heid

      smite off his head

      (c1440, *Prose Life Alexander* (EETS) 16, 7; Visser § 1220)

   b. uirtue **makeþ wynne** heuene

      vitrue makes win   haven

      (1340, *Ayenbite*, 84/14; Visser § 1235)

   c. He **leet brennen** the cite of Rome

      He let burn   the city of Rome

      (c1374, Chaucer, *Boece* II, 6, 3; Visser § 1232)

The 'FP' construction was lost in the early 16th century for all these verbs. Guasti (1990) correlates this with the disappearance of the infinitival affix (cf. 3.1.2.); this correlation holds up well cross-linguistically in that all the other Western European languages (notably including MSc, cf. 3.3.2.) have a causative construction of this type and have identifiable infinitival affixes, while ENE and NE lack both. The fact that Guasti (1990) identifies this construction as depending on a nominal infinitive is consistent with Lightfoot's (1979) account of the history of the English infinitive that we discussed in 3.1.2. We suggest that these are cases of TP-complementation where the affix in T^{-1} licenses *pro* as the subject of VP* (under government; cf. our account of Nominative-assignment to this position in 1.2.). When T^{-1} was lost, so was this construction as *pro* could no longer be licensed. This meant that *make* and *let* became restricted to AgrP (ECM) complements. For *do*, many FP cases became raising cases, owing to the equivocation in the nature of the empty complement subject (see below), contributing to the DR to be discussed in 3.2.3

*c) Raising **do***. There are a number of cases where *do* has an empty
complement subject where a causative interpretation is implausible or
impossible. The following are examples of this kind:

(81) a.   They worschipped the sonne whanne he **dede arise**
          They worshipped the sun   when   he did   arise
          (Ellegård 1953: 78, 327/8; Kroch 1989)

     b.   In Faguell, . . . A great lord somtyme **dyd dwell**
          In F., . . .   a great lord once   did live
          (1480+, *The Knight of Curtsey*, McCausland 1922; Gray 1985:
          185, 1–2)

It does not seem that *do* is causative here. The most natural analysis is
to treat it as a raising verb. Similarly, the examples of ME *do* in interrogatives and negatives given in 3.3.1. (23), (27) and (28) are, on semantic
grounds, implausible causatives but plausible instances where *do* is functioning as a raising verb.

There is in fact evidence that *do* was able to be a raising verb in
ME. Unfortunately, the most direct kind of evidence, the presence of a
pleonastic subject and a finite complement, is unavailable, since *do* always
had a non-finite complement. Assuming that the FP construction involves
a null pronominal of some kind (probably *pro*, see above), and that these
elements must always bear a Θ-role (*pro* can be expletive, as we have
seen, but arbitrary *pro* never can, and the *pro* postulated in the FP
construction has arbitrary reference), we can nevertheless infer the presence of a raising construction from the presence of a verb which assigns
no external Θ-role in the complement to *do*. So evidence for raising *do*
comes from cases where the verb in *do*'s complement is either a raising
verb or an ergative verb. The following are relevant examples:

(82) a.   We hereth of miracles al day þat of sent Agace **doth**
          We hear   of miracles all day that of St.   Agatha do
          falle
          fall
          (c1300 *South English Legendary* (EETS) 16, 63; V § 1418)

     b.   Alle þe tyme þat þy lyffe **doth last**
          All the time that thy life   does last
          (c1450 *St. Editha* (ed. Horstmann) 811; V § 1418)

     c.   The sterre to shyne **did be-gynne**
          The star   to shine did begin

(13 ... *Curs M.* (G) 11481)

Denison (1985: 53f) says that raising *do* (his periphrastic *do*) was functionally a perfective marker. In support of this, he points to the frequent
diachronic development from causative to perfective, and the fact that the
OE prefixal aspect- (or Aktionsart-) marking system became obsolescent
during ME (cf. Samuels 1972: 160f); Denison suggests that *do* could have
been a functional replacement for the prefixes. As we mentioned earlier,
raising *do* is the ergative counterpart of ECM *do*; as such it does not
assign Case to its complement subject, triggering raising, and it assigns no
external Θ-role of its own. Hence *do*'s only contribution to the Θ-structure
of the clause is by assigning the role 'Event Caused', or perhaps 'Event
Happened', to its complement.

Denison also observes that the overwhelming majority of 13th- and 14th-
century complements to *do* are either accomplishments or achievements in
the terminology of Vendler (1967), Dowty (1979); that is, they are of the
two classes of verbs most naturally compatible with a perfective marker.
Finally, Denison points out that the assumption that *do* is a perfective
marker can explain the absence of examples where *do* precedes *have*, *be*
or modals, since these are all stative verbs, and so incompatible with a
perfective marker. We can explain in the same way the comparative rarity
of *do* with 'classic' raising verbs of the *seem*-class (although examples like
(27), (73) and (81b) indicate that this ban is not categorical; however, the
aspectual property of *do* may account for the rarity or absence of examples
with modals, etc., in the texts).

The cognates of *do* seem to behave similarly to ME *do* in other West
Germanic varieties. This is the case in some contemporary Alemannic and
Bavarian dialects of German, as well as Middle High German (MHG)
and Middle Dutch (Denison 1985, Stein 1989, Visser 1963–73), as the
following examples illustrate (the Welsh example in (5a) of Chapter One
may be a further case of a similar type, but it is unclear what the aspectual
value of *gwneud* (= 'do') is):

(83) a.   Modern German (South-Western dialect (Stein 1989: 34):

        Er **tut**   nicht singen, er **tut**   springen

        He does not   sing   he does jump

        'He doesn't sing, he jumps'

   b.   MHG (Stein 1989: 4):

        I **tun** evr   wirdikeit zc wizzen

        I do always truth   to know

        'I always know the truth'

    c. MIddle Dutch (Visser 1963–73: 1502, n. 2):

        . . . ende hi **dede** den brief leesen

        . . . *and he did   the letter read*

        '. . . and he read the letter'

        (1516: Margarieta van Limborch *Volksboek*)

According to Stein (1989: 30), *tun* in current South-Western and Northern Italian German (Monte Rosa Dutch) can be a marker of habitual aspect, as in the following examples:

    (84) a. Morgens **tun** wir zuerst die Kartoffeln schälen . . .

           Mornings do we first   the potatoes   peel . . .

           'In the morning, first we peel the potatoes . . .'

      b. Da **tuet** er geschwin logu . . .

           Then does he quickly   look . . .

This is not the case for all examples; Stein additionally isolates uses as an irrealis marker and as an 'intensity' marker, suggesting that these are all semantically or pragmatically related. Whatever the precise details of the semantics of 'dummy' *tun*, these are most compatible with a syntactic analysis treating this element as a raising verb. So we see that, even if the semantic value may differ, some West Germanic cognates of *do* should be treated as raising verbs (also, it is not clear that *do* did not have an imperfective aspectual value in ME; Poussa (op. cit.) argues for this, and cf. (27) and (28), which favour this interpretation over a perfective one. Moreover, certain cases of 'free' *do*-insertion in contemporary Somerset dialect indicate imperfectivity, according to Trudgill 1990: 95).

    As a raising verb marking aspect, *do* was clearly close in function to T° (especially if we can maintain that its sole function was to assign an Event-role to its complement; cf. Higginbotham 1985, Pollock 1989). However, *do* could not be reanalysed as a member of T° as long as the infinitival *-en* remained in T^{-1}, *to* was not an infinitive marker, and the 'FP' construction was still possible. All of these circumstances changed early in the 16th century, when, as we shall see in the next section, *do* was reanalysed as a functional element base-generated in T°. In ME, there are occurrences of dummy *do* where the complement contains the *-e(n)* affix. Since *-e(n)* is T^{-1}, the complement here must be AgrP (since raising *do* is the ergative counterpart of ECM *do*; see above). This kind of evidence that dummy *do* was a main verb was no longer available in the 16th century, after the loss of the infinitival ending.

    We can summarize the discussion of ME *do* by showing the syntactic frames associated with each kind of *do* (without giving a very fine-grained analysis of the structure of the complement):

(85) a. ECM: NP_1 do [$_{AgrP}$ NP_2 VP]   (cf. *let, make, gar*)

  b. FP: NP_1 do [$_{TP}$ [$_{VP*}$ *pro* VP]]   (cf. idem)

  c. Raising: NP_i do [$_{AgrP}$ t_i VP]   (cf. WGmc cognates)

As mentioned earlier, there was an equivocation between FP and raising *do*. Superficially the two forms appear in identical strings. The one thing which can distinguish them is the relation between the matrix subject and the phonologically empty complement subject; this relation must be one of coreference in the case of raising *do*, and must be one of disjoint reference with FP *do* (if FP *do* is like the comparable causativizers in other languages, as we are assuming). Thus where the complement subject of FP *do* is interpretable as coreferential with the matrix subject, raising is preferred. So examples of the following type are ambiguous between the structure in (85b) and the one in (85c), since either interpretation seems to be possible:

(86) a. . . . a kastell he **did reyse**

  . . . a castle he did build

  (Ellegård 1953: 81, 96/24; Milton 1988: 60)

  b. he **did carye** grete quantitee of Armure to the Guyldehalle

  he did carry great quantity of armour to the Guildhall

  (1386: *RParl. FM* in *Bk. Lond. E.* 34, 25; Denison 1985: 46)

  c. Henry . . . þe walles **did doun felle**

  Henry . . . the walls did down fell

  (?a1400 (a1338): Mannyng *Chron. Pt. 2* 97, 22; Denison ibid.).

The two interpretations of these examples can be given by the modern paraphrases of (86b):

(87) a. He had a great quantity of armour carried to the Guildhall

  b. He carried a great quantity of armour to the Guildhall

The difference resides in the Θ-role borne by the (matrix) subject; the causative reading in (86a) arises when *do* assigns a Θ-role to this NP, while the non-causative reading of (86b) arises when the subject is Θ-marked by the other verb and undergoes raising. In the former case, the lower verb Θ-marks the empty pronominal subject of the lower clause. This thematic characterization of the ambiguity in (86) giving rise to the structural ambiguity between (85b) and (85c) leads to a clear prediction, given the Least Effort Stategy of 2.2.2. (115). Raising *do*, but not FP *do*, will be analysed as a functional head if there is one available, since such a reanalysis will save one chain position in the movement of *do*, one in the raising of the subject, and possibly one in the movement of the lower verb. The loss of T^{-1} in the early 16th century made $T°$ available as a position of lexical insertion of dummy *do*, which gave rise to the reanalysis of *do* as an auxiliary with essentially the distribution of the modals. It is now time to see exactly how this development took place, and what led to the subsequent restriction in the distribution of *do* to its contemporary contexts.

3.2.3. *Do in ENE*

If we compare the distribution of *do* in the 16th century — up to roughly 1575 — with the ME situation, we see two major dlfferences: (i) causative *do* dies out; (ii) 'dummy' *do* becomes extremely widespread both in frequency and distribution (for the moment we use the term 'dummy' rather than the term 'raising', since, as we shall see, the 16th-century dummy *do* is probably not a raising verb but an auxiliary). Both of these developments are related to the changes in infinitives that we discussed in 3.1.2.: the loss of the infinitive affix *-en* and the development of *to* as a 'pure' infinitival marker. Development (ii) above is of most interest to us, as this led to a further reanalysis of *do* as an obligatorily inserted element from about 1575 on, with the consequence that the contemporary system of *do*-support emerges in the 17th century. We will discuss this later development in the 3.2.4. Here we concentrate on the prior development of *do* as an auxiliary.

Causative *do* dies out in the 16th century. Barber (1976: 267) gives two examples, involving the two different syntactic kinds of causative *do*:

(88) a.   He hes **done** petuously **devour** The noble Chaucer

(1505: Dunbar, *Lament for the Makaris*)

b.   So matter did she make of nought
To stirre vp strife, and **do** them **disagree**

(1596: Spenser, *The faerie Queene*)

(88a) is clearly ambiguous between an FP reading and a raising sense. Moreover, it is Scots (a variety which apparently retained the 'FP' construction longer than Southern and Midland English; cf. Denison 1985: 55) and from very early in the 16th century; what is important about this example is not so much that *do* might be causative, but rather that it occurs in a non-finite form, a matter that we return to later. (88b) is an example of ECM *do* from a text known to contain many deliberate archaisms.

Speaking of the FP causatives, Visser (§ 1212) says "Just after 1500 this construction with *do* + infinitive . . . becomes obsolete." We suggested in 3.2.2. that the loss of FP, which was not restricted to *do* but affected all the ME causative verbs, was related to the loss of infinitival morphology. So the loss of *-en* led more or less directly to the loss of the FP construction, and so to the loss of FP *do*.

ECM *do* continues to appear sporadically in the 16th century, often with *to* in its complement. One such case is the following:

(89)   Oft the boisteous winds **did** them to stay

        (1547, Surrey, *Aeneid* II; *OED*, *do*, 22)

It is unclear why this kind of *do* should have disappeared, since the other causative verbs have survived as ECM verbs. We continue to suppose that the other V retained AgrP complements, which *do* lost. Presumably, (89) is a rare example of *do* with an AgrP complement after it has otherwise lost all complementation possibilities — this is an instance of 'lexical split' caused by the DR of the kind we will see again when we discuss the modals in 3.3.

On the other hand, 'dummy' *do* becomes extremely widespread at this period, as is well-known. Visser (§ 1419) gives evidence that this kind of *do* is found in all 16th-century authors, major and minor. At this period, *do* appears to be like NE *do*, in lacking semantic content (see below), but with the striking difference that it appears freely in positive declaratives. Since V-raising is still possible (in 3.1.1. we saw that it is found in texts throughout the 16th century), this means that ENE is more liberal than NE both in allowing *do*-insertion where it is no longer allowed, i.e. in positive declaratives, and in not requiring it where it is now required, i.e. in negatives and interrogatives. These extra possibilities in ENE can be illustrated from a single play by Shakespeare (*Hamlet*, 1605), as follows (Shakespeare was born in 1564 and thus lived through the period where Agr^{-1} was lost; since he was a professional writer, one can thus expect that he could control both the old system and the new system in his writing, cf. 3.1.1.):

(90) a. **Looks** it **not** like the king?

        (*Hamlet*, I, i, 43)

    b. Thus cónscience **does** make cówards of us áll

        (ibid. II, i, 83; cf. (6a))

    c. whose sore task **Does not** divide the Sunday from the week

        (ibid. I, i, 75–6)

(As mentioned in the discussion of (6a), the metre in (90b) shows us that *do* is not stressed here).

Do appears so frequently in positive declaratives at this period that it is difficult to give a small number of representative examples. The following quotations from contemporary grammars (cited in Visser § 1419) give a better indication of the situation at the time:

> *I do* is a verbe muche comenly used in our tonge to be before other verbes, as, **it is all one to say** [Visser's emphasis] *I do speake* and such like, and *I speake* . . . The preter impefit tense *je parloye*, *I did speake* . . . We use to circumlocute the presente and the preter imparfite tenses of all our verbes actyves parsonalles with the same tenses of this verbe *I do*.
>
> (1530, Palsgrave, *Esclaircissement de la langue françoyse* 84, 380, 523).
>
> They [viz. the verbs] haue also some signes in their moodes and tenses, to know, for the present indicative, *doe, doest, doeth, doe.* For the imperfect . . . *Did, didest, did* . . . For the perfect *haue, haste, hath.*
>
> (1580, Bellot, *Le Maistre d'Ecole Anglais*)
>
> *I did learn* discebam et *I learned* aequipollent
>
> (1565, Cooper *Gramm. Ling. Anglic.*)

In terms of the different kinds of ME *do* discussed in the preceding section, it is clear that the 16th century 'dummy' *do* is a continuation of raising *do* and of the equivocal cases of FP *do*. There is no reason to suppose that dummy *do* had any (nominal) Case- or Θ-role-assigning capacity, and so the question that arises is: is 16th-century dummy *do* an auxiliary or a raising verb?

There is one important piece of evidence that 16th-century *do* was an auxiliary. Visser (§ 419) notes that non-finite dummy *do* disappears early in the 16th century. We saw in the previous section that this was possible in ME. However, the following is one of the last examples of the order Modal — *do*:

(91)   Now if I would then **doe** . . . **tel** hym

         (1534, St. Th. More, *Wks* (1557) 1192, F4; Visser, ibid.)

Significantly, Thomas More is also one of the last authors to use sequences of modals (cf. Lightfoot 1979: 2.1). Moreover, sequences of the following kind disappear early in the 16th century:

(92)   A grete toure &   bigge, whiche Julius Caesar **dide doo make**

  A great tower and big, which J. C. did do make

  (c1500, *Melusine* xix, 103; *OED*, DO I. B, III, 25aß)

Taking together *do* and the modals, then, we can see that three of the four logically possible sequences given in (93) disappear early in the 16th century (cf. Note 3 and 3.3.1. on contemporary dialects which allow double-modal sequences):

(93) a. do do

  b. do Modal

  c. Modal do

  d. Modal Modal

We saw in the previous subsection that the sequence *do* — Modal was probably excluded on semantic grounds in ME. Aside from this, however, we expect that, as raising verbs, *do* and modals should be able to freely iterate. This iteration is attested up until the early 16th century but not afterwards.

  The obvious interpretation of this fact is that the raising verbs became auxiliaries in complementary distribution in a given position in the clause. We articulate this idea in terms of the following Diachronic Reanalysis, which took place around the 1530s (cf. Roberts 1985a: 38, Denison 1985 for essentially this idea; Denison, unlike Roberts, explicitly links the development of dummy *do* in the 16th century to the development of modal auxiliaries):

(94) a. NP_i $[_{T°}$ do/M_j $T^{-1}]$ t_j $[t_i$ VP] $\Rightarrow$

  b. NP $[_{T°}$ did/M] VP

This reanalysis was possible since T^{-1} had ceased to be instantiated by morphological material with the demise of the infinitive affix around 1500, and since *to* was inserted in $T°$ from this time on (cf. the discussion of *for to* constructions in 3.1.2.). Thus there was a position available for insertion of the modals and *do*.

  A further precondition for (94) concerns the nature of the items involved. We defer discussion of the peculiar morphological and semantic properties of modals until 3.3.1. (cf. also Lightfoot 1979, Roberts 1985). Raising *do* was amenable to reanalysis as $T°$ since the Θ-role it assigned to its complement had essentially temporal/aspectual content; a verb whose sole lexico-semantic content consists in assigning an Event role to a clausal complement is functionally very close to a temporal or aspectual operator. Thus the semantic conditions certainly did not hamper the re-

analysis of *do* as a member of T°. We will elaborate on the relation
between temporal or modal operators and temporal and modal verbs
which assign Θ-roles in 3.3.2.

So the DR in (94) was allowed by changes in the infinitive system and
by the intrinsic lexico-semantic properties of *do* and modals. Once these
preconditions were met, it was required by the Least Effort Strategy (LES;
cf. Chapter 2, (115)). The LES requires that DRs always operate in such
a way as to choose the structural option which has the least number of
chain-positions. The structure in (94a) has at least the following chain-
positions:

(95) a. (do/M, t)   matrix verb-movement

   b. (NP, t)   subject raising

The structure in (94b), on the other hand, appears to have no movement
at all. In fact, this is probably not quite correct, since we must take into
account the fact that the subject is base-generated in a VP-projection, and
that *do* or the modal raise through both T and Agr as main verbs, while
raising only from T to Agr after being reanalysed as auxiliaries (it is
actually unclear why modals raise to Agr in NE, but the evidence unambiguously shows that they do). In terms of these assumptions, we have
the following chains in (94a):

(96) a. (do/M, t, t)   matrix verb-movement

   b. (NP, t, t, t)   subject raising

This gives a total of 7 chain-positions. On the other hand, the structure
in (94b) has only 4 positions:

(97) a. (do/M, t) matrix T-to-Agr

   b. (NP, t)   subject raising

Clearly, then, the LES will dictate a preference for the structure in (94b)
wherever possible.[18]

After the DR in (94), *do* has the distribution of a modal auxiliary. One
consequence of this is that it can no longer take complements, hence it is
no more able to appear with AgrP, and so the ECM *do* disappears. It is
important to stress, however, that at this point *do* is distributionally on a
par with the modals; it does not yet have the peculiar distribution it has
in contemporary English. 16th-century *do*, then (until after 1575), was
intermediate between the ME main verb and the NE 'supporting' auxiliary
in terms of its distribution. The next thing to determine concerns the
function of 16th-century *do*: was it an aspect marker like ME raising *do*,
or was it entirely devoid of semantic content, as in NE?

Unsurprisingly, this question is rather hard to answer with any confidence. However, the indications are that 16th-century *do* was semantically empty. The only real test we have for the aspectual meaning of *do* concerns the classes of verbs that occur under it. We saw in the previous section that, following Denison (1985), ME *do* tended to occur only with verbs of particular aspectual classes, and in particular that it did not occur with certain kinds of statives or with modals, *have* or *be*. Once *do* became an auxiliary, the ban on cooccurence with modals, *have* and *be* remained, although now it held for syntactic reasons, where previously it had been semantically motivated. Thus it is hard to say when *do* lost its content on the basis of the nature of the verbs that it cooccurs with.

Fortunately, little really depends on this point. As we shall see in the next section, it is important that *do* have no content by 1575, when it begins to have its present-day distribution. So we conclude that at the beginning of the 16th century, (raising) *do* has some kind of aspectual meaning, while by 1575 it has no semantic content at all. At some point in between the 1530s, when it underwent (94), and 1575, whatever aspectual content *do* had had was lost. Another thing to stress about the grammar of English at this period is that Agr^{-1} was still present. We can infer this from the fact that V-to-Agr movement was still the norm for main verbs (cf. the discussion in 3.1.1.). This is the case despite the fact that the agreement paradigms had been dramatically reduced early in the 16th century, so that the morphological trigger for Agr^{-1} was no longer present (see 3.1.1., 3.1.3.). Nevertheless, from the early part of the century up to 1550–75, an abstract Agr^{-1} seems to have been posited (see Figures 1 and 2). It is striking that this period corresponds almost exactly to that of auxiliary *do*, suggesting that *do*, once reanalysed as an auxiliary, was interpreted as a functional substitute for agreement marking (arguably in this way it lost its aspectual meaning). We can articulate this intuition in terms of the notion of 'verbal Case' introduced in 3.2.1., and say that *do* became a semantically empty marker of verbal Case at a period when the morphological cues for verbal Case-marking (Agr^{-1}) were opaque. In this way, *do* may have contributed to the demise of abstract Agr^{-1} (although other factors were also at work, cf. 3.1.3., 3.2.4.) by rendering V-to-Agr movement unnecessary, in a situation where there was no clear morphological trigger for it either. The LES would also play a role in favouring raising of *do* from T to Agr over raising of V through T to Agr.

So we see that while ENE had an auxiliary *do*, this auxiliary was very different from contemporary *do*, which carries agreement marking only in well-defined contexts, and does so obligatorily in those contexts. However, we are now in a position to see the development of the modern *do*-support system as the rendering obligatory of a previously optional process.

To summarize, we have seen two major developments concerning *do* in the 16th century. First, the causative *do* dies out; for FP *do* this was

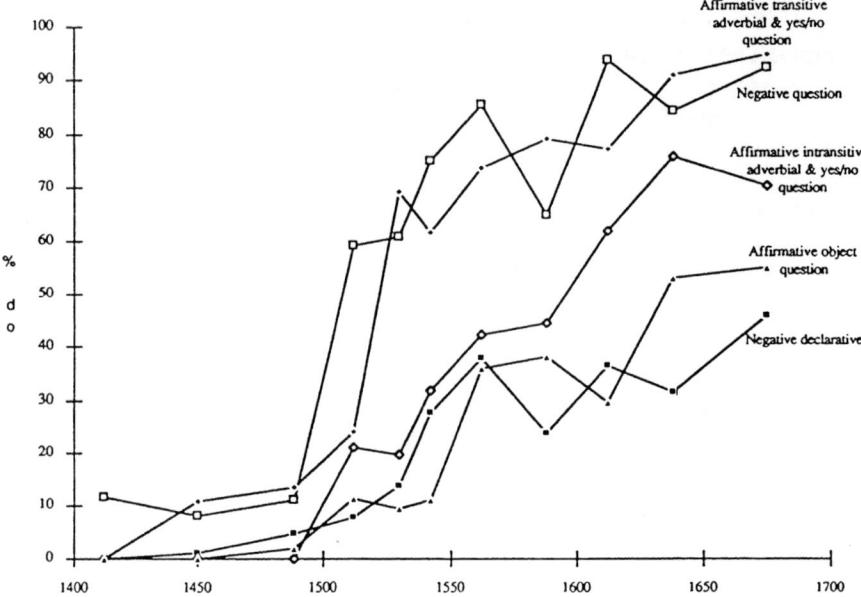

Figure 2. The rise of periphrastic *do* (adapted from Ellegård 1953). From Kroch (forthcoming: 22).

just a case of the general loss of the FP construction, while in the case of ECM *do* it seems that it lost its AgrP-complement. Second, the former raising *do*, and presumably at least some occurrences of equivocal FP *do*, were reanalysed as an auxiliary along with the modals. As far as we can tell, auxiliary *do* had little or no semantic content, but functioned as an optional verbal Case-marker in a system where PF-identification of verbs had become opaque owing to the erosion of the agreement endings. To sum up, we repeat the syntactic contexts of ME *do* given in (85), showing what each of them became in ENE:

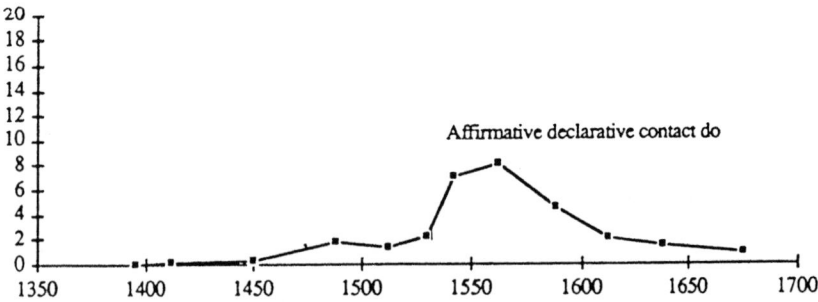

Figure 1. Percent *do* in unemphatic affirmative declarative sentences (contact cases only[24]). From Kroch (forthcoming: 28).

(85′) a. ECM: NP_1 do [NP_2 VP] $\Rightarrow \varnothing$

  b. FP: NP_1 do [proVP] $\Rightarrow \varnothing$ OR (94b)

  c. Raising: NP_i do [t_i VP] $\Rightarrow$ (94b)

We now turn to the question of how optional *do*-insertion became categorical, and became restricted to a specific set of contexts.

3.2.4. *Agr-Lowering and **Do**-Support*

In this section, we will propose an account of the diachronic origin of the NE *do*-support phenomenon. The task is to try to explain how the ENE auxiliary *do*, an element base-generated in T° with essentially the distribution of modern modals and functioning primarily as a morphological-identifier of V, came to be obligatorily base-generated in that position only in a certain class of contexts, and forbidden in all others.

We proposed an analysis of NE *do*-support in 3.2.1. The leading idea of that analysis, in common with a number of other recent approaches to *do*-support (cf. the references given in 3.2.1.), is that the properties of *do*-support are intimately related to the rule of Agr/T-lowering. In negative contexts, QR of V (i.e. T) at LF cannot take place after V has been lowered at SS into VP because Neg° blocks movement to C, and so *do* is inserted to PF-identify V. In this way, Agr/T-lowering does not have to take place and so QR of T does not cross Neg. In interrogatives, the *wh*-criterion forces T-to-Agr-to-C movement; because of this downward movement of Agr and T is impossible (cf. 3.2.1. for details). Moreover, we assumed that a lexical auxiliary is necessary for PF-identification of V (in the absence of SS V-movement), hence, if no other auxiliary is base-generated in T°, *do* must be inserted.

A very important aspect of this analysis is that *do*-insertion is taken to be a 'last resort' operation in the precise sense that it involves post-DS lexical insertion of *do* in order to save the structure. We proposed in terms of the condition on lexical insertion in (66) that it is this property of *do*-insertion which makes the operation impossible where it is not obligatory; Agr/T-lowering, since it does not entail post-DS lexical insertion, is preferred over *do*-insertion wherever the lowering operation does not lead to an ill-formed derivation.

If it is true that it is post-DS lexical insertion which is responsible for the categorical nature of *do*-support in NE, then, in order to see how the freely inserted 16th-century auxiliary became the obligatorily inserted modern auxiliary, we have to see how a given element could diachronically develop the property of post-DS lexical insertion. One precondition for this, given the standard conception of DS (cf. Chomsky 1981, Ch. 2), is that the item in question have no Θ-roles to assign. However, this does not distinguish *do* from other auxiliaries, given our conception of auxiliaries (see 1.3.3.). A stronger precondition would be to say that the item in question can have no inherent semantic content at all. Put this way, we can claim that 16th-century *do* fulfilled this precondition while other auxiliaries did not, as we saw in the previous section that there is no clear evidence that 16th-century *do* had any semantic content. In fact, we can perhaps frame this requirement, and modify the definition of DS, in an interesting way. Hale and Keyser (1986, 1987) distinguish Lexical Conceptual Structure (LCS) from Predicate-Argument Structure (PAS). LCS is a level of representation of lexical items at which their inherent semantic content is specified. This level interfaces with extralinguistic aspects of knowledge and cognition. PAS, on the other hand, encodes the argument structure properties of lexical items, essentially their Θ-grids. While it is unclear exactly how the mapping between these two levels functions, it is clear that there is some non-trivial relation between LCS and PAS, such that lexical items with certain types of inherent content (e.g. action verbs, or 'psych-verbs') tend to have certain types of Θ-grids.

In these terms, it is clear that the characterization of auxiliaries that we have been assuming is one which holds for PAS representations: auxiliaries are items with empty Θ-grids. It is also clear that all the English auxiliaries aside from *do* have some semantic content, of either an aspectual or a modal nature. Thus all the auxiliaries other than *do* have an LCS representation. However, it seems natural to say that *do* lacks an LCS representation, in addition to lacking a PAS representation. Now, if we informally define DS as the syntactic level at which LCS properties are syntactically instantiated, we understand how *do* can fail to be present at this level, while modal and aspectual auxiliaries cannot. This informal characterization of DS retains Chomsky's (1981, Ch. 2) idea that DS is the pure representation of Θ-properties, since these are properties of PAS, which is in turn derived from LCS.

In these terms, then, we see how *do* emerged as a candidate for post-DS lexical insertion once it had lost its earlier aspectual meaning, which seems to have happened by the mid-16th century. However, we have not yet seen why *do* should be forced to be inserted after DS, clearly a crucial facet of the development of modern *do*-support. Here the condition on lexical insertion in 3.2.1. (66) is relevant, so we repeat it here:

(66)   DS lexical insertion is always optional.

As we saw in 3.2.1., (66) means that once *do*-insertion became obligatory, *do* could no longer be inserted at DS. In terms of the characterization of DS just given, (66) is a very natural statement; if DS is a syntactic expression of LCS, i.e. of the content of lexical items, there is no syntactic reason to expect any particular content, therefore any particular lexical item, to be obligatory. Hence, any item which is obligatorily inserted must be both contentless and inserted after DS; both of these conditions are satisfied by NE *do*.[19] Moreover, as a reviewer points out, there is no notion of 'obligatoriness' in current syntactic theory: *do* is only obligatory to the extent that it is a 'last-resort' item.

In NE, Agr/T-lowering creates contexts in which *do* is obligatorily inserted, as we saw in 3.2.1. Once *do* lost its semantic content, then, it was the introduction of Agr/T-lowering which made *do* obligatory in certain contexts. And, given (66), it was this development which made *do* impossible in all other contexts.

The evidence in Figures 1 and 2 at the end of the previous section shows that free *do*-insertion began to decline after 1575, while *do*-insertion in other contexts, particularly interrogatives, continues to increase. As we said in 3.1.1., we — like Kroch — interpret this differential trend in the incidence of positive declarative *do* as an indication that V-to-Agr raising was lost in this period. Since, as we saw in 3.1.3., the agreement paradigms of English were severely weakened by the early 16th century, the morphological trigger for V-to-Agr had clearly been lost. In fact, we are forced to postulate an abstract Agr^{-1} for the period from the loss of the plural agreement endings up to 1575. We suggested in the previous section that freely-inserted positive declarative *do* acted as a functional substitute for the abstract Agr^{-1}, since it provided a morphosyntactically less opaque mode of PF-identification of V. What we interpret Kroch's figures as showing is that another form PF-identification of V became available from 1575 on: Agr/T-lowering.

We propose that Agr-lowering resulted from a Diachronic Reanalysis of Stylistic Fronting (the same proposal is made for the loss of V-to-Agr movement in MSc in Vikner 1990: 2.5.2). We saw in 3.1.1., partly drawing on evidence from Platzack (1990), that ME had an Icelandic-style rule of Stylistic Fronting. This is shown in the following examples:

(31) For many   are that **never** kane halde the

For many (there) are that never can   hold   the

ordyre of lufe

ordure of love

(32) that ladyes . . . might se Who that **beste** were of dede

that ladies . . . might see who   were were of deed

(Platzack 1990)

Moreover, we are obliged to allow that ME had the order Adv-V even in cases which cannot be treated as Stylistic Fronting (see 3.1.1. for examples and discussion).

Our proposal is that the ME cases of Stylistic-Fronting were reanalysed as Agr-lowering by the following DR (where we substitute I for T and Agr for ease of exposition):

(98)   [subj [$_{I'}$ YP$_i$ [$_{I'}$ [$_{I°}$ V$_j$] [$_{VP}$ t$_j$ t$_i$]]]] $\Rightarrow$
        [subj. I° [$_{VP}$ YP [$_{VP}$ V]]]

It is clear that this DR saved at least two chain-positions: the one moving V to I, and the one fronting YP. One precondition for (98) was the lack of a morphological trigger for V-to-I. As we saw in 3.1.3., the relevant trigger was lost early in the 16th century. However, dating (98) at the beginning of the 16th century would mean that, once *do* was reanalysed as an auxiliary, it should have immediately become impossible in non-obligatory contexts, given (66). In other words, we cannot claim that the sole trigger for (98) was the breakdown of the agreement paradigm, as this deprives us of any account of the appearance of auxiliary *do* in 16th-century positive declaratives. In fact, once again following Kroch's interpretation of Ellegard's data, we should date (98) as taking place around 1575. As things stand, this poses a problem: why was Agr-lowering introduced more than half a century after the loss of the morphological trigger for V-raising? We have seen how and why the consequence of this time lag was, in Jespersen's (1938: 195) phrase, the 'exuberant' use of positive declarative *do*. What remains unclear, however, is how and why an abstract Agr^{-1} was retained for this short period, and what may have caused its final disappearance. Of course, it is possible to claim that time lags of this sort are an inevitable part of syntactic change (or language change more generally), and to some extent this is true. However, this is most likely not the whole story.

One possibility would be to claim that Agr-lowering was indeed introduced early in the century, but that *do* retained some semantic content until 1575. On this view, it would be the loss of *do*'s content that led to the NE-style interaction with Agr-lowering after 1575. However, we saw in the previous section that 16th-century *do* had no discernable semantic content, so this approach does not seem promising.

Another solution is to capitalize on the idea that positive declarative *do* functioned as a substitute for abstract Agr^{-1} as a PF-identifier of V. When the agreement paradigm collapsed, certain agreement affixes remained (and remain): 2sg -(*e*)*st* and 3sg -(*e*)*th*/-(*e*)*s* (the choice between these depending on region and, in East Midland English, to some extent on register; cf. Barber 1976: 237f). We suggested in 3.1. that these elements were reanalysed as Agr° when the paradigm collapsed, pointing out that these elements (and the past tense morpheme) must be X° for Agr/T-lowering to be possible without violating the Structure Preservation Condition. Suppose now that these items remained as Agr^{-1} for some time after the collapse of the agreement paradigm, and that it was the use of *do* as a functional substitute for the opaque Agr^{-1} which triggered their reanalysis as $Agr°$, creating the conditions for the DR in (98). From this perspective, the introduction of Agr-lowering depends on three things which happened one after the other: (i) the breakdown of the agreement paradigm (with the retention of some endings); (ii) the development of *do* as a functional substitute for Agr^{-1}; (iii) the DR in (98). Also, this account depends on the characterization of the trigger for Agr^{-1} given in 3.1.3., since it is because of the morphological opacity of Agr^{-1}, defined in 3.1.3., that *do* begins to act as a PF-identifier for V.

Let us now consider the effects of the introduction of Agr/T-lowering. We will take each of the relevant contexts one by one.

In positive declarative clauses, (66) forbids *do*-insertion. We saw that positive declarative *do* reduces in frequency from 1575 on. Following Kroch, and with the provisos regarding the continued attestations of the conservative system into the 17th century that we mentioned in 3.1.1., we take this as the point at which V-to-Agr raising was replaced by Agr/T-lowering. Once Agr/T-lowering is introduced, (66) makes *do*-insertion impossible where it is not required. Since it is not required in positive declaratives, it is therefore ruled out.[20]

In interrogatives, on the other hand, the frequency of *do* rises steadily. Kroch says "Questions . . . show only small deviations from a continued monotonic increase in the use of *do*." As we saw in our discussion of Milton in 3.1.1., interrogatives with V-to-Agr are certainly attested in texts of the 17th century and after, but this can be attributed to extragrammatical factors. Once Agr-lowering is introduced and V-raising is lost, *do*-insertion becomes obligatory in interrogatives for the reasons we saw in 3.2.1.: the *wh*-criterion requires T/Agr-raising, while, in the absence of an auxiliary, the PF-identification requirement of the V requires Agr/T-lowering. Since *do* was available as a PF identifier of V, it was required to be inserted in order to resolve this paradox.

The situation concerning negative clauses is more complex and more intriguing. Kroch (ibid.) reports a decline in *do*-insertion in negative clauses in 1575–1600 (Ellegård's Period 8) and it does not start to increase significantly in frequency until Period 11, i.e. 1650. So *do*-insertion in negatives lags behind *do*-insertion in declaratives from 1575 to 1650.

A related point is that negative clauses provide some of the clearest evidence for Agr/T-lowering, since we find a number of 16th-century cases of 'MSc-style' negation with *not* preceding the main verb. We discussed such examples briefly in 3.1.1. (29), and repeat them here:

(29) a.   Thairwith he **nocht growit**

    At this   he not   shrunk (i.e. in fear)

(c1448: Richard Holland, *The Buke of the Howlat*, 7; Gray 1985: 152)

b. y so **not presuppose**

    I so not presuppose

    (1450s? Pecock *Repressor of Overmuch Blaming*; Gray 1985: 124)

c. Or if there were, it **not belongs** to you

    (1600: Shakespeare, *2 Henry IV*, IV, i, 98; in Battistella and Lobeck 1988: 33)

d. Safe on this ground we **not fear** today to tempt your laughter by our rustic play

    (1637: Ben Jonson *Sad Shepherd*, Prologue 37; in Kroch 1989).

As (29a–b) show, a small number of cases of this kind is also found in the 15th century. It is striking that all the 15th-century occurrences of this order given in Visser (§ 1440, p. 1532) have either subject gaps or pronominal subjects. If we allow that subject pronouns could cliticize to C° in syntax (cf. 2.1.2., 2.2.2. on OF subject pronouns), then we see that this order is related to the presence of a gap in subject position. In that case, it is natural to treat the 15th-century examples as cases of Stylistic-Fronting of *not*.

This account of (29a–b) has two consequences. First, it entails that 15th-century *not* was an XP, since only XPs undergo Stylistic-Fronting. Second, it predicts that the 16th-century examples of the construction in (29) result from the DR in (98). This is confirmed by the examples given in Visser (§ 1440); only two examples are earlier than 1550, one of which is a clear case of Styl-F of *not* since it involves a subject relative. The other example, from 1535, may have to be treated as an early example of Agr/T-lowering.

Let us suppose, then, that in the 16th century *not* was an XP which occupied SpecNeg' (it could presumably also occupy other specifier positions, giving rise to the possibility of constituent negation). In fact, Kroch proposes essentially the same treatment of *not*, and, as he says, this explains the time lag regarding *do*-insertion in negatives compared with interrogatives. The obligatory *do*-insertion in negatives is triggered in NE by the presence of *not* in Neg° blocking QR of T° from inside VP, but if *not* is a specifier rather than a head it will not have such a blocking effect. Given our analysis of *do*-support, then, in a system just like contemporary English with the single difference that *not* is in SpecNeg' rather than in Neg°, negative declaratives would pattern like positive declaratives. This is what Kroch's interpretation of Ellegård's figures shows; the occurrence of *do* in negative declaratives drops with positive declarative *do* from 1575 to 1600. For this period, then, we assume exactly the system just described; a grammar with NE-style *do*-support but in which *not* has a different status.

After 1600 the situation changes, and the modern situation of obligatory *do*-insertion emerges. Significantly, the reduced form of sentential negation, *n't*, emerges at this period. Jespersen (*MEG*, V: 429) makes the following remark:

> The contracted forms seem to have come into use in speech, though not yet in writing, about the year 1600. In a few instances (extremely few) they may be inferred from the metre in Sh[akespeare], though the full form is written.

Jespersen goes on to say that the first written occurrences of *n't* are found in the 1660s, so we take it that *n't* was established in the spoken language by then. In the prose of the late 17th-century Restoration dramatists we find a number of examples, e.g.:

(99)   **Mayn't** my cousin stay with me?

(1697, Congreve; cf. Plank 1984: 1330)

Significantly, as Plank (ibid.) indicates, we never find any case of a main verb negated by *n't* (in Standard English), even in the late 17th century when main verb could be raised over *not* in literary style (cf. 3.1.1). This suggests that the grammar which cliticizes *not* is separate from the one which raises main verbs to Agr, even though both may have existed (the latter somewhat marginally) in different registers at this time.

To sum up, negative *do*-support lags behind interrogative *do*-support during the late 16th and early 17th centuries. Following Kroch, we interpret this fact to mean that *not* was not a head at this time, and so did not block QR of V° and did not trigger *do*-support; instead, negative clauses pattern with positive ones in the last years of the 16th century, and so *do*-insertion in this context in fact declines. In the 17th century, *not* becomes a head, as the emergence of the reduced form *n't* reveals. As a head, *not/n't* blocks QR of T° and triggers *do*-support. So we find that by the late 17th century we have the NE situation in negatives.[21]

The above paragraphs give the essential elements of our account of *do*-support. Our proposal is that *do* became restricted to its present-day contexts because it became obligatory in those contexts, given (66). *Do* became obligatory in the contexts in question because of the introduction of the Agr-lowering rule, and the interaction of this rule with LF-raising of V° and with the conditions on the PF-identification of verbs. Agr-lowering was introduced as a result of the DR in (98), which, in conditions where the PF-identification of V was either opaque or carried out by an auxiliary (recall that modal and aspectual auxiliaries also played this role from the 16th century on), converted the former Stylistic Fronting structure into an Agr-lowering configuration. *Do*-support in interrogatives was the immediate consequence of this DR, with *do*-support in negatives following only when *not* began to regularly appear in (or cliticize to — cf. Note 21) Neg°. The other consequence of this DR was the elimination of unstressed positive declarative *do*.

Before leaving this topic we should make two more brief remarks concerning the introduction of Agr-lowering.

The first point concerns the form of the 3sg present ending. We saw in 3.1. that, in ME, this ending was -(*e*)*s* in the North and -(*e*)*th* in the Midlands and the South. Moreover, we noted in 3.1.3. in our discussion of the Scots agreement paradigm that the agreement inflection in this variety was apparently in complementary distribution with a subject pronoun (cf. the examples in (54)). During the 16th century, the -(*e*)*s* inflection gradually spread southward, so that by 1600 it was probably the usual colloquial form. Barber (1976: 239) discusses the competition between the two endings, concluding:

It is probable that, by the 1590s, -*es* was normal in educated speech. As early as 1500 there is evidence for its use in familiar speech even in the London area, and in the course of the 16th century it became the normal form. The continued use of -*eth* in writing after about 1590 is an example of the conservatism of the written language. By about 1600 there are clear indications that people often wrote -*eth* but expected it to be read as -*es*.

Bambas (1947) discusses the timing of the introduction of -(*e*)*s* for -(*e*)*th* in the following terms:

The -*s* inflection had been in use in Northern dialects since the thirteenth century, but didn't appear in London writing until the second half of the sixteenth century. Northern migrants had been bringing this peculiarity of their speech to London ears for three hundred years before the south-easterners inexplicably adopted it as a variant.

This development could of course be completely independent of the introduction of Agr-lowering. However, the fact that a new ending was borrowed at the precise time that the syntactic behaviour of that ending changed, and not before, is suggestive.

We very tentatively suggest that the introduction of -(*e*)*s* for -(*e*)*th* may have been related to the changes we have seen owing to the peculiar property of this ending in Northern dialects. As we saw in (54), non-2sg/3sg -*s* (or -*is*) was in complementary distribution with subject pronouns. Although it is unclear what underlies this peculiarity of Northern syntax, we suggest that it was conducive to treating the -*s* ending as Agr° (we saw in 3.1.3. that treating Northern -*s* as a clitic may explain V-to-Agr in that variety). If we grant this, then we would expect -*s* to increase in frequency at the expense of -*th* as the 3sg (and 2sg) endings start to be treated as instantiations of Agr rather than Agr^{-1} (we also expect to find -*s* in other persons, which we certainly do; cf. Note 9). What is unclear in this account is the precise mechanism of borrowing from the Northern dialect, if indeed that is what happened. The facts nevertheless suggest that something of this sort may have happened.

A further, possibly related remark concerns certain rural English dialects. These dialects, although less in use in the late 20th century than formerly, were certainly viable earlier in this century. In a large area of South-Western England (an area covering West Hampshire, Dorset, Wiltshire, Gloucestershire, Somerset, Devon and Cornwall according to Wright 1898–1905) *do* has a distribution quite different from that found in Standard English since the 17th century. The general characteristic of this area is that *do* appears frequently in positive declarative sentences. So we find the following:

(100) a. Thee do look.

b. They do be fighting up yonder.

c. I do do.

d. I do eat.

e. I do go.   (Wright 1970: *DO*)

In some dialects, positive declarative *do* seems general. This may be true of the Gloucestershire dialect, given the following quotation, again from Wright (ibid.):

Almost invariably used in the present tense of verbs. 'Did' is also used in the same way as 'I did go' for 'I went'.

(Cf. also Wakelin 1986, Visser § 421, Palmer 1974: 25). On the other hand, Trudgill (1990) says that in Somerset dialect *do* is used to mark habitual aspect. Of course, it is entirely possible that there is no contradiction here, and that *do* has a different status in the two dialects.

Our account of the development of Standard English *do* support makes it possible to understand this dialectal variation, if the facts we have reported are accurate. For a system of the kind Trudgill describes for the Somerset dialect, we can treat *do* as an aspectual auxiliary on a par with modals. The immediate prediction of such an analysis is that *do* should block *have/be* raising, just as modals do, and this appears to be true (cf. (100b)). As we mentioned in 3.2.2., the existence of this construction may cast some doubt on the idea that (East Midland) ME *do* was an perfective marker, in favour of the idea proposed by Poussa (1990) that it was a habitual marker.

A system of the type that, according to Wright, exists (or existed) in Gloucestershire is minimally distinct from that of Standard English. In fact, we can hypothesize that this system arises where Agr-lowering fails to be introduced. In that case, *do* comes to be inserted obligatorily in all clauses in order to PF-identify V (or to carry the agreement affix, but there appears to be variation across dialects, with many completely lacking agreement affixes (Wakelin 1986: 38)). Since *do* is obligatorily inserted, (66) means that it cannot be inserted at DS; however, this restriction has no consequences in a system without Agr-lowering. Thus we can postulate exactly the developments we have seen for Standard English, minus the DR in (98). Concerning the lack of this DR, it is interesting to note that the dialects that have this property are all in South-Western England, clearly outside the area of linguistic influence from Scandinavia. If Stylistic Fronting were a borrowing from Scandinavian (which is probable, although we cannot establish this here), then we would expect it to be absent in the parts of the country where Scandinavian had hardly, or never, been spoken. And we have seen that the introduction of Agr-Lowering depends on the prior existence of Stylistic-Fronting. Clearly, establishing or refuting these speculative points is a matter for future research; but this seems to be a place where the concerns of syntactic theory meet those of traditional dialectology.

In the preceding pages, we have attempted a kind of syntactic history of the auxiliary *do*. We have seen that in ME *do* had three syntactic instantiations: as an ECM verb, a raising verb, and something similar to the verbs which take '*faire-par*' complements in Romance languages. In ENE, ECM *do* disappears, FP-type constructions disappear with all causative verbs, plausibly because of the disappearance of the infinitive affix *-en*, and raising *do* is reanalysed (along with some equivocal FP cases) as an auxiliary. In ENE the auxiliary *do* loses the aspectual meaning characteristic of ME raising *do*, and appears to function as a substitute for the opaque Agr^{-1}, PF-identifying V. This function actually makes Agr^{-1} still more opaque, and around 1575 this position is lost and Agr-lowering is introduced via a DR affecting Stylistic Fronting. Agr-lowering creates contexts in which the formerly optional *do*-insertion is obligatory, and so, given (66), *do*-insertion is prevented in all contexts where it is not required. As the Kroch/Ellegård data shows, the modern *do*-support system was introduced in interrogatives before it was introduced in negatives, a fact we attribute, following Kroch, to the different status of negation at this period. By the mid-17th century, *not* has its modern syntax (as shown by the written occurrences of *n't*), and the system is essentially as it is now.

The NE system of *do*-support is cross-linguistically very unusual. However, the above account makes it possible to see how this system arose by a series of natural steps from a system where interrogatives and negation were marked in a more cross-linguistically frequent way. In fact, we can maintain that *do*-support is the result of a combination of North Germanic and West Germanic properties, and so it is no more surprising than the English pronoun system, or the forms of the verb *be*, both of which are a mixture of West Germanic and North Germanic forms. The elements shared with North Germanic in what we have seen are (i) the breakdown of agreement paradigms (cf. 3.1.3. on MSc), and (ii) the loss of Stylistic Fronting (although this factor may be only apparently North Germanic; cf. the discussion of Styl-F in OF in Dupuis 1990, Platzack 1990 and 2.2.1.). The element shared with West Germanic is the aspectual auxiliary *do*. It is essentially the interaction of these three elements with our assumptions regarding the PF-identification of V that gave rise to the NE situation. We regard this view of the origins of *do* as more plausible than the one put forward by Poussa (1990), who postulates an Anglo-Celtic creole influencing later varieties of English, since, although Welsh has a raising verb *do* with little discernable semantic content (cf. (5a) of Chapter 1), Celtic influence on English has been extremely slight in other areas (e.g. in the lexicon). On the other hand, our account suggests that the NE situation may owe something, indirectly, to Scandinavian influence; it is plausible that Scandinavian influenced English syntax since the incidence of lexical borrowing in this case is very high (cf. Perrenoud 1990 on another possible case of Scandinavian influence on the development of English syntax). We have seen that the development of (part of) the NE auxiliary system is intimately connected with the breakdown in the agreement system. This is not a particularly novel idea: cf. Lightfoot (1979) and Roberts (1985), among others. However, a point which has been neglected up to now by those who maintain this position regarding the history of English is that MSc has lost its agreement system, but has developed neither *do*-support nor modal auxiliaries of the NE kind. We will now turn to this question, as we take up the topic of the development of English modals.

3.3. MODALS

Our final topic in this chapter is the history of the English modals. Since Lightfoot (1979), the development of the modals has been taken as a prime case of categorial reanalysis. In 3.3.1., we will briefly recapitulate the main ideas of the account of this reanalysis given in Roberts (1985) in terms of the assumptions made here. The essential fact is that the DR given in 3.2.3. (93) took place in the first part of the 16th century, and so the modals, formerly raising/control verbs, became auxiliaries.

In 3.3.2. we take up a topic that was neglected in Roberts (1985): the question of the comparative history of English and MSc. As we saw in 3.0. (cf. (14)), MSc modals do not have the distributional peculiarities of NE modals, and yet many of the properties that have been held to be responsible for the English development hold in MSc, notably the lack of agreement (cf. 3.1.3.) and the lack of a subjunctive (see Roberts 1985 and below). However, we will see that there is a crucial difference between English and MSc in that MSc still has T^{-1} and so main verbs move to T in MSc. In fact, we will propose that the absence of T^{-1} is responsible for various NE traits that distinguish NE from MSc (and so from the rest of Germanic and Romance).

3.3.1. *The Historical Reanalysis of English Modals*

In this section, we take up once more the question of the well-known developments in the English modal auxiliary system. These facts are treated in Lightfoot (1979, Ch. 2) and Roberts (1985), while different views on the matter are taken in Plank (1984), van Kemenade (to appear) and Warner (1982, 1983, 1987). These approaches appear to be very different from one another, but this is in large part due to the fact that the history of the modals involves two separate but linked kinds of change, and the different accounts have concentrated more on one aspect than on the other. On one hand, there is a change in syntactic distribution: modals were formerly much closer in distribution to main verbs than they are in present-day English. On the other hand, these items have changed their lexico-semantic properties in subtle and complex ways, involving a general drift towards epistemic modality to the exclusion of root modality.

We will suggest that modals underwent a Diachronic Reanalysis in the first part of the 16th century, a change which did not really manifest itself until the later changes involving the loss of V-to-Agr and the introduction of Agr-lowering had taken place. The lexico-semantic changes are gradual, and have been going on throughout the recorded history of English. The complexity arises from the fact that the two kinds of changes interact; for example, if a modal loses the capacity to take a direct object, this is both a change in syntactic distribution and a change in lexico-semantic properties (subcategorization, or more precisely, PAS properties). The Diachronic Reanalysis that took place in the 16th century prevented modals from taking direct objects since they became functional heads. It says nothing about the transitivity of modals prior to the reanalysis; and, indeed, some of them were clearly unable to take direct objects anyway as they had already lost this capacity owing to the drift towards epistemic modality. Similarly, as we shall see in more detail below, the reanalysis created the potential for lexical splits, whereby a premodal (to use Lightfoot's 1979 term for the verbs which are the historical antecedents of the NE modals) was reanalysed as a modal in some positions, and became a 'pure' main verb in other cases.

Although related, the syntactic and lexico-semantic developments are independent of one another. It is clear that elements with the semantic properties of NE modals can be main verbs; a cursory glance at the syntax of their Romance or Germanic equivalents shows this. Conversely, as our discussion of *do* in 3.2.3. showed, the reanalysis that converted the modals into auxiliaries did not depend on the fact that they express modality since *do*, which at the time had an aspectual meaning, was affected by the same reanalysis. Neither was the reanalysis sensitive to the kind of modality expressed; both root and epistemic modals were reanalysed.

We can capture the different nature of the syntactic and lexico-semantic changes in the modals in terms of the different notions of the theory of change introduced in 2.3.1.: the syntactic change in the history of modals was a Diachronic Reanalysis, while the lexico-semantic changes are Steps. As we have said, the parametric change relevant to the history of modals was the loss of X^{-1}-level projections, where X is a functional head. The development of the modals is of interest in connection with this change, as it sheds further light on the loss of T^{-1}. As we will see in 3.3.2., English has the negative value of the T^{-1} parameter, unlike the rest of Germanic.

We now briefly recapitulate the basic facts concerning the distribution of the modals prior to the 16th century.

First, inversion and negation contexts indicate clearly that modals were able to raise to Agr:

(101) a. . . . so **mote** they nedes go home on fote

. . . *so must they needs go home on foot*

(cl464, Capgrave, *Chronicle of England*; Visser § 1694; Roberts 1985a: 22, cf. (11b))

b. **Wilt thow**   ony thinge with hym?

Wilt thou [do] any thing with him?

(1470–85, Malory, *Morte d'Arthure* III, iii, 120; Visser, § 559; Roberts ibid.: 23)

(102) a. A blynde man **kan nat** juggen wel in hewis

A blind   man cannot judge   well in colours

(cl387: Chaucer, *Troilus* 2, 21, Roberts ibid., cf. (11a))

b. Thy   godfadirs   wyff thow **shalt not** take

Your godfather's wife you   shall not take

(cl 450: *Idley Instructions* 2a, 1757, Roberts ibid.)

As we saw in 3.1.1., in these respects modals did not differ from all other verbs. However, NE modals have of course retained the ability to raise to Agr. No property of modals forces raising to Agr; it seems that finite T is always combined with Agr (either by raising or lowering) probably for reasons connected with the phonological realization, if any, of verbal affixes; cf. Johnson (1990).

In ME, all verbs raised to Agr; this movement was triggered by the presence of Agr^{-1}, as we saw in 3.1. In the 16th century, Agr^{-1} was lost. After that time, any verb which continued to raise to Agr productively (allowing for the effects of literary conservatism and fossilization of certain expressions that we mentioned in 3.1.1.) cannot be a Θ-role assigner for the reasons that we saw in 1.3. and 3.0. Hence, we deduce that NE modals are not Θ-assigners (or, more precisely, they are not assigners of main Θ-roles; cf. below and Chapter 1, n. 13, on the distinction between main Θ-roles and adjunct Θ-roles).

As is well-known, the NE aspectual auxiliaries *have* and *be* raise to Agr. The fact that these elements are independent of properties of Tense (cf. 3.0.) suggests that they are best treated as base-generated as heads of their own VPs. Modals, on the other hand, are clearly sensitive to the finiteness of the clause they appear in (cf. (9–10)), and as such are best treated as base-generated in T°, in fact T° [+finite]. The restriction of modals to finite clauses did not apply to the pre-modals, however, as the examples given in (12), repeated here, show:

(12) a. I shall not **konne**   answere

      I shall not be-able-to answer

      (1386: Chaucer *CT*, B, in Visser § 1649, Roberts ibid.)

    b. They are doumbe dogges, not **mowende**   berken

      They are dumb   dogs,   not being-able-to bark

      (cl1380: Wyclif, *Prov.* 7, 11: Visser § 1684)

    c. if he **had wolde**

      if he had wanted to

      (1525 Ld. Berners, *Froiss.* II, 402, Visser § 1687, Roberts ibid.)

This suggests that at least some of the premodals were able to be base-generated in V. However, various authors (Mitchell 1983, Warner 1982, van Kemenade to appear) have pointed out that evidence is lacking for certain premodals; for example, there are no attested non-finite forms of *shall*. More generally, in OE non-finite forms of premodals are rare, and non-finite forms of epistemic premodals are non-existent. In ME, however, non-finite forms become more frequent (cf. van Kemenade to appear). Since we are concerned with the changes taking place between ME and NE, the latter fact is what is relevant here. Cf. Note 22 for a possible analysis of the difference between OE and ME regarding non-finite modals.

Another important difference between ME and NE is that (some) premodals were able to take direct objects, as illustrated in (13):

(13) a. She **koude** much of   wandrynge by the weye

      She knew much about wandering by the way

      (Chaucer; Lightfoot op. cit.: 99)

b. euerych bakere of þe town . . . **shal** to þe clerke of þe

town a   baker   of the town . . . owes to the clerk   of the

town a penny

town a peny

(al400: Usages of Winchester (Engeroff), p. 64: Visser § 549)

c. **Wultu** kastles and kinedomes?

Wilt thou [i.e. do you want] castles and kingdoms?

(cl225: *Ancr. R.* 389: Visser, § 559)

Again, this was not a property of all premodals, but it nevertheless represents a clear difference between the ME premodals and the NE modals.

The last two points can be accounted for together if we assume that at least some of the premodals were Θ-assigning verbs base-generated in V. Since we have no evidence that a given premodal was not base-generated in V, we extend this account to all premodals. So we treat the ME premodals as a class as main verbs with sentential complements; the evidence in (13) indicates that some premodals also allowed nominal complements.

The premodals most commonly (although not exclusively) had infinitival complements, and it is clear that the superficial subject of the modal is to be interpreted as the subject of the complement verb. This is the case in the examples in (12), (101) and (102) given above. So the question arises of whether they were raising or control verbs. Van Kemenade (to appear: 26), basing her discussion in part on Denison (1987) and Warner (1987), gives some OE examples which indicate that some premodals were raising verbs at this period:

(103) a. ða   cwæð ic: Hwy ne **sceolde** me swa ðyncan?

then said I: Why neg should me so   seem?

'Then I said: Why should it not seem so to me?'

b. Me mæig . . . gif hit **mot** gewiderian,   mederan settan . . .

One can . . . if it must be-fair-weather, madder plant

'One can, in case of fair weather, plant madder'

In these cases, the complement of the premodal has an expletive subject (in (103a) this is an expletive *pro*). This rules out the possibility of control, and so we treat these as cases where the expletive is raised from the lower subject position to the subject position of the premodal.[22]

Similarly, in ME we find examples where a premodal has a complement verb whose subject is non-thematic (unaccusative, passive, raising, or copular):

(104) a. . . . agens   whom **it schal be argued** and concluded . . .

      . . . against whom it shall be argued and concluded . . .

      (c1443: Pecock, *Reule* 96; Visser § 1489)

    b. . . . a cubite of geometrie conteyneth six comoun cubites, þat

      . . . a cubit of geometry contains   six common cubits   that

      wil be **nyne foot long**

      will be nine feet long

      (1387: Trevisa, tr. Higden (*Rolls*) II, 235; Visser § 1586)

    c. Hu   **mai it be** þat vr   language spek þai þus

      How may it be that our language speak they thus

      (c1300: Havelok 18966, Visser §1674)

Evidence of this kind, combined with the epistemic meaning of the pre-modals here, indicates that the premodals were raising verbs.

One class of examples that may be interpretable as cases of modals appearing in a control structure is constituted by the impersonal uses of premodals with a dative Experiencer argument that seems to act as a controller, as in the following cases:

(105) a. Mee **moste** nedys   been dampned for this

      Me must needs [I must] be   damned for this

      (1455: *Speculum Misercordie*, 251, Visser § 1715; Roberts 1985: 38)

    b. hwi me **ouh**   and hwi me **schal** iesu crist luuien

      why me ought and why me shall J.C.   love

      (*Ancr. R.* (EETS 1952) 6, 23; Visser § 1712)

    c. þe   **þar**   not dowt þo warlocke wyld

      Thee should not doubt the warlock wild

      (c1450: *Sir Gowther* (ed. Breul), 673; Visser § 1343)

(In (105c), *þar* is a form of *thurfen*, a premodal cognate with German *dürfen* which is obsolete in Standard English, but which meant roughly 'should'). In each of these examples, the expletive is *pro*, occupying SpecAgr' with the inflected verb in C° (cf. Note 8 on null subjects in ME). Such examples could not be treated in terms of raising, since raising cannot place an NP in indirect object position (on the assumption that no operation of 'quirky raising' creating dative subjects exists; we assume that it does not since this would allow dative expletives, something we do not find).

Many cases of premodals are formally ambiguous between raising and control interpretations. It is plausible to identify root readings (ability, volition, obligation) with control and epistemic readings (necessity and possibility) with raising since in root readings the subject receives a Θ-role (roughly Experiencer) from the premodal, while in the epistemic reading it does not. This correlation holds for the examples in (104) and (105). Most of the ME premodals allowed both epistemic and root readings (cf. Lightfoot 1979: 2.1), and so this further indicates that the premodals were both raising and control verbs. One consequence of this analysis of premodals is that we do not expect to find passive forms of premodals (with sentential complements) since raising verbs (and impersonal dative-control verbs) very rarely passivize cross-linguistically (cf. Perlmutter and Postal 1984, Baker, Johnson and Roberts 1989) and subject-control verbs do not passivize at any period of English.[23]

In the early 16th century, the premodals underwent the DR schematized in (96), which we repeat here:

(96) a.   NP$_i$ [$_{T^\circ}$ do/M$_j$ T^{-1}] t$_j$ [t$_i$ VP]
     b.   NP [$_{T^\circ}$ did/M] VP $\Rightarrow$

As we saw in our discussion of how this DR affected *do* in 3.2.3., this reanalysis was possible since T^{-1} was no longer morphologically triggered, once the infinitive marker *-en* had been lost (cf. 3.1.2.), and replaced by the X° element *to*. This development made finite T a possible site for the insertion of modals and *do*.

Of course, not just any raising verb could be reanalysed as an auxiliary inserted in T°. We saw in 3.2.3. that *do* underwent this reanalysis because of its aspectual meaning. In the case of the modals, various morphological and semantic factors seem to have contributed to making them susceptible to (96). Following Roberts (1985), we consider the most important factors to have been the morphological irregularity of premodals, the loss of the subjunctive inflection, and the fact that, owing to their epistemic content, the premodals were used as functional substitutes for the subjunctive. We will briefly discuss each of these factors in turn.

First, the premodals as a class showed highly irregular tense/agreement morphology, owing to the fact that they form the residue of class of Proto-Germanic 'preterit-present' verbs; verbs whose present tense was diachronically a preterit. In ME, this meant that they had no 3sg present ending; the only verbs in the language to lack this ending. This morphological peculiarity distinguished the modals as a class from all other verbs.

Second, another morphological peculiarity was that their past tenses were irregularly formed and, as in NE, were not in the regular semantic relationship with the present but could be used to express nuances of doubt, etc. This means that the premodals did not interact in the usual way with T, which may have favoured an analysis of them in which they did not interact with the tense morpheme in T°, but instead were in complementary distribution with this morpheme. A natural consequence of this would have been to treat them as base-generated in T°.

Third, the premodals began to act as functional substitutes for subjunctive inflections as these inflections eroded during the ME period. Because of phonological changes, it seems, the subjunctive inflections gradually fell out of use in ME (cf. Visser (789ff)). The premodals functioned as periphrastic substitutes in all the former subjunctive contexts (cf. Roberts 1985: 41, Note 13 for a list of these).

So it was possible on both formal and semantic grounds to treat the modals as base-generated in T°. Once T^{-1} had been lost, a development indicated by the changes in infinitives that we discussed in 3.1.2., T° was available for lexical insertion of X°, and the DR in (96) became possible. As we saw in detail in 3.2.3., once this DR became possible it was favoured by the LES, since it reduced the number of chain-positions in the structure by three (cf. (97)).

(96) is formulated for the raising cases of premodals. However, as we saw, the premodals also appeared in control structures. We can assume that the same reanalysis affected these cases, leading to the same reduction in the number of chain positions. The root readings of some modals were retained, however. If we continue to analyse root modality as involving a thematic relation between the modal and the (surface) subject (cf. Roberts 1985: 50 for evidence that this is the case at least for ability *can* and volitional *will* in NE), then we are led to the conclusion that these elements assign an adjunct Θ-role in the sense of Zubizarreta (1982); cf. Chapter 1, Note 13 for more on this point. Thus we see that the DR in (96) was insensitive to the raising or control properties of the modals.

The most important consequence of the DR in (96) was that modals were no longer found in non-finite forms: in the infinitive, in participial forms, or in sequence (in Standard English, cf. Note 3 and below). This was because, once the reanalysis took place, they, like *do*, could only be inserted in a [+ finite] T°. There are a few examples of non-finite modals from the late 16th century and the 17th century. However, as pointed out in Roberts (1985: 49), these examples are all root modals:

(106) a. Where we **would** no pardon they laboured to punish us.

(1643: Angier *Lanc. Vall. Achor* 18, *OED*, WILL, B 22)

b. In evill, the best condicioun is not **to wille,** and the second not **to canne.**

(1607: Bacon *G. Pl. Ess. Arb.* 242; *OED*, CAN, A5)

(106a), and possibly (106b), are moreover cases of modals with a direct object. Plank (1984: 311) gives a similar example with *may*:

(107)   If it had been the pleasure of him who **may** all things.

(1597 Morley)

The evidence suggests that the three properties of (i) root modality, (ii) non-finite forms, and (iii) the ability to take direct objects group together in the 16th and 17th centuries. This is entirely compatible with our proposed reanalysis in (96). (96) says nothing about modals with direct objects, and so we may expect them to remain alongside the newly-created auxiliaries, but as essentially different lexical items, with distinct syntactic and semantic properties. In particular, we expect that where such a split takes place the main verb retains the root readings and the auxiliary retains the epistemic readings, since root readings are associated with a richer thematic structure than epistemic readings. This is in fact what has happened to *need* and *dare* (cf. Note 2); that transitive *will, can* and *may* did not survive is an accident of the lexicon.

In fact, Plank (op. cit.: 316), citing Ščur (1968), points out that *can* has retained non-finite forms in various dialects of England and Scotland. What Plank does not point out, however, is that these forms all have root meanings, as is clear from the context:

(108) a. Nobody seems **to can** understand it. (Leicestershire)

 b. She's use to **couldn't** sit nur stan'. (Leicestershire)

 c. We'll **can** agree fine. (Scots)

 d. If wey had **cuid** cum. (Scots)

(Note that (108b) may be a counterexample to the claim we made in 3.2.4. that no Θ-assigning verb ever hosts *n't*; however, that claim was made for Standard English, so (106b) can be interpreted as indicating that *n't* has a different status in the Leicestershire dialect).

At this point, it could be objected that our proposed reanalysis of the modals has very little empirical content, since, as both van Kemenade (to appear) and Plank (1984) point out, it is true for many Germanic languages that epistemic modals are rare in non-finite forms and never have direct objects. If (96) is compatible with the retention of root modals in non-finite forms and with direct objects, and if epistemic modals never occurred in these contexts, then what is the result of (96)? In the short term, between the time of the DR and the introduction of Agr-lowering around 1575 (see 3.2.4.), (96) may indeed have had only rather slight effects on the distribution of modals (although it affected the distribution of *do*, as we saw in 3.2.3). However, after the loss of V-to-Agr and the introduction of Agr-lowering, the striking differences in the syntax of modals and main verbs that are familiar from NE emerged as a consequence of (96), since modals were base-generated in T° and verbs in V°. This, and the parallels with the behaviour of *do*, justify the postulation of (96).

In this section, we have sketched an account of the development of English modals that is consistent with what we said in previous sections concerning the development of *do*-support and the loss of V-to-Agr movement. There is little here that adds to the earlier accounts of Lightfoot (1979) and Roberts (1985), except where we have tried to take into account various objections raised by other scholars. The essential point is that modals underwent the DR in (96), which converted premodals which were raising verbs into auxiliaries devoid of thematic content and premodals which were control verbs into auxiliaries with an adjunct Θ-role to assign to a derived subject. This DR interacted with the developments described in 3.1. and 3.2., the loss of V-to-Agr raising and the introduction of Agr-lowering, to give rise to the sharp syntactic division between modals and main verbs that is characteristic of NE.

Like *do*-support, the sharp division between modals and main verbs is unique to NE among Germanic and Romance languages. For all the Romance languages and the other West Germanic languages this is not surprising, since these languages have rich agreement systems (they all have Agr^{-1}, cf. (65)). On the other hand, it remains to be seen why MSc, which also lacks Agr^{-1}, does not have anything comparable to NE modals. This is our next topic.

3.3.2. Modals and T^{-1} in MSc

In the previous subsection we saw how the syntactically distinct subclass of NE modals developed as a result first of the DR in (98) and then as a consequence of the loss of V-to-Agr and the introduction of Agr-lowering. In this section, we compare the development of English modals as outlined in the previous section with the situation in the MSc languages (we base our discussion primarily on Danish data, from Vikner (1988, pers. comm.); as far as we are aware, the syntax of Danish modals is representative of the syntax of modals in MSc as a whole).

The basic fact about MSc is that the modal verbs are not subject to the constraints that hold of their NE counterparts. Modals occupy the same range of finite-verb positions as main verbs: second position in matrix clauses, and post-negative position in subordinate clauses (cf. 1.0., 1.3.2., 1.4. on MSc word order). The following examples (from Vikner 1988) illustrate this:

(100) a. Han **skal** være rejst   til London
          He   shall be   travelled to L.
          'He is supposed to have gone to L.'

b. Det **skal** han ikke

   That shall he   not

c. [En   af de ting   han **ikke kan**] er at svømme over Kanalen

   One of the things he   not can   is to swim   over Channel

   'One of the things he cannot do is swim the Channel'

There are thus no grounds in MSc for assigning modals to a special syntactic position, in the way that there are in NE.

   Moreover, although subject to certain restrictions (see below), we find modals in non-finite forms (cf. Vikner op. cit.: 6f), and (14)):

(110) a. ?Han **har skullet** bo i Århus

   He   has should live in Å.

   'He has been said to live in A.'

b. Det måtte **have kunnet** stå på en   side

   It   must have could fit on one page

   'It must have been possible to fit it onto one page'

c. Han **har villet**   tjene   mange penge

   He has wanted to-earn much   money

   'He has wanted to make a lot of money'

(111) a. De   **skal ville** bygge et hus

   They shall will build a house

   'They are said to want to build a house'

b. Det **må   kunne** stå på en   side

   It   must can   fit on one side

   'It must be possible to fit it into one page'

c. Han **skal kunne** svømme for at få jobbet

   He   must can   swim   for to get job-the

   'He must be able to swim to get the job'

d. Det ser   ud til at **ville** blive   godt vejr   i eftermiddag

   It   seems out to   will become good weather in afternoon

   'This afternoon seems to be going to be nice'

Also, at least in pseudo-cleft constructions, we find modals with direct objects (Vikner, p. 11):

(112)   Det eneste han **vil**   er at svare   på spørgsmålet
         The only   he   will is to answer on question-the
         'The only thing he wants to do is answer the question'

The non-finite and transitive modals are subject to interesting restrictions. Epistemic modals are questionable in the perfect (cf. (110a)), with the exception of *kunne* (Vikner in fact argues that the perfect tense applies to the main verb in (110a), but this does not affect the point that the modal is formally a participle). In sequences, epistemics cannot be embedded under root modals (again with the exception of *kunne*), but can be embedded under other epistemics ((111b)), and root modals can be embedded under other root modals ((111c)). In other kinds of infinitivals, Vikner shows (pp. 8–9) that epistemics cannot have a PRO subject, but root modals can, and that the epistemic modals vary in acceptability in raising contexts. We will comment further on these peculiarities of epistemic modals below.

The data in (109–112) clearly show that MSc modals are much closer to ME modals than to NE modals in their overall distribution, and in the relation between their distribution and the distribution of main verbs. As a first approximation, we can take this fact to mean that MSc modals are lexically inserted in V rather than in T. This analysis captures the similarities between MSc and ME, and the differences between both of these systems and NE. What it further implies, of course, is that MSc modals have not undergone the DR in (98), which we claimed to be responsible for the peculiarities of NE modals. Given that, as we saw in 3.1.3., MSc has undergone a development parallel to English in losing its agreement system and in losing V-to-Agr, this in turn means that the DR in (98) must be independent of the loss of the agreement system and the loss of V-to-Agr. This conclusion is consistent with what we have said in this chapter, but is notably inconsistent with the claims of Roberts (1985).

The independence of the loss of Agr^{-1} and the development of a syntactically distinct class of modals (and, given 3.2.3., auxiliary *do*), as shown by the facts of MSc, leads to a further implication. Other things being equal, the property of 16th-century English that led to the development of NE modals does not hold of MSc. In the previous subsection we attributed the development of the NE modals to the reanalysis in (98). This reanalysis was triggered by the loss of the infinitival affix, making $T°$ a possible site of lexical insertion of $X°$-elements. In MSc, we find that an infinitival affix has been preserved, as the ending *-e/-a*, e.g. Da. *køb-e* Nor. *kjøp-e*, Sw. *köp-a* ('buy'). That this is the infinitive ending can be seen by comparing the imperative forms, which are just the bare stems *køb, kjøp, köp* with the infinitive forms. So we take *-e/-a* to be a realization of T^{-1} in MSc.[24] Another prediction that clearly holds up concerns the existence of an 'FP' construction in MSc. Following Guasti (1990), we take it that the existence of an infinitival affix is essential for this construction. As we saw in 3.2.3., this construction existed in ME but died out in the 16th century. As is well-known, it exists in MSc (cf. Taraldsen 1983, Vikner 1987) (applying Guasti's analysis of causatives, the suggestion for InfP in Note 24 is supported).

So we arrive at the following comparative picture of the development of English and of MSc:

(113) a. Loss of agreement = loss of Agr^{-1} (Cf. 3.1.3.)

b. Development of modals/*do* = loss of T^{-1}

(113a) holds for both English and MSc. (113b) holds only for English. (113b) explains four comparative correlations that hold across Germanic (and Romance):

(114) a. NE is the only language with a syntactically distinct class of modals (and *do*-support).

b. NE is the only language with a bare-stem form of the infinitive.

c. NE is the only language with a *for NP to VP* construction.

d. NE is the only language with no "FP" construction.

Moreover, these properties correlate diachronically; they were all innovated in English in the early 16th century. We attribute these developments to the loss of T^{-1} around 1500, and the introduction soon after of insertion of $X°$ items, first *to* and later *do* and modals, into $T°$. These synchronic and diachronic correlations are strong evidence for the T^{-1} parameter.

(113a) explains the correlations summarized 3.1.3. (65a). It is worth noting that the generalizations in (113), and the fact we must clearly distinguish the T^{-1} parameter from the Agr^{-1} parameter in order to account for the attested cross-linguistic variation, constitute an indirect argument in favour of Pollock's 'split-Infl' hypothesis (*contra*, for example, the alternative in Iatridou 1990).

The idea that NE has no T^{-1} implies that past-tense morphology, like 3sg present -*s*, does not trigger V-movement. We saw in 3.1.3. why it might be that 3sg -*s* is too weak to trigger this movement: essentially, it is an affix without a paradigm. On the other hand, at first sight it is less obvious that past-tense -*ed* is 'weak'. However, if we think of the paradigm of tense/nontense inflection in NE, and compare it with MSc, we can see that it is. The English past-tense morpheme alternates with no overt ending, either in the present tense (where the only marking is for 3sg agreement), or with respect to the infinitival form of the verb. In other words, the crucial point about NE is that there is no overt, equipollent present/past opposition, and no overt equipollent finite/non-finite opposition. In MSc, on the other hand, both present and past tense are overtly marked: the present ending is -er (e.g. Da. *kast-er* 'throw' (present, all persons)), and the past ending is -ede (*kast-ede* 'threw' (past, all persons)). Moreover, the infinitive is also overtly marked, as we saw. The parallel between these observations and the morphological condition for the postulation of Agr^{-1} given in (58) should be clear. The generalization over the two cases is that, for X^{-1} to be postulated (where X is a functional category), the morphological feature fundamental to X must be equipollently realized.

The above comparison of NE and MSc implies that contemporary MSc has V-movement in subordinate clauses as well as in matrix clauses. This movement places the verb in T, as V is morphologically selected by T°. This proposal is consistent with the available evidence from MSc. Negation is in any case higher than T°, and so V-movement does not interact in any way with NegP. Floated quantifiers are arguably able to appear in all positions except the base position of the subject (see Deprez 1990); cf. the fact that in English they must precede the lowest VP-adverbs (*They have all hardly eaten* vs. *They have hardly all eaten*). VP-adverbs show a strong tendency to appear to the right of VP, and hence they do not interact with verb-placement. So, the MSc evidence, taken alone, is equivocal regarding V-to-T movement, but the comparison with NE, taking into account the diachronic facts, suggests that these languages have V-to-T.

A further question which comes up when comparing NE and MSc is why aspectual auxiliaries do not raise to Agr in MSc as they do in NE. In other words, we have seen why MSc lacks modals and *do*, but it remains unclear why we should not find an NE-style dichotomy between aspectual auxiliaries and main verbs, which the evidence clearly indicates that we do not. We suggested in Note 5 that *have* and *be* raise in NE, but not in MSc, precisely because NE has a small amount of residual morphological agreement in Agr. More generally, as we saw, the fact that *do*-support is not sensitive to person indicates that Agr carries morphologically null person features in NE. In MSc, there is no evidence for such a postulate, so we can treat MSc Agr as present but always empty (except for its Case feature). As such it does not attract even those verbs that could move there without violating the Θ-criterion or the Projection Principle, namely aspectuals (and epistemic modals).

One further diachronic development in English is related to the loss of T^{-1}. This concerns the subjunctive mood. The OE and ME subjunctive (present) was characterized by -e endings throughout the singular and -en endings in the plural. As in the case of the indicative and infinitive endings, these endings eroded during ME, so that by ENE the subjunctive was marked by a bare verb. The following examples illustrate this:

(115) a. thou shalt not come out thence till thou **have** payed the vtmost farthinge

(1534: Tyndale, *Newe Testament*; Barber 1976: 246)

b. excepte it **do** contayne in it degrees

(1531: Eliot, *Governor*; Barber op. cit.: 247)

(Note that (115b) is a case of the subjunctive of auxiliary *do*, which is impossible in NE, cf. (118c)).

In ME and ENE, subjunctives raised to T and to Agr, as shown by the fact that subjunctive verb forms precede *not*:

(116) a. And gif he **be noght** so, then . . .

And if   he be not   so, then . . .

(1420s: James I, *Kingis Quair*, 62; Gray 1985: 73)

b. Beware that thou **bring not** my son thither again.

(1611: *Bible*, Gen 24, 6; Visser 1973, § 869)

The obvious conclusion to draw here is that the subjunctive is an inflection in T. By ENE, then, this inflection had no overt realization.

In NE, verbs cannot move in the subjunctive:

(117)   I require that he **not leave** before 6.

Moreover, *have/be* raising and *do*-insertion are both impossible in this context:

(118) a. I require that he **not have/*have not** what he wants.

b. I require that he **not be/*be not** here before 6.

c. I require that he **(*do) not** arrive late.

The only other context in NE in which *have/be*-raising and *do*-support are both blocked is when a modal or *to* appears in T°. So, as argued independently in Culicover (1976), Emonds (1976) and Roberts (1985, Note 12), we take the NE 'subjunctive' to be a phonologically null modal, or, more precisely, a null realization of T°.

In addition to the evidence provided by the position and behaviour of *have*, *be* and *do*, a further argument comes from embedded residual V2 with negative adverbs, discussed in 1.4. Negative adverbs of the relevant type obligatorily trigger inversion, in matrix contexts and under bridge verbs:

(119)   ?*I said that in no circumstances he would do that

The same is true if we embed an overt modal like *should* under a subjunctive-taking verb:

(120) ?*I require that under no circumstances he should do that.

Inversion is required in (121):

(121)   I require that under no circumstances should he do that

With the subjunctive, negative adverbs apparently drop the requirement for inversion:

(122)   I require that under no circumstances he do that

We can regularize this fact if we suppose that the empty $T°$ inverts in (122).

The empty-$T°$ hypothesis is consistent with our proposed parametric change. The subjunctive was earlier realized as a null inflection in T^{-1}; because of the loss of T^{-1} and the reanalysis of the modals, it was later realized as a null $T°$. Schematically, the change was as follows:

(123) $[_{T^{-1}}\varnothing] \Rightarrow [T°\varnothing]$

The element $[_{T°}\varnothing]$ acts like a modal in blocking *do*-insertion and *have/be* raising. Furthermore, this element does not seem to carry any morphological features, as verbs governed by it appear in their base forms (nevertheless, we must assume that it is capable of PF-identifying V; in this sense it genuinely acts like an auxiliary). MSc has lost the subjunctive (in the 16th century, cf. Skautrup 1948–53), showing that the reanalysis in (123) was not triggered simply by morphological erosion, but depends on the loss of T^{-1}, and the innovation of auxiliaries.

One necessary condition for the development of a class of modal auxiliaries is thus the loss of T^{-1}. However, the verbs which are reanalysed as auxiliaries must be semantically compatible with an auxiliary function. We alluded to this point in 3.2.3. and the previous section, but we have not yet fully spelled out what it means for a verb to be able to take on an 'auxiliary function'. Let us see now what this means in terms of the assumptions we have made so far, restricting ourselves for the sake of discussion to the case of epistemic modality.

It is clear that certain semantic notions are frequently expressed by functional heads: tense, aspect, modality, negation, possession, definiteness, quantification, etc. These notions can also be expressed by lexical heads, of course. Rather than attempt a characterization, or even a list, of the possible content of functional heads, we tentatively suggest that functional heads carry the content that they do simply because the notions in question are not necessarily mapped into thematic relations. We can capture this idea, and capture the cross-linguistic variation in the realization of certain notions like modality, by saying that these notions may be mapped from LCS to PAS or may, in a sense, 'bypass' PAS and map directly onto syntax.

To give a concrete example, assume that epistemic modals have the following LCS and PAS representations:

(124) a. LCS: ■, ◆

    b. PAS: {Θ} OR { }

(The empty Θ-grid in (124b) is a way of representing the idea that PAS is bypassed). As (124) indicates, we take it that the LCS of epistemic modals represents them as corresponding to the modal operators of some kind of modal logic. What (124) says is that epistemic modality can be syntactically expressed either through assigning a Θ-role or not. Since epistemic modality is an operator, where the Θ-assignment option is not taken, the modal will occupy an operator position in syntax, typically $T°$. The former choice gives rise to a raising verb; the latter to a modal auxiliary.

If we put the above remarks together with our ideas about the functioning of DRs and the Least Effort Strategy, we can see why raising verbs expressing epistemic modality can be reanalysed as modal auxiliaries, and also why, for a given modal, there is a tendency to 'drift' towards epistemic and away from root readings; epistemic readings are associated with simpler syntactic representations since, typically, less chain-positions will be induced by a modal auxiliary than by a raising verb with an infinitival complement (e.g. in that the lower subject will move to the matrix subject position in less steps). More generally, we assume that the semantic notions that make up the 'grey area' for Θ-theory are precisely those notions that can also be syntactically instantiated on functional heads. Possession is a further example of this kind, as we noted in Chapter 1, Note 13.[25]

It is clear that we have not exhausted the topic of the syntax of expressions of epistemic modality with these remarks. The constraints on the distribution of non-finite epistemics in Danish noted by Vikner that we discussed above (and hinted at for Dutch and German by van Kemenade (to appear) and Plank 1984 respectively) suggest that epistemic modals strongly favour appearing in tensed contexts. In fact, the available evidence strongly suggests that epistemic modals must be associated with [+finite] $T°$. If this could be established in full generality, it would clearly be a further factor contributing to the DR which created English modals.

Along these lines, suppose that epistemic modals, whether realized as verbs or as T, are required to associate with finite Tense. All the evidence we have seen points in the direction of such a constraint. If so, then given that V raises to T in MSc, epistemic modals *qua* verbs have the distribution of Tense in MSc. On the other hand, NE main verbs do not raise, and so items which instantiate epistemic modality cannot be verbs. We cannot use these suggestions in accounting for the DR of the modals (and we do not need to), since the reanalysis of the modals happened before V-raising was lost. However, the reanalysis of the modals could have further facilitated the loss of V-raising by removing one motivation for it; after modals were in T, there was no need to raise V to T to satisfy the conditions on the representation of epistemic modality.

In this section we have seen that MSc lacks NE-style modals (and *do*) because it retains T^{-1}. In fact, we saw that the hypothesis that NE lacks T^{-1} establishes a synchronic and diachronic correlation between four properties that distinguish NE from the rest of Germanic, from Romance, and from ME. This correlation is strong evidence in favour of the proposed T^{-1} parameter. We also saw how the English subjunctive developed into an empty $T°$, and, more speculatively, how certain kinds of semantic content are naturally encoded on functional heads independently of Θ-relations.

3.4. CONCLUSION: THE LOSS OF V2 IN ENGLISH

In this chapter we have discussed the historical development of the English agreement and auxiliary systems between ME and NE, concentrating in particular on the 16th century, which seems to be the period in which a series of changes took place in this area. We have seen that these changes can be accounted for in terms of a change in the value of the parameter which determines whether an $X°$ has an X^{-1}-level projection: ENE lost both T^{-1} and Agr^{-1} in quick succession.

As in the case of the Nominative-assignment parameter discussed in Chapter 2, the proposed account of the diachronic development in terms of parametric change has several kinds of consequences.

First, we hope that the foregoing sheds new light on well-known facts of the history of English. We have related together the (near-) loss of the morphological agreement system and the introduction of *do*-support (as opposed to the optional insertion of the empty auxiliary *do*) in terms of the loss of Agr^{-1}. We also connected the four cross-linguistically distinctive properties of NE syntax listed in (114) above. So we have provided an account of the historical development of several major features of English syntax.

In fact, if V2 depends on the presence of C^{-1} (cf. 1.4.), the fact that English has also lost that syntactic constraint seems to indicate a further case where X^{-1} has been lost. We have said very little about the loss of V2 in English in this chapter, mainly because we have been dealing with changes that took place later than this (V2 was lost in the 15th century — cf. van Kemenade 1987: 219f). However, it is worth briefly saying something about this development since it is indirectly connected with what we have seen concerning English, and of some comparative interest given our account of French in Chapter 2. As is well-known, OE was very similar to the modern Continental West Germanic languages in having a basic

SOV order with V2 (cf. 1.1., 1.4. on German). Van Kemenade (1987: 29ff) discusses OE word order in detail, making consistent comparisons with Modern Dutch in order to show the fundamental similarities. Concerning V2, she gives the following examples (p. 42; compare the German examples in 1.1. (7–9) and the OF text in 2.1.2. (25)):

(125) a. we **sculon** swiðe smealice ðissa ægðer underðencean   (SV)
       we must   very   narrowly these both   consider
       'we must consider both of these very carefully'

    b. Maran cyððe   **habbað** englas to Gode þonne men   (OV)
       more   affinity have   angels to God than men
       'angels have more affinity to God than people'

    c. On twam þingum **hæfde** God þæs mannes
       in   two   things   had   God the man's
       sawle gegodod   (PP V)
       soul   endowed
       'With two things God had endowed the man's soul'

    d. þonne **boeð** eowere eagan geopenode   (Adv V)
       then   are   your   eyes   opened
       'Then your will be opened'

    e. Hwi **wolde** God swa lytles þinges him forwyrnan?   (WH V)
       why would God such small thing   him deny
       'Why would God deny him such a small thing?'

The following table presents the results of Bean's (1983) study of OE word order for main clauses (we have rearranged the presentation to facilitate comparison with the OF figures in 2.1.2. (26), although Bean gives no figures for *Pred V* order; the figures do not add up to 100% because Bean has a category for 'miscellaneous' orders which we have disregarded):

(126)

	Subj V	Compl V	Adv V	V1	V > 2
Anglo-Saxon *Chronicle* (c.891–c.1154)	38%	2.5%	34.5%	4%	18.5%
Alfred's *Letter* *on Learning*	25%	3%	19%	6%	26%

Ohthere	48%	5%	19%	8%	8%
Wulfstan	40%	0%	50%	4%	8%
Ælfric's *Preface* to Genesis	59%	1%	20%	8%	11%

These figures are similar to those for OF in major respects: an overwhelming majority of matrix declaratives place the inflected verb in second position. There are nevertheless two differences: OE, especially the later texts, resembles MidFr more than OF in having greater frequency of SV orders and rarer Compl — V orders (cf. 2.3.1., 2.3.2.,); and OE, especially in earlier texts, shows a striking frequency of V > 2 orders.

The first of these points simply shows that V2 began to erode in English earlier than in French. The second point is more important. The large proportion of V > 2 in OE is surprising at first sight (especially in comparison with OF). However, these orders fall into three distinct types, one of which involves *XP — subject pronoun — V*. Both Stockwell (1977) and Van Kemenade analyse these subject pronouns as clitics (we refer to them as SCLs henceforth).

Van Kemenade (p. 198f) (followed by van Kemenade and Hulk 1990 and Platzack 1990) relates this cliticization phenomenon to the loss of V2 in English. The basic idea is that all clitics were lost in ME (a development which van Kemenade insightfully relates to the overall loss of inflectional morphology during this period), and therefore either the *XP — SCL — V* sequences were reinterpreted as *XP — NP — V* orders, or these orders were simply lost and subject pronouns began to behave like regular NPs. In the first case, the loss of SCLs leads to an increase in the proportion of V > 2 orders where there were two full constituents preceding the verb.

In 2.3.2. and 2.4.3., we discussed the loss of V2 in French. We proposed that the elimination of V2 was caused by the change in the Nominative-assignment parameter, which made it impossible for C^{-1} to be hypothesized by acquirers. A major factor contributing to the parameter change was the DR which converted SVO V2 CPs into AgrPs, which took place in the 15th century (cf. 2.3.2. (119)). This DR saved chain-positions by eliminating string-vacuous subject- and verb-movement in matrix SVO clauses. The preconditions for this reanalysis were as follows:

(127) a. Agr/T to the left of VP;

b. V-to-Agr movement;

c. No Agr-recursion.

After the change in base word-order in Early ME (c1200), ME fulfilled (127a). As we saw in detail in 3.1.3., ME had V-to-Agr movement, fulfilling (127b). We will consider (127c) directly.

Despite the similarities with French, it is clear that English retains Nominative-assignment under government (cf. 1.2.). Hence the parametric change that led to the loss of V2 in French is not what caused its loss in English. We tentatively propose that the change in 15th-century English was in fact a change in the opposite direction from that which took place in 16th-century French with respect to the Nominative parameter: ME innovated Nominative-assignment under agreement, when Agr1P was lost. As in OF/MidFr (cf. the discussion in 2.3.1.), this innovation led to the DR eliminating string-vacuous verb and subject-movement in matrix clauses. The loss of Agr1P meant that ME fulfilled condition (127c) for the DR.

To see how this account works, we must first go back to OE. In OE, both subject and object clitics could occupy the 'Wackernagel position' between C and the usual subject position, as they do in Modern German (van Kemenade's (32e–f), p. 130):

(128) a. þa   stickode **him** mon   þa eagan ut

      then stuck   him someone the eyes   out

      'Then his eyes were gouged out'

      (*Orosius*, 90, 14)

    b. þæt **him** his fiend   wæren æfterfylgende

      that him his enemies were   following

      'that his enemies were chasing him'

      (*Orosius*, 48, 12)

We take this as *prima facie* evidence for the Agr1 position in OE (cf. Cardinaletti and Roberts (forthcoming) on comparable data in German, and 1.3.2.). So we suggest that OE had Agr-recursion, in the sense argued for Icelandic in 1.4., and for 'conservative' OF in 2.1.2. and 2.2.4.

The order $XP - SCL - V$ is not found in all matrix clauses in OE. If XP is a *wh*-constituent, the negative element *ne*, or the adverb *þa*, we find the order $V - SCL$ (van Kemenade's (42b, d, f), pp. 138–9):

(129) a. Hwæt sægest þu   yrþlincg?

      What saist   thou, earthling?

      'What do you say, ploughman?'

      (AColl., 22)

    b. þa   wearð **he** to deofle awend

      Then was   he to devil changed

'Then he was changed into a devil'

(AHTh, I, 12)

c. Ne worhte **he** þeah nane wundra openlice

Not wrought he yet   no   wonders openly

'He didn't perform any miracles openly'

(AHTh, I,26)

The same is true for object clitics; note that the object clitic in (128a) follows V, and XP is *þa*. Compare the following (van Kemenade's (7c, f), p. 114):

(130) a. God **him** worhte þa reaf   of fellum

God them wrought than garments of skin

'God then made them garments of skin'

(AHTh, I, 18)

b. Ne geseah **hine** nan man nates-hwon yrre

Not saw   him no man so little   angry

'Noone ever saw him so little angry'

(ASL, XXXI, 306)

The evidence, then, is that the Wackernagel position precedes the tensed verb in matrix clauses unless the initial consituent is a *wh*-constituent, *ne* or *þa*, in which case it follows the tensed verb.

The class of elements that triggers verb-clitic order (i.e. verb-Wackernagel position order) is clearly a class of elements associated with C cross-linguistically; this is clearest in the case of *wh*-constituents, but very plausible also for *ne*. *þa* seems to be rather like OF *si*, a kind of dummy discourse marker associated with SpecC'. Accordingly, we assume that verb — clitic order is the consequence of the presence of an element in SpecC' which triggers V-movement to C (presumably by some generalization of Rizzi's 1990b *wh*-criterion). Otherwise, when we see the order clitic — verb, V is in Agr1 with the clitic. This means that many V2 orders in OE and early ME were the result, not of V-movement to C, but of V-movement to Agr1. In this system, as we suggested for early OF and for Icelandic in 1.2., 2.1.2. and 2.2.4., Agr1 assigns Nominative under government, and so the (non-clitic) subject occupies SpecAgr2'. Spec-Agr1', however, does not seem to be a topic position, since we do not find clear cases of embedded V2 other than under bridge verbs (cf. van Kemenade 1991). It is unclear why this should be, but this system is reminiscent of the possible 'intermediate' OF system discussed in 2.1.2.

In ME, the clitic system was lost. As a result of this, there was no further evidence for the Wackernagel position Agr1, and so this projection was no longer postulated (as mentioned in 2.2.4., Cardinaletti and Roberts relate the existence of Agr1 to generalized morphological nominative case, something which was lost by ME). This led to the 'decliticization' of preverbal SCLs, and their reanalysis as NPs, outlined above. As a result, the Nominative-assignment parameter changed to allow for Case-assignment to preverbal pronouns and to preverbal NPs in subordinate clauses. This change led to a DR like that in 2.3.2. (121) (but not fully identical to it) which reanalysed many former Agr1Ps, and perhaps some CPs, as AgrPs. More generally, this account implies that English never had V2 in the sense that Modern German (or OF) does, i.e., in the sense of having a C^{-1}. So the statement that English has lost V2, although superficially correct, is rather misleading.

Why did English not retain some reduced form of V2, perhaps involving *do*-insertion after the loss of V-to-Agr for main verbs? Here, the proposals in this chapter become relevant. In French, after Agr1P was lost, $C°$ 'took over' some of the abstract properties of $Agr1°$, in that it attracted the finite verb. In other words, as we said in 2.3.1., $C°$ took on the [Agr] feature characteristic of Germanic V2 systems (cf. 1.4.). Hence, C^{-1} was postulated. It seems that, at the time English lost Agr1, the inflectional system was sufficiently decadent that the innovation of X^{-1} was impossible. It is not clear how exactly to instantiate this notion formally, but it is based on the clear fact that, at the time of the loss of Agr1P, English lost all clitics and had weak, and declining, verbal inflection. French, on the other hand, retained a clitic system (although the clitics changed their status; cf. the discussion of the Tobler-Mussafia Law in 2.2.4.), and retained somewhat richer verbal inflection.

Old High German (OHG) showed similar clitic-placement phenomena to those of OE, as shown in Tomaselli (1990). We could apply the same analysis to these data. However, German has not lost its clitic system (or its inflectional system). In terms of the ideas above, German has developed C^{-1} in its recorded history, rather in the way late OF did.

MSc, too, may have developed from an 'double Agr' system (comparative considerations would suggest this, given the situation in Icelandic). Here it is tempting to propose that what was lost when clitics and inflection were lost was Agr2, not Agr1: the present-day Agr corresponds to Agr1, a position which had never carried verbal inflection.

We suggest, then, that English may never have had C^{-1}. Nevertheless, the loss of the prevalent V2 orders is related to the other changes we have discussed here, since, as van Kemenade (1987) shows, it was connected to the overall loss of inflectional morphology in English.

More generally, if the ideas developed in this chapter can be maintained, we may able to conclude the following for NE:

(131)   For X a functional category, NE has no X^{-1}

Another change which has taken place in English, and which may be related to (131), is the development of the genitive marker *'s*. This element developed from a Case-marker which originally attached directly to head nouns. However, in NE, as is well-known, *'s* attaches to whole nominals:

(132) a. the king of England's crown

b. the man I met yesterday's dog

c. the destruction of Rome's consequences

One way to treat this development would be to say that *'s* used to be in D^{-1}, but is now an $X°$ element of some kind (possibly a postposition). This is yet another matter that we must leave open.

(131) is tantamount to the claim that NE is a partially isolating language, from a well-defined X'-theoretic perspective. Again, our conclusions approach those of more traditional work, to which we hope to have added theoretical depth.

NOTES

[1] We cite English examples in the same way as we cited French examples in Chapter 2: references are given to page or line number of primary sources, and full reference is given to secondary sources. In both cases, dates are given where relevant. We used less primary sources for English than we did for French, in part because we are concerned with a much shorter period (solely the 16th century, as opposed to 1110–1600 in the case of French), and in part because there are more high-quality secondary sources available. In particular, we have consulted Barber (1976) on ENE, the excellent collection of texts of various types from the period 1400–1520 in Gray (1985), the *Oxford English Dictionary* (*OED*), Visser (1963–73) (which we cite giving section numbers), Jespersen (1909–49; henceforth *MEG*). Since this chapter (especially 3.3.1.) is in part a reworking of ideas in Roberts (1985), we also re-use a number of examples that appeared in that paper. We treat Old English (OE, pre-1066) examples as examples from a foreign language, giving a word-for-word gloss and a translation. We give Middle English (ME, 1066–1520) examples word-for-word glosses only. We treat Early Modern English (ENE, 1520–1650) as NE, giving no gloss.

[2] Some modals are homophonous with main verbs. This is true of *need* and *dare* in some contemporary varieties of (British) English. Modal *need* does not have 3sg present, inverts, precedes *not* and cannot be followed by *to*; non-modal *need* has 3sg present, triggers *do*-support and can be followed by *to*. Hence the following paradigms emerge:

(i) a.   Need he (*to) talk like that?

b.   He needn't (*to) talk like that

c.   He need (*s) talk like that

(ii) a.   Does he need *(to) talk like that?

b.   He doesn't need *(to) talk like that

c.   He need *(s) to talk like that

There are thus clear syntactic and morphological (and semantic, cf. Roberts 1983) differences

between the two *needs*. This is a different state of affairs to that with *be* and British *have*, cf. Chapter 1, Note 13 and Note 25 below.
[3] Some dialects of American English, in the Southern States of the USA, allow double modals. Nagel (1989) has shown convincingly that this is an innovation, rather than a retention of an ENE trait. Battistella (1991) discusses double-modal constructions in some detail. The most widespread (but not the only) sequences feature *might* as the first modal. These constructions show an intriguing pattern with respect to negation, inversion and tag-formation. In inversion, *could* preferentially inverts:

(i)　　　Could you might possibly use a teller machine?

　　　　(Battistella's (4), p. 4)

Also, we find the following pattern with tags:

(ii) a.　　I might could do that, couldn't I?

　b.　　*I might could do that, might couldn't I?

　c.　　?*I might could do that, couldn't I?

　　　　(Battistella's (5), p. 5)

(i) and (ii) justify considering *might* as a 'spurious' modal and *could* as the 'true' modal. Indeed, we could follow Labov (1972) (and Plank 1984, who does not attribute it to Labov) and treat *might* as a kind of adverb here. The problem with this is the fact that negation can associate with *might* (as well as with *could*), while of course this is impossible with adverbs:

(iii) a.　　They might not could have gone over the state line.

　b.　　I was afraid you might couldn't find this address.

　　　　(Battistella's (6a, 7a), p. 6)

Moreover, *might* appears to be impossible in infinitives:

(iv)　　　*I expect us to might be able to get you one.

　　　　(Battistella's (9b), p. 10)

Battistella proposes an analysis of these facts which is not directly compatible with the assumptions about clause structure we make here (cf. his article for details, and also for references to the descriptive literature on the relevant dialects).

　　We leave this question of the analysis of double modals open, noting only that these dialects seem to have no bearing on the historical development of modals that we will discuss below since what appears to be going here is that the first modal is being reanalysed as a 'tertiary' element of some kind (in fact, Nagel argues that this phenomenon could not have occurred without some previous categorial reanalysis of modals of the type proposed in Lightfoot 1979, Roberts 1985 and 3.3.1.; Battistella's analysis of the double-modal construction is also most naturally compatible with this view). Double modals are also found in some contemporary varieties of English spoken in Britain, notably in Northumbrian and Scots English (Trudgill 1990: 96). We discuss this phenomenon in 3.3.1. (cf. (108)).
[4] There is no gerundive form of progressive *be*, owing to the very interesting and mysterious doubl-*ing* filter (Ross 1972, Pullum 1974, Reuland 1983), which prevents a large class of aspectual verbs with -*ing* participles as complements from themselves carrying *ing*:

(i)　　　*Starting/keeping/continuing writing is difficult

(ii)　　　To start/keep/continue writing is difficult

(iii)　　　*Being writing a book, I am irritable

As with other matters concerning English participles, we have nothing to say on this matter here.

[5] It is noteworthy that, with the isolated exception of *say*, exactly the verbs that are able to resist *do*-support are the verbs that have morphologically irregular realizations of 3sg present: *has*, not **haves*, the internal vowel-change of *do*, and the suppletive forms of *be*. Moreover, *have*, *say* and *do* are exactly the verbs that retained 3sg present *-th* long after *-s* had taken over everywhere else (cf. Jespersen, *MEG*, VI: 17f, Barber 1976: 37f, and 3.2.4. on the *-(e)s*/*-(e)th* alternation in Standard English in the 16th century). This suggests that *have*, *do* and *be* may have retained the capacity to be morphologically selected by Agr. *Say* is the crucial counterexample here which shows that Θ-theory is relevant, not morphology. *Say* is a Θ-assigner and neither inverts nor precedes *not*; if morphological selection were the relevant factor we would expect this verb to act like *have* and *be* given its formal irregularity. We can nevertheless integrate these observations into our system by saying that *do*, *have* and *be* are V^{-1}, and are able to raise since they are not Θ-assigners, so this overrides *do*-support. On the other hand, *say* may also be a V^{-1} but is nevertheless unable to raise for the Θ-theoretic reasons we have seen. This account implies that verbs which raise are V^{-1} generally, an idea which introduces a further strand into the historical discussion which we will not explore in full. However, it is clear that NE differs from earlier stages of English, and all other Germanic and Romance languages (including MSc, cf. 3.2.2.) in that the base form of the verb occurs very frequently at SS. This result partially 'falls out' from the proposals we will make, but the case of *have*/*be* raising suggests that this possibility needs further investigation in order to be teased apart from the proposals in the text.

[6] C° is a different case, of course. Here, following the analysis of V2 given in 1.4., C^{-1} appears whenever it can. Overt complementizers, elements inserted at the C°-level, appear in the contexts where C^{-1} cannot. The only situation where there is a genuine choice (assuming that overt complementizers are in general excluded in matrix C°s, for reasons that are ill-understood) is in the complements to bridge verbs, and here we indeed find both possibilities.

[7] ME also had a preverbal negative element *ne*. This element immediately preceded the inflected verb:

(i) a   **He ne held** it **noght**

      He neg held it not

      (Minot, *Song of Edward* (*The Poems of Lawrence Minot* J. Hall, ed., Oxford, 3rd ed., 1915), 36; Mossé 1968; Roberts 1985: 23)

    b.   the grettness therof **ne couthe I not** gesse nor acounte

      the greatness of it   neg could I not guess nor account

      (1400/1413: Anon. translation of de Deguilleville *Pèlerinage de l'Ame*; Gray 1985: 97)

This element is presumably parallel to French *ne*. In the text of (ib), its use seems somewhat inconsistent; it is possible to find examples of *ne V*, *V not* and *ne V not* in the one-page excerpt given by Gray (pp. 97–8):

(ii) a.   There **nys   no** thing in erthe that **ne wolde** have hasted thider

      There neg-is no thing on earth that neg would have hurried there

    b.   I suppose that stones **shulde not** have kept hem   fro   syngyng

      I suppose that stones should not have kept themselves from singing

Compare also (ib) and the contemporary (25a). According to Jespersen (*MEG*, V: 427) "The practical disappearance of *ne* and the exclusive use of *not* was reached in the fifteenth century." Indeed, the *OED* gives only one clear 16th-century example of *ne* (NE, A.a).

This element survived as a component of the verb *nill* (< *ne* + *will*), meaning 'to not want', found in isolated examples in Spenser and Shakespeare. Kroch (1989), citing Mossé (1968), says that *ne* disappears "at about the time that *do* began to spread." In terms of Pollock's proposed functional category NegP, *ne* can be treated as Neg° (cf. Moritz 1989 for an analysis of *ne* of this type, and a proposal for the diachronic development of negation in English).

[8] English has always allowed Nominative to be assigned under government by Agr (cf. 1.2. on NE; examples like (19) and (20) clearly establish that this was the case in ME and ENE). In that case, given the approach to licensing null subjects that we developed in 2.2.3. and 2.4.3., one might wonder at this point why ME was not a null-subject language. The necessary conditions for licensing null subjects under government appear to have been satisfied: a [+MU] agreement paradigm and the ability to assign Nominative under government. In these respects, ME was just like contemporary Continental West Germanic, and, like those languages, ME allowed expletive null subjects in certain contexts:

(i)   him drempte *pro*   ðorquiles he slep
           he   dreamed (i.e. it dreamed him) while   he slept

           (c1250: Gen and Ex, 1941; Visser § 29, p. 21)

Compare the German example in 1.4. (80a), 2.2.3. (86a) (we cannot reproduce the German example in (86b), as English appears never to have had impersonal passives). As we proposed in 1.4., we take this to indicate that C° is the licenser for null subjects in these languages. The conditions regarding Agr that we just mentioned are necessary, but not sufficient, for null subjects; a further condition concerns the choice of which head(s) can formally license *pro*. It is clear that West Germanic languages which have null subjects uniformly choose C° (a matter clearly related to V2, as pointed out in 1.4.; it may be possible to articulate this relation in terms of C^{-1}, but see Note 12). So ME patterns with the rest of West Germanic with respect to null subjects, while NE, once again, does not.

But cf. the discussion at the end of 2.2.3. for the suggestion that Agr may be the licenser here (also Chapter 2, Notes 5 and 32).

[9] The situation is complicated by the tendency, which persists in sub-standard varieties to the present, for the historically Northern -(*e*)*s* ending to appear in the plural even in Midland and Southern writers during the 16th century. This is undoubtedly related to the adoption of -(*e*)*s* as the 3sg ending, which was going on at this time (on which see 3.2.4.). Barber points to the following cases in the First Folio (1623) version of Shakespeare's *The Tempest*, which were corrected in the later Folios (1632, 1663, 1685):

(i)   My old bones akes
           His teares runs

Barber (op. cit.: 244) comments "such forms occur too frequently for them to be dismissed as printers' or copyists' errors."

[10] Thanks to Sten Vikner for invaluable help in locating and translating the relevant parts of the works by Danish scholars.

[11] French might be thought to raise the question of a series of distinct plural endings where one of the distinctions is manifested by the absence of an ending, i.e. 3pl. However, there is good phonological evidence that at least /ə/ is present underlyingly in the 3pl (cf. the references given in Chapter 2, Note 33).

[12] Given the presence of expletive null subjects licensed by a [+wh] C° in French (cf. 1.2., 2.4.4.1.) and Italian (1.5.), this suggests that these Cs also have a C^{-1}. If so, then one could envisage, *contra* the proposals in Rizzi and Roberts (1989) and in 1.3., the possibility of treating verb-movement to C in interrogatives as triggered by an abstract affix. Given our assumptions so far, this abstract C^{-1} would trigger Agr-to-C raising. However, Agr-to-C raising (i.e. verb-movement to C) is a strictly root phenomenon in French and Italian (cf. 1.2.,

1.5.), something which is directly captured by the assumption that head-to-head movement is free substitution, but cannot be directly captured if the substitution is held to be selected. Because of this, we retain the view that the *wh*-criterion is at work in interrogatives, at the cost of weakening the general relation between X^{-1} and *pro*. Note that, as in the discussion of (6a′) in 2.3.5., C seems to be the category with exceptional properties as regards licensing *pro*.

[13] In the light of the discussion surrounding (58), one may question the postulation of an abstract affix as the trigger for V2 (cf. 1.4.). However, there are two related differences between Agr and C that are relevant here. First, (58) states what morphological content is necessary for the postulation of Agr^{-1}, based on the idea that morphological content forms the crucial trigger. In the case of C^{-1}, the crucial trigger is syntactic rather than morphological: C^{-1} triggers XP-movement to SpecC′ (cf. 1.4.), and bars topicalization to positions outside CP (cf. 2.3.1.). C^{-1} thus has clear syntactic reflexes in terms of XP-movement, while Agr^{-1} does not. Second, the postulation of Agr^{-1} is related to the potential presence of an agreement paradigm; it seems to be an irreducible fact about Agr that it instantiates phi-features (and may play a pronominal role, cf. 2.4.3. and below). C, on the other hand, is not intrinsically related to the notion of paradigm in the same way (although it is associated with agreement paradigms in (some) V2 languages, precisely the property which justifies an abstract agreement feature — cf. 1.4.).

[14] The analogue of (63) in the C-system is (i):

(i)   If a language has null expletives (where it cannot have null subjects), then it is V2.

The clear counterexample to (i) is ModFr (and Italian, if the analysis of interrogatives in this language given in 1.5. is correct). Cf. Note 12 for discussion of C^{-1} and the *wh*-criterion in these languages.

[15] Chinese might be a counterexample to (63). According to Huang (1989), it has null subjects and an 'Infl' node. However, there is to my knowledge no evidence for V-to-I movement, and, given (58), we would not expect this movement since there is no agreement morphology at all. However, the latter fact most likely lets us off the hook here; Chinese is so entirely lacking in agreement morphology that it is most likely correct to identify Huang's 'Infl' position with $T°$ rather than with $Agr°$, and conclude that Chinese lacks Agr altogether. This is consistent with the fact that the elements which motivate the postulation of Infl for Huang are aspect and tense markers. In that case, (63) is simply not applicable. Clearly, on this view, Chinese null subjects, however they are identified, are not identified by $Agr°$. Cf. Huang (1989) for discussion of null subjects and null objects in Chinese. Notice that in order to maintain this view and distinguish Chinese from MSc we should posit that MSc has Agr, but no Agr^{-1}, as we have been assuming (cf. Rizzi 1986a for similar considerations).

This line of reasoning probably applies for other Oriental languages. Cf. Kuroda's (1988) proposal that Japanese, another likely counterexample to (63), lacks Agr. As Kuroda suggests (followed by Fukui 1986), the usual subject position in Japanese is within VP*; our system predicts this outcome if there is no AgrP and if SpecT′ is universally an A′-position (cf. 1.2., 1.3.2.).

[16] T containing an auxiliary raises across negation to Agr. This does not cause a problem with our conception of relativized minimality applying to heads because this movement is not QR but rather X°-movement of the A-type. Note that this is the inverse case (A-movement skipping an A′-position) compared to Lema and Rivero's Long Head Movement discussed in 1.3.2. or Aux-to-Comp discussed in 1.2. (A′-movement skipping an A-position). Note further that we follow Kayne (1989b) in taking unstressed, uncontracted *not* as being ungrammatical. Contracted *not* fills Neg° and triggers *do*-insertion in the manner outlined in the text, and emphasis does the same in examples like (i):

(i)   I do NOT like pizza

Strictly speaking, then, emphatic stress triggers *do*-insertion here, not *not*. On varieties which allow subject-aux inversion to 'strand' *not*, as in (ii), cf. Note 21:

(ii)   Have they not done it?

[17] More needs to be said about *wh*-questions on the subject, where *do*-support is impossible (without emphasis):

(i) a.   Who left?

   b.   *Who did leave?

The usual combination of *wh*-movement and inversion, shown in (ib), can be ruled out here because the trace in SpecAgr′ cannot be head-governed (cf. 1.5.). Rizzi (1990b) proposes the following representation for examples like (i):

(ii) $[_{CP}$ who$_i$ C$°_i$ $[_{IP}$ t$_i$ I$°_i$ . . .]]

I° is [+wh] here. If the *wh*-criterion is stated in terms of chains (in fact, the important point for present purposes is that Part B of the *wh*-criterion be stated in terms of chains, i.e. 'Each X° [+wh] must be in a chain whose head is in a Spec-head configuration with a [+wh] operator'; compare 1.4. (98b)), then it can be satisfied without movement of I° to C°, as I° can form an extended chain (in the sense of Chomsky 1986b) with C°, a position which is clearly in a spec-head configuration with the *wh*-operator. This can only happen when the index for spec-head agreement between C° and SpecC′ is equivalent to that which manifests spec-head agreement between I° and SpecI′, i.e. in cases where the *wh*-operator corresponds to the (possibly derived) subject. This possibility is limited to subjects; if the *wh*-operator were the object, transitivity of indexing would give rise to a Strong Crossover configuration:

(iii)   *wh$_i$ C$_i$ $[_{IP}$ NP$_i$ I$_i$ $[_{VP}$ V t$_i]$

Here the *wh*-trace in object position is A-bound by the subject NP, in violation of Principle C of the binding theory (cf. Chomsky (1981, Chapter 3)).

   Given our assumption of a 'split-Infl' clause structure and the idea that [+wh] is base-generated on T°, the above account requires some further technical elaboration. The relation with the derived subject position is formed by Agr°, not T°. Thus, Agr° can join the extended chain with C°. T° becomes part of this chain since Agr° passes through T° as it downgrades, as we saw above. Because of this, T and Agr share an index. So Rizzi's proposal for (i) carries over to the 'split-Infl' system.

[18] As noted by Plank (1984), Ramat (1987) and others, the development of English modals is a paradigm case of a crosslinguistically very common syntactic change known as auxiliarization. The notion of DR as formulated here, coupled with the LES, tells us why such changes are so common. We will return to this point in 3.3.2.

[19] This account of *do*-insertion has implications for the theory of expletives. Essentially, we expect genuine expletives, i.e. elements with no content and no Θ-role, to be either optional, in the sense of being in alternation with a structure without an expletive, or inserted after DS. It is clear that many instances of expletives are optional in this sense (e.g. nearly all cases of *there*-insertion in English, other than with existential *be*); what is not clear is whether there is evidence that the few cases of apparently obligatory expletives are inserted after DS. We leave this matter open, noting that the predictions our system for *do*-insertion makes are clear.

[20] As we mentioned in 3.2.1., *do* is possible in NE positive declaratives with emphatic stress. According to Kroch, who again bases his discussion on Ellegård (1953), this construction is not found before late ME. It is unclear how the kind of emphasis signalled by modern emphatic *do* was conveyed earlier, and so we cannot speculate on the origins of this construction. For NE, as we suggested in 3.2.1., the natural interpretation of the connection between

do-support and emphasis involves generalizing the account of *do*-support in negatives to positive-polarity contexts, perhaps by postulating a Polarity Phrase.
[21] If we want to retain Rizzi's (1990a) account of the 'inner-island' phenomenon, we must complicate our assumptions about the syntax of *not* and *n't* somewhat. Inner islands are islands for adjunct-extraction created by certain negative elements, as in:

(i)   *How didn't you say [John fixed the car t]?

Here *how* cannot be construed with scope over the lower clause. Rizzi (op. cit.: 1.5.) accounts for this in terms of RM (cf. 1.3.2. (58)) by saying that negation occupies an A'-specifier. Hence negation blocks antecedent-government of the adjunct trace in an example like (i). This account does not distinguish between *not* and *n't*. Since, for our account of *do*-support, we must treat *not/n't* as Neg° in NE, we have to explain (i). We suggest that *not* is indeed generated in SpecNeg', but obligatorily cliticizes to Neg° (this unifies sentential negation and constituent negation, since we can now say that *not* is always a specifier, and when it is in SpecNeg' it cliticizes). The trace resulting from this operation is c-commanded by *n't* at SS because Neg° containing *n't* always attaches to an inflected auxiliary, hence at SS the trace will be c-commanded by *n't*. This trace nevertheless counts as an A'-specifier position for RM and so blocks antecedent-government of the adjunct trace in (i).
    In these terms, the 17th-century development was just the innovation of the cliticization rule. This leads to the plausible conclusion that, although the SS (and LF) status of the negative morpheme has changed, the nature of inner-island phenomena has not (we have no data on ENE inner islands, but we can confidently assume that the situation was as in NE). As mentioned earlier (Note 16) our view of negation implies that we agree with Kayne (1989b) in treating sentences like (ii) with non-emphatic negation as ungrammatical:

(ii)   I do not like pizza

Although Kayne's judgement for examples like (ii) seems sound, some dialects of NE (including my own) allow *not* to be 'stranded' when subject-aux inversion takes place (at least with aspectuals):

(iii)   Have they not done it?

This kind of case is difficult to reconcile both with Kayne's proposals and with the above. We suggest that what is at stake is purely phonological: in these varieties *not* cliticizes syntactically to Neg° as in other post-17th-century varieties. However, phonological cliticization to Agr° (or, more precisely, a c-commanding T [+fin]) is optional rather than obligatory. When, as in (iii), *not* does not attach to Agr°, its trace is properly governed at LF by QR of *not* (which presumably takes place for reasons connected to determining its scope domain; the trace of QR of Neg° still blocks T-to-C movement, of course).
[22] Van Kemenade (p. 27) uses these facts to argue that the OE premodals were auxiliaries, rather than raising verbs. She argues against a raising analysis on the grounds that raising verbs in OE usually have a *to*-infinitival, while modals always have a bare infinitival complement. However, since we take OE *to* to be a complementizer (cf. 3.1.2.), we do not expect it to be systematically present in clausal infinitival complements in the way that it is in NE, and it is possible to treat this difference between premodals and other raising verbs as a simple difference in selection for a complementizer. This seems to be the most plausible view since OE had rich system of verbal inflection and no NE-style auxiliary phenomena. However, the rarity of nonfinite modals as compared with ME, as well as the fact that OE modals are obligatory triggers for Verb (Projection) Raising suggest, as van Kemenade points out, that OE premodals were somewhat auxiliary-like. A plausible conclusion is that OE modals were rather like the 'restructuring verbs' of Italian and other Romance languages (cf. Rizzi (1982, Ch. 1)). Arguably the change in base word-order from SOV to SVO in early ME eradicated the evidence for V(P)R, and so in a sense "normalized" the syntax of

premodals for a few centuries by making them more like other infinitival-taking verbs than they had been in OE. In any case, it is clear that the NE situation is completely distinct from that in OE and ME.
[23] Both Plank (1984) and van Kemenade (to appear) object to Lightfoot's (1979) account of premodals on the grounds that no passive forms are found, but this objection seems spurious since Lightfoot treats premodals essentially as we do here. It is, however, unclear why there are no cases of passives of premodals with NP complements (although little in our account of modals depends on this). Since, as van Kemenade (p. 8) notes, the cognates of the premodals in other West Germanic languages which have NP-complements do not passivize either, the question clearly should not be confined to ME. Note also that NE *want*, a main verb close in meaning to ME root *will*, does not passivize although it clearly allows a direct object:

(i)   *A pie is wanted by me

Whatever is going on here, it is clearly something independent of Lightfoot's claims about premodals.
[24] In light of what we said in 3.2.1. concerning the status of *for* and *to* in ME, and its relation with the presence of an infinitival marker, we predict that MSc should lack *for NP to VP* constructions but allow *for to* sequences. Equating *at* with *to*, we see from (109c) that *for to* sequences are possible in Modern Danish. Similarly, *for NP to VP* sequences (of the NE type) are impossible (Vikner, pers. comm.). Following Platzack (1986) and Beukema and den Dikken (1989), it seems clear that *att* is in C° in Swedish. However, in Norwegian and Danish the situation is less clear. Here, it appears that *at/å* occupies a lower position than C°. The contrasts in contexts of negation indicate this (Beukema and den Dikken, p. 65):

(i) a.   Han lovade **att inte** läsa boken   (Swedish)

   b.   Han lovede **ikke at** lese bogen   (Danish)

   c.   Han lovet **ikke å** lese bogen   (Norwegian)

   He promised not to/to not read the-book

Here we see that Sw. *att* precedes *inte*, while in Da. and Nor. *at/å* follows the cognate morpheme. Also, Da./Nor. *at/å* at least preferentially precedes adverbs like *never* (Beukema and den Dikken, p. 66). Third, Da./Nor. *at/å* is obligatory with raising verbs and ECM verbs, while *att* is impossible in these contexts in Sw. We illustrate with raising verbs (cf. Beukema and den Dikken, p. 67):

(ii) a.   Han verkar (*att) ha   läst boken   (Sw.)
         He   seems   to   have read the-book

   b.   Han siges *(at) tale   svensk flydende   (Da.)
         He   seems   to   speak Swedish fluently

   c.   Jon synes *(å) ha   drukket vin   (Nor.)
         J.   seems   to have drunk   wine

From this evidence *at/å* resembles NE *to* more closely than any complementizer, and so one might be led, as are Beukema and den Dikken, to the conclusion that these elements are in some functional projection lower than C°. However, given our claims up to now, we cannot say that this functional projection is T°, because, as we have seen, Da. and Nor. have an infinitive affix. One possibility would be that *at/å* are base-generated in C° and lowered to T° in the syntax. We could incorporate both the Beukema/den Dikken analysis of Dutch *te* and Giusti's analysis of German *zu* into our framework of assumptions in terms of a similar notion.

A major objection to this approach emerges from Giusti's work. As Giusti points out (pp. 19–20), German and MSc disallow infinitival [+wh] clauses:

(iii)   *Ich weiß nicht, was   zu kaufen   (German)

           *Jeg ved   ikke   hvad at købe   (Danish)

           '*I don't know what to buy*'

In terms of the lowering analysis just suggested, one could think that lowering of [+wh] C° would be ruled out by the *wh*-criterion (cf. 1.4.). However, the ban on [+wh] infinitivals seems to be more general, in that the counterparts to (iii) without *at/zu* are also ungrammatical. Giusti proposes that in these languages the zero-complementizer that introduces infinitivals is inherently [−wh], rather like NE *that*.

An alternative to the lowering analysis, which certainly seems more promising, although its implications would take us too far afield here, would be to consider *zu/te/at/å* as heads of an InfP (cf. Kayne 1990: 5) with the various infinitival affixes as T^{-1}. This allows us to preserve the idea that *zu* (etc.) are not complementizers, and that in these languages T^{-1} is occupied by the infinitival affix. So we can incorporate Giusti's account of the lack of [+wh] infinitivals into our system. In these terms, NE lacks both InfP and T^{-1}, and *to*, *do* and modals occupy $T°$ — as we have proposed. The loss of infinitival *-en* c1500 could thus be viewed as triggering a DR which led to the elimination of InfP. Clearly, more comparative research on Germanic infinitives, including ME [+wh] infinitivals, is needed.

[25] In that Note, we suggested that the possessive *have* of conservative (British) English does not assign Θ-roles, but rather has a small-clause complement internally to which the possession relation is realized. This gives (i):

(i) a.   Have you any money?

    b.   I haven't any money

The contemporary American English construction with *do*-support dates from the 19th century (Visser § 1467 gives the first American attestation as 1880, and the first British one as 1897). This clearly results from a reanalysis of the construction in (i) such that *have* Θ-marks the Possessor and the Possessee arguments, triggering *do*-support. Note also that in this way one chain-position is saved, since *do* raises only from T to Agr, while *have* in (i) raises from V to T to Agr.

The contemporary British construction in *have got* dates from just before 1800. This construction reanalyses *have* as a perfect auxiliary and regularizes the Θ-assignment relations by treating *got* as the Θ-assigner. Here, however, if perfect *have* heads its own VP, as we have been assuming in this chapter, there is no saving in terms of chain-positions.

APPENDIX: TEXTS CONSULTED

Here we list the primary sources we used in the historical chapters, i.e. the texts we referred to directly for example sentences. Our secondary sources feature texts from many other sources, to which references are provided in the text.

Chapter 2: French

Late c11	*La Chanson de Roland*, Société des Anciens Textes Français, Paris.
Early c12	*Le Charroi de Nîmes*, J.-L. Perrier (ed.), Champion, Paris, 1972.
Early c12	Béroul *The Romance of Tristran*, Volume 1, Ewert (ed.), Blackwell, Oxford.
Late c12	*Le Roman de Perceval*, Roach (ed.), *Textes Littéraires Français*, Droz, Genève.
Early c13	*Aucassin et Nicolette*, M. Roques (ed.), Champion, Paris, 1962.
1212	Villehardouin *La Conquête de Constantinople*, E. Faral (ed.), 'Les Belles Lettres', Paris, 1961.
c13	*Merlin*, Société des Anciens Textes Français, Paris.
c1400	Froissart, *Chroniques*, *Textes Littéraires Français*, George T. Diller (ed.), Droz, Genève, 1972.
c1400	*Les Quinze Joyes de Mariage*, *Textes Littéraires Français*, J. Rychner (ed.), Droz, Genève, 1967.
1422	Alain Chartier *Le Quadrilogue Invectif*, E. Droz (ed.), Champion, Paris, 1950.
1462	Gréban *Le Mystère de la Passion*, Gaston Paris and Gaston Raynaud, Slatkine Reprints, Genève, 1970.
1466	*Les Cent Nouvelles Nouvelles*, *Textes Littéraires*, F. Sweetser (ed.), Droz, Genève, 1966.*
1495	*Le Roman de Jehan de Paris*, E. Wichersheimer (ed.), Champion, Paris, 1923.
1505-15	de Vigneulles, P. *Les Cent Nouvelles Nouvelles*, Droz, Genève, 1972.*
1530s	Rabelais Excerpts from *Gargantua*, *Pantagruel* (*Tiers Livre*, *Quart Livre*, *Cinquième Livre*), Bordas, Paris, 1987.
1536	Calvin *Insitution de la Religion Chrestienne*, Tome I, Société des belles Lettres, Paris, 1936.
1549	du Bellay *Deffence et Illustration de la Langue Françoyse*, Genève, Droz, 1950 (fac-similé de l'édition originale de 1549).
1592–1627	d'Aubigné *Lettres Diverses* in *Oeuvres Complètes*, Tome I, Réaume and Caussade (eds.), Slatkine Reprints, Genève, 1967.

Maupas, C.: 1607, *Grammaire française*, Blois.
Vaugelas: 1647, *Remarques sur la langue française*, Chassang (ed.), Paris, 1880, 2 volumes.

* For these texts, we used a computerized corpus, which Paul Hirschbuhler kindly made available.

Godefroy, F.: 1893, *Dictionnaire de l'ancienne langue française et de tous ses dialectes du IXe and XVe siècle*, Vieweg, Paris.

Brunot, F.: 1905, *Histoire de la langue française des origines à nos jours*, Armand Colin, Paris.

Foulet, L.: 1982, *Petite syntaxe de l'ancien français*, Editions Champion, Paris (3ème édition).

Chapter 3: English

Chaucer, *Complete Works* F. M. Robinson (ed.), Oxford University Press, 1957.

Shakespeare, *Complete Works*, 2 Volumes, M. J. Adler (ed.), *Great Books of the Western World*, Chicago University Press.

Milton, *English Minor Poems, Paradise Lost, Samson Agonistes, Areopagitica*, 2 Volumes, M. J. Adler (ed.), *Great Books of the Western World*, Chicago University Press.

Barber, C.: 1976, *Early Modern English*, André Deutsch, London.

Ellegård, A. 1953, *The Auxiliary do: The Establishment and Regulation of its Use in English*, edited by F. Behre, *Gothenburg Studies in English*. Almqvist and Wiksell, Stockholm.

Gray, D.: 1985, *The Oxford Book of Late Medieval Prose and Verse*, Oxford University Press.

Jespersen, O.: 1938, *Growth and Structure of the English Language*, Basil Blackwell, Oxford.

Jespersen, O.: 1909–49, *A Modern English Grammar on Historical Principles*, George Allen & Unwin, London.

Kottler, B. and Markman, A.: 1966, *A Concordance to Five Middle English Poems*, University of Pittsburgh Press.

The Oxford English Dictionary, 1933, J. A. H. Murray *et al.* (eds.), Clarendon Press, Oxford.

Tatlock, J. and Kennedy, A.: 1927, *A Concordance to the Complete Works of Geoffrey Chaucer*. The Carnegie Institution, Washington.

Visser, Th.: 1963–73, *An Historical Syntax of the English Language*, 4 Volumes. E. J. Brill, Leiden.

Wright, J. (ed.): 1899–1905, *The English Dialect Dictionary*, 6 Volumes. Frowde and Corner, London and Oxford; G. P. Putnam, New York.

REFERENCES

Abney, S.: 1987, *The English Noun Phrase in its Sentential Aspect*, Ph.D. dissertation, MIT.

Adams, M.: 1987a, 'From Old French to the Theory of Pro-Drop', *Natural Language and Linguistic Theory* **5**, 1–32.

Adams, M.: 1987b, *Old French, Null Subjects and Verb Second Phenomena*, Ph.D. dissertation, UCLA.

Adams, M.: 1988a, 'Embedded *pro*', in Blevins, J. and Carter, J. (eds.), *Proceedings of Nels 18*, GSLA, University of Massachusetts, Amherst, pp. 1–21.

Adams, M.: 1988b, 'Les effets V2 en ancien et en moyen français', in Hirschbuhler, P. and Rochette, A. (eds.), *Aspects de la syntaxe historique du français*, *Revue québécoise de linguistique théorique et appliquée* **7**, 13–40.

Adams, M.: 1988c, 'Word Order and Null Subjects: Contributions from Old French', ms. UCLA.

Alberton, S.: 1990, *Enclise du pronom objet en français et en italien antique ou la loi Tobler-Mussafia*, Mémoire de Licence, Université de Genève.

Andersen, H.: 1973, 'Abductive and Deductive Change', *Language* **49**, 567–595.

Anderson, S.: 1982, 'The Analysis of French schwa, or How to Get Something for Nothing', *Language* **58**, 534–573.

Aoun, J., Hornstein, N., Lightfoot, D. and Weinberg, A.: 1987, 'Two Types of Locality', *Linguistic Inquiry* **18**, 537–577.

Arquint, J. C.: 1964, *Vierv Ladin: Grammatica elementara dal rumantsch d'Engiadina bassa*, Lia Rumantscha, Chur.

Aspland, C. W.: 1979, *A Medieval French Reader*, Oxford Unviersity Press.

Bach, E. and Horn, G. G.: 1976, "Remarks on 'Conditions on Transformations'", *Linguistic Inquiry* **7**, 265–299.

Baker, M.: 1985, *Incorporation: A Theory of Grammatical Function Changing*, Ph.D. dissertation, MIT.

Baker, M.: 1988, *Incorporation: A Theory of Grammatical Function Changing*, University of Chicago Press.

Baker, M., Johnson, K. and Roberts, I.: 1989, 'Passive Arguments Raised', *Linguistic Inquiry* **20**, 219–251.

Bambas, R. C.: 1947, 'Verb Forms in *-s* and *-th* in Early Modern English Prose', *Journal of English and Germanic Philology* XLVI, 183–7.

Barber, C.: 1976, *Early Modern English*, André Deutsch, London.

Barnes, M.: 1987, 'Some Remarks on Subordinate-Clause Word Order in Faroese', *Scripta Islandica* **38**, 3–35.

Barnes, M.: 1989, 'Faroese Syntax – Achievements, Goals, Problems', ms. University College, London (to appear in *Proceedings of the 7th Conference of Nordic and General Linguists, Tórshavn, August 1989*).

Battistella, E.: 1991, 'INFL, Head Feature Licensing, and the Double Modal Construction', ms. University of Birmingham at Alabama.

Battistella, E. and Lobeck, A.: 1988, 'On Verb Fronting, Inflection Movement, and Aux Support', *Canadian Journal of Linguistics/Revue Canadienne de Linguistique* **36**(3), 255–267.

Bayer, J.: 1984, 'COMP in Bavarian Syntax', *The Linguistic Review* **3**, 209–274.

Bean, M.: 1983, *The Development of Word Order Patterns in Old English*, Croom Helm, London.

Belletti, A.: 1990, *Generalized Verb Movement: Aspects of Verb Syntax*, Rosenberg & Sellier, Turin.

Belletti, A. and Rizzi, L.: 1988, 'Psych Verbs and Θ-Theory', *Natural Language and Linguistic Theory* **6**, 291–352.

Benincà, P.: 1983, 'Osservazioni sulla sintassi dei testi di Lio Mazor', in Angelet, C. *et al.* (eds.), *Langue, Dialecte et Littérature. Etudes romanes à la mémoire de Hugo Plomteux*, Leuven University Press, pp. 187–197.

Benincà, P.: 1984, 'Un'ipotesi sulla sinassi delle lingue romanze medievali', *Quaderni Patavini di Linguistica*, 3–19.

Benincà, P.: 1986, 'L'interferenza sintattica: di un aspetto della sintassi ladina considerata di origine tedesca', ms. Università di Padova.

Benincà, P.: 1989, 'L'ordine delle parole nelle lingue romanze medievali', XIX Congreso Internacional de Lingüística e Filoloxia Romanicas, Santiago de Compostela.

Benincà, P.: 1990, 'TOP and SpecCP in Medieval and Modern Romance', paper presented at the First Generative Diachronic Syntax Conference, York.

Benincà, P. and Cinque, G.: 1990, 'On Certain Differences between Enclisis and Proclisis', ms. Università di Padova/Università di Venezia.

Bennis, H.: 1984, 'Pro and Pronoun in Celtic Languages', in Bennis, H. and van Lessen-Kloecke, W. U. S. (eds.), *Linguistics in the Netherlands*, Foris, Dordrecht.

Bergman, G.: 1968, *Kortfattad Svensk Språkhistoria*, Prisma, Stockholm.

Berwick, R.: 1985, *The Acquisition of Syntactic Knowledge*, MIT Press, Cambridge, Mass.

den Besten, H.: 1983, 'On the Interaction of Root Transformations and Lexical Deletive Rules', in Abraham, W. (ed.), *On the Formal Syntax of the Westgermania*, John Benjamins, Amsterdam, pp. 47–131.

Beukema, F. and den Dikken, M. 1989, 'The Position of the Infinitival Marker in the Germanic Languages', in Jaspers, D. *et al.* (eds.), *Sentential Complementation and the Lexicon: Studies in Honour of Wim de Geest*, Foris, Dordrecht, pp. 57–76.

Borer, B.: 1984, *Parametric Syntax*, Foris, Dordrecht.

Brandi, L. and Cordin, P.: 1989, 'Two Italian Dialects and the Null Subject Parameter', in Jaeggli, O. and Safir, K. (eds.), *The Null Subject Parameter*, Kluwer, Dordrecht.

Brunot, F.: 1905, *Histoire de la langue française des origines à nos jours*, Armand Colin, Paris.

Buchli, S.: 1989, 'Les formes interrogatives dans les *Poésies* de Froissart', ms. Université de Genève.

Burzio, L.: 1986, *Italian Syntax: a Government Binding Approach*, Kluwer, Dordrecht.

Cardinaletti, A.: 1990a, *Impersonal Constructions and Sentential Arguments in German*, Unipress, Padua.

Cardinaletti, A.: 1990b, *Pronomi nulli e pleonastici nelle lingue germaniche e romanze: Saggio di sintassi comparata*, Dottorato di Ricerca in Linguistica, Università di Padova.

Cardinaletti, A. and Roberts, I.: forthcoming, 'Clause Structure and X-Second', to appear in Chao, W. and Horrocks, G. (eds.), *Levels, Principles and Processes: The Structure of Grammatical Representations*, Foris, Dordrecht.

Carroll, S.: 1983, 'Remarks on FOR-TO Infinitives', *Linguistic Analysis* **12**, 415–451.

Chomsky, N.: 1957, *Syntactic Structures*, Mouton, The Hague.

Chomsky, N.: 1964, *Current Issues in Linguistic Theory*, Mouton, The Hague.

Chomsky, N.: 1981, *Lectures on Government and Binding*, Foris, Dordrecht.

Chomsky, N.: 1982, *Some Concepts and Consequences of the Theory of Government and Binding*, MIT Press, Cambridge, Mass.

Chomsky, N.: 1986a, *Knowledge of Language*, Praeger, New York.

Chomsky, N.: 1986b, *Barriers*, MIT Press, Cambridge, Mass.

Chomsky, N.: 1989, 'Some Notes on Economy of Derivations and Representations', in Laka, I. and Mahajan, A. (eds.), *MIT Working Papers in Linguistics*, Volume 10, MIT, Cambridge, Mass, reprinted in Friedin, R. (ed.), *Principles and Parameters in Comparative Grammar*, MIT Press, Cambridge, Mass, pp. 417–454.

Chomsky, N. and Lasnik, H.: 1977, 'Filters and Control', *Linguistic Inquiry* **8**, 425–504.

Chung, S.: 'VPs and Verb Movement in Chamorro', to appear in *Natural Language and Linguistic Theory*.

Cinque, G.: 1991, *Types of A'-Dependencies*, MIT Press, Cambridge, Mass.

Clark, R.: 1990, *Papers on Learnability and Natural Selection*, Technical Reports on Formal and Computational Linguistics, 1, Université de Genève.

Culicover, P.: 1976, *Syntax*, Academic Press, New York.

Dell, F.: 1973, *Les règles et les sons: Introduction à la phonologie générative*, Hermann, Paris.

Denison, D.: 1985, 'The Origins of Periphrastic *Do*: Ellegård and Visser Reconsidered', in Eaton, R. *et al.* (eds.), *Papers from the 4th International Conference on Historical Linguistics, Amsterdam, April 10–13, 1985*, John Benjamins, Amsterdam, pp. 45–60.

Denison, D.: 1987, 'Aux + impersonal in OE', ms. University of Manchester.

Denison, D.: forthcoming, *English Historical Syntax: Verbal Constructions*, Longmans, London.

Deprez, V.: 1989, 'Stylistic Inversion and Verb Movement', ms. MIT.

Deprez, V.: 1990, *On the Typology at Syntactic Positions and the Nature of Chains* PH.D. dissertation, MIT.

Derbyshire, D. C. and Pullum, G. (eds.): 1986, *Handbook of Amazonian Languages*, Mouton, The Hague.

De Vincenzi, M.: 1989, *Syntactic Parsing Strategies in a Null Subject Language*, Ph.D. dissertation, University of Massachusetts, Amherst.

Diesing, M.: 1988, 'Word Order and the Subject Position in Yiddish', in Blevins, J. and Carter, J. (eds.), *Proceedings of NELS 18*, GSLA, University of Massachusetts, Amherst, pp. 124–140.

Diesing, M.: 1990, 'Verb Second in Yiddish and the Nature of the Subject Position', *Natural Language and Linguistic Theory* **8**, 41–80.

Dowty, D.: 1979, *Word Meaning and Montague Grammar: The Semantics of Verbs and Times in Generative Semantics and Montague's PTQ*, Kluwer, Dordrecht.

Dupuis, F.: 1988, 'Pro-drop dans les subordonnées en ancien français', in Hirschbuhler, P. and Rochette, A. (eds.), *Aspects de la syntaxe historique du français*, Revue québécoise de linguistique théorique et appliquée **7**, 41–62.

Dupuis, F.: 1989, *L'expression du sujet dans les subordonnées en ancien français*, thèse de Ph.D., Université de Montréal.

Einhorn, E.: 1974, *Old French: A Concise Handbook*, Cambridge University Press.

Ellegård, A.: 1953, *The Auxiliary do: The Establishment and Regulation of its Use in English*, Behre, F. (ed.), *Gothenburg Studies in English*, Almqvist and Wiksell, Stockholm.

Emonds, J.: 1976, *A Transformational Approach to English Syntax: Root, Structure-Preserving and Local Transformations*, Academic Press, New York.

Emonds, J.: 1978, 'The Complex V – V' in French', *Linguistic Inquiry* **9**, 151–175.

Emonds, J.: 1981, 'Word Order in Generative Grammar', *Journal of Linguistic Research* **1**, 33–54.

Everett, D.: 1986, 'Pirahã Clitic Doubling and the Parameterization of Nominal Clitics', in Rapoport, T., Fukui, N., and Sagey, B. (eds.), *MIT Working Papers in Linguistics Volume 8*, MIT, Cambridge, Mass., pp. 85–127.

Everett, D.: 1989, 'Clitic Doubling, Reflexives and Word Order Alternations in Yagua', *Language* **65**, 339–372.

Fabb, N.: 1984, *Syntactic Affixation*, Ph.D. dissertation, MIT.

Falk, H. and A. Torp (1900) *Dansk-Norskens Syntaks*, H. Aschehoug, Kristiana.

Foulet, L.: 1919, *Petite syntaxe de l'ancien français*, Editions Champion, Paris (1ère édition).
Foulet, L.: 1921, 'Comment ont évolué les formes de l'interrogaton?' *Romania* **47**, 243–348.
Foulet, L.: 1935/6, 'L'extension de la forme oblique du pronom personnel en ancien français', *Romania* **61**, 257–315; 401–463; *Romania* **62**, 27–91.
Foulet, L.: 1982, *Petite syntaxe de l'ancien français*, Editions Champion, Paris (3ème édition).
Franzén, T.: 1939, *La syntaxe des pronoms personnels sujets en ancien français*, Almqvist, Uppsala.
Friedemann, M.-A.: 1989, 'Le pronom interrogatif *que*', ms. Université de Genève.
Fukui, N.: 1986, *A Theory of Category Projection and Its Applications*, Ph.D. dissertation, MIT.
Fukui, N. and Speas, M.: 1986, 'Specifiers and Projections', in Rapoport, T., Fukui, N. and Sagey, B. (eds.), *MIT Working Papers in Linguistics*, Volume **8**, MIT, Cambridge, Mass.
Giorgi, A. and Longobardi, G.: 1991, *The Syntax of Noun Phrases: Configuration, Parameters and Empty Categories*, Cambridge University Press, Cambridge.
Giupponi, E.: 1989, *Pro-Drop-Parameter und Restruktierung im Trentino*, Diplomarbeit zur Erlangung des Magistergrades an der Geisteswissenschaftliche Fakultät der Universität Wien.
Giusti, G.: 1989, '*Zu*-infinitivals and the Structure of IP in German', ms. Università di Venezia.
Godefroy, F.: 1893, *Dictionnaire de l'ancienne langue française et de tous ses dialectes du IXe au XVe siècle*, Vieweg, Paris.
Gray, D.: 1985, *The Oxford Book of Late Medieval Prose and Verse*, Oxford University Press.
Greenberg, J.: 1963, 'Some universals of grammar with particular reference to the order of meaningful elements', in Greenberg, J. (ed.), *Universals of Language*, MIT Press, Cambridge, Mass.
Grimshaw, J.: 1979, 'Complement Selection and the Lexicon', *Linguistic Inquiry* **10**, 279–326.
Gruber, G.: 1965, *Studies in Lexical Relations*, Indiana University Linguistics Club, Bloomington.
Guasti, M.-T.: 1989, 'Romance Infinitive Complements of Perception Verbs', in Branigan, P. *et al.* (eds.), *MIT Working Papers in Linguistics*, Volume **11**, MIT, Cambridge, Mass, pp. 31–45.
Guasti, M.-T.: 1990, 'The *faire-par* Construction in Romance and Germanic', in Halpern, L. (ed.), *Proceedings of the Ninth West Coast Conference on Formal Linguistics*, CSLI, pp. 205–217.
Guéron, J.: 1986, 'Le verbe *avoir*', *Recherches Linguistiques*, 16.
deHaan, G. and Weerman, F.: 1986, 'Finiteness and Verb Fronting in Frisian', in Haider & Prinzhorn, 1986, pp. 77–110.
Haegeman, L.: 1990, *Generative Syntax: Theory and Description. A Case Study from West Flemish*, Cambridge University Press.
Haider, H.: 1986, 'V-Second in German', in Haider & Prinzhorn, 1986, pp. 49–76.
Haider, H.: 1989, 'Matching Projections', in Cardinaletti, A., Giusti, G. and Cinque, G. (eds.), *Proceedings of the 10th Annual GLOW Colloquium*, Venice, Annali di Ca' Foscari.
Haider, H. and Prinzhorn, M. (eds.): 1986, *Verb Second Phenomena in Germanic Languages*, Foris, Dordrecht.
Haiman, J.: 1971, 'Targets and Paradigmatic Borrowing in Romantsch', *Language* **47**, 797–808.
Haiman, J.: 1974, *Targets and Syntactic Change*, Mouton, The Hague.
Haiman, J.: 1988, 'From V/2 to subject clitics: Evidence from Northern Italian', ms. University of Manitoba.
Hale, K. and Keyser, S.: 1986, 'Three Cases of Transitivity Alternation in English', *Lexicon Project Working Paper*, **7**, MIT Center for Cognitive Science.

Hale, K. and Keyser, S.: 1987, 'The View from the Middle', *Lexicon Project Working Paper*, **10**, MIT Center for Cognitive Science.

Harris, M.: 1978, *The Evolution of French Syntax: A Comparative Approach*, Longmans, London and New York.

Hendrick, R.: 1988, *Anaphora in Celtic and Universal Grammar*, Kluwer, Dordrecht.

Henry, A.: 1988, 'Infinitives in a For-To Dialect', ms. University of Ulster at Jordanstown/MIT.

Heny, F.: 1979, *Binding and Filtering*, MIT Press, Cambridge, Mass. and Croom Helm, London.

Higginbotham, J.: 1985, 'On Semantics', *Linguistic Inquiry* **16**, 547–593.

Higginbotham, J. and May, R.: 1981, 'Questions, Quantifiers and Crossing', *The Linguistic Review* **1**, 41–79.

Hirschbuhler, P.: 1990, 'La légitimation de la construction V1 à sujet nul dans la prose et la vers en ancien français', *Revue québécoise de linguistique* **19**, 32–55.

Hirschbuhler, P.: 1991, 'Null subjects in V1 embedded clauses in Philippe de Vigneulles' *Cent Nouvelles Nouvelles*', ms. University of Ottawa.

Hirschbuhler, P. and Junker, M.-O.: 1988, 'Remarques sur les sujets nuls en subordonnées en ancien et en moyen français', in Hirschbuhler, P. and Rochette, A. (eds.), *Aspects de la syntaxe historique du français*, *Revue québécoise de linguistique théorique et appliquée* **7**, 63–84.

Hoekstra, T. and Roberts, I.: 1990, 'The Mapping from the Lexicon to Syntax: Null Arguments', ms. University of Leiden/Université de Genève.

Holmberg, A.: 1986, *Word Order and Syntactic Features in the Scandinavian Languages*, Department of General Linguistics, University of Stockholm.

Holmberg, A.: 1990, 'Scandinavian Weak Pronouns', paper given at Eurotyp Group 8 Meeting "Clitics and Their Hosts", Université de Genève.

Holmberg, A. and Platzack, C.: 1988, 'On the Role of Inflection in Scandinavian Syntax', *Working Papers in Scandinavian Syntax*, 42. Reprinted in Abraham, W. and Reuland, E. (eds.), (1991), *Germanic Syntax Workshop*, John Benjamins, Amsterdam.

Huang, C.-T. J.: 1984, 'On the Distribution and Reference of Empty Pronouns', *Linguistic Inquiry* **15**, 531–574.

Huang, C.-T. J.: 1989, 'Pro-Drop in Chinese: A Generalized Control Theory', in Jaeggli & Safir, 1989, 185–214.

Humphreys, H.: 1932, *A Study of the Dates and Causes of Case Reduction in the Old French Pronoun*, New York.

Hyams, N.: 1985, *Language Acquisition and the Theory of Parameters*, Kluwer, Dordrecht.

Iatridou, S.: 1990, 'About Agr(P)', *Linguistic Inquiry* **21**, 551–576.

Jackendoff, R.: 1972, *Semantic Interpretation in Generative Grammar*, MIT Press, Cambridge, Mass.

Jaeggli, O.: 1982, *Topics in Romance Syntax*, Foris, Dordrecht.

Jaeggli, O. and Hyams, N.: 1987, 'Morphological Uniformity and the Setting of the Null Subject Parameter', in Blevins, J. and Carter, J. (eds.), *Proceedings of NELS 18*, GSLA, University of Massachusetts, Amherst, pp. 238–253.

Jaeggli, O. and Hyams, N.: 1989, 'On the Independence and Interdependence of Syntactic and Morphological Properties: English Aspectual *Come* and *Go*', ms. USC/UCLA.

Jaeggli, O. and Safir, K. (eds.): 1989, *The Null Subject Parameter*, Kluwer, Dordrecht.

Jespersen, O.: 1938, *Growth and Structure of the English Language*, Basil Blackwell, Oxford.

Jespersen, O.: 1909–49, *A Modern English Grammar on Historical Principles*, George Allen & Unwin, London.

Johnson, K.: 1990, 'On the Syntax of Inflectional Paradigms', ms., University of Wisconsin, Madison.

Jones, M.: 1988, 'Auxiliary Verbs in Sardinian', *Transactions of the Philological Society* **86**, 173–203.

Karker, A.: 1974, 'Sproghistorisk oversigt', Oxenvad, E. (ed.), *Nudansk Ordbog*, Politikens Forlag, Copenhagen.

Kato, M. and Tarallo, F. 1986, 'Anything You Can Do in Brazilian Portuguese', in Jaeggli, O. and Silva-Corvalàn, C. (eds.), *Studies in Romance Syntax*, Foris, Dordrecht.

Kayne, R.: 1972, 'Subject Inversion in French Interrogatives', in Casagrande, J. and Saciuk, B. (eds.), *Generative Studies in Romance Languages*, Newbury House, Rowley, Mass., pp. 70–126.

Kayne, R.: 1975, *French Syntax*, MIT Press, Cambridge, Mass.

Kayne, R.: 1982, 'Predicates and Arguments, Verbs and Nouns', abstract of paper presented at the 5th Annual GLOW Colloquium, *GLOW Newsletter* **8**, 24.

Kayne, R.: 1983, 'Chains, Categories External to S, and French Complex Inversion', *Natural Language and Linguistic Theory* **1**, 109–37.

Kayne, R.: 1984, *Connectedness and Binary Branching*, Foris, Dordrecht.

Kayne, R.: 1986, 'Connexité et l'inversion du sujet', in Ronat, M. and Couquaux, D. (eds.), *La Grammaire Modulaire*, Editions de Minuit, Paris, 127–147.

Kayne, R.: 1989a, 'Null Subjects and Clitic Climbing', in Jaeggli and Safir, 1989, pp. 239–261.

Kayne, R.: 1989b, 'Notes on English Agreement', *CIEFL Bulletin*, Hyderabad, India.

Kayne, R.: 1990, 'Romance Clitics and PRO', in Carter, J. *et al.* (eds.), *Proceedings of NELS 20*, GLSA, University of Massachusetts, Amherst, pp. 255–302.

Kayne, R. and Pollock, J.-Y.: 1978, 'Stylistic Inversion, Successive Cyclicity and Move-NP in French', *Linguistic Inquiry* **9**, 595–621.

Keenan, E.: 1978, 'Subject Final Languages', in Lehmann, W. P. (ed.), *Syntactic Typology: Studies in the Phenomenology of Language*, University of Texas Press.

van Kemenade, A.: 1987, *Syntactic Case and Morphological Case in the History of English*, Foris, Dordrecht.

van Kemenade, A.: 'The Diffusion and Implementation of the Category 'Modal' in Middle English', to appear in Rissanen, M. *et al.* (eds.), *Papers from the Sixth International Conference on English Historical Linguistics*, Mouton, The Hague.

van Kemenade, A.: 1991, 'Verbal Position in Old English: Evidential Problems', *Studia Anglica Posnaniensa*, 24.

van Kemenade, A. and Hulk, A.: 1990, 'Licensing V2, Case Systems and Pro-drop', paper presented at the First Generative Diachronic Syntax Conference, York.

Kitagawa, Y.: 1986, *Subject in Japanese and English*, Ph.D. dissertation, University of Massachusetts, Amherst.

Klima, E.: 1964, 'Relatedness between Grammatical Systems', in Reibel and Schane (eds.), *Modern Studies in English*, Prentice-Hall, New Jersey.

de Kok, A.: 1985, *La place du pronom personnel régime conjoint en français. Une étude diachronique*, Rodopi, Amsterdam.

Koopmann, H. and Sportiche, D.: 1990, 'The Position of Subjects', to appear in *Lingua*.

Koster, J.: 1975, 'Dutch as an SOV Language', *Linguistic Analysis* **1**, 111–136.

Kroch, A.: 1989, 'Reflexes of Grammar in Patterns of Language Change', *Journal of Language Variation and Change* **1**, 199–244.

Kuroda, Y.: 1988, 'Whether We Agree or Not: a Comparative Syntax of English and Japanese', in Poser, W. (ed.), *Papers From the Second International Workshop on Japanese Syntax*, CSLI, Stanford University.

Labov, W.: 1972, *Language in the Inner City*, University of Pennsylvania Press, Philadelphia.

Lema, J. and Rivero, M.-L. 1989, 'Inverted Conjugations and V-second effects in Romance', to appear in *Proceedings of the 19th Linguistic Symposium on Romance Languages*, John Benjamins, Amsterdam.

Lema, J. and Rivero, M.-L. 1990a, 'Long Head Movement: ECP *vs.* HMC', in Carter, J. *et al.* (eds.), *Proceedings of NELS 20*, GLSA, University of Massachusetts, Amherst, pp. 333–347.

Lema, J. and Rivero, M.-L.: 1990b, 'Types of Verbal Movement in Old Spanish: Modals, Futures and Perfects', ms., University of Ottawa.

Leiber, R.: 1980, *On the Organization of the Lexicon*, Ph.D. dissertation, MIT; distributed by the Indiana University Linguistics Club, Bloomington.

Lieber, R.: 1983, 'Argument Linking and Compounds in English', *Linguistic Inquiry* 14, 251–286.

Lightfoot, D.: 1979, *Principles of Diachronic Syntax*, Cambridge University Press.

Lightfoot, D.: 1989, 'The Child's Trigger Experience: Degree-O Learnability', *Behavioral and Brain Sciences* 12, 321–334; commentary 334–375.

Lockwood, W.: 1955, *An Introduction to Modern Faroese*.

Maling, J.: 1980, 'Inversion in Embedded Clauses in Modern Icelandic', *Islenskt mál og almenn málfræði* 2, 175–193. Reprinted in Maling, J. and Zaenen, A. (eds.), 1990, *Modern Icelandic Syntax, Syntax and Semantics Volume 24*, Academic Press, New York.

Manzini, M.-R.: 1986, abstract of a paper presented at the 1986 GLOW Colloquium.

Marantz, A.: 1984, *On the Nature of Grammatical Relations*, MIT Press, Cambridge, Mass.

Marchello-Nizia, C.: 1979, *Histoire de la langue française aux XIVe et XVe siècles*, Bordas, Paris.

Martineau, F.: 1990, *La montée du clitique en moyen français: une étude de la syntaxe des constructions infinitives*, thèse de doctorat, Université d'Ottawa.

Martinet, A.: 1974, *Le français sans fard*, Presses Universitaires de France, Paris, 2ème édition.

Mattos e Silva, R.: 1989, *Estructuras Trecentistas*, Livraria Camões, Rio de Janeiro.

Maupas, C.: 1607, *Grammaire française*, Blois.

May, R.: 1977, *The Grammar of Quantification*, Ph.D. dissertation, MIT.

May, R.: 1985, *Logical Form. Its Structure and Derivation*, MIT Press, Cambridge, Mass.

McCawley, J.: 1968, 'Lexical Insertion in a Transformational Grammar without Deep Structure', in *Papers from the Fourth Regional Meeting of the Chicago Linguistics Society*, University of Chicago.

McCloskey, J.: 1986, 'Inflection and Conjunction in Modern Irish', *Natural Language and Linguistic Theory* 4, 245–281.

McCloskey, J.: 1990, 'Clause Structure, Ellipsis and Proper Government in Irish', to appear in *Lingua*.

McCloskey, J. and Hale, K.: 1984, 'On the Syntax of Person-Number Inflection in Modern Irish', *Natural Language and Linguistic Theory* 1, 487–533.

Mikkelsen, K.: 1911, *Dansk Ordföjningslære*, Lehmann & Stage, Copenhagen (reprinted 1975).

Milton, J.: 1988, 'DO Perifrástico em Shakespeare', *DELTA* 4, 59–84.

Mitchell, B.: 1985, *Old English Syntax*, 2 volumes, Clarendon Press, Oxford.

Mohammad, M.: 1989, 'The Problem of Subject Verb Order in Arabic: Towards a Solution', in Eid, M. (ed.), *Perspectives in Arabic Linguistics*, John Benjamins, Amsterdam.

Moignet, G.: 1965, *Le pronom personnel français*, Klincksieck, Paris.

Moignet, G.: 1973, *Grammaire de l'ancien français*, Klincksieck, Paris.

Moritz, L.: 1989, *Aperçu de la syntaxe de la négation en français et en anglais*, Mémoire de licence, Université de Genève.

Mossé, F.: 1968, *Manual of Middle English*, Johns Hopkins Press, Baltimore.

Motapanyane, V.: 1991, *Theoretical Implications of Complementation in Rumanian*, Thèse de Doctorat, Université de Genève.

Mussafia, A.: 1983, *Scritti di filologia e linguistica*, Daniele, A. and Renzi, L. (eds.), Padua.

Mustanoja, T.: 1960, *A Middle English Syntax*, Philological Society, Helsinki.

Nagel, S.: 1989, *Inferential Change and Syntactic Modality in English*, Peter Lang, Berne.

Noonan, M.: 1989, 'The [+WH]-IP/CP Parameter: a Comparison of Standard and Quebec French', paper presented at the 12th Annual GLOW Colloquium, Utrecht.

Offord, M.: 1971, 'The Use of Personal Pronoun Subjects in Post-Position in Fourteenth Century French', *Romania* **92**, 37–64; 200–245.

Ouhalla, J.: 1990, 'Sentential Negation, Relativised Minimality and the Aspectual Status of Auxiliaries', *The Linguistic Review* **7**, 183–231.

Murray, J. A. H. *et al.* (eds.): 1933, *The Oxford English Dictionary*, Clarendon Press, Oxford.

Palmer, F.: 1974, *The English Verb*, Longmans, London and New York.

Pearce, E.: 1990, *Parameters in Old French Syntax: Infinitival Complements*, Kluwer, Dordrecht.

Penner, Z.: 1990, 'Raising Verbs in Bernese: Doubling Verbs, Modals, Auxiliaries, and the Third Construction Verbs: Description and Analysis', ms., University of Berne.

Perlmutter, D.: 1971, *Deep and Surface Structure Constraints in Syntax*, Holt, Reinhart and Winston, New York.

Perlmutter, D. and Postal, P.: 1984, 'The 1-Advancement Exclusiveness Law', in Perlmutter, D. and Rosen, C. (eds.), *Studies in Relational Grammar*, Volume 2, University of Chicago Press.

Perrenoud, M.: 1990, *Extragrammatical Causes of Language Change: Did Scandinavian Languages Influence the Structure of English?* Mémoire de Licence, Université de Genève.

Pesetsky, D.: 1987, 'Wh in situ: Movement and Unselective Binding', in Reuland, E. and ter Meulen, A. (eds.), *The Representation of (In)definiteness*, MIT Press, Cambridge, Mass, pp. 98–129.

Pesetsky, D.: 1990, 'Language-Particular Processes and the Earliness Principle', ms., MIT.

Plank, F.: 1984, 'The Modals Story Retold', *Studies in Language* **8**, 305–364.

Platzack, C.: 1987, 'The Scandinavian Languages and the Null-Subject Parameter', *Natural Language and Linguistic Theory* **5**, 377–401.

Platzack, C.: 1988, 'The Emergence of a Word-Order Difference in Scandinavian Subordinate Clauses', in Fakete, D. and Laubitz, Z. (eds.), *McGill Working Papers in Linguistics: Special Issue on Comparative Germanic Syntax*, pp. 215–238.

Platzack, C.: 1990, 'The Loss of V2 in English and French', talk given at the First Generative Diachronic Syntax Conference, University of York.

Platzack, C. and Holmberg, A.: 1989, 'The Role of AGR and Finiteness', *Working Papers in Scandinavian Syntax* **43**, 51–76.

Poletto, C.: 1990a, 'The Subject Clitic System in Basso Polesano and the Theory of *pro*'.

Poletto, C.: 1990b, 'Subject-Clitic Inversion in the Dialects of North-Eastern Italy', to appear in Belletti, A. (ed.), *Dialects of Italy*, Rosenberg & Sellier, Turin.

Poletto, C.: 1991, 'Diachronic Development of Subject Clitics', ms. Università di Venezia.

Pollock, J.-Y.: 1986, 'Sur la syntaxe de *en* et le paramètre du sujet nul', in Ronat, M. and Couquaux, D. (eds.), *La Grammaire Modulaire*, Editions de Minuit, Paris, pp. 211–246.

Pollock, J.-Y.: 1989, 'Verb Movement, UG and the Structure of IP', *Linguistic Inquiry* **20**, 365–424.

Pollock, J.-Y.: in progress, Monograph on Verb-movement.

Poussa, P.: 1990, 'A Contact-Universals Origin for Periphrastic *do*, with Special Consideration for OE-Celtic Contact', in Adamson, K. *et al.* (eds.), *Papers from the Fifth International Conference on English Historical Linguistics, Cambridge, 6–9 April, 1987*, John Benjamins, Amsterdam, pp. 407–434.

Price, G.: 1961, 'Aspects de l'ordre des mots dans les *Chroniques* de Froissart', *Zeitschrift für Romanische Philologie* **77**, 15–48.

Price, G. 1971, *The French Language: Present and Past*, Edward Arnold, London.

Priestley, L.: 1955, 'Reprise Constructions in French', *Archivum Linguisticum* **7**, 1–28.

Pullum, G.: 1974, 'Restating Doubl-*ing*', *Glossa* **8**, 109–120.

Ramat, P.: 1987, 'Introductory Paper', in Harris, M. and Ramat, P. (eds.), *Historical Development of Auxiliaries*, Mouton de Gruyter, The Hague.

Reinhart, T.: 1976, *The Syntactic Domain of Anaphora*, Ph.D. dissertation, MIT.

Reis, M.: 1985, 'Satzeinleitende Strukturen im Deutschen: über COMP, Haupt- und Nebensätze, w-Bewegung und die Rest', in Abraham, W. (ed.), 1985, *Erklärende Syntax des Deutschen*, Narr, Tübingen.

Reuland, E.: 1983, 'Governing -*ing*', *Linguistic Inquiry* **14**, 101–136.

Ribeiro, I.: 1990, 'Evidence for a V2 Phase in Old Portuguese', ms. UNICAMP, Brazil.

Rivero, M.-L.: 1988, 'The Structure of IP and V-movement in the Languages of the Balkans', ms., University of Ottawa.

Rivero, M.-L.: 1990, 'Patterns of V°-raising in Long Head Movement, and Negation: Serbo-Croatian *vs*. Slovak', to appear in the *International Journal of Basque Linguistics and Philosophy*.

Rizzi, L.: 1982, *Issues in Italian Syntax*, Foris, Dordrecht.

Rizzi, L.: 1986a, 'Null Objects in Italian and the Theory of *pro*', *Linguistic Inquiry* **17**, 501–557.

Rizzi, L.: 1986b, 'On the Status of Subject Clitics in Romance', in Jaeggli, O. and Silva-Corvalàn, C. (eds.), *Studies in Romance Syntax*, Foris, Dordrecht, pp. 391–419.

Rizzi, L.: 1987, 'Three Issues in Romance Dialectology', talk given at the GLOW Workshop on Dialectology, 10th GLOW Colloquium, Venice.

Rizzi, L.: 1988, 'The Structural Uniformity of Syntactic Categories', in *Proceedings of the Conference on the Basque Language*, Eusko Jaurlaritzaren Argitalpen-Zerbitzu Nagusia/Servicio Central de Publicaciones del Gobierno Vasco, Vitoria/Gasteiz.

Rizzi, L.: 1990a, *Relativized Minimality*, MIT Press, Cambridge, Mass.

Rizzi, L.: 1990b, 'Speculations on Verb-Second', in Nespor, M. *et al*. (eds.), *Grammar in Progress: A Festschrift for Henk van Riemsdijk*, Foris, Dordrecht.

Rizzi, L. and Roberts, I.: 1989, 'Complex Inversion in French', *Probus* **1**, 1–30.

Roberts, I.: 1983, 'The Syntax of English Modals', in Flickinger, D. *et al*. (eds.), *Proceedings of the Second West Coast Conference on Formal Linguistics*, Stanford, pp. 227–246.

Roberts, I.: 1985, 'Agreement Parameters and the Development of English Modal Auxiliaries', *Natural Language and Linguistic Theory* **3**, 21–58.

Roberts, I.: 1987, *The Representation of Implicit and Dethematized Subjects*, Foris, Dordrecht.

Roberts, I.: 1990, 'Inversion and Subject Clitics in Valdôtain', in Engdahl, E. *et al*. (eds.), *Parametric Variation in Germanic and Romance: Proceedings from a DYANA Workshop, September 1989, Edinburgh Working Paper in Cognitive Science*, Volume 6, pp. 155–168.

Roberts, I.: 1991, 'Excorporation and Minimality', *Linguistic Inquiry* **22**, 209–218.

Roberts, I.: 'The Nature of Clitics in Franco-Provençal Valdôtain', to appear in Belletti, A. (ed.), *Dialects of Italy*, Rosenberg & Sellier, Turin.

Rochette, A.: 1988, 'Réseau de corrélations: sujet nul, montée et placement des clitiques et le caractère nominal des infinitives', in Hirschbuhler, P. and Rochette, A. (eds.), *Aspects de la syntaxe historique du français*, *Revue québécoise de linguistique théorique et appliquée* **7**, 175–192.

Rögnvaldsson, E. and Thráinsson, H.: 1990, 'On Icelandic Word Order Once More', in Maling, J. and Zaenen, A. (eds.), 1990, *Modern Icelandic Syntax, Syntax and Semantics*, Volume **24**, Academic Press, New York.

Ross, J. R.: 1969, 'Auxiliaries as Main Verbs', in Todd, W. (ed.), *Studies in Philosophical Linguistics*, series 1, Evanston, Ill., Great Expectations Press.

Ross, J. R.: 1972, 'Doubl-*ing*', *Linguistic Inquiry* **3**, 61–86.

Ross, J. R.: 1982, 'Pronoun Deleting Processes in German', paper presented at the Annual Meeting of the Linguistic Society of America, San Diego.

Rossi, A.: 1990, 'A perdida do fenomeno V-front no português do Brasil', ms., UNICAMP, Brazil.

Rouveret, A.: 1982, 'Structure argumentale et stratégies d'identification en gallois', ms., Université de Paris VIII.

Rouveret, A.: 1987, *Syntaxe des Dépendences Lexicales. Identité et Identification dans la Théorie Syntaxique*. Thèse de Doctorat d'Etat, Université de Paris VII.

Rouveret, A.: 1988, 'X-bar Theory and Barrierhood in Welsh', ms., Université de Paris VIII.

Rouveret, A. and Vergnaud, J.-R.: 1980, 'Specifying Reference to the Subject: French Causatives and Conditions on Representations', *Linguistic Inquiry* 11, 97–202.

Safir, K.: 1982, 'Inflection-Government and Inversion', *The Linguistic Review* 1, 417–467.

Samuels, M.: 1972, *Linguistic Evolution: With Special Reference to English*, Cambridge University Press.

Sandfeld, K.: 1970, *Syntaxe du français contemporain, I: les pronoms*, Paris.

Santorini, B.: 1988, 'Against a Uniform Analysis of All Verb-Second Clauses', ms., University of Pennsylvania.

Santorini, B.: 1989, *The Generalization of the Verb-Second Constraint in the History of Yiddish*, Ph.D. dissertation, University of Pennsylvania.

Schönenberger, M.: 1990, 'Doubling Constructions', ms., Université de Genève.

Schulze, R.: 1888, *Die Altfranzösische Direkte Fragesatz*, Leipzig.

Schwartz, B. and Vikner, S.: 1989, 'All Verb Second Clauses are CPs', *Working Papers in Scandinavian Syntax* 43, 27–49.

Ščur, G.: 1968, 'On the Non-finite Forms of the Verb *can* in Scottish', *Acta Linguistica Hafniensa* 11, 211–218.

Selkirk, E.: 1982, *The Syntax of Words*, MIT Press, Cambridge, Mass.

Shlonsky, U.: 1989, 'The Hierarchical Representation of Subject Verb Agreement', ms., University of Haifa.

Sigurðsson, H.: 1985, 'Subordinate V/1 in Icelandic. How to Explain a Root Phenomenon', *Working Papers in Scandinavian Syntax*, 18.

Skårup, P.: 1975, 'Les premières zones de la proposition en ancien français', *Revue Romaine*, numéro spécial 6.

Skautrup, P.: 1948–53, *Det danske sprog historie*, Vol. I–IV, Gyldendal, Copenhagen. Reprinted 1968.

Sportiche, D.: 1988a, 'A Theory of Floating Quantifiers and Its Corollaries for Constituent Structure', *Linguistic Inquiry* 19, 33–60.

Sportiche, D.: 1988b, 'Conditions on Silent Categories', ms., UCLA.

Sproat, R.: 1985, 'Welsh Syntax and VSO Structure', *Natural Language and Linguistic Theory* 3, 173–216.

Stein, D.: 1989, '*Do* and *tun*: A Semantics and Varieties-Based Approach to Syntactic Change', paper given at the 9th International Conference on Historical Linguistics, Rutgers University, New Jersey.

Stephens, J.: 1982, *Word Order in Breton*, Ph.D. dissertation, University of London.

Stockwell, R.: 1977, 'Motivations for Exbraciation in Old English', in Li, C. (ed.), *Mechanisms of Syntactic Change*, University of Texas Press.

Stowell, T.: 1981, *Origins of Phrase Structure*, Ph.D. dissertation, MIT.

Taraldsen, K. T.: 1978, 'On the NIC, Vacuous Application and the That-Trace Filter', Indiana University Linguistics Club, Bloomington.

Taraldsen, K. T.: 1983, *Variation in Phrase Structure: A Case Study*, Doctoral Dissertation, University of Tromsø.

Tarallo, F. and Kato, M.: 1989, *Harmonia trans-sistémica: Variação intra- e inter-lingüística*, Preedição 5, Departamento de Lingüística, Unicamp, Brazil.

Thöni, G.-P.: 1969, *Rumantsch-Surmeir*, Lia Rumantscha, Chur.

Thráinsson, H.: 1986, 'V1, V2, V3 in Icelandic', in Haider & Prinzhorn, 1986.

Thurneysen, R.: 1892, 'Die Stellung des Verbums im Altfranzösischen', *Zeitschrift für Romanische Philologie* 16, 289–371.

Tomaselli, A.: 1989, *La Sintassi del verbo finito nelle lingue germaniche*, Dottorato di Ricerca in Linguistica, Università di Pavia.

Tomaselli, A.: 1990, 'Cases of V3 in Old High German', paper presented at the First Generative Diachronic Syntax Conference, York.

Traugott, E.: 1972, *A History of English Syntax*, Holt, Reinhart and Winston, New York.

Travis, L.: 1984, *Parameters and Effects of Word Order Variation*, Ph.D. dissertation, MIT.

Travis, L.: 1986, 'Parameters of Phrase Structure and V2 Phenomena', ms., McGill University. (Presented at the First Princeton Workshop on Comparative Syntax, to appear in the Proceedings).

Trosterud, T.: 1989, 'The Null Subject Parameter and the New Mainland Scandinavian Word Order – A Possible Counterexample from a Norwegian Dialect', ms., University of Trondheim. (To appear in *Proceedings of the 11th Scandinavian Conference on Linguistics, Joensuu 1988*).

Trudgill, P.: 1990, *Dialects of England*, Longman, London.

Vance, B.: 1988, 'L'évolution du pro-drop en français médiéval', in Hirschbuhler, P. and Rochette, A. (eds.), *Aspects de la syntaxe historique du français*, *Revue québécoise de linguistique théorique et appliquée* 7, 85–112.

Vance, B.: 1989, *Null Subjects and Syntactic Change in Medieval French*, Ph.D. dissertation, Cornell University.

Vance, B.: 1990, 'Inversion and Pro-drop in Middle French', paper presented at the First Generative Diachronic Syntax Conference, York.

Vanelli, L.: 1987, 'I pronomi soggetto nei dialetti italiani settentrionali dal Medio Evo a oggi', *Medioevo Romanzo*, 12.

Vanelli, L., Renzi, L. and Benincà, P.: 1986, 'Typologie des pronoms sujets dans les langues romanes', *Actes du XIIe Congrès de Linguistique et Philologie Romanes*, Aix-en-Provence.

Vaugelas: 1647, *Remarques sur la langue française*, Chassang (ed.), Paris, 1880, 2 volumes.

Vendler, Z.: 1967, *Linguistics in Philosophy*, Cornell University Press.

Vikner, S.: 1987, 'Case Assignment Differences between Danish and Swedish', in Allan, R. and Barnes, M. (eds.), *Proceedings of the Seventh Conference of Scandinavian Studies in Great Britain*, University College London, pp. 262–281.

Vikner, S.: 1988, 'Modals in Danish and Event Expressions', *Working Papers in Scandinavian Syntax*, 39.

Vikner, S.: 1990, *Verb Movement and the Licensing of NP-Positions in the Germanic Languages*, Thèse de Doctorat, Université de Genève.

Visser, Th.: 1963–73, *An Historical Syntax of the English Language*, 4 Volumes, E. J. Brill, Leiden.

Wackernagel, J.: 1892, 'Über ein Gesetz der indogermanischen Wortstellung', *Indogermanische Forschungen* 1, 333–435.

Warner, A.: 1982, *Complementation in Middle English and the Methodology of Historical Syntax*, The Pennsylvania State University Press.

Wakelin, M. F.: 1986, *The Southwest of England*, Varieties of English Around the World 5, John Benjamins, Amsterdam.

Warner, A.: 1983, Review of Lightfoot (1979), *Journal of Linguistics* 19, 187–209.

Warner, A.: 1987, 'Reworking the History of English Auxiliaries', to appear in Adamson, S. *et al.* (eds.), *Papers from the Fifth International Conference on English Historical Linguistics*, Amsterdam, Benjamins.

von Wartburg, W.: 1934, *Evolution et structure de la langue française*, Larousse, Paris.

Weerman, F.: 1989, *The V 2 Conspiracy*, Foris, Dordrecht.

Williams, E.: 1974, *Rule Ordering in Syntax*, Ph.D. dissertation, MIT.

Williams, E.: 1984, '*There*-Insertion', *Linguistic Inquiry* 15, 131–153.

Wright, J. (ed.): (1899–1905) *The English Dialect Dictionary*, 6 Volumes. Frowde and Corner, London and Oxford; G. P. Putnam, New York.

Zagona, K.: 1982, *Government and Proper Government of Verbal Projections*, Ph.D. dissertation, University of Washington, Seattle.

Zagona, K.: 1988, *Verb Phrase Syntax*, Kluwer, Dordrecht.

Zanuttini, R.: 1989, 'The Structure of Negative Clauses in Romance', ms., University of Pennsylvania.

Zubizarreta, M.-L.: 1982, *On the Relation of the Lexicon to Syntax*, Ph.D. dissertation, MIT.

Zwanenburg, W.: 1978, 'L'ordre des mots en français médiéval', in Martin, R. (ed.), *Etudes de syntaxe de moyen français*, Paris, Klincksieck.

INDEX OF NAMES

INDEX OF SUBJECTS

Studies in Natural Language and Linguistic Theory

Managing Editors

Joan Maling, *Brandeis University*
James McCloskey, *University of California, Santa Cruz*
Ian Roberts, *University of Wales, Bangor*

Publications

1. L. Burzio: *Italian Syntax*. A Government-binding Approach. 1986.
   ISBN Hb 90-277-2014-2; Pb 90-277-2015-0

2. W.D. Davies: *Choctaw Verb Agreement and Universal Grammar*. 1986.
   ISBN Hb 90-277-2065-7; Pb 90-277-2142-4

3. K. É. Kiss: *Configurationality in Hungarian*. 1987.
   ISBN Hb 90-277-1907-1; Pb 90-277-2456-3

4. D. Pulleyblank: *Tone in Lexical Phonology*. 1986.
   ISBN Hb 90-277-2123-8; Pb 90-277-2124-6

5. L. Hellan and K. K. Christensen: *Topics in Scandinavian Syntax*. 1986.
   ISBN Hb 90-277-2166-1; Pb 90-277-2167-X

6. K. P. Mohanan: *The Theory of Lexical Phonology*. 1986.
   ISBN Hb 90-277-2226-9; Pb 90-277-2227-7

7. J. L. Aissen: *Tzotzil Clause Structure*. 1987.
   ISBN Hb 90-277-2365-6; Pb 90-277-2441-5

8. T. Gunji: *Japanese Phrase Structure Grammar*. A Unification-based Approach. 1987.   ISBN 1-55608-020-4

9. W. U. Wurzel: *Inflectional Morphology and Naturalness*. 1989
   ISBN Hb 1-55608-025-5; Pb 1-55608-026-3

10. C. Neidle: *The Role of Case in Russian Syntax*. 1988   ISBN 1-55608-042-5

11. C. Lefebvre and P. Muysken: *Mixed Categories*. Nominalizations in Quechua. 1988.   ISBN Hb 1-55608-050-6; Pb 1-55608-051-4

12. K. Michelson: *A Comparative Study of Lake-Iroquoian Accent*. 1988
    ISBN 1-55608-054-9

13. K. Zagona: *Verb Phrase Syntax*. A Parametric Study of English and Spanish. 1988   ISBN Hb 1-55608-064-6; Pb 1-55608-065-4

14. R. Hendrick: *Anaphora in Celtic and Universal Grammar*. 1988
    ISBN 1-55608-066-2

15. O. Jaeggli and K.J. Safir (eds.): *The Null Subject Parameter*. 1989
    ISBN Hb 1-55608-086-7; Pb 1-55608-087-5

16. H. Lasnik: *Essays on Anaphora*. 1989
    ISBN Hb 1-55608-090-5; Pb 1-55608-091-3

17. S. Steele: *Agreement and Anti-Agreement*. A Syntax of Luiseño. 1990
    ISBN 0-7923-0260-5

Studies in Natural Language and Linguistic Theory

18. E. Pearce: *Parameters in Old French Syntax.* Infinitival Complements. 1990
ISBN Hb 0-7923-0432-2; Pb 0-7923-0433-0

19. Y.A. Li: *Order and Constituency in Mandarin Chinese.* 1990
ISBN 0-7923-0500-0

20. H. Lasnik: *Essays on Restrictiveness and Learnability.* 1990
ISBN 0-7923-0628-7; Pb 0-7923-0629-5

21. M.J. Speas: *Phrase Structure in Natural Language.* 1990
ISBN 0-7923-0755-0; Pb 0-7923-0866-2

22. H. Haider and K. Netter (eds.): *Representation and Derivation in the Theory of Grammar.* 1991
ISBN 0-7923-1150-7

23. J. Simpson: *Warlpiri Morpho-Syntax.* A Lexicalist Approach. 1991
ISBN 0-7923-1292-9

24. C. Georgopoulos: *Syntactic Variables.* Resumptive Pronouns and A' Binding in Palauan. 1991
ISBN 0-7923-1293-7

25. K. Leffel and D. Bouchard (eds.): *Views on Phrase Structure.* 1991
ISBN 0-7923-1295-3

26. C. Tellier: *Licensing Theory and French Parasitic Gaps.* 1991
ISBN 0-7923-1311-9; Pb 0-7923-1323-2

27. S.-Y. Kuroda: *Japanese Syntax and Semantics.* Collected Papers. 1992
ISBN 0-7923-1390-9; Pb 0-7923-1391-7

28. I. Roberts: *Verbs and Diachronic Syntax.* A Comparative History of English and French. 1992
ISBN 0-7923-1705-X

Kluwer Academic Publishers – Dordrecht / Boston / London